Foundations of Theological Study: A Sourcebook

Richard Viladesau
Mark Massa, S.J.

PAULIST PRESS
New York / Mahwah, N.J.

Book design by Nighthawk Design.

Copyright © 1991 by Richard Viladesau and Mark Massa, S.J.

Library of Congress Cataloging-in-Publication Data

Viladesau, Richard.
    Foundations of theological study: a sourcebook/Richard
Viladesau, Mark Massa.
      p. cm.
    Includes bibliographical references.
    ISBN 0-8091-3281-8 (pbk.)
    1. Theology. I. Massa, Mark Stephen. II. Title.
BT80.V55 1991
230—dc20   91-30807
                                                   CIP

Published by Paulist Press
997 Macarthur Boulevard
Mahwah, New Jersey 07430

Printed and bound in the
United States of America

Pg 23

CONTENTS

iii

C. Conversion Experiences

Chapter Two: Speaking About God

A. Religion: The Symbolic Dimension

B. Theology

Chapter Three: Revelation and Faith

A. General Revelation: The Knowledge of God Through Reason

B. Special Revelation

C. Christian Life

Acknowledgments

The articles reprinted in Foundations of Theological Study first appeared in the following publications and are reprinted with permission:

St. Augustine: Confessions, pp. 3–5. Sheed & Ward, Kansas City, Mo.

"The Life of the Holy Mother Teresa of Jesus," in *The Complete Works of St. Teresa,* vol. 1, translated and edited by E. Allison Peers, pp. 119, 121, 125, 126. Sheed & Ward, Kansas City, Mo.

Thomas a Kempis: Imitation of Christ, pp. 19, 60–62, 73, 75–76. Sheed & Ward, Kansas City, Mo.

A Haggadah for the School, by Hyman Chanover, pp. 5–9, 11, 14–15, 17–18, 33, 37, 41–48, 59, 66. Illustrated by Uri Shulevitz, and published by the United Synagogue Commission on Jewish Education, New York, 1964.

From *The Way of Torah: An Introduction to Judaism,* by Jacob Neusner, pp. 7–8, 13–18. Dickenson Publishing Company, Inc., 1970. Reprinted by permission of Wadsworth, Inc., Belmont, Ca. 94002.

From: *Meditations on Freedom and the Spirit,* by Karl Rahner. English translation © 1977 Search Press Ltd. Reprinted by permission of The Crossroad Publishing Company, New York, N.Y.

Excerpts from the English translation of *The Roman Missal.* Copyright © 1973. International Committee on English in the Liturgy, Inc., Washington, D.C. 20005-1202.

From: *The Documents of Vatican II.* Abbott-Gallagher edition. America Press, New York, N.Y.

Excerpt from *The Gulag Archipelago,* volume 1, by Alexander Solzhenitsyn. Copyright © 1973 by Alexander Solzhenitsyn. HarperCollins Publishers, New York, N.Y.

Excerpt from *Making Religion Real,* by Neis Ferre. Copyright © 1955, Harper & Row, Publishers, Inc. By permission, HarperCollins Publishers, New York, N.Y.

Excerpt from *Catholicism,* volume II, by Richard McBrien. Copyright © 1982 by Richard McBrien. By permission, HarperCollins Publishers, New York, N.Y.

Reprinted with permission of Charles Scribner's Sons, an imprint of Macmillan Publishing Company from *I And Thou,* by Martin

Buber, translated by Ronald Gregor Smith, pp. 3–4, 76–79. Copyright © 1958, Charles Scribner's Sons, New York, N.Y.

Reprinted with permission as published in *God Struck Me Dead: Religious Conversion Experiences and Autobiographies of Ex-Slaves*, edited by Clifton H. Johnson. Copyright © 1969, United Church Press, New York, N.Y.

Excerpts from *Economic Justice for All: Catholic Social Teaching and the U.S. Economy.* Copyright © 1987 by the United States Catholic Conference, Washington, D.C. Used with permission.

From *Voice of the Voiceless,* by Oscar Romero, pp. 177–187. Orbis Books, Maryknoll, N.Y.

Excerpt from *Do You Believe in God?* by Karl Rahner. English edition published by Paulist Press © 1969. Original German edition published by Ars Sacra Verlag, Munich, Germany.

From *About Love,* by Josef Pieper, pp. 22–23. Franciscan Herald Press, Chicago, Il. 60609.

From *The Courage to Be,* by Paul Tillich, pp. 32–39. Yale University Press, New Haven, Ct. 06520.

From *Interpreting the Old Testament,* by Daniel Harrington, S.J., pp. 11–17, 69–88. Copyright © by The Order of St. Benedict, Inc. Published by The Liturgical Press, Collegeville, Mn. 56321.

From the poem "Der Schauende," by Rainer Maria Rilke. Copyright Insel Verlag, Frankfurt, Germany.

From Essay On The Development of Christian Doctrine, by John Henry Newman, pp. 58–65. Copyright © 1989 by the University of Notre Dame Press, Notre Dame, In.

Excerpt(s) from *Models of Revelation,* by Avery Dulles. Copyright © 1983 by Avery Dulles. Used by permission of Doubleday, a Division of Bantam Doubleday, Dell Publishing Group, Inc., New York, N.Y.

Excerpt(s) from *On Being A Christian,* by Hans Küng. Copyright © 1976 by Doubleday, a division of Bantam Doubleday, Dell Publishing Group, Inc., New York, N.Y.

From *Systematic Theology,* vol. 1, by Paul Tillich, pp. 3–8 & 11–15. The University of Chicago Press, Chicago, Il. 60637.

From *Comment Je Crois,* by Pierre Teilhard de Chardin, pp. 125–126. Georges Borchardt, Inc., New York, N.Y.

From "Jesus Among the Historians," by John P. Meier. December 21, 1986, *New York Times*, New York, N.Y.

From The *Idea of the Holy*, by Rudolf Otto, translated by John W. Harvey (2nd ed., 1950). Reprinted by permission of Oxford University Press, Oxford, England.

From *The Epistle to the Romans*, by Karl Barth, translated by Edwyn C. Hoskyns (1933). Reprinted by permission of Oxford University Press, Oxford, England.

From *America: Religion and Religions*, by Catherine Albanese. Wadsworth Pub. Co., Belmont, Ca. 94002.

From *Foundations of Christian Faith*, by Karl Rahner. The Crossroad Publishing Co., New York, N.Y.

INTRODUCTION

This Sourcebook

In his little essay "On the Reading of Old Books," C. S. Lewis notes that the average student will almost invariably avoid reading primary sources, much preferring the mediation of some contemporary scholar's explanation. Lewis considers this mistake—as he calls it—to be based on a kind of misplaced humility. The student presupposes that the great thinkers and great books will necessarily be far beyond his or her ability, and that the modern interpreter will clarify the subject, make it contemporary, and ease the process of learning. In fact, the opposite is frequently the case. The classics are often more intelligible and more interesting than their expositors; to which one might add that they are not infrequently more relevant to life than the most recent academic fashions, particularly in areas like theology and philosophy. "It has always therefore been one of my main endeavors as a teacher," Lewis concludes, "to persuade the young that first-hand knowledge is not only more worth acquiring than second-hand knowledge, but is usually much easier and more delightful to acquire."[1]

Most teachers of theology would probably concur, at least in large measure. Even those who believe that the level of undergraduates' reading skills has seriously declined since Lewis' time would probably agree that an encounter with the great minds of religious tradition—however challenging and sometimes frus-

---

1. C. S. Lewis, "On the Reading of Old Books," in *God in the Dock: Essays on Theology and Ethics,* ed. Walter Hooper. Grand Rapids: William B. Eerdmans Publishing Co., 1970, 200.

trating—is ultimately more fruitful educationally than a total program of pre-digested material. A problem for contemporary college teachers of theology, however, is the dearth of readily
accessible material at the appropriate level. It is in an attempt to
address at least partially this perceived lack that this volume of
readings is presented.

The purpose of this collection is to provide a wide selection of
materials suitable for an introductory course in Christian theology. We have attempted to include readings relevant to the principal areas that such a source might cover. Because of consider-
ations of length, we have not included readings from the
scriptures, presuming that a Bible should be part of the equipment
of every theological student. We have instead indicated, wherever
appropriate, a number of biblical passages which might be used in
the consideration of particular topics. In selecting the readings
themselves, we have attempted to stay with presentations that are
in some sense "classic" and/or that give basic introductory perspectives that will be helpful in pursuing further study.

After much consideration, we have decided not to attempt to
include readings from non-Christian religions in this volume. On
the one hand, we are convinced that an introductory course in
theology—rather than, for example, religious studies or compara-
tive religions—in the contemporary situation must include some
apposite comparisons with non-Christian traditions. On the other
hand, it is impossible to do justice to the richness of those traditions and also to the Christian tradition which is our main focus in
the limited space that could be afforded here. We have therefore
planned to follow this volume with a second collection of texts
drawn from the scriptures and theological writings of the major
non-Christian religions.

This Sourcebook and the Study of Theology

Answering questions about the origin ("why") and purpose
("whither") of life might qualify with motherhood as the "world's
oldest profession." The cave paintings of the Neolithic Period that
mark the beginning of a distinctly "human" history witness to our

species' perennial passion for understanding the forces (or Force) that structures and controls the universe. Those haunting and powerful paintings of the cave dwellers witness to theological as well as to artistic impulses at work at the dawn of history, being both *creeds* (statements about how the world really operates) and forms of *worship* ("prayers" for good hunting in return for painting faithful likenesses of bison and bears). Broadly conceived, then, theology began with human history itself, and represents one of those constituitive factors that makes humans "human." As Chapter I of this sourcebook attests, the "religious question" is co-terminous with the "human question" itself, and forms one of the central questions pursued in literature (Dickinson, Solzhenitsyn, Rilke) in examining the "reflective life."

But while theology may be rooted in the most basic needs of being human (our need for knowing *why*), it is also a science. Like all sciences, the practice of theology demands painstaking study, a close observation of experience, and disciplined reflection. As Section B of Chapter I seeks to show, it is the "experimental" factor in theology that *grounds* it in human experience. But as in all sciences, a disciplined reflection on this very real experience is also necessary—a disciplined study that allows us to speak of its study as a "science." Thus, basic to "speaking about God" (the title for Chapter II of the text) is both a rigorous examination of the records of religious experience, and an ongoing reflection on the meaning(s) of those records. Our name for this science thus derives from the Greek, *theos logos,* meaning "speaking about the holy," or, more specifically, "speaking about God."

In western culture, at least since Plato and Moses, the object of this disciplined study has traditionally been labeled "God"—that utterly transcendent yet immanent Reality that most western theologians present as the answer to the ancient human questions about the "why" and the "whither" of life. But it is important to keep in mind that theology's task, while focused on that realm of human experience where we encounter the "Other," invariably involves the theologian in studying the records and tools of human beings. Much of the theologian's task, therefore, is defined by studying and interpreting the historical tradition through which the sacred encounter is celebrated and remembered. As

Chapter II of this sourcebook outlines, the religious tradition en-compasses symbols, myths, rituals, and scriptures that both hu-mankind in general (Section A) and specific human communities (Section B) construct to speak about their experience of the Holy. This experiential factor that undergirds theology links revelation (Chapter I of this text) with the community's attempt to speak critically about that revelation (Chapter II), an attempt that forms the heart of theology as a scientific discipline.

The revealing of this "Other" ("revelation") usually leads to the "conversion" of those involved in the experience; it also in-variably leads to the founding of a community to remember and celebrate the revelation. As Chapter III of this text illustrates, the "revealing" often discloses knowledge that can be formulated and analyzed in intellectual categories (Thomas Aquinas and An-selm); often the revelation eludes dogmatic formulation, and takes the form of a more basic, pre-conceptual reorganization of how "reality" itself is approached and understood (Tillich); some-times it is both (Pascal). Whatever the form of the revelation, the community arising out of the revelation usually celebrates the Other encountered as "sacred" or "holy" ("set apart") from other categories of human knowing—less a "being" in the normal sense (even the greatest and most perfect of all beings), than Being itself.

While theology as a human science begins with, and rests upon, a careful consideration of the human experience of the Holy, most theologians pursue their task from within a specific religous community—a group of believers called together in re-sponse to a shared encounter with the Holy. Thus, while all theol-ogies address the universal human questions of "why" and "whither," they all nonetheless proceed from, and speak to, a specific religious group. This twofold obligation that all theolo-gians face—to both a specific religious community and to the universal human experience of the sacred—creates the fruitful tension within which theology is done. Indeed, one might say that a theology is valid or not to the extent that it emerges from the real experience of a community, engages the general human religious experience in an ongoing discussion, using certain agreed-upon analytic tools, and then returns to the community's experience for verification and clarification.

As Chapters IV, V, and VI of the following sourcebook of readings will witness, this text is rooted in, and is addressed to, students engaged in the "study of the holy" from within a specific religious community (Christianity); it likewise reflects the communal interests and commitments of its authors to a specific religious family within that community (Roman Catholicism). As such, the sacred encounter that this text seeks to explicate is rooted in the Judeo-Christian tradition of symbols and myths as that tradition has been celebrated and analyzed within Roman Catholicism.

How To Use This Sourcebook

While each professor will no doubt use an anthology in his or her own way, it will perhaps be worthwhile to explain briefly the rationale behind our selection and ordering of the readings. This text grounds the study of theology in the most basic questions and needs of the human person, questions that arise in literature, in the discussion of the sacred as a category in philosophy, and in existential "encounters" with the holy from several sources. The readings are thus arranged in an order from less to more thematically "religious." Section A of Chapter I intends to confront the student with the elements in common human experiences which evoke "the riddle of life, the riddle of death": the question of the meaning of existence itself. Rainer Maria Rilke's poem and Aleksandr Solzhenitsyn's reflection on suffering explicitly raise the issue of depth of life vs. superficiality. Emily Dickinson and Miguel de Unamuno, in different ways, draw our attention to the "restlessness" of spirit—the perpetual wondering, the desire for "more" than life—that St. Augustine saw as the expression of our need for God. Paul Tillich's category of "ultimate concern" identifies more precisely the goal of our longing, while Martin Buber reminds us that the reflective life must go beyond objectification and categorization to personal relation. In Section B, the readings examine various ways in which the "sacred" is experienced or pointed to: negatively, in anxiety about existence (Tillich); positively, in beauty (Plato), as the explanation of the evolutionary dynamism of the world (Teilhard), in love which desires to be eteneral (Pieper), in the courage and self-sacrifice of everyday life (Rahner), in awe and fascination (Otto). Finally, Section C presents several biographical examples of explicitly religious conversion experiences.

Chapters II and III likewise offer several approaches to understanding how theologians speak about the holy. Section A of Chapter II offers readings that analyze how symbols and ritual behavior operate in religious systems generally: Catherine Albanese attempts a definition and classification of religion. Nels Ferré emphasizes the need for personal engagement with God in prayer if religion is to be real, and not merely an object of study. Victor Warnach's article gives a concrete example of the symbolic dimension of religious discourse by addressing the issue of the eucharist. This section, focused on the constituent elements of all theological systems, forms the bridge between Chapter I, which grounds the religious quest in the human person, and Chapter II, Section B, which considers the critical and conceptual aspect of religion which is theology. We are presented with St. Anselm's classical definition of theology as *fides quarens intellectum*, St. Thomas' analysis of theology as a science, and Paul Tillich's view of the theological task as "correlation" of revealed truth with the contemporary situation. Together, these two sections of Chapter II offer a consideration of the *parts* of theological systems (how symbols and ritual function in theology), and how theologians attempt a *synthesis* of these parts in what is usually called "systematic theology."

Chapter III centers on revelation. Section A examines the question of "general revelation"—that knowledge of the sacred that all human beings experience by virtue of their historical experience. After presenting Aquinas' distinction between knowledge and faith, this section offers some of the classical "ways" of reason to God: the "five ways"; Anselm's and Descartes' versions of the *a priori* argument, and Pascal's "wager." This section concludes with Hans Küng's way to God from "fundamental trust," a contemporary development of Kant's "moral argument" to God as a postulate of "practical reason." (This section might be used in conjunction with Chapter I of the text, as the reflections of Aquinas, Descartes, and Pascal that are included in IIIA represent the formal *theological* systematizing of the universal human "sense" of the sacred explored in Chapter I.)

Section B of Chapter III builds on this universal knowledge and experience of the holy to examine God's self-revelation as received and interpreted in the Judeo-Christian tradition, leading up to its culmination in Jesus. This section offers both a systematic analysis of the "models" of Christian revelation (Dulles), and two specific examples of these models—the "vertical" model explored by Karl Barth and the more immanentist model offered by the Second Vatican Council in *Dei Verbum*. In considering these various models, instructors may wish to utilize the readings in the Hebrew and Christian scriptures suggested in Chapter I (reading 14).

Chapter IV of the text explores a central theological question that emerges from the encounter with the holy—that of the "nature of God." This question, which forms the core of "systematic" or "constructive" theology in all religious traditions, is explored utilizing the western Judeo-Christian scriptures and the "doctors" of Christian theology (Augustine and Aquinas). A selection from Karl Rahner's *Foundations of Christian Theology* develops the classical position in terms of a contemporary "transcendental" approach, in which God is seen as the immanent source and goal of each human being's existential dynamism toward knowledge and love. This part of the text might be seen as representing the culmination of the first four chapters of the sourcebook—an extended examination of how theology utilizes human experience, revelatory encounters, the communal traditions of celebration and reflection, and philosophical traditions to speak *systematically* about *who* this sacred Other is, both in Itself and in relation to us. As such, Chapter IV might be used as the "bridge" between the study of general revelation and the examination of the Christian tradition, or it might be used after an examination of the person and work of Jesus of Nazareth, depending on the nature and subject of the course.

Chapters V and VI of this text focus specifically on Christian tradition, and can be utilized in conjunction with suggested readings in the New Testament. Chapter V examines the "person and teaching of Jesus" from several standpoints—from that of his

Jewish origins (A), from the record of creedal statements constructed by the community to "unpack" the implications of his
person and work (C), and that of contemporary theologians engaged in examining the implications of his teaching for "moral
theology" (B). One of the goals of all three of these sections in
Chapter V is to introduce students to the problem of "exegesis"—
the critical examination of the records of a religious tradition—
and how the community and its theologians interpret those records. This interpretive, *textual* question is presented in a
multi-valent way in these three sections: Jesus in the context of
the late classical world, where Judaism itself provides the "text"
for understanding who Jesus might have thought himself to be;
Jesus himself as the "text" for considering the moral implications
of his teachings; and Jesus as the object of the Christian community's worship and belief in its creedal texts.

Chapter VI of the sourcebook, building on Chapter V, examines how the person and message of Jesus has been incarnated in
the institutional tradition of the Catholic Church. This final part
of the text represents the most "specific" of the subsections of the
sourcebook—examining in a sustained way the Catholic tradition
in its historical, doctrinal, and ethical manifestations. It might
thus be used early in a course syllabus (to provide a specific framework for studying the general human phenomenon of religion),
or as the end of a course, where the categories of symbol, ritual,
and myth can be examined as they are applied in a specific way to
the Catholic Christian tradition.

Chapter VI looks at the early historical development of the
realization of who this Jesus was in worship (*Pange Lingua* and
Didache), and in the Christian community's relationship to the
classical world (Justin Martyr). Section B examines two of the
most important documents in the recent history of the Catholic
community—documents that, in very different ways, have
shaped the theological reflections of theologians: Newman's *Essay on Development* and Vatican II's *Lumen Gentium*. These two
documents offer valuable insight into the ways in which the contemporary Catholic community reflects on its existence in history.
Finally, Section C looks at several applications of the tradition to
Christian life in the world: the classic work on "imitating Christ"

by Thomas à Kempis; the Vatican statements on birth control and the rights of women; the statement of the U.S. Bishops' Conference on economic justice; and the prophetic witness of Martin Luther King and Archbishop Oscar Romero on the political implications of living a Christian life in the modern world.

A Postscript

As with any anthology, there are limitations, of which we are keenly aware. Reasons of length, copyrights, cost, repetition, and other factors have eliminated many readings that we would have liked to include. We are also aware that an introductory course could have very different emphases, and that many topics (for example, faith and unbelief; the problem of evil; the doctrine of grace—to name but a few) and authors could profitably have been included. A primary concern, however, has been to produce a text which is modest in cost; hence we have sacrificed many possible options. Nevertheless, we hope that these offerings will be useful for a variety of ways of presenting an introductory course in theology.

Another kind of limitation imposed by our sources regards language. In our introductions and commentaries, we have attempted to use gender-inclusive terminology. The same is not true, however, of some of the authors and/or translators of the selections. In particular, many follow the (once standard) practice of using "man" as a common-gender noun and "he" as a common-gender pronoun to refer to humanity. It is our hope that instructors will put such passages in their historical linguistic context, and use them as an occasion to raise the issue of inclusive language with their students.

Chapter One

The Reflective Life
and Religious Experience

A. The Reflective Life and the Question of God

1. The question of existence

Love, death and nature were the main themes of the poetry of **Emily Dickinson (1830–1886),** one of the American masters of the short lyric poem. A recluse who lived her adult life almost exclusively in her home and gardens, Dickinson manifests in her poetry a meditative quality basic to the "reflective life."

This World is not Conclusion.
A Species stands beyond—
Invisible, as Music—
But positive, as Sound—
It beckons, and it baffles—
Philosophy—don't know—
And through a Riddle, at the last—
Sagacity, must go—
To guess it, puzzles scholars—
To gain it, Men have borne
Contempt of Generations
And Crucifixion, shown—
Faith slips—and laughs, and rallies—
Blushes, if any see—
Plucks at a twig of Evidence—

1

And asks a Vane, the way—
Much Gesture, from the Pulpit—
Strong Hallulujahs roll—
Narcotics cannot still the Tooth ⁻⟨ʙₑₐ⟩
That nibbles at the soul—

                              [ca. 1862]

2. The struggle of contemplation

The poetry of **Rainer Maria Rilke (1875–1926)** is frequently called "metaphysical" and "existential." He challenges the reader to a meditative stance in which the most ordinary realities take on eternal significance. In this poem, the effort to live life deeply is compared to the struggle of the patriarch Jacob with an angel (Gen 32:24).

The Contemplative

Through the trees I watch the storms
that out of days grown tepid
come to beat against my frightened windows
and I hear far-off places saying things
that I cannot bear without a friend,
cannot love without a sister.

There goes the storm, an overturner;
it goes through the forest and through time
and everything becomes as though ageless:
the landscape is like a verse of the psalms:
grave, weighty, eternal.

How small is that with which we wrestle;
what wrestles with us—how great it is!
if, more like things, we let ourselves
be swayed, so, by the great storm—
we would become wide and beyond name.

What we conquer are the small things;
and our very successes make us small.
The eternal and mysterious

will not be bent by us.
That is the angel who appeared
to the wrestlers of the Old Testament:
when the sinews of his opponents
stretch like metal in battle,
he feels them under his fingers
like the chords of deep melodies.

Whoever is defeated by this angel—
who so often renounces battle—
he goes forth erect and just
and great from that hard hand
which closed upon and formed him.
Victories do not tempt him.
His growth is this: to be
deeply defeated by the ever-greater One.
                    [*Collected Works*; trans. R. Viladesau]

3. *Awareness through suffering*

The Russian writer **Aleksandr Solzhenitsyn** was awarded the Nobel
Prize for literature in 1972 for his works of fiction and history. Imprisoned for many years under the Stalinist regime, he had first-
hand experience of the forced labor camps (the "*Gulag*") whose
very existence was a well-kept secret from most of the world. To the
experience of suffering and survival Solzhenitsyn attributes his spiritual awakening; "that is why," he writes, "I turn back to the years of
my imprisonment and say, sometimes to the astonishment of those
about me: 'Bless you, prison!' "

In this passage Solzhenitsyn describes a "special-convoy" trip: a
transfer from one labor camp to another. The prisoners and their
guards travel by ordinary train. For the sake of secrecy, they are
dressed in ordinary clothes, and are outwardly indistinguishable
from the people around them.

If the souls of those who have died sometimes hover among us, see us,
easily read in us our trivial concerns, and we fail to see them or guess at
their incorporeal presence, then that is what a special-convoy trip is like.

You are submerged in the mass of *freedom*, and you push and shove with the others in the station waiting room. You absentmindedly examine announcements posted there, even though they can hardly have any relevance for you. You sit on the ancient passenger benches, and you hear strange and insignificant conversations: about some husband who beats up his wife or has left her; and some mother-in-law who, for some reason, does not get along with her daughter-in-law; how neighbors in communal apartments make personal use of the electric outlets in the corridor and don't wipe their feet; and how someone is in someone else's way at the office; and how someone has been offered a good job but can't make up his mind to move—how can he move bag and baggage, is that so easy? You listen to all this, and the goose pimples of rejection run up and down your spine: to you the true measure of things in the Universe is so clear! The measure of all weaknesses and all passions! And these sinners aren't fated to perceive it. The only one there who is alive, truly alive, is incorporeal you, and all these others are simply mistaken in thinking themselves alive.

And an unbridgeable chasm divides you! You cannot cry out to them, nor weep over them, nor shake them by the shoulder: after all, you are a disembodied spirit, you are a ghost, and they are material bodies.

And how can you bring it home to them? By an inspiration? By a vision? A dream? Brothers! People! Why has life been given you? In the deep, deaf stillness of midnight, the doors of the death cells are being swung open—and great-souled people are being dragged out to be shot. On all the railroads of the country this very minute, right now, people who have just been fed salt herring are licking their dry lips with bitter tongues. They dream of the happiness of stretching out one's legs and of the relief one feels after going to the toilet. In Orotukan the earth thaws only in summer and only to the depth of three feet—and only then can they bury the bones of those who died during the winter. And you have the right to arrange your own life under the blue sky and the hot sun, to get a drink of water, to stretch, to travel wherever you like without a convoy. So what's this about unwiped feet? And what's this about a mother-in-law? What about the main thing in life, all its riddles? If you want, I'll spell it out for you right now. Do not pursue what is illusory—property and position: all that is gained at the expense of your nerves decade after decade, and is confiscated in one fell night. Live with a steady superiority over life—don't be afraid of misfortune; and do not yearn after happiness; it is, after all, all the same: the bitter doesn't last forever, and the sweet never fills the cup to overflowing. It is enough if you don't freeze in the cold and if thirst and hunger don't claw at your insides. If your back isn't broken, if your feet can walk, if both arms can bend, if both eyes see, and if both ears hear, then whom should you envy? And why? Our envy of others devours us most of all. Rub your eyes and purify your heart—and prize above all else in the world those who love you and who wish you well. ["From Island to Island." *The Gulag Archipelago, I*]

4. The hunger for immortality

Miguel de Unamuno (1864–1936) was a poet, essayist, novelist, philosopher, professor of Greek and Rector of the University of Salamanca in Spain. In his most famous philosophical work, he puts forth the thesis that the hunger for immortality is not only the source of religion, but is the most profound desire of every human being. Our reason, Unamuno says, tells us that immortality is impossible; yet our heart cannot accept death as the final reality. Unamuno holds that human beings must live as if we were destined by God for eternity, even while reason denies the possibility. It is consciousness of this conflict which constitutes the "tragic sense of life."

Let us pause to consider this immortal yearning for immortality—even though the gnostics or intellectuals may be able to say that what follows is not philosophy but rhetoric. Moreover, the divine Plato, when he discussed the immortality of the soul in his *Phædo*, said that it was proper to clothe it in legend, μυθολογεῖν.[1]

First of all let us recall once again—and it will not be for the last time—that saying of Spinoza that every being endeavours to persist in itself, and that this endeavour is its actual essence, and implies indefinite time, and that the soul, in fine, sometimes with a clear and distinct idea, sometimes confusedly, tends to persist in its being with indefinite duration, and is aware of its persistency (*Ethic*, Part III., Props. VI.–X.).

It is impossible for us, in effect, to conceive of ourselves as not existing, and no effort is capable of enabling consciousness to realize absolute unconsciousness, its own annihilation. Try, reader, to imagine to yourself, when you are wide awake, the condition of your soul when you are in a deep sleep; try to fill your consciousness with the representation of no-consciousness, and you will see the impossibility of it. The effort to

---

1. mythologein: to make myths (ed.).

comprehend it causes the most tormenting dizziness. We cannot conceive ourselves as not existing.

The visible universe, the universe that is created by the instinct of self-preservation, becomes all too narrow for me. It is like a cramped cell, against the bars of which my soul beats its wings in vain. Its lack of air stifles me. More, more, and always more! I want to be myself, and yet without ceasing to be myself to be others as well, to merge myself into the totality of things visible and invisible, to extend myself into the illimitable of space and to prolong myself into the infinite of time. Not to be all and for ever is as if not to be—at least, let me be my whole self, and be so for ever and ever. And to be the whole of myself is to be everybody else. Either all or nothing!

All or nothing! And what other meaning can the Shakespearean "To be or not to be" have, or that passage in *Coriolanus* where it is said of Marcius "He wants nothing of a god but eternity"? Eternity, eternity!— that is the supreme desire! The thirst of eternity is what is called love among men, and whosoever loves another wishes to eternalize himself in him. Nothing is real that is not eternal.

From the poets of all ages and from the depths of their souls this tremendous vision of the flowing away of life like water has wrung bitter cries—from Pindar's "dream of a shadow," σκιᾶς ὄναρ, to Calderón's "life is a dream" and Shakespeare's "we are such stuff as dreams are made on," this last a yet more tragic sentence than Calderón's, for whereas the Castilian only declares that our life is a dream, but not that we ourselves are the dreamers of it, the Englishman makes us ourselves a dream, a dream that dreams.

The vanity of the passing world and love are the two fundamental and heart-penetrating notes of true poetry. And they are two notes of which neither can be sounded without causing the other to vibrate. The feeling of the vanity of the passing world kindles love in us, the only thing that triumphs over the vain and transitory, the only thing that fills life again and eternalizes it. In appearance at any rate, for in reality . . . And love, above all when it struggles against destiny, overwhelms us with the feeling of the vanity of this world of appearances and gives us a glimpse of another world, in which destiny is overcome and liberty is law.

Everything passes! Such is the refrain of those who have drunk, lips to the spring, of the fountain of life, of those who have tasted of the fruit of the tree of the knowledge of good and evil.

To be, to be for ever, to be without ending! thirst of being, thirst of being more! hunger of God! thirst of love eternalizing and eternal! to be for ever! to be God!

"Ye shall be as gods!" we are told in Genesis that the serpent said to the first pair of lovers (Gen. iii. 5). "If in this life only we have hope in Christ, we are of all men most miserable," wrote the Apostle (I Cor. XV. 19); and all religion has sprung historically from the cult of the dead—that is to say, from the cult of immortality.

The tragic Portuguese Jew of Amsterdam[2] wrote that the free man thinks of nothing less than of death; but this free man is a dead man, free from the impulse of life, for want of love, the slave of his liberty. This thought that I must die and the enigma of what will come after death is the very palpitation of my consciousness. When I contemplate the green serenity of the fields or look into the depths of clear eyes through which shines a fellow-soul, my consciousness dilates, I feel the diastole of the soul and am bathed in the flood of the life that flows about me, and I believe in my future; but instantly the voice of mystery whispers to me, "Thou shalt cease to be!" the angel of Death touches me with his wing, and the systole of the soul floods the depths of my spirit with the blood of divinity.

Like Pascal, I do not understand those who assert that they care not a farthing for these things, and this indifference "in a matter that touches themselves, their eternity, their all, exasperates me rather than moves me to compassion, astonishes and shocks me," and he who feels thus "is for me," as for Pascal, whose are the words just quoted, "a monster."

It has been said a thousand times and in a thousand books that ancestor-worship is for the most part the source of primitive religions, and it may be strictly said that what most distinguishes man from the other animals is that, in one form or another, he guards his dead and does not give them over to the neglect of teeming mother earth; he is an animal that guards its dead. And from what does he thus guard them? From what does he so futilely protect them? The wretched consciousness shrinks from its own annihilation, and, just as an animal spirit, newly severed from the womb of the world, finds itself confronted with the world and knows itself distinct from it, so consciousness must needs desire to possess another life than that of the world itself. And so the earth would run the risk of becoming a vast cemetery before the dead themselves should die again.

When mud huts or straw shelters, incapable of resisting the inclem-

2. The philosopher Spinoza (ed.).

ency of the weather, sufficed for the living, tumuli were raised for the dead, and stone was used for sepulchres before it was used for houses. It is the strong-builded houses of the dead that have withstood the ages, not the houses of the living; not the temporary lodgings but the permanent habitations.

This cult, not of death but of immortality, originates and preserves religions. In the midst of the delirium of destruction, Robespierre induced the Convention to declare the existence of the Supreme Being and "the consolatory principle of the immortality of the soul," the Incorruptible being dismayed at the idea of having himself one day to turn to corruption.

A disease? Perhaps; but he who pays no heed to his disease is heedless of his health, and man is an animal essentially and substantially diseased. A disease? Perhaps it may be, like life itself to which it is thrall, and perhaps the only health possible may be death; but this disease is the fount of all vigorous health. From the depth of this anguish, from the abyss of the feeling of our mortality, we emerge into the light of another heaven, as from the depth of Hell Dante emerged to behold the stars once again—

   e quindi uscimmo a riveder le stelle.[3]

Although this meditation upon mortality may soon induce in us a sense of anguish, it fortifies us in the end. Retire, reader, into yourself and imagine a slow dissolution of yourself—the light dimming about you—all things becoming dumb and soundless, enveloping you in silence—the objects that you handle crumbling away between your hands—the ground slipping from under your feet—your very memory vanishing as if in a swoon—everything melting away from you into nothingness and you yourself also melting away—the very consciousness of nothingness, merely as the phantom harbourage of a shadow, not even remaining to you.

I have heard it related of a poor harvester who died in a hospital bed, that when the priest went to anoint his hands with the oil of extreme unction, he refused to open his right hand, which clutched a few dirty coins, not considering that very soon neither his hand nor he himself would be his own any more. And so we close and clench, not our hand, but our heart, seeking to clutch the world in it.

A friend confessed to me that, foreseeing while in the full vigour of physical health the near approach of a violent death, he proposed to

3. "and then we emerged to see the stars again" (ed.).

concentrate his life and spend the few days which he calculated still remained to him in writing a book. Vanity of vanities!

If at the death of the body which sustains me, and which I call mine to distinguish it from the self that is I, my consciousness returns to the absolute unconsciousness from which it sprang, and if a like fate befalls all my brothers in humanity, then is our toil-worn human race nothing but a fatidical procession of phantoms, going from nothingness to nothingness, and humanitarianism the most inhuman thing known.

And the remedy is not that suggested in the quatrain that runs—

Cada vez que considero
que me tengo de morir,
tiendo la capa en el suelo
y no me harto de dormir.[4]

No! The remedy is to consider our mortal destiny without flinching, to fasten our gaze upon the gaze of the Sphinx, for it is thus that the malevolence of its spell is discharmed.

If we all die utterly, wherefore does everything exist? Wherefore? It is the Wherefore of the Sphinx; it is the Wherefore that corrodes the marrow of the soul; it is the begetter of that anguish which gives us the love of hope.

Among the poetic laments of the unhappy Cowper there are some lines written under the oppression of delirium, in which, believing himself to be the mark of the Divine vengeance, he exclaims—

Hell might afford my miseries a shelter.

This is the Puritan sentiment, the preoccupation with sin and predestination; but read the much more terrible words of Sénancour, expressive of the Catholic, not the Protestant, despair, when he makes his Obermann say, "L'homme est périssable. Il se peut; mais périssons en résistant, et, si le néant nous est réservé, ne faisons pas que ce soit une justice."[5] And I must confess, painful though the confession be, that in the days of the simple faith of my childhood, descriptions of the tortures of hell, however terrible, never made me tremble, for I always felt that nothingness was much more terrifying. He who suffers lives, and he who lives suffering, even though over the portal of his abode is written "Abandon all hope!" loves and hopes. It is better to live in pain than to cease to be in

4. Each time that I consider that it is my lot to die, I spread my cloak upon the ground and am never surfeited with sleeping.
5. "Humans must perish. Perhaps; but let us perish while resisting, and, if annihilation is our fate, let us not make it a just one" (ed.).

peace. The truth is that I could not believe in this atrocity of Hell, of an eternity of punishment, nor did I see any more real hell than nothingness and the prospect of it. And I continue in the belief that if we all believed in our salvation from nothingness we should all be better.

What is this *joie de vivre* that they talk about nowadays? Our hunger for God, our thirst of immortality, of survival, will always stifle in us this pitiful enjoyment of the life that passes and abides not. It is the frenzied love of life, the love that would have life to be unending, that most often urges us to long for death. "If it is true that I am to die utterly," we say to ourselves, "then once I am annihilated the world has ended so far as I am concerned—it is finished. Why, then, should it not end forthwith, so that no new consciousnesses, doomed to suffer the tormenting illusion of a transient and apparential existence, may come into being? If, the illusion of living being shattered, living for the mere sake of living or for the sake of others who are likewise doomed to die, does not satisfy the soul, what is the good of living? Our best remedy is death." And thus it is that we chant the praises of the never-ending rest because of our dread of it, and speak of liberating death.

Leopardi, the poet of sorrow, of annihilation, having lost the ultimate illusion, that of believing in his immortality—

> Peri l'inganno estremo.
> ch'eterno io mi credei,[6]

spoke to his heart of *l'infinita vanitá del tutto*,[7] and perceived how close is the kinship between love and death, and how "when love is born deep down in the heart, simultaneously a languid and weary desire to die is felt in the breast." The greater part of those who seek death at their own hand are moved thereto by love; it is the supreme longing for life, for more life, the longing to prolong and perpetuate life, that urges them to death, once they are persuaded of the vanity of this longing.

The problem is tragic and eternal, and the more we seek to escape from it, the more it thrusts itself upon us. Four-and-twenty centuries ago, in his dialogue on the immortality of the soul, the serene Plato—but was he serene?—spoke of the uncertainty of our dream of being immortal and of the *risk* that the dream might be vain, and from his own soul there escaped this profound cry—Glorious is the risk!—καλὸς γὰρ ὁ κίνδυνος, glorious is the risk that we are able to run of our souls never

---

6. "Then perished the ultimate illusion: thinking myself eternal." (ed.)
7. "the infinite vanity of everything" (ed.)

dying—a sentence that was the germ of Pascal's famous argument of the wager.

Faced with this risk, I am presented with arguments designed to eliminate it, arguments demonstrating the absurdity of the belief in the immortality of the soul; but these arguments fail to make any impression upon me, for they are reasons and nothing more than reasons, and it is not with reasons that the heart is appeased. I do not want to die—no; I neither want to die nor do I want to want to die; I want to live for ever and ever and ever. I want this "I" to live—this poor "I" that I am and that I feel myself to be here and now, and therefore the problem of the duration of my soul, of my own soul, tortures me.

I am the centre of my universe, the centre of the universe, and in my supreme anguish I cry with Michelet, "Mon moi, ils m'arrachent mon moi!"[8] What is a man profited if he shall gain the whole world and lose his own soul? (Matt. xvi. 26). Egoism, you say? There is nothing more universal than the individual, for what is the property of each is the property of all. Each man is worth more than the whole of humanity, nor will it do to sacrifice each to all save in so far as all sacrifice themselves to each.   ["The Hunger for Immortality" from *The Tragic Sense of Life*]

5. *Ultimate concern*

Theologian **Paul Tillich (1886–1965)** holds that behind all the many desires and concerns of life, there is something that is of "ultimate" and infinite concern: the concern for being itself, and for what is capable of threatening or saving our very existence. It is this object of ultimate concern which defines religion.

Ultimate concern is the abstract translation of the great commandment: "The Lord, our God, the Lord is one; and you shall love the Lord your God with all your heart, and with all your soul and with all your mind, and with all your strength."[9] The religious concern is ultimate; it excludes all other concerns from ultimate significance; it makes them preliminary. The ultimate concern is unconditional, independent of any conditions of character, desire, or circumstance. The unconditional con-

8. "My self, they are taking away my self!" (literally, my "I") (ed.).
9. Mark 12:29.

cern is total: no part of ourselves or of our world is excluded from it; there is no "place" to flee from it.[10] The total concern is infinite: no moment of relaxation and rest is possible in the face of a religious concern which is ultimate, unconditional, total, and infinite.

The word "concern" points to the "existential" character of religious experience. We cannot speak adequately of the "object of religion" without simultaneously removing its character as an object. That which is ultimate gives itself only to the attitude of ultimate concern. It is the correlate of an unconditional concern but not a "highest thing" called "the absolute" or "the unconditioned," about which we could argue in detached objectivity. It is the object of total surrender, demanding also the surrender of our subjectivity while we look at it. It is a matter of infinite passion and interest (Kierkegaard), making us its object whenever we try to make it our object. For this reason we have avoided terms like "*the* ultimate," "*the* unconditioned," "*the* universal," "*the* infinite," and have spoken of ultimate, unconditional, total, infinite concern. Of course, in every concern there is *something* about which one is concerned; but this something should not appear as a separated object which could be known and handled without concern. This, then, is the first formal criterion of theology: *The object of theology is what concerns us ultimately. Only those propositions are theological which deal with their object in so far as it can become a matter of ultimate concern for us.*

The negative meaning of this proposition is obvious. Theology should never leave the situation of ultimate concern and try to play a role within the arena of preliminary concerns. Theology cannot and should not give judgments about the aesthetic value of an artistic creation, about the scientific value of a physical theory or a historical conjecture, about the best methods of medical healing or social reconstruction, about the solution of political or international conflicts. The theologian *as* theologian is no expert in any matters of preliminary concern. And, conversely, those who are experts in these matters should not *as such* claim to be experts in theology. The first formal principle of theology, guarding the boundary line between ultimate concern and preliminary concerns, protects theology as well as the cultural realms on the other side of the line.

But this is not its entire meaning. Although it does not indicate the content of the ultimate concern and its relation to the preliminary concerns, it has implications in both respects. There are three possible rela-

10. Psalm 139.

tions of the preliminary concerns to that which concerns us ultimately. The first is mutual indifference, the second is a relation in which a preliminary concern is elevated to ultimacy, and the third is one in which a preliminary concern becomes the vehicle of the ultimate concern without claiming ultimacy for itself. The first relation is predominant in ordinary life with its oscillation between conditional, partial, finite situations and experiences and moments when the question of the ultimate meaning of existence takes hold of us. Such a division, however, contradicts the unconditional, total, and infinite character of the religious concern. It places our ultimate concern beside other concerns and deprives it of its ultimacy. This attitude sidesteps the ultimacy of the biblical commandments and that of the first theological criterion. The second relation is idolatrous in its very nature. Idolatry is the elevation of a preliminary concern to ultimacy. Something essentially conditioned is taken as unconditional, something essentially partial is boosted into universality, and something essentially finite is given infinite significance (the best example is the contemporary idolatry of religious nationalism). The conflict between the finite basis of such a concern and its infinite claim leads to a conflict of ultimates; it radically contradicts the biblical commandments and the first theological criterion. The third relation between the ultimate concern and the preliminary concerns makes the latter bearers and vehicles of the former. That which is a finite concern is not elevated to infinite significance, nor is it put beside the infinite, but in and through it the infinite becomes real. Nothing is excluded from this function. In and through every preliminary concern the ultimate concern can actualize itself. Whenever this happens, the preliminary concern becomes a possible object of theology. But theology deals with it only in so far as it is a medium, a vehicle, pointing beyond itself.

Pictures, poems, and music can become objects of theology, not from the point of view of their aesthetic form, but from the point of view of their power of expressing some aspects of that which concerns us ultimately, in and through their aesthetic form. Physical or historical or psychological insights can become objects of theology, not from the point of view of their cognitive form, but from the point of view of their power of revealing some aspects of that which concerns us ultimately in and through their cognitive form. Social ideas and actions, legal projects and procedures, political programs and decisions, can become objects of theology, not from the point of view of their social, legal, and political form, but from the point of view of their power of actualizing some aspects of that which concerns us ultimately in and through their social, legal, and political forms. Personality problems and developments, educational aims and methods, bodily and mental healing, can become objects of theology, not from the point of view of their ethical and technical form, but from the point of view of their power of mediating some aspects of that which concerns us ultimately in and through their ethical and technical form.

The question now arises: What is the content of our ultimate concern? What *does* concern us unconditionally? The answer, obviously, cannot be a special object, not even God, for the first criterion of theology must remain formal and general. If more is to be said about the nature of our ultimate concern, it must be derived from an analysis of the concept "ultimate concern." *Our ultimate concern is that which determines our being or not-being. Only those statements are theological which deal with their object in so far as it can become a matter of being or not-being for us.* This is the second formal criterion of theology.

Nothing can be of ultimate concern for us which does not have the power of threatening and saving our being. The term "being" in this context does not designate existence in time and space. Existence is continuously threatened and saved by things and events which have no ultimate concern for us. But the term "being" means the whole of human reality, the structure, the meaning, and the aim of existence. All this is threatened; it can be lost or saved. Man is ultimately concerned about his being and meaning. "To be or not to be" in *this* sense is a matter of ultimate, unconditional, total, and infinite concern. Man is infinitely concerned about the infinity to which he belongs, from which he is separated, and for which he is longing. Man is totally concerned about the totality which is his true being and which is disrupted in time and space. Man is unconditionally concerned about that which conditions his being beyond all the conditions in him and around him. Man is ultimately concerned about that which determines his ultimate destiny beyond all preliminary necessities and accidents.

The second formal criterion of theology does not point to any special content, symbol, or doctrine. It remains formal and, consequently, open for contents which are able to express "that which determines our being or nonbeing." At the same time it excludes contents which do not have this power from entering the theological realm. Whether it is a god who is a being beside others (even a highest being) or an angel who inhabits a celestial realm (called the realm of "spirits") or a man who possesses supranatural powers (even if he is called a god-man)—none of these is an object of theology if it fails to withstand the criticism of the second formal criterion of theology, that is, if it is not a matter of being or nonbeing for us. [*Systematic Theology*, Vol. 1]

6. Relationship poses the ultimate question

The Jewish philosopher **Martin Buber (1878–1965)** made a lasting contribution to modern religious thought in emphasizing "dialogue" as the key to understanding the divine/human relationship. In his classic work *I and Thou* Buber made a crucial distinction between "I-Thou" relations, characterized by trust, directness, and mutual concern, and "I-It" relations, in which persons merely know and use one another as impersonal objects. According to Buber, then, God is the "Eternal Thou," whom one can know in mutual relationship but not as an object of knowledge.

To man the world is twofold, in accordance with his twofold attitude.

The attitude of man is twofold, in accordance with the twofold nature of the primary words which he speaks.

The primary words are not isolated words, but combined words.

The one primary word is the combination *I-Thou.*

The other primary word is the combination *I-It;* wherein, without a change in the primary word, one of the words *He* and *She* can replace *It.*

Hence the *I* of man is also twofold.

For the *I* of the primary word *I-Thou* is a different *I* from that of the primary word *I-It.*

Primary words do not signify things, but they intimate relations.

Primary words do not describe something that might exist independently of them, but being spoken they bring about existence.

Primary words are spoken from the being.

If *Thou* is said, the *I* of the combination *I-Thou* is said along with it.

If *It* is said, the *I* of the combination *I-It* is said along with it.

The primary word *I-Thou* can only be spoken with the whole being.

The primary word *I-It* can never be spoken with the whole being.

There is no *I* taken in itself, but only the *I* of the primary word *I-Thou* and the *I* of the primary word *I-It.*

When a man says *I* he refers to one or other of these. The *I* to which he refers is present when he says *I*. Further, when he says *Thou* or *It,* the *I* of one of the two primary words is present.

The existence of *I* and the speaking of *I* are one and the same thing.

When a primary word is spoken the speaker enters the word and takes his stand in it.

The life of human beings is not passed in the sphere of transitive verbs alone. It does not exist in virtue of activities alone which have some *thing* for their object.

I perceive something. I am sensible of something. I imagine something. I will something. I feel something. I think something. The life of human beings does not consist of all this and the like alone.

This and the like together establish the realm of *It*.

But the realm of *Thou* has a different basis.

When *Thou* is spoken, the speaker has no thing for his object. For where there is a thing there is another thing. Every *It* is bounded by others; *It* exists only through being bounded by others. But when *Thou* is spoken, there is no thing. *Thou* has no bounds.

When *Thou* is spoken, the speaker has no *thing*; he has indeed nothing. But he takes his stand in relation.

The extended lines of relations meet in the eternal *Thou*.

Every particular *Thou* is a glimpse through to the eternal *Thou*; by means of every particular *Thou* the primary word addresses the eternal *Thou*. Through this mediation of the *Thou* of all beings fulfilment, and non-fulfilment, of relations comes to them: the inborn *Thou* is realized in each relation and consummated in none. It is consummated only in the direct relation with the *Thou* that by its nature cannot become *It*.

Men have addressed their eternal *Thou* with many names. In singing of Him who was thus named they always had the *Thou* in mind: the first myths were hymns of praise. Then the names took refuge in the language of *It*; men were more and more strongly moved to think of and to address their eternal *Thou* as an *It*. But all God's names are hallowed, for in them He is not merely spoken about, but also spoken to.

Many men wish to reject the word God as a legitimate usage, because it is so misused. It is indeed the most heavily laden of all the words used by men. For that very reason it is the most imperishable and most indispensable. What does all mistaken talk about God's being and works (though there has been, and can be, no other talk about these) matter in comparison with the one truth that all men who have addressed God had God Himself in mind? For he who speaks the word God and really has *Thou* in mind (whatever the illusion by which he is held), addresses the true *Thou* of his life, which cannot be limited by another *Thou*, and to which he stands in a relation that gathers up and includes all others.

But when he, too, who abhors the name, and believes himself to be godless, gives his whole being to addressing the *Thou* of his life, as a *Thou* that cannot be limited by another, he addresses God.

If we go on our way and meet a man who has advanced towards us and has also gone on *his* way, we know only our part of the way, not his—his we experience only in the meeting.

Of the complete relational event we know, with the knowledge of life lived, our going out to the relation, our part of the way. The other part only comes upon us, we do not know it; it comes upon us in the meeting. But we strain ourselves on it if we speak of it as though it were some thing beyond the meeting.

We have to be concerned, to be troubled, not about the other side but about our own side, not about grace but about will. Grace concerns us in so far as we go out to it and persist in its presence; but it is not our object.

The *Thou* confronts me. But I step into direct relation with it. Hence the relation means being chosen and choosing, suffering and action in one; just as any action of the whole being which means the suspension of all partial actions, and consequently of all sensations of actions grounded only in their particular limitation, is bound to resemble suffering.

This is the activity of the man who has become a whole being, an activity that has been termed doing nothing: nothing separate or partial stirs in the man any more, thus he makes no intervention in the world; it is the whole man, enclosed and at rest in his wholeness, that is effective —he has become an effective whole. To have won stability in this state is to be able to go out to the supreme meeting.

To this end the world of sense does not need to be laid aside as though it were illusory. There is no illusory world, there is only the world— which appears to us as twofold in accordance with our twofold attitude. Only the barrier of separation has to be destroyed. Further, no "going beyond sense-experience" is necessary; for every experience, even the most spiritual, could yield us only an *It*. Nor is any recourse necessary to a world of ideas and values; for they cannot become presentness for us. None of these things is necessary. Can it be said what really is neces- sary?—Not in the sense of a precept. For everything that has ever been devised and contrived in the time of the human spirit as precept, alleged preparation, practice, or meditation, has nothing to do with the primal, simple fact of the meeting. Whatever the advantages in knowledge or the wielding of power for which we have to thank this or that practice, none of this affects the meeting of which we are speaking; it all has its place in the world of *It* and does not lead one step, does not take *the* step, out of it. Going out to the relation cannot be taught in the sense of precepts being given. It can only be indicated by the drawing of a circle which excludes everything that is not this going out. Then the one thing that matters is visible, full acceptance of the present.

To be sure, this acceptance presupposes that the further a man has wandered in separated being the more difficult is the venture and the more elemental the turning. This does not mean a giving up of, say, the *I*, as mystical writings usually suppose: the *I* is as indispensable to this, the supreme, as to every relation, since relation is only possible between *I* and *Thou*. It is not the *I*, then, that is given up, but that false self-asserting instinct that makes a man flee to the possessing of things before the unreliable, perilous world of relation which has neither density nor duration and cannot be surveyed.

Every real relation with a being or life in the world is exclusive. Its *Thou* is freed, steps forth, is single, and confronts you. It fills the heavens. This does not mean that nothing else exists; but all else lives in *its* light. As long as the presence of the relation continues, this its cosmic range is inviolable. But as soon as a *Thou* becomes *It*, the cosmic range of the relation appears as an offense to the world, its exclusiveness as an exclusion of the universe.

In the relation with God unconditional exclusiveness and unconditional inclusiveness are one. He who enters on the absolute relation is concerned with nothing isolated any more, neither things nor beings, neither earth nor heaven; but everything is gathered up in the relation. For to step into pure relation is not to disregard everything but to see everything in the *Thou*, not to renounce the world but to establish it on its true basis. To look away from the world, or to stare at it, does not help a man to reach God; but he who sees the world in Him stands in His presence. "Here world, there God" is the language of *It*; "God in the world" is another language of *It*; but to eliminate or leave behind nothing at all, to include the whole world in the *Thou*, to give the world its due and its truth, to include nothing beside God but everything in him —this is full and complete relation.

Men do not find God if they stay in the world. They do not find Him if they leave the world. He who goes out with his whole being to meet his *Thou* and carries to it all being that is in the world, finds Him who cannot be sought.

Of course God is the "wholly Other"; but He is also the wholly Same, the wholly Present. Of course He is the *Mysterium Tremendum* that appears and overthrows; but He is also the mystery of the self-evident, nearer to me than my *I*.

If you explore the life of things and of conditioned being you come to the unfathomable, if you deny the life of things and of conditioned being you stand before nothingness, if you hallow this life you meet the living God.   [*I and Thou*]

B. Experiences of Transcendence and the Sacred

7. The experience of the sacred in the scriptures

The call of Abraham: **Genesis 12:1–8**

Jacob wrestles with the angel: **Genesis 32:24–30**

Moses and the burning bush: **Exodus 3:1–22**

The event at the Red Sea: **Exodus 14:10–15:18**

The call of Jeremiah: **Jeremiah 1:4–19**

The vision of Isaiah: **Isaiah 6:1–13**

The vision of Ezekiel: **Ezekiel 1:1–28**

Daniel's vision of the four beasts: **Daniel 7:1–22**

Jesus and the demoniacs: **Matthew 8:28–34**

Jesus walks on water: **Matthew 14:22–32**

The transfiguration of Jesus: **Matthew 17:1–13**

The resurrection accounts: **Matthew 28:1–10   Mark 16:1–8   Luke 24:1–35   John 21:1–19**

The vision of John: **Revelation 1:10–20**

8. Anxiety and courage

The notion of "anxiety" (or "*Angst*") was first developed as a theological category by the Danish philosopher Søren Kierkegaard, and became a major theme of the Existentialists. Here **Paul Tillich** presents an ontology of anxiety as the unavoidable reaction of the human person to the threat of non-being implied in our very finitude. For Tillich, it is only when we have faced this threat that we can understand what the notion of "God" really means: the absolute Ground of Being, the object of our "ultimate concern" [see

#5]. In this sense, anxiety may be seen as a negative sign of transcendence, for it is the revolt of the human spirit against non-being and an intimation of the dynamism toward God.

Courage is usually described as the power of the mind to overcome fear. The meaning of fear seemed too obvious to deserve inquiry. But in the last decades depth psychology in cooperation with Existentialist philosophy has led to a sharp distinction between fear and anxiety and to more precise definitions of each of these concepts. Sociological analyses of the present period have pointed to the importance of anxiety as a group phenomenon. Literature and art have made anxiety a main theme of their creations, in content as well as in style. The effect of this has been the awakening of at least the educated groups to an awareness of their own anxiety, and a permeation of the public consciousness by ideas and symbols of anxiety. Today it has become almost a truism to call our time an "age of anxiety." This holds equally for America and Europe.

Nevertheless it is necessary for an ontology of courage to include an ontology of anxiety, for they are interdependent. And it is conceivable that in the light of an ontology of courage some fundamental aspects of anxiety may become visible. The first assertion about the nature of anxiety is this: anxiety is the state in which a being is aware of its possible nonbeing. The same statement, in a shorter form, would read: anxiety is the existential awareness of nonbeing. "Existential" in this sentence means that it is not the abstract knowledge of nonbeing which produces anxiety but the awareness that nonbeing is a part of one's own being. It is not the realization of universal transitoriness, not even the experience of the death of others, but the impression of these events on the always latent awareness of our own having to die that produces anxiety. Anxiety is finitude, experienced as one's own finitude. This is the natural anxiety of man as man, and in some way of all living beings. It is the anxiety of nonbeing, the awareness of one's finitude as finitude.

THE INTERDEPENDENCE OF FEAR AND ANXIETY

Anxiety and fear have the same ontological root but they are not the same in actuality. This is common knowledge, but it has been emphasized and overemphasized to such a degree that a reaction against it may occur and wipe out not only the exaggerations but also the truth of the distinction. Fear, as opposed to anxiety has a definite object (as most authors agree), which can be faced, analyzed, attacked, endured. One can act upon it, and in acting upon it participate in it—even if in the form of struggle. In this way one can take it into one's self-affirmation. Courage can meet every object of fear, because it is an object and makes participation possible. Courage can take the fear produced by a definite object into itself, because this object, however frightful it may be, has a side with which it participates in us and we in it. One could say that as long as there is an *object* of fear love in the sense of participation can conquer fear.

But this is not so with anxiety, because anxiety has no object, or rather, in a paradoxical phrase, its object is the negation of every object. Therefore participation, struggle, and love with respect to it are impossible. He who is in anxiety is, insofar as it is mere anxiety, delivered to it without help. Helplessness in the state of anxiety can be observed in animals and humans alike. It expresses itself in loss of direction, inadequate reactions, lack of "intentionality" (the being related to meaningful contents of knowledge or will). The reason for this sometimes striking behavior is the lack of an object on which the subject (in the state of anxiety) can concentrate. The only object is the threat itself, but not the source of the threat, because the source of the threat is "nothingness."

One might ask whether this threatening "nothing" is not the unknown, the indefinite possibility of an actual threat? Does not anxiety cease in the moment in which a known object of fear appears? Anxiety then would be fear of the unknown. But this is an insufficient explanation of anxiety. For there are innumerable realms of the unknown, different for each subject, and faced without any anxiety. It is the unknown of a special type which is met with anxiety. It is the unknown which by its very nature cannot be known, because it is nonbeing.

Fear and anxiety are distinguished but not separated. They are immanent within each other: The sting of fear is anxiety, and anxiety strives toward fear. Fear is being afraid of something, a pain, the rejection by a person or a group, the loss of something or somebody, the moment of dying. But in the anticipation of the threat originating in these things, it is not the negativity itself which they will bring upon the subject that is frightening but the anxiety about the possible implications of this negativity. The outstanding example—and more than an example—is the fear of dying. Insofar as it is *fear* its object is the anticipated event of being killed by sickness or an accident and thereby suffering agony and the loss of everything. Insofar as it is *anxiety* its object is the absolutely unknown "after death," the nonbeing which remains nonbeing even if it is filled with images of our present experience. The dreams in Hamlet's soliloquy, "to be or not to be," which we may have after death and which make cowards of us all are frightful not because of their manifest content but because of their power to symbolize the threat of nothingness, in religious terms of "eternal death." The symbols of hell created by Dante produce anxiety not because of their objective imagery but because they express the "nothingness" whose power is experienced in the anxiety of guilt. Each of the situations described in the *Inferno* could be met by courage on the basis of participation and love. But of course the meaning is that this is impossible; in other words they are not real situations but symbols of the objectless, of nonbeing.

The fear of death determines the element of anxiety in every fear. Anxiety, if not modified by the fear of an object, anxiety in its nakedness, is always the anxiety of ultimate nonbeing. Immediately seen, anxiety is the painful feeling of not being able to deal with the threat of a special situation. But a more exact analysis shows that in the anxiety about any special situation anxiety about the human situation as such is implied. It is the anxiety of not being able to preserve one's own being which underlies every fear and is the frightening element in it. In the moment, therefore, in which "naked anxiety" lays hold of the mind, the previous objects of fear cease to be definite objects. They appear as what they always were in part, symptoms of man's basic anxiety. As such they are beyond the reach of even the most courageous attack upon them.

This situation drives the anxious subject to establish objects of fear. Anxiety strives to become fear, because fear can be met by courage. It is impossible for a finite being to stand naked anxiety for more than a flash of time. People who have experienced these moments, as for instance some mystics in their visions of the "night of the soul," or Luther under the despair of the demonic assaults, or Nietzsche-Zarathustra in the experience of the "great disgust," have told of the unimaginable horror of it. This horror is ordinarily avoided by the transformation of anxiety into fear of something, no matter what. The human mind is not only, as Calvin has said, a permanent factory of idols, it is also a permanent factory of fears—the first in order to escape God, the second in order to escape anxiety; and there is a relation between the two. For facing the God who is really God means facing also the absolute threat of nonbeing. The "naked absolute" (to use a phrase of Luther's) produces "naked anxiety"; for it is the extinction of every finite self-affirmation, and not a possible object of fear and courage. But ultimately the attempts to transform anxiety into fear are vain. The basic anxiety, the anxiety of a finite being about the threat of nonbeing, cannot be eliminated. It belongs to existence itself.   [*The Courage To Be*]

9. The ascent of the mind from beauty to God

In his dialogue *The Symposium*, the Greek philosopher **Plato (ca. 427–ca. 347 B.C.)** discusses the nature of love and beauty. A mysterious woman named Diotima instructs Socrates, Plato's master, on the nature of eros—the Greek term for love or desire. For Plato, things are beautiful (or good) and lovable because they participate, in varying degrees, in an ultimate and divine beauty which is the final goal of all human desire. Therefore, while eros begins as physical ("erotic") love, it is essentially a dynamism that goes beyond physical beauty to spiritual beauty, and finally to the ultimately beautiful and lovable, which is God.

"The one who has been instructed in the matter of love, and has learned to see the beautiful in its proper order, when he comes toward the end will suddenly perceive a nature of wondrous beauty—and this beauty, Socrates, is the final cause, the goal of all our prior striving. First of all, this beauty is everlasting: not increasing and decreasing or growing and decaying. Furthermore, it is not attractive in one aspect or relation and repulsive in another, or beautiful in some times or places and ugly in others . . . rather, it is pure beauty: absolute, separate, simple, and everlasting. It is without decrease or increase or any change at all, and it is the source of the ever-growing and perishing beauty of all other things.

He who, under the influence of true *eros*, ascends from perishable things and begins to see that final beauty, is not far from the goal. And the true order of proceeding, or being led, to the things of love is this: to use the beauties of earth as steps along which one ascends toward that other beauty; going from one to two; from two to all beautiful forms; from beautiful forms, to beautiful actions; from beautiful or good actions, to beautiful ideas; and from beautiful ideas, one arrives at the notion of absolute beauty, and at last knows what the essence of beauty is. This, my dear Socrates, is that life above all others that a person should live: the life of contemplation of absolute beauty. . . . If one had eyes to see true beauty—the divine beauty, pure and clear and unmixed, not polluted with mortality and all the different vanities of human life . . . in that communion, seeing beauty with the mind's eye, one would be enabled to bring forth not mere images of beauty, but realities; for one would have hold not of a reflection, but of reality itself, and one would bring forth and educate true virtue, and would become the friend of God and be immortal, if mortal beings can. . . ." [*The Symposium*]

10. *Love desires eternity*

The Catalan author **José Maria Gironella** in his novel *The Cypresses Believe in God* writes of an atheist who comes to believe in God because "he loved his wife so much that suddenly the idea that everything should end with death horrified him. It seemed impossible to him that she should not be eternal; and he in turn desired with all his heart to have an eternity to continue living in union with her. After ten years of marriage, his desire had become conviction. . . ."

Contemporary German thinker **Josef Pieper** examines the thought of a number of philosophers and theologians who hold that the nature of love is to will the good of the other. This means to will the other's existence—even that the other should "be" forever. The biblical *Song of Solomon* says that "love is stronger than death" (8:6). Is this merely poetry, or wishful thinking? Or can human love give us a true intimation of eternity?

What is it that I really "will" by loving? What do I want when I turn to another person and say: It's good that you exist? It is clear, as has already been noted, that this can be said and meant with very different kinds of orchestration. *In concreto* many different degrees of intensity are conceivable. Still, even the weakest degree evidently testifies to approval of the mere existence of the other person; and that certainly is no small thing. We need only try to answer with complete sincerity the test question: Do I really in my heart of hearts have "nothing against" (this being probably the minimal degree of approval) the existence of this particular, unique associate, neighbor, or housemate? And to move from that to: "How wonderful that you exist!" In saying that, what do I really have in mind? What am I really getting at? What precisely is it that I am "willing"?

Such writers as Thomas Aquinas, Ortega y Gasset, Vladimir Soloviev, and Maurice Blondel have replied to this question with astonishing unanimity in basic intent, although the radicality of some of their statements sometimes makes their point too strongly and renders their answers of dubious value if not downright wrong. Thomas Aquinas in his now famous beginner's textbook avers: The first thing that a lover "wills" is for the beloved to exist and live. "The 'I' who loves above all wants the existence of the 'You.' " The somewhat forgotten phenomenologist and logician Alexander Pfänder, a magnificient analyst of the mental processes, calls love "an act of partisanship for the existence of the beloved," and even "a continual affirmative keeping the beloved in existence"; the lover "confers upon the beloved the right to exist on his own authority."

It is true that we read these last two sentences with a feeling of uneasiness; something seems to be wrong. Is this not sentimentally overestimating the powers of a loving person? Ortega y Gasset, although basically intending to make the same point, puts it much more precisely and circumspectly: As lovers, he says, we "continually and intentionally give life to something which depends on us." The lover "refuses to accept the possibility of a universe without it. Maurice Blondel boldly asserts: "*L'amour est par excellence ce qui fait être*"—love is above all what "makes be," that is, what makes something or someone exist. But again we can accept this sententious phrase only if we understand it as bespeaking the lover's *intention*.

By far the most extreme formulation of the idea that is struggling to emerge through all these different phrases is to be found in Vladimir Soloviev's essay "On the meaning of Sexual Love," in which he describes love as a force that excludes death, protests against it, and actually denies it. I confess that I react to such a statement with perplexed astonishment. Perhaps we may say that true love makes us realize, more directly than any theorizing can, that the beloved as a person cannot simply drop out of reality, and even—though this to be sure will be evident only to the believer—the beloved will be physically resurrected and live forever, through death and beyond it. This at any rate, is the way I have always understood Gabriel Marcel's moving words: "To love a person means to say: You will not die." [*About Love*]

11. The dynamism of the world toward Spirit

Pierre Teilhard de Chardin (1881–1955), a Jesuit priest, was a noted paleontologist. His scientific researches into the evolution of the human species, far from diminishing his faith, led him to see the entire cosmos not as a mere collection of individual beings, but as a unified process in which all things are related together in an upward evolutionary movement, each stage of which brings increased complexity and subjectivity. Ontogenesis (the evolution of individual beings) is a small-scale reflection of a universal cosmogenesis (the evolution of the universe). The world of matter progresses toward the appearance of conscious and free subjects, who are the "face," the personal expression of the universe itself. Persons in turn tend to a higher unity, a communion among themselves and with the universal whole. For Teilhard, the question that arises from modern science is: What is the source and the goal of this dynamism that we see active in the cosmos? This question can only finally be answered in religious terms: the "point Omega" of evolution is the unity of all things in God's love.

The unity of the world is of a dynamic or evolutionary nature. . . . In the past, we regarded ourselves and the things around us as "points" closed in on themselves. But now beings are revealed as something like fibers woven together in a universal process. Everything plunges backward into the abyss of the past. And everything thrusts forward toward the abyss of the future. Through its history, each being is coextensive with all Time; and its ontogenesis is only an infinitesimal element in a Cosmogenesis in which, finally, individuality expresses itself as the face of the Universe.

Thus the universal Whole, as well as each element within it, is defined for me by a particular movement which animates it. But what can this movement be? Where is it taking us? In facing this question, I find the suggestions and the evidence gathered throughout the course of my professional researches moving and coming together. And it is as an historian of Life, at least as much as a philosopher, that I reply, from the depths of my reason and from the depths of my heart: "It is moving toward Spirit." [How I Believe; trans. R. Viladesau]

12. Experience of God in the ordinary

The German Jesuit **Karl Rahner (1904–1984)** remains one of the most influential theologians of the twentieth century. At the center of his theology is the conviction that God actually shares his own life with humanity, and that we can experience that life as the depth of our own being, even if we are not explicitly aware of it. Wherever a person lives with radical courage and love, there is an experience of God and an "implicit" faith response, even if God remains unacknowledged or is denied on the conceptual level.

First let us ask: Have you ever experienced the spiritual element in man? And the answer may be: Yes, I have had this experience and have it every day. I think, I decide, I love, I rejoice over values like knowledge and art. So I know what spirit is. Now the matter is not so simple. For in the examples that have been cited "spirit" is only a kind of extra benefit from earthly life which makes it beautiful and in some way significant. But this does not mean that we are experiencing anything at all of the transcendent divine Spirit. Where are we to find experience of that Spirit who is anything but an intrinsic element of natural life? Only a modest word or two can be said about this, perhaps by mentioning cases where a spiritual experience of God seems credible.

Have we ever kept silent, despite the urge to defend ourselves, when we were being unfairly treated? Have we ever forgiven another although we gained nothing by it and our forgiveness was accepted as quite natural? Have we ever made a sacrifice without receiving any thanks or acknowledgment, without even feeling any inward satisfaction? Have we ever decided to do a thing simply for the sake of conscience, knowing that we must bear sole responsibility for our decision without being able to explain it to anyone? Have we ever tried to act purely for love of God when no warmth sustained us, when our act seemed a leap in the dark, simply nonsensical? Were we ever good to someone without expecting a trace of gratitude and without the comfortable feeling of having been "unselfish"?

If we can find such experiences in our life, then we have had that very experience of the Spirit which we are after here—the experience of the Eternal, the experience that the Spirit is something more than and different from a part of this world, the experience that happiness in this world is not the whole point of existence, the experience of trust as we sink into darkness, the experience of a faith for which this world provides no reason. In this context we can understand what secret passion burns in the real men of the Spirit and in the saints. Penetrated though they be with the "Lord, I am not worthy," they are bent on having this experience. At their vitals gnaws a fear of sticking in this world, and so they crave a pledge that they have already begun to live in the Spirit. Whereas for ordinary men such experiences are only unpleasant interruptions of normal life which cannot quite be avoided, the men of the Spirit and the saints find in them a taste of the pure Spirit—hence their strange life, their poverty, their cult of humility, their longing "to depart and be with Christ" (cf. Phil. 1, 23; 3, 12ff.). They well know that grace can bless even the reasonable doings of everyday life; they know that on earth we are not angels and are not meant to be. But by faith they know that man as a spirit must really live on the frontier between the world and God, between time and eternity. And by their messages to this person or that, they try to prove to themselves that the Spirit in them is something other than a means of living earthly life well.

Now if we have *this* experience of the Spirit—by accepting it—then we who live in faith have in fact experienced the supernatural, perhaps without quite realizing it.   [*Do You Believe in God?*]

In making himself the dynamism and the goal of our hope in his grace, God is truly revealed to us. Grace, which is given to the spirit, the possibility of hope granted by that grace, which reaches out towards that goal, God himself, is truly revelation. It does not need to be consciously understood as such, nor to be distinguished consciously from all the other experiences of a man who is spiritually free, nor even to be explicitly recognized as different by the individual concerned. Nothing alters the fact that it is a truly personal and divine revelation. It does not, in this instance, result directly from the communication of certain dogmas, but springs from the heart and soul of the free person, breaks open this heart through its dynamism and exposes it directly to God and so gives it the courage to hope for everything, that is, to hope for God himself. This inner spiritual dynamism of man should be accepted and not retarded and reduced by any false modesty (implying a last secret fear of life), so that no other good is sought as the final goal of life. If it is accepted, then what we call faith, in theological terms, is already present.

This acceptance of unrestricted and unconditional hope in freedom must not initially be considered as an explicitly religious occurrence. Whenever a man is true to the dictates of his conscience, whenever he does not reject an unconditional hope in the final moment of decision in spite of all disappointments and disasters in his experience of life, that is revelation. That is faith. In Christian terminology, that is the work of the Holy Spirit, no matter whether it is put explicitly into words or not. The acceptance of life in courage and hope sets a person free into the saving and incomprehensible greatness of God and his freedom. It can take place in the midst of the dull everyday life of the ordinary man, because even this everyday average man cannot avoid such ultimate decisions, even when they seem usually to be very unobtrusive. Faith of this sort can therefore flourish in courageous unconditional hope, where religion as such is scarcely or not at all formalized. This faith can even flourish where a man, for whatever reasons, draws back from giving a name to what is inconceivable and so nameless in his life. Hope in courage, which is what true faith is, is in demand everywhere and is found everywhere, even among those who are only anonymous Christians. True faith in the full sense of the word is only possible in free hope, which is absolute courage; and such absolute courage in unconditional hope is, conversely, faith in a real Christian sense.   [*Meditations on Freedom and the Spirit*]

13. The fascinating and awesome mystery

In *The Idea of the Holy*, German Protestant theologian **Rudolf Otto (1869–1937)** sought to describe scientifically the nature of the human encounter with the divine; that is, Otto sought a description of religious experience in "neutral" language that built on, but transcended, all religious traditions. Drawing on his studies of many world religions, Otto posited a human encounter with some *"Mysterium Tremendum"* (Latin for "awesome mystery") as the foundational experience in religion. This awesome mystery is usually described in religious tradition and scripture as "holy"—"set apart"—to distinguish it from all other human experiences. This encounter gives rise to a human awareness of the "numinous" (from the Latin *numen*, "divine spirit") that provokes a "creature-feeling" of both attraction and fear (*tremor*) before such overpoweringness (*majestas*) and energy (*orge*). Otto argued that this fascinating (*fascinans*) but frightening mystery that is encountered —external to the human, awe-inspiring, but benevolent—is what the word "God" in western religious language points to. His book, originally published in 1917, is now regarded as a classic statement on the nature of religious life.

"MYSTERIUM TREMENDUM"

The Analysis of "Tremendum"

Let us consider the deepest and most fundamental element in all strong and sincerely felt religious emotion. Faith unto salvation, trust, love—all these are there. But over and above these is an element which may also on occasion, quite apart from them, profoundly affect us and occupy the mind with a wellnigh bewildering strength. Let us follow it up with every effort of sympathy and imaginative intuition wherever it is to be found, in the lives of those around us, in sudden, strong ebullitions of personal piety and the frames of mind such ebullitions evince, in the fixed and ordered solemnities of rites and liturgies, and again in the atmosphere that clings to old religious monuments and buildings, to temples and to churches. If we do so we shall find we are dealing with something for which there is only one appropriate expression, *"myste-rium tremendum."* The feeling of it may at times come sweeping like a gentle tide, pervading the mind with a tranquil mood of deepest worship. It may pass over into a more set and lasting attitude of the soul, continuing, as it were, thrillingly vibrant and resonant, until at last it dies away and the soul resumes its 'profane', nonreligious mood of everyday experience. It may burst in sudden eruption up from the depths of the soul with spasms and convulsions, or lead to the strangest excitements, to intoxicated frenzy, to transport, and to ecstasy. It has its wild and demonic forms and can sink to an almost grisly horror and shuddering. It has its crude, barbaric antecedents and early manifestations, and again it may be developed into something beautiful and pure and glorious. It may become the hushed, trembling, and speechless humility of the creature in the presence of—whom or what? In the presence of that which is *mystery* inexpressible and above all creatures.

It is again evident at once that here too our attempted formulation by means of a concept is once more a merely negative one. Conceptually *mysterium* denotes merely that which is hidden and esoteric, that which is beyond conception or understanding, extraordinary and unfamiliar. The term does not define the object more positively in its qualitative character. But though what is enunciated in the word is negative, what is meant is something absolutely and intensely positive. This pure positive we can experience in feelings, feelings which our discussion can help to make clear to us, in so far as it arouses them actually in our hearts.

The Element of Awefulness

Tremor is in itself merely the perfectly familiar and 'natural' emotion of fear. But here the term is taken, aptly enough but still only by analogy, to denote a quite specific kind of emotional response, wholly distinct from that of being afraid, though it so far resembles it that the analogy of fear may be used to throw light upon its nature. There are in some languages special expressions which denote, either exclusively or in the first instance, this "fear" that is more than fear proper. The Hebrew *hiqdish* (hallow) is an example. To "keep a thing holy in the heart" means to mark it off by a feeling of peculiar dread, not to be mistaken for any ordinary dread, that is, to appraise it by the category of the numinous.

But the Old Testament throughout is rich in parallel expressions for this feeling. Specially noticeable is the *"emah* of Yahweh" ("fear of God"), which Yahweh can pour forth, dispatching almost like a daemon, and which seizes upon a man with paralysing effect: . . . Compare Exodus 23:27—"I will send my fear before thee, and will destroy all the people to whom thou shalt come . . ."; also Job 9:34; 13:21 ("let not his fear terrify me"; "let not thy dread make me afraid"). Here we have a terror fraught with an inward shuddering such as not even the most menacing and overpowering created thing can instil. It has something spectral in it. . . .

Of modern languages English has the words "awe," "aweful," which in their deeper and most special sense approximate closely to our meaning. The phrase, "he stood aghast," is also suggestive in this connexion. . . . [The] antecedent stage [of "religious dread" or "awe"] is "daemonic dread" (cf. the horror of Pan) with its queer perversion, a sort of abortive offshoot, the "dread of ghosts." It first begins to stir in the feeling of "something uncanny," "eerie," or "weird." It is this feeling which, emerging in the mind of primeval man, forms the starting-point for the entire religious development in history. "Daemons" and "gods" alike spring from this root, and all the products of "mythological apperception" of "fantasy" are nothing but different modes in which it has been objectified. And all ostensible explanations of the origin of religion in terms of animism or magic or folk-psychology are doomed from the outset to wander astray and miss the real goal of their inquiry, unless they recognize this fact of our nature—primary, unique, underivable from anything else—to be the basic factor and the basic impulse underlying the entire process of religious evolution.

Not only is the saying of Luther, that the natural man cannot fear God perfectly, correct from the standpoint of psychology, but we ought to go farther and add that the natural man is quite unable even to "shudder" (*grauen*) or feel horror in the real sense of the word. For "shuddering" is something more than "natural," ordinary fear. It implies that the mysterious is already beginning to loom before the mind, to touch the feelings. It implies the first application of a category of valuation which has no place in the everyday natural world of ordinary experience, and is only possible to a being in whom has been awakened a mental predisposition, unique in kind and different in a definite way from any "natural" faculty. And this newly-revealed capacity, even in the crude and violent manifestations which are all it at first evinces, bears witness to a completely new function of experience and standard of valuation, only belonging to the spirit of man.

Before going on to consider the elements which unfold as the "tremendum" develops, let us give a little further consideration to the first crude, primitive forms in which this "numinous dread" or awe shows itself. It is the mark which really characterizes the so-called "religion of primitive man," and there it appears as "daemonic dread." This crudely naive and primordial emotional disturbance, and the fantastic images to which it gives rise, are later overborne and ousted by more highly developed forms of the numinous emotion, with all its mysteriously impelling power. But even when this has long attained its higher and purer mode of expression it is possible for the primitive types of excitation that were formerly a part of it to break out in the soul in all their original naivete and so to be experienced afresh. That this is so is shown by the potent attraction again and again exercised by the element of horror and "shudder" in ghost stories, even among persons of high all-round education. It is remarkable that the physical reaction to which this unique "dread" of the uncanny gives rise is also unique, and is not found in the case of any "natural" fear or terror. We say: "my blood ran icy cold," and "my flesh crept." The "cold blood" feeling may be a symptom of ordinary, natural fear, but there is something non-natural or supernatural about the symptom of "creeping flesh." And any one who is capable of more precise introspection must recognize that the distinction between such a "dread" and natural fear is not simply one of degree and intensity. The awe or "dread" *may* indeed be so overwhelmingly great that it seems to penetrate to the very marrow, making the man's hair bristle and his limbs quake. But it may also steal upon him almost unobserved as the gentlest of agitations, a mere fleeting shadow passing across his mood. It has therefore nothing to do with intensity, and no natural fear passes over into it merely by being intensified. I may be beyond all measure afraid and terrified without there being even a trace of the feeling of uncanniness in my emotion. . . .

Though the numinous emotion in its completest development shows a world of difference from the mere "daemonic dread," yet not even at the highest level does it belie its pedigree or kindred. Even when the worship of "daemons," has long since reached the higher level of worship of "gods," these gods still retain as *numina* something of the "ghost" in the impress they make on the feelings of the worshipper, viz., the peculiar quality of the "uncanny" and "aweful," which survives with the quality of exaltedness and sublimity or is symbolized by means of it. And this element, softened though it is, does not disappear even on the highest level of all, where the worship of God is at its purest. Its disappearance would be indeed an essential loss: The shudder reappears in a form ennobled beyond measure where the soul, held speechless, trembles inwardly to the farthest fibre of its being. It invades the mind mightily in Christian worship with the words: "Holy, Holy, Holy"; it breaks forth from the hymn of Tersteegen:

God Himself is present:
Heart, be stilled before Him:
Prostrate inwardly adore Him.

The "shudder" has here lost its crazy and bewildering note, but not the ineffable something that holds the mind. It has become a mystical awe, and sets free as its accompaniment, reflected in self-consciousness, that "creature-feeling" that has already been described as the feeling of personal nothingness and submergence before the awe-inspiring object directly experienced.

The referring of this feeling of numinous tremor to its object in the numen brings into relief a property of the latter which plays an important part in our Holy Scriptures, and which has been the occasion of many difficulties, both to commentators and to theologians, from its puzzling and baffling nature. This is the . . . *orge*, the Wrath of Yahweh, which recurs in the New Testament as *orge theou* [wrath of God], and which is clearly analogous to the idea occurring in many religions of a mysterious *va deorum* [God's anger]. To pass through the Indian Pantheon of gods is to find deities who seem to be made up altogether out of such an *orge;* and even the higher Indian gods of grace and pardon have frequently, beside their merciful, their "wrath" form. But as regards the "wrath of Yahweh," the strange features about it have for long been a matter for constant remark. In the first place, it is patent from many passages of the Old Testament that this "wrath" has no concern whatever with moral qualities. There is something very baffling in the way in which it "is kindled" and manifested. It is, as has been well said, "like a hidden force of nature," like stored-up electricity, discharging itself upon anyone who comes too near. It is "incalculable" and "arbitrary." Anyone who is accustomed to think of deity only by its rational attributes must see in this "wrath" mere caprice and wilful passion. But such a view would have been emphatically rejected by the religious men of the Old Covenant, for to them the Wrath of God, so far from being a diminution of His Godhead, appears as a natural expression of it, an element of "holiness" itself, and a quite indispensable one. And in this they are entirely right. This *orge* is nothing but the *tremendum* itself, apprehended and expressed by the aid of a naive analogy from the domain of natural experience, in this case from the ordinary passional life of men. "Wrath" here is the "ideogram" of a unique emotional moment in religious experience, a moment whose singularly daunting and awe-inspiring character must be gravely disturbing to those persons who will recognize nothing in the divine nature but goodness, love, and a sort of confidential intimacy, in a word, only those aspects of God which turn toward the world of men. . . .

The Element of "Overpoweringness" ("Majestas")

We have been attempting to unfold the implications of that aspect of the mysterium tremendum indicated by the adjective, and the result so far may be summarized in two words, constituting, as before, what may be called an "ideogram," rather than a concept proper, viz. "absolute unapproachability."

It will be felt at once that there is yet a further element which must be added, that, namely, of "might," "power," "absolute overpowering-ness." We will take to represent this the term *majestas*, majesty—the more readily because anyone with a feeling for language must detect a last faint trace of the numinous still clinging to the word. The *tremendum* may then be rendered more adequately *tremenda majestas*, or "aweful majesty." This second element of majesty may continue to be vividly preserved, where the first, that of unapproachability, recedes and dies away, as may be seen, for example, in mysticism. It is especially in relation to this element of majesty or absolute overpoweringness that the creature-consciousness, of which we have already spoken, comes upon the scene, as a sort of shadow or subjective reflection of it. Thus, in contrast to "the overpowering" of which we are conscious as an object over against the self, there is the feeling of one's own submergence, of being but "dust and ashes" and nothingness. And this forms the numinous raw material for the feeling of religious humility. . . .

The Element of "Energy" or Urgency

There is, finally, a third element comprised in those of *tremendum* and *majestas*, awefulness and majesty, and this I venture to call the "urgency" or "energy" of the numinous object. It is particularly vividly perceptible in the *orge* or "wrath"; and it everywhere clothes itself in symbolical expressions—vitality, passion, emotional temper, will, force, movement, excitement, activity, impetus. These features are typical and recur again and again from the daemonic level up to the idea of the "living" God. We have here the factor that has everywhere more than any other prompted the fiercest opposition to the "philosophic" God of mere rational speculation who can be put into a definition. And for their part the philosophers have condemned these expressions of the energy of the numen, whenever they are brought on to the scene, as sheer anthropomorphism. . . .

For wherever men have been contending for the "living" God or for voluntarism, there, we may be sure, have been non-rationalists fighting rationalists and rationalism. It was so with Luther in his controversy with Erasmus; and Luther's *omnipotentia Dei* [omnipotence of God] in his [essay] *De Servo Arbitrio* is nothing but the union of "majesty"—in the sense of absolute supremacy—with this "energy," in the sense of a force that knows not stint nor stay, which is urgent, active, compelling, and alive. In mysticism, too, this element of "energy" is a very living and vigorous factor at any rate in the "voluntaristic" mysticism, the mysticism of love, where it is very forcibly seen in that "consuming fire" of love whose burning strength the mystic can hardly bear, but begs that the heat that has scorched him may be mitigated, lest he be himself destroyed by it. And in this urgency and pressure the mystic's "love" claims a perceptible kinship with the *orge* itself, the scorching and consuming wrath of God; it is the same "energy," only differently directed. "Love," says one of the mystics, "is nothing else than quenched wrath." . . .

THE ANALYSIS OF "MYSTERIUM"

"A God comprehended is no God." (Tersteegen)

We gave to the object to which the numinous consciousness is directed the name *mysterium tremendum,* and we then set ourselves first to determine the meaning of the adjective *tremendum*—which we found to be itself only justified by analogy—because it is more easily analyzed than the substantive idea *mysterium.* We have now to turn to this, and try, as best we may, by hint and suggestion, to get to a clearer apprehension of what it implies.

The "Wholly Other"

It might be thought that the adjective itself gives an explanation of the substantive; but this is not so. It is not merely analytical; it is a synthetic attribute to it; i.e., *tremendum* adds something not necessarily inherent in *mysterium*. It is true that the reactions in consciousness that correspond to the one readily and spontaneously overflow into those that correspond to the other; in fact, anyone sensitive to the use of words would commonly feel that the idea of "mystery" (*mysterium*) is so closely bound up with its synthetic qualifying attribute "aweful" (*tremendum*) that one can hardly say the former without catching an echo of the latter, "mystery" almost of itself becoming "aweful mystery" to us. But the passage from the one idea to the other need not by any means be always so easy. The elements of meaning implied in "awefulness" and "mysteriousness" are in themselves definitely different. The latter may so far preponderate in the religious consciousness, may stand out so vividly, that in comparison with it the former almost sinks out of sight; a case which again, could be clearly exemplified from some forms of mysticism. Occasionally, on the other hand, the reverse happens, and the *tremendum* may in turn occupy the mind without the *mysterium*.

This latter, then needs special consideration on its own account. We need an expression for the mental reaction peculiar to it; and here, too, only one word seems appropriate, though, as it is strictly applicable only to a "natural" state of mind, it has here meaning only by analogy: it is the word "stupor." *Stupor* is plainly a different thing from *tremor*; it signifies blank wonder, an astonishment that strikes us dumb, amazement absolute. Taken, indeed, in its purely natural sense, *mysterium* would first mean merely a secret or a mystery in the sense of that which is alien to us, uncomprehended and unexplained; and so far *mysterium* is itself merely an ideogram, an analogical notion taken from the natural sphere, illustrating, but incapable of exhaustively rendering, our real meaning. Taken in the religious sense, that which is "mysterious" is—to give it perhaps the most striking expression—the "wholly other" . . . , that which is quite beyond the sphere of the usual, the intelligible, and the familiar, which therefore falls quite outside the limits of the "canny," and is contrasted with it, filling the mind with blank wonder and astonishment. . . .

Even on the lowest level of religious development the essential characteristic . . . lies . . . in a peculiar "moment" of consciousness, to wit, the *stupor* before something "wholly other," whether such an other be named "spirit" or "daemon" or "deva," or be left without any name. Nor does it make any difference in this respect whether, to interpret and preserve their apprehension of this "other," men coin original imagery of their own or adapt imaginations drawn from the world of legend, the fabrications of fancy apart from and prior to any stirrings of daemonic dread.

In accordance with laws of which we shall have to speak again later, this feeling or consciousness of the "wholly other" will attach itself to, or sometimes be indirectly aroused by means of, objects which are already puzzling upon the "natural" plane, or are of a surprising or astounding character; such as extraordinary phenomena or astonishing occurrences or things in inanimate nature, in the animal world, or among men. But here once more we are dealing with a case of association between things specifically different—the "numinous" and the "natural" moments of consciousness—and not merely with the gradual enhancement of one of them—the "natural"—till it becomes the other. As in the case of "natural fear" and "daemonic dread" already considered, so here the transition from natural to daemonic amazement is not a mere matter of degree. But it is only with the latter that the complementary expression *mysterium* perfectly harmonizes, as will be felt perhaps more clearly in the case of the adjectival form "mysterious." No one says, strictly and in earnest, of a piece of clockwork that is beyond his grasp, or of a science that he cannot understand: "That is 'mysterious' to me."

It might be objected that the mysterious is something which is and remains absolutely and invariably beyond our understanding, whereas that which merely eludes our understanding for a time but is perfectly intelligible in principle should be called, not a "mystery," but merely a "problem." But this is by no means an adequate account of the matter. The truly "mysterious" object is beyond our apprehension and comprehension, not only because our knowledge has certain irremovable limits, but because in it we come upon something inherently "wholly other," whose kind and character are incommensurable with our own, and before which we therefore recoil in a wonder that strikes us chill and numb.

This may be made still clearer by a consideration of that degraded offshoot and travesty of the genuine "numinous" dread or awe, the fear of ghosts. Let us try to analyze this experience. We have already specified the peculiar feeling-element of "dread" aroused by the ghost as that of grisly horror. Now this grisly horror obviously contributes something to the attraction which ghost-stories exercise, in so far, namely, as the relaxation of tension ensuing upon our release from it relieves the mind in a pleasant and agreeable way. So far, however, it is not really the ghost itself that gives us pleasure, but the fact that we are rid of it. But obviously this is quite insufficient to explain the ensnaring attraction of the ghost-story. The ghost's real attraction rather consists in this, that of itself and in an uncommon degree it entices the imagination, awakening strong interest and curiosity; it is the weird thing itself that allures the fancy. But it does this, not because it is "something long and white" (as someone once defined a ghost), nor yet through any of the positive and conceptual attributes which fancies about ghosts have invented, but because it is a thing that "doesn't really exist at all," the "wholly other," something which has no place in our scheme of reality but belongs to an absolutely different one, and which at the same time arouses an irrepressible interest in the mind.

But that which is perceptibly true in the fear of ghosts, which is, after all, only a caricature of the genuine thing, is in a far stronger sense true of the "daemonic" experience itself, of which the fear of ghosts is a mere off-shoot. And while, following this main line of development, this element in the numinous consciousness, the feeling of the "wholly other," is heightened and clarified, its higher modes of manifestation come into being, which set the numinous object in contrast not only to everything wanted and familiar (i.e., in the end, to nature in general), thereby turning it into the "supernatural," but finally to the word itself, and thereby exalt it to the "supramundane," that which is above the whole world-order.

The Element of Fascination

The qualitative *content* of the numinous experience, to which "the mysterious" stands as *form* is in one of its aspects the element of daunting "awefulness" and "majesty," which has already been dealt with in detail; but it is clear that it has at the same time another aspect, in which it shows itself as something uniquely attractive and *fascinating*.

These two qualities, the daunting and the fascinating, now combine in a strange harmony of contrasts, and the resultant dual character of the numinous consciousness, to which the entire religious development bears witness, at any rate from the level of the "daemonic dread" onwards, is at once the strangest and most noteworthy phenomenon in the whole history of religion. The daemonic-divine object may appear to the mind an object of horror and dread, but at the same time it is no less something that allures with a potent charm, and the creature, who trembles before it, utterly cowed and cast down, has always at the same time the impulse to turn to it, nay to even make it somehow his own. The "mystery" is for him not merely something to be wondered at but something that entrances him; and besides that in it which bewilders and confounds, he feels a something that captivates and transports him with a strange ravishment, rising often enough to the pitch of dizzy intoxication; it is the Dionysiac-element in the numen.

The ideas and concepts which are the parallels or "schemata" on the rational side of this non-rational element of "fascination" are love, mercy, pity, comfort; these are all "natural" elements of the common psychical life, only they are here thought as absolute and in completeness. But important as these are for the experience of religious bliss or felicity, they do not by any means exhaust it. It is just the same as with the opposite experience of religious infelicity—the experience of the *orge* or "wrath" of God:—both alike contain fundamentally non-rational elements. Bliss or beautitude is more, far more, than the mere natural feeling of being comforted, of reliance, of the joy of love, however these may be heightened and enhanced. Just as "wrath," taken in a purely rational or a purely ethical sense, does not exhaust that profound element of *awefulness* which is locked in the mystery of deity, so neither does "graciousness" exhaust the profound element of *wonderfulness* and rapture which lies in the mysterious beatific experience of deity. The term "grace" may indeed be taken as its aptest designation, but then only in the sense in which it is really applied in the language of the mystics, and in which not only the "gracious intent" but "something more" is meant by the word. This "something more" has its antecedent phases very far back in the history of religions.   [*The Idea of the Holy*]

C. Conversion Experiences

14. *Conversion in the scriptures*

2 Kings 5:1–15—Naaman the Syrian

Isaiah 6:1–13—The Call of Isaiah

Matthew 3:1–12; John 1:19–36—John the Baptizer

Luke 5:27–32—The Call of Levi

Matthew 19:16–26—The Prodigal Son   Luke 15:11-3~

Luke 18:18–27—The Rich Young Man

Luke 19:1–10—Zacchaeus

John 4:7–42—The Woman at the Well

John 8:3–11—The Woman Caught in Adultery

Acts 8:26–39—The Conversion of the Ethiopian

Acts 9:1–22—The Conversion of St. Paul

15. The restless heart

The influence of **St. Augustine (354–430)** on western theology and civilization is enormous. Born in North Africa of a pagan father and Christian mother, he lived a turbulent youth and young manhood, finally establishing himself in Carthage where he lived with his mistress and fathered a son. For a time he became a Manichee (a follower of Mani, a Persian prophet who preached that there are two conflicting supreme forces, a good God, the source of spirit and light, and an evil principle, the source of matter). Traveling to Italy, he left this sect and went through a period of skepticism. Eventually, under the influence of St. Ambrose, bishop of Milan, he discovered that his mother's religion had dimensions that he had hitherto not suspected. He became a Christian and was later ordained a priest and finally bishop of Hippo in North Africa. His voluminous writings became the basis for medieval theology. His autobiography, *The Confessions*, from which the following excepts are taken, is acknowledged as one of the great books of western literature.

I

Great art Thou, O Lord, and greatly to be praised; great is Thy power, and of Thy wisdom there is no number. And man desires to praise Thee. He is but a tiny part of all that Thou hast created. He bears about him his mortality, the evidence of his sinfulness, and the evidence that *Thou dost resist the proud:* yet this tiny part of all that Thou hast created desires to praise Thee.

Thou dost so excite him that to praise Thee is his joy. For Thou hast made us for Thyself and our hearts are restless till they rest in Thee. Grant me, O Lord, to know which is the soul's first movement toward Thee—to implore Thy aid or to utter its praise of Thee; and whether it must know Thee before it can implore. For it would seem clear that no one can call upon Thee without knowing Thee, for if he did he might invoke another than Thee, knowing Thee not. Yet may it be that a man must implore Thee before he can know Thee? But, *how shall they call on Him in Whom they have not believed? or how shall they believe without a preacher?* And, *they shall praise the Lord that seek Him;* for those that seek shall find; and finding Him they will praise Him. Let me seek Thee, Lord, by praying Thy aid, and let me utter my prayer believing in Thee:

for Thou hast been preached to us. My faith, Lord, cries to Thee, the faith that Thou hast given me, that Thou hast inbreathed in me, through the humanity of Thy Son and by the ministry of Thy Preacher.

II

But how can I call unto my God, my God and Lord? For in calling unto Him, I am calling Him to me: and what room is there in me for my God, the God, who made heaven and earth? Is there anything in me O God that can contain You? All heaven and earth cannot contain You for You made them, and me in them. Yet, since nothing that is could exist without You, "You must in some way be in all that is:" [therefore also in me, since I am]. And if You are already in me, since otherwise I should not be, why do I cry to You to enter into me? Even if I were in Hell You would be there *for if I go down into hell, Thou art there also.* Thus, O God, I should be nothing, utterly nothing, unless You were in me—or rather unless I were in You, *of Whom and by Whom and in Whom are all things.* So it is, Lord; so it is. Where do I call You to come to, since I am in You? Or where else are You that You can come to me? Where shall I go, beyond the bounds of heaven and earth, that God may come to me, since He has said: *Heaven and earth do I fill.*

III

But if You fill heaven and earth, do they contain You? Or do You fill them, and yet have much over since they cannot contain You? Is there some other place into which that overplus of You pours that heaven and earth cannot hold? Surely You have no need of any place to contain You since You contain all things, and fill them indeed precisely by containing them. The vessels thus filled with You do not render You any support: for though they perished utterly. You would not be spilt out. And in pouring Yourself out upon us, You do not come down to us but rather elevate us to You: You are not scattered over us, but we are gathered into one by You. You fill all things: but with Your whole being? It is true that all things cannot wholly contain You: but does this mean that they contain part of You? and do they all contain the same part at the same time? or do different parts of creation contain different parts of You— greater parts or smaller according to their own magnitude? But are there in You parts greater and smaller? Or are You not in every place at once in the totality of Your being, while yet nothing contains You wholly?

IV

What then is my God, what but the Lord God? *For Who is Lord but the Lord, or Who is God but our God?* O Thou, the greatest and the best, mightiest, almighty, most merciful and most just, utterly hidden and utterly present, most beautiful and most strong, abiding yet mysterious, suffering no change and changing all things: never new, never old, making all things new, *bringing age upon the proud and they know it not;* ever in action, ever at rest, gathering all things to Thee and needing none; sustaining and fulfilling and protecting, creating and nourishing and making perfect; ever seeking though lacking nothing. Thou lovest without subjection to passion, Thou are jealous but not with fear; Thou canst know repentance but not sorrow, be angry yet unperturbed by anger. Thou canst change the works Thou hast made but Thy mind stands changeless. Thou dost find and receive back what Thou didst never lose; art never in need but dost rejoice in Thy gains, art not greedy but dost exact interest manifold. Men pay Thee more than is of obligation to win return from Thee, yet who has anything that is not already Thine? Thou owest nothing yet dost pay as if in debt to Thy creature, forgivest what is owed to Thee yet dost not lose thereby. And with all this, what have I said, my God and my Life and my sacred Delight? What can anyone say when he speaks of Thee? Yet woe to them that speak not of Thee at all, since those who say most are but dumb.

Late have I loved Thee, O Beauty so ancient and so new, late have I loved Thee! And behold, Thou wert within and I was without. I was looking for Thee out there, and I threw myself, deformed as I was, upon those well-formed things which Thou hast made. Thou wert with me, yet I was not with Thee. These things held me far from Thee, things which would not have existed had they not been in Thee. Thou didst call and cry out and burst in upon my deafness; Thou didst shine forth and glow and drive away my blindness; Thou didst send forth Thy fragrance, and I drew in my breath and now I pant for Thee; I have tasted, and now I hunger and thirst; Thou didst touch me, and I was inflamed with desire for Thy peace. [*The Confessions I, 1–4; X, 27*]

16. Desire and resistance

The leading poet of the "Metaphysical School" of British poetry and a renowned preacher, **John Donne (1572–1631)** wrote verse fa-

mous for its fusion of human passion with profound religious sentiment. For Donne, the basic human issues—mastering a divided
self, finding salvation and meaning in a sinful world—were the ones
that mattered, so that his poetry was much less concerned with the
external world than the internal one where the great battles of the
spirit were fought. In the famous poem below, Donne reflects ironi-
cally on the pain involved in the human response to the divine.

Batter my heart, three person'd God; for, you
As yet but knocke, breathe, shine, and seeke to mend;
That I may rise, and stand, o'erthrow mee, and bend
Your force, to breake, blowe, burn and make me new.
I, like an usurpt towne, to another due,
Labour to admit you, but Oh, to no end,
Reason your viceroy in mee, mee should defend,
But is captiv'd, and proves weake or untrue.
Yet dearely I love you, and would be loved faine,
But am betroth'd unto your enemie:
Divorce mee, untie, or breake that knot againe,
Take mee to you, imprison mee, for I
Except you enthrall mee, never shall be free,
Nor ever chast, except you ravish mee.

[*Divine Meditations*, 14]

17. *The invitation of love*

A devotional poet of the Metaphysical School of Donne, **George
Herbert (1593–1633)** described his poems as "pictures of the many
spiritual conflicts that have passed between God and my soul, before I could subject mine to the will of Jesus my master." Like many
of his poems, the one below records the conflict between the divine call and the awareness of human sinfulness that forms a component in all religious experience.

Love bade me welcome: yet my soul drew back,
    Guiltie of dust and sinne.
But quick-ey'd Love, observing me grow slack

From my first entrance in,
Drew nearer to me, sweetly questioning,
    If I lack'd any thing.
A guest, I answer'd, worthy to be here:
    Love said, you shall be he.
I the unkinde, ungrateful? Ah my deare,
    I cannot look on thee.
Love took my hand, and smiling did reply,
    Who made the eyes but I?
Truth Lord, but I have marr'd them: let my shame
    Go where it doth deserve.
And know you not, sayes Love, who bore the blame?
    My deare, then I will serve.
You must sit down, sayes Love, and taste my meat:
    So I did sit and eat.

18. Mystical union

In contrast to the intellectual apprehension of the Holy that shaped
the conversion of St. Augustine, **St. Teresa of Avila (1515–1582)**
offers a different model of personal religious experience—the af-
fective experience of mysticism. In the selection below, taken from
her spiritual autobiography, St. Teresa describes the mystical raptures that accompanied her prayer, during which she was physically
overwhelmed by an awareness of the Holy. Teresa here concen-
trates on her emotions and on the ways in which she "felt" the
divine calling during these rapturous prayer periods. Famous as a
reformer of the Carmelite Order and spiritual writer, Teresa is one
of the most famous mystics of the Christian tradition.

I should like, with the help of God, to be able to describe the difference
between union and rapture, or elevation, or what they call flight of the
spirit, or transport—it is all one. I mean that these different names all
refer to the same thing, which is also called ecstasy. It is much more
beneficial than union: the effects it produces are far more important and,
it has a great many more operations, for union gives the impression of
being just the same at the beginning, in the middle and at the end, and it
all happens interiorly. But the ends of these raptures are of a higher

degree, and the effects they produce are both interior and exterior. May the Lord explain this, as He has explained everything else, for I should certainly know nothing of it if His Majesty had not shown me the ways and manners in which it can to some extent be described.

Let us now reflect that this last water which we have described is so abundant that, were it not that the ground is incapable of receiving it, we might believe this cloud of great Majesty to be with us here on this earth. But as we are giving Him thanks for this great blessing, and doing our utmost to draw near to Him in a practical way, the Lord gathers up the soul, just (we might say) as the clouds gather up the vapours from the earth, and raises it up till it is right out of itself (I have heard that it is in this way that the clouds or the sun gather up the vapours) and the cloud rises to Heaven and takes the soul with it, and begins to reveal to it things concerning the Kingdom that He has prepared for it. I do not know if the comparison is an exact one, but that is the way it actually happens.

In these raptures the soul seems no longer to animate the body, and thus the natural heat of the body is felt to be very sensibly diminished: it gradually becomes colder, though conscious of the greatest sweetness and delight. No means of resistance is possible, whereas in union, where we are on our own ground, such a means exists: resistance may be painful and violent but it can almost always be effected. But with rapture, as a rule, there is no such possibility: often it comes like a strong, swift impulse, before your thought can forewarn you of it or you can do anything to help yourself; you see and feel this cloud, or this powerful eagle, rising and bearing you up with it on its wings.

You realize, I repeat, and indeed see, that you are being carried away, you know not whither. For, though rapture brings us delight, the weakness of our nature at first makes us afraid of it, and we need to be resolute and courageous in soul, much more so than for what has been described. For, happen what may, we must risk everything, and resign ourselves into the hands of God and go willingly wherever we are carried away, for we are in fact being carried away, whether we like it or no. In such straits do I find myself at such a time that very often I should be glad to resist, and I exert all my strength to do so, in particular at times when it happens in public and at many other times in private, when I am afraid that I may be suffering deception. Occasionally I have been able to make some resistance, but at the cost of great exhaustion, for I would feel as weary afterwards as though I had been fighting with a powerful giant. At other times, resistance has been impossible: my soul has been borne away, and indeed as a rule my head also, without my being able to prevent it: sometimes my whole body has been affected, to the point of being raised up from the ground. . . .

When I tried to resist these raptures, it seemed that I was being lifted up by a force beneath my feet so powerful that I know nothing to which I can compare it, for it came with a much greater vehemence than any other spiritual experience and I felt as if I were being ground to powder. It is a terrible struggle, and to continue it against the Lord's will avails very little, for no power can do anything against His. At other times His Majesty is graciously satisfied with our seeing that He desires to show us this favour, and that, if we do not receive it, it is not due to Himself. Then, if we resist it out of humility, the same effects follow as if we had given it our entire consent.

These effects are very striking. One of them is the manifestation of the Lord's mighty power: as we are unable to resist His Majesty's will, either in soul or in body, and are not our own masters, we realize that, however irksome this truth may be, there is One stronger than ourselves, and that these favours are bestowed by Him, and that we, of ourselves, can do absolutely nothing. This imprints in us great humility. Indeed, I confess that in me it produced great fear—at first a terrible fear. One sees one's body being lifted up from the ground; and although the spirit draws it after itself, and if no resistance is offered does so very gently, one does not lose consciousness—at least, I myself have had sufficient to enable me to realize that I was being lifted up. The majesty of Him Who can do this is manifested in such a way that the hair stands on end, and there is produced a great fear of offending so great a God, but a fear over-powered by the deepest love, newly enkindled, for One Who, as we see, has so deep a love for so loathsome a worm that He seems not to be satisfied by literally drawing the soul to Himself, but will also have the body, mortal though it is, and befouled as is its clay by all the offences it has committed. . . .

I can testify that after a rapture my body often seemed as light as if all weight had left it: sometimes this was so noticeable that I could hardly tell when my feet were touching the ground. For, while the rapture lasts, the body often remains as if dead and unable of itself to do anything: it continues all the time as it was when the rapture came upon it—in a sitting position, for example, or with the hands open or shut. The subject rarely loses consciousness: I have sometimes lost it altogether, but only seldom and for but a short time. As a rule the consciousness is disturbed; and, though incapable of action with respect to outward things, the subject can still hear and understand, but only dimly, as though from a long way off. I do not say that he can hear and understand when the rapture is at its highest point—by "highest point" I mean when the faculties are lost through being closely united with God. At that point, in my opinion, he will neither see, nor hear, nor perceive; but, as I said in describing the preceding prayer of union, this complete transformation of the soul in God lasts but a short time, and it is only while it lasts that none of the soul's faculties is able to perceive or know what is taking place. We cannot be meant to understand it while we are on earth— God, in fact, does not wish us to understand it because we have not the capacity for doing so. I have observed this myself. . . .

I believe myself that a soul which attains to this state neither speaks nor does anything of itself, but that this sovereign King takes care of all that it has to do. Oh, my God, how clear is the meaning of that verse about asking for the wings of a dove and how right the author was—and how right we shall all be!—to ask for them! It is evident that he is referring to the flight taken by the spirit when it soars high above all created things, and above itself first of all; but it is a gentle and a joyful flight and also a silent one.

What power is that of a soul brought hither by the Lord, which can look upon everything without being ensnared by it! How ashamed it is of the time when it was attached to everything! How amazed it is at its blindness! How it pities those who are still blind, above all if they are persons of prayer to whom God is still granting favours! It would like to cry aloud to them and show them how mistaken they are, and some- times it does in fact do so and brings down a thousand persecutions upon its head. Men think it lacking in humility and suppose that it is trying to teach those from whom it should learn, especially if the person in question is a woman. For this they condemn it, and rightly so, since they know nothing of the force by which it is impelled. Sometimes it cannot help itself nor endure failing to undeceive those whom it loves and desires to see set free from the prison of this life; for it is in a prison, nothing less—and it realizes that it is nothing less—that the soul has itself been living.

It is weary of the time when it paid heed to niceties concerning its own honour, and of the mistaken belief which it had that what the world calls honour is really so. It now knows that to be a sheer lie and a lie in which we are all living. It realizes that genuine honour is not deceptive, but true; that it values what has worth and despises what has none; for what passes away, and is not pleasing to God, is worth nothing and less than nothing. [*The Life of the Holy Mother Teresa of Jesus*]

19. A sudden call

Conversion—the "turning around" (Latin, *conversio*) that results from an encounter with the Holy—exposes the crucial importance of personal experience in empowering ordinary people to respond joyfully and courageously to a divine "call." The account below, an autobiographical transcription of a former American slave's call from God, highlights both the role of cultural presuppositions in the shaping of our experience of the divine, and the emotional power of such experiences in freeing people from their past.

One day while in the field plowing I heard a voice. I jumped because I thought it was my master coming to scold and whip me for plowing up some more corn. I looked but saw no one. Again the voice called, "Morte! Morte!" With this I stopped, dropped the plow, and started running, but the voice kept on speaking to me saying, "Fear not, my little one, for behold! I come to bring you a message of truth."

Everything got dark, and I was unable to stand any longer. I began to feel sick, and there was a great roaring. I tried to cry and move but was unable to do either. I looked up and saw that I was in a new world. There were plants and animals, and all, even the water where I stooped down to drink, began to cry out, "I am blessed but you are damned! I am blessed but you are damned!" With this I began to pray, and a voice on the inside began to cry, "Mercy! Mercy! Mercy!"

As I prayed an angel came and touched me, and I looked new. I looked at my hands and they were new; I looked at my feet and they were new. I looked and saw my old body suspended over a burning pit by a small web like a spider web. I again prayed, and there came a soft voice saying, "My little one, I have loved you with an everlasting love. You are this day made alive and freed from hell. You are a chosen vessel unto the Lord. Be upright before me, and I will guide you unto all truth. My grace is sufficient for you. Go, and I am with you. Preach the gospel, and I will preach with you. You are henceforth the salt of the earth."

I then began to shout and clap my hands. All the time a voice on the inside was crying, "I am so glad! I am so glad!" About this time an angel appeared before me and said with a loud voice, "Praise God! Praise God!" I looked to the east, and there was a large throne lifted high up, and thereon sat one, even God. He looked neither to the right nor to the left. I was afraid and fell on my face. When I was still a long way off I heard a voice from God saying, "My little one, be not afraid, for lo! many wondrous works will I perform through thee. Go in peace, and lo! I am with you always." All this he said but opened not his mouth while speaking. Then all those about the throne shouted and said, "Amen."

I then came to myself again and shouted and rejoiced. After so long a time I recovered my real senses and realized that I had been plowing and that the horse had run off with the plow and dragged down much of the corn. I was afraid and began to pray, for I knew the master would whip me most unmercifully when he found that I had plowed up the corn.

About this time my master came down the field. I became very bold and answered him when he called me. He asked me very roughly how I came to plow up the corn, and where the horse and plow were, and why I had got along so slowly. I told him that I had been talking with God Almighty, and that it was God who had plowed up the corn. He looked at me very strangely, and suddenly I fell for shouting, and I shouted and began to preach. The words seemed to flow from my lips. When I had finished I had a deep feeling of satisfaction and no longer dreaded the whipping I knew I would get. My master looked at me and seemed to tremble. He told me to catch the horse, stumbling down the corn rows. Here again I became weak and began to be afraid for the whipping. After I had gone some distance down the rows, I became dazed and again fell to the ground. In a vision I saw a great mound and beside it or at the base of it, stood the angel Gabriel. And a voice said to me, "Behold your sins as a great mountain. But they shall be rolled away. Go in peace, fearing no man, for lo I have cut loose your stammering tongue and unstopped your deaf ears. A witness shalt thou be, and thou shalt speak to multitudes, and they shall hear. My word has gone forth, and it is power. Be strong, and lo! I am with you even until the world shall end. Amen."

I looked, and the angel Gabriel lifted his hand, and my sins, that had stood as a mountain, began to roll away. I saw them as they rolled over into the great pit. They fell to the bottom, and there was a great noise. I saw old Satan with a host of his angels hop from the pit, and there they began to stick out their tongues at me and make motions as if to lay hands on me and drag me back into the pit. I cried out, "Save me! Save me, Lord!" And like a flash there gathered around me a host of angels, even a great number, with their backs to me and their faces to the outer world. Then stepped one in the direction of the pit. Old Satan and his angels, growling with anger and trembling with fear, hopped back into the pit. Finally again there came a voice unto me saying, "Go in peace and fear not, for lo! I will throw around you a strong arm of protection. Neither shall your oppressors be able to confound you. I will make your enemies feed you and those who despise you take you in. Rejoice and be exceedingly glad, for I have saved you through grace by faith, not of yourself but as a gift of God. Be strong and fear not. Amen."

I rose from the ground shouting and praising God. Within me there was a crying, "Holy! Holy! Holy is the Lord!"

I must have been in this trance for more than an hour. I went on to the barn and found my master there waiting for me. Again I began to tell him of my experience. I do not recall what he did to me afterwards. I felt burdened down and that preaching was my only relief. When I had finished I felt a great love in my heart that made me feel like stooping and kissing the very ground. My master sat watching and listening to me, and then he began to cry. He turned from me and said to me, in a broken voice, "Morte, I believe you are a preacher. From now on you can preach to the people here on my place in the old shed by the creek. But tomorrow morning, Sunday, I want you to preach to my family and neighbors. So put on your best clothes and be in front of the big house early in the morning, about nine o'clock."

I was so happy that I did not know what to do. I thanked my master and then God, for I felt that he was with me. Throughout the night I went from cabin to cabin, rejoicing and spreading the news.

The next morning at the time appointed I stood up on two planks in front of the porch of the big house and, without a Bible or anything, I began to preach to my master and the people. My thoughts came so fast that I could hardly speak fast enough. My soul caught on fire, and soon I had them all in tears. I told them that God had a chosen people and that he had raised me up as an example of his matchless love. I told them that they must be born again and that their souls must be freed from the shackles of hell.

Ever since that day I have been preaching the gospel and am not a bit tired. I can tell anyone about God in the darkest hour of midnight, for it is written on my heart. Amen.   [from *God Struck Me Dead*]

Chapter Two

Speaking About God

A. Religion: The Symbolic Dimension

20. The notion of religion

Analyzing and interpreting the faith and worship of a specific religious community for other members of the community is the formal task of theology—the critical discipline that seeks to "speak about God" in faith. Theology, however, builds on the insights of another discipline: the history of religions—a discipline that examines the symbols, myths, and rituals of all religious traditions in order to understand how religion functions in human culture. **Catherine Albanese,** an historian of American religions, attempts below to offer a definition of religion that does justice to the many faiths of humanity by defining religion as a "boundary-making function" of the human animal. Such boundary making, she argues, manifests itself both horizontally (ordinary religion) and vertically (extraordinary religion). These two religions, moreover, always find expression in what she calls the "4 Cs" of creed, code, cultus, and community. Theologians use the insights of historians of religion like Albanese to examine how the symbols, myths, and rituals of their own religious tradition perform such boundary making.

DEFINING RELIGION

From the viewpoint of common sense, every one of us knows what religion is. Surely, it is one of those obvious realities that we have either grown up practicing or observing others practice. It is just there—a fact as unavoidable in the social landscape as a mountain or a tree would be in a natural setting. Everyone knows what religion is—that is, until one tries to define it. It is in the act of defining that religion seems to slip away.

We might want to limit it to a relationship that humans consider themselves to have had with God or the Gods, but someone could point out that the oldest Buddhists did not believe in any God, while another person might ask if atheists were religious. We might want to call religion a way of living, an ethical system such as Confucius taught, but somebody could counter that all people had some way of living or other and that meant all of them had a religion. We might say religion had to do with a quality of experience, a powerful feeling that people have had when they have confronted something totally "other." Yet a few in our group would be sure to suggest that the most powerful experience that they could remember at a religious service on many a Saturday or Sunday morning was being lost in a daydream. We might become very brave and venture that religion was the thing in life a person was most ultimately concerned about, but one sarcastic member of our group would be sure to ask if that meant race horses and the lottery as well as less material realities.

Why is it that so common a feature of human life proves so baffling? What is it about religion that eludes our grasp? Is the inability to define, like the optical illusion, simply because we are staring too long into the religious landscape? Or are there other problems as well, intrinsic to the nature of religion? A definition, says *Webster's Third New International Dictionary*, is an "act of determining or settling." It is "the action or the power of making definite and clear or of bringing into sharp relief." Definition, in fact, comes from the Latin word *finis*, which means an end or limit—a boundary. A definition tells us where some reality ends; it separates the world into what is and what is not that reality. So a definition certainly works to end optical illusions, firming up the object in its landscape rather than dissolving it.

But there are special reasons why religion eludes definition that move beyond the general problem of staring at it too long. Religion cannot be defined very easily because it thrives both within and outside of boundaries. It crosses and crisscrosses the boundaries that definitions want to set up because, paradoxically, it, too, concerns boundaries. The boundaries of religion, however, are different from the logical boundaries of good definitions. In the end, religion is a feature that encompasses *all* of human life, and therefore it is difficult and, indeed, impossible to define it.

Rather than continuing to try to square the religious circle, it might be more fruitful to think not of defining religion but, instead, of trying to describe it. To describe something is to say what it generally looks like and how it usually works. It is not to say what its innermost realities are, and it is not to say definitely what separates these realities from every other object in the world. Still, describing a thing can tell us much about what it is. Looking at the past and present appearances of religion can tell us what clusters or sets of functions and forms go along with it. Learning to recognize these functions and forms helps us to know when we are looking at religion. Hence, in what follows, we will not so much try to define religion as to describe it.

Religion and Boundaries

What we know about various kinds of religions suggests that they arose in the context of dealing with boundaries. For many peoples, physical boundaries that marked the limits of the territory of one or another group were highly charged with emotional significance. They divided land that was safe and secure, the source of nurture and sustenance, from land that was alien and unfriendly, the home of hostile spirits and strange or warring tribes. So it was that any exchanges conducted across these boundaries were stressful occasions, and so it was that people strengthened themselves for these exchanges through the use of ritual. In the formula of word and act, people at a dangerous place on the physical landscape could call on special help and assistance; they could ease their encounter with whatever was alien to themselves.

This special assistance came from the mysterious and fearful unknown, from forces that transcended, or went beyond, ordinary life. In other words, alien land and people were countered by a second form of "otherness," more powerful than the first. By enlisting the help of this second "otherness," the first was overcome, and life could go on as intended. These "other" forces that saved a difficult situation by their power were called religious. And the rituals through which they were contacted were religious rituals.

But territorial boundaries were only one kind of border with which people dealt. There were also the limits of their own bodies, the boundaries of skin and tissue which separated each person in a group from every other person. Crossing the boundary of one's body could not be avoided: it happened every day in the simple acts of eating and drinking, of defecating, or of enjoying sexual intercourse. It occurred even when words passed from one person out into the air to the next, and rituals like prayer before a solemn speech or meeting grew up around these exchanges of language. In many cultures, prayer also accompanied the taking of food and drink. Similarly, the products of human bodies at their boundaries—hair, spittle, nail parings, feces—were invested with a power that made them dangerous or helpful, depending on the circumstances and the talents of the user. Thus, in a number of cultures, people feared that an enemy who found strands of their hair or their nail parings could bring evil upon their persons. Hair and nail parings, along with the other "boundary" products of the body, possessed a mysterious energy that made them focuses for ritual. Religious specialists learned to use them in magical ceremonies, and people stood in awe of these products of their own bodies.

Finally, there were the temporal boundaries in the life cycle that any person passed through. In events such as birth, puberty, marriage, and death, a person crossed the border between one form of life, which was known and secure, and a new kind of life, which was perhaps somewhat fearful. These were crisis events, and so there were rites that would ease the passage across the boundaries from one stage in the life cycle to another. In our own society, we are familiar with ceremonies of baptism for infants and with Bar/Bat Mitzvahs and confirmation rites at adolescence. Marriage brings us its solemnity as even in the simplest of ceremonies two people exchange their commitment to each other for life. At death, both wakes and funerals form the usual rites of passing.

In general, throughout the history of human societies, the concern for boundaries was apparent. Borders continued to be places invested with religious awe—the imposing birdlike garudas at the entrances of Hindu temples or the equally ferocious gargoyles at the outside corners of medieval Christian cathedrals. These signs and boundary markers like them warned all comers that they were crossing a frontier into a sacred precinct. They effectively divided one world from another. In a striking example from the United States, many Roman Catholics in the Upper Midwest placed on their lawns statues of the Virgin Mary, which performed a similar function. Anyone who has seen the vast sameness of the prairie and has imagined its unending wildness for Europeans before the creation of their towns can understand why a Virgin would be wanted on the lawn—defining the sacred space of the family and separating it from the far reaches of unnamed territory.

Even in the realm of language, religious or theological discourse has always tried to speak about the unspeakable. It has been "limit" language, language that pushed to the edge of human knowledge and tried to talk about what went beyond. Death, judgment, heaven, hell, these were the last things in Christian theology. They were also passes across the boundary of the world we know, attempts to make sense of mysterious realities from a different world. When religious people used such language, they were trying to describe a landscape they had only seen, as Paul said, "in a mirror dimly" (I Cor. 13:12). They were trying to name through language signs and symbols features of a country they had not seen with bodily eyes.

It should be clear by now that we are part of a long tradition of mixing boundary questions with religious questions. Thus, our religion concerns the way we locate ourselves in space through the arrangement of sacred rites and holy places as boundary markers. It concerns, too, the way we locate ourselves in time through origin stories or theological traditions that also express boundaries. But location is always social. It concerns our place among other human beings, and it means staking out a claim on the landscape of identity.

This internal landscape provides a new territory in which boundaries become important. So an especially fascinating modern version of the religion/boundary theme is the quest for identity. As social beings who turn within, people act out the same concerns about boundaries that they do in external space. By searching for identity and finding it, individuals metaphorically establish inner boundaries, discover through testing who they are not, and begin to affirm who they are. In the process, each individual finds that these personal boundaries overlap with those of other people and groups, so that there can be a free process of exchange. In other words, a person locates others who occupy the same inner territory and, because of the shared internal space, feels at one with them and their concerns. This is the meaning of identification with others.

Religion throughout the ages has tried to answer the continuing human question, Who am I? More particularly, religious writers of our century have made much of the issue of identity, since the intense pluralism of the modern world has given people many choices about the boundaries of the inner space they will occupy. In more traditional societies, most people grew up in a culture that took the inner world for granted, with ancient and prescribed rules for living. But in a mobile society, as in our postindustrial era, this picture of fixed inner space rapidly disappears. The presence of many possibilities for finding a land of one's own means that many decisions have to be made, some of them for alternatives not traditionally religious. Many interior regions must be denied, and others must be affirmed. Hence, in our era, identity has become a problem in a way that it was not during much of the past.

Two Kinds of Religion

The preoccupation with boundaries that comes with the search for identity points to an important fact. People are concerned not just about how to cross boundaries but also about how to live well within them. Finding one's identity means finding the inner space and social space within which it is possible to thrive and grow. And so, if religion is about boundaries, it is not just about crossing them but, as in the question of identity, about respecting them, too. Therefore, learning to live well within boundaries and learning how to cross them safely gives rise to two kinds of religion. The first kind is *ordinary religion*—the religion that is more or less synonymous with culture. Ordinary religion shows people how to live well within boundaries. The second is *extraordinary religion*—the religion that helps people to transcend, or move beyond, their everyday culture and concerns. Extraordinary religion grows at the frontiers of life as we know it and seeks to cross over into another country and another form of life. In the West, extraordinary religion helps us to contact God. Let us look briefly at each of these two kinds of religion.

Ordinary religion, we might say with the scholar Joachim Wach, is the trunk of the tree of culture. In the most general sense, ordinary religion is the source of distinguishable cultural forms and the background out of which the norms arise that guide us in our everyday lives. Yet ordinary religion is obstinate to precise definition. The reason is that it is the taken-for-granted reality that we all assume the statements and actions that make up our picture of the way the world is and is not, the things we do not have to think about or would not dream of arguing over because they are so obvious. Ordinary religion puts its premium on the things which are deeply present and unconsciously revered here within the borders of everyday culture. So this kind of religion can reveal itself in intuitive statements and vague sayings about the meaning of life: "Whatever will be, will be"; "It is better to give than to receive"; "Every cloud has its silver lining"; and the like. This kind of religion is better at being implicit than explicit.

In a more specific sense, ordinary religion can reveal itself in the many customs and folkways that are part of a culture: expected ways of greeting people; wedding etiquette concerning clothes, manners, and obligations; habits of diet; and holiday behavior, to mention a few. Each of these, if examined, can tell worlds about the main values of a society.

Each is a concrete expression of the way in which people are accustomed to think and act. As such, each is a boundary marker that helps people to locate themselves and make sense of the everyday world. For example, a bridal gown suggests the traditional values of the importance of marriage and family for a young woman. The distinctiveness of wedding attire speaks for how significant such values still are in America, for how strongly the bride—and the culture—uses the institution of marriage to mark social space.

In other words, ordinary religion is at home with the way things are. It functions as the (mostly unexamined) religion of a community as community. Because it is about living well within the boundaries, it values the social distinctions that define life in the community and respects the social roles that people play. It honors the ranks that they hold and the general institutions of government, education, family, and recreation to which they assent.

Extraordinary religion, on the other hand, involves an encounter with some form of "otherness," whether natural or supernatural. It is specific and particular, easily recognizable as religion, and possible to separate from the rest of culture. Indeed, if ordinary religion is diffused throughout culture, extraordinary religion is condensed—present in clear and strongly identified religious forms that stand out from their background. Extraordinary religion encourages a special language that also distinguishes it from the rest of culture, and its sense of going beyond the boundaries often finds expression in universal statements, intended to apply to all peoples. The special (theological) language of extraordinary religion maps a landscape that living people have not clearly seen. It gives people names for the unknown and then provides access to the world beyond. It assures people that the "other" world does touch this one but is never merely the same as it. In Christianity, for example, God, grace, and salvation all describe realities beyond the material world. These terms chart the unknown and suggest how it beckons people away from their more ordinary concerns. Moreover, extraordinary religion often encourages religious activity not only on the part of the community as a whole but also on the part of separate individuals who tune themselves with particular intensity to the message delivered to the community. Mystics and prophets, who have seen visions and experienced special mental states, are its heroes and heroines.

Yet we call this religion extraordinary not because it is hard to find or to express but because it concerns itself with what is extraordinary in our day-to-day existence. That is, it deals with how to negotiate boundaries and still return to the ordinary world. Extraordinary religion may involve ecstasy, but it may also involve a simple and uneventful Sunday morning church service. The point is that people in some symbolic way voice their concern with crossing boundaries to the "other" side. Such concern is what makes the religion extraordinary, and as we shall see, such concern is what makes it very visible, very easy to find.

As we move through the religious landscape of the United States, we will find that here, as elsewhere, ordinary and extraordinary religion are often difficult to separate. In fact, in traditional societies the two were often very closely blended, and people used the same or similar symbols to express both everyday and transcendent concerns. For instance, in Judaism the most repeated ritual of extraordinary religion was the Sabbath meal, a weekly family observance which joined a formal framework of prayer and blessings to ordinary conversation and enjoyment around the dinner table.

One sign of modernity in the West has been the increasing separation of extraordinary from ordinary religion. And as we will notice, Protestantism, more than any other religious movement, tried to bring a clear distinction between the two. However, even with this Protestant goal and even with the overall Protestant character of the United States, there were numerous examples of the fusion of ordinary and extraordinary religion. Sometimes, as in the Jewish example of the Sabbath meal, people tried to make the extraordinary world easy and familiar by setting it in the midst of ordinary reality. At other times, people became so involved in the extraordinary claims of the "other" world that they drew everything possible along with them. For example, in the cult movements of the later twentieth century, many people were making a radical break with their former lives to embrace a total commitment to extraordinary concerns.

Components of a Religious System

Both ordinary and extraordinary religion exist as religious systems; that is to say, they are composed of parts related to other parts, which together add up to one whole. For convenience, we can think of these parts as the four Cs: creed, code, cultus, and community. These four terms, taken together, express the collection of related symbols that make up a religious system. Each of these, therefore, is present in both ordinary and extraordinary religion.

First of all, religion is expressed in *creeds*, or explanations about the meaning of human life in the universe. Such creeds may take various forms from highly developed theologies and sacred origin myths to informal oral traditions and unconscious affirmations that surface in casual conversation. Secondly, religion is expressed in *codes,* which are rules that govern everyday behavior. These may take the form of the great moral and ethical systems of antiquity, but they may also be the customs which have become acceptable in a society, the ethos in which people live. Thirdly, religion is expressed in *cultuses,* which are *rituals* to act out the insights and understandings that are expressed in creeds and codes. Not to be confused with small and intense religious groups known as cults, ritual cultuses, with their formal and repeated character, underline and reinforce the meanings evoked by creeds and codes.

Finally, religion is expressed in *communities,* groups of people either formally or informally bound together by the creed, code, and cultus they share. In ordinary religion, such communities tend to be ethnic or cultural (Indians, blacks, Polish people), informally knitting together people who share a common land, history, and language. In extraordinary religion, such communities, especially in the West, have tended to be formal institutions (Catholicism, Methodism, Adventism), designated in terms of their social organization as churches, denominations, sects, and cults.   [from *America: Religion and Religions*]

21. *Speaking of God through symbol*

All religious traditions utilize symbols to both signal and effect the presence of the Holy. **Victor Warnach,** a Roman Catholic theologian, distinguishes between "sign" and "symbol" in order to discuss how the Holy (Christ) is present during ritual (the celebration of the eucharist). Basic to the author's argument is his contention that the power of symbols (as opposed to signs) transcends the "subjective" in bringing about a divine-human encounter.

SYMBOL AND REALITY

The modern usage of the word "symbol" and its derivative is very confusing. It is frequently used to mean a pure sign (whether a semantic sign, or a logical or scientific expression, figure or term), for something which is not immediately present. The function of a sign, however, is to bring to mind the reality for which it stands. This reality is something essentially different from the sign itself. Signs are abstract and in the logic of intention, for instance, they stand at the greatest possible distance from reality. The word "symbol" is also used of the images by which we refer to supersensual realities. If we then go on to use "symbol" of "emblems" such as flags, coats of arms, insignia, and so on, this is because these, too, represent an institution office or group which has some sort of power or influence. In depth-psychology "symbol" is used of suppressed elements of conscious life or of the sublimated forms by which drives manifest themselves in dreams, neurotic traits and awkward behavior. "Symbol" here involves a greater degree of reality than the earlier examples and borders of its full significance as seen in religious and artistic traditions. Here, especially in the older cultures, it does not mean an abstract instrument of our understanding but principally a means by which a higher, frequently divine, reality is made present or accessible—a means therefore by which living contact with the "other" world can be achieved. Symbol properly so called, therefore, is not something man has chanced upon, nor the result of human invention as are most signs, but owes its symbolic character either to the created or natural order (natural symbol) or to God's presence in saving history. The two worlds of God and man, heaven and earth, spirit and matter meet preeminently in the religious symbol. Even the etymology of *symbolon*, from *symballein* (to cast together), suggests this.

The "real symbol," the full correct meaning of "symbol," is therefore a form that can be experienced by the senses and through which a higher transcendent reality announces itself as present and active. It is distinguishable from a sign in that it is of its nature a self-expression in which something of the reality of what is expressed, or expresses itself, is present or "appears." For this reason it is distinguishable from the mere expression through which some inner experience spontaneously becomes visible but whose nature can only be gathered from its effects. To be sure, as an exact phenomenological analysis shows, both the significative and the expressive function are included within the complex phenomenon of the symbol. Nevertheless its fundamental character derives from its roots in space and time; it must be the visible and sensible "appearance" (*epiphaneia*)—as an ontological presence—of a (higher) being. The use of "appearance" here neither weakens nor questions the reality of the symbolic presence—a conclusion too frequently found in platonic thinkers. Rather it emphasizes the inadequacy of the material levels of being by indicating that spiritual (pneumatic) being cannot be directly present in space and time since its nature is essentially beyond the bounds of space and time. A symbol, accordingly, is the making visible and present of a reality, of its nature divisible, in a form that though inadequate, discloses what it signifies.

Our conception of what a symbol is, therefore, determines whether we see a contradiction between symbol and reality, or can conceive of the possibility of a synthesis encompassing and complementing both aspects. This latter possibility is easier to visualize if we avoid a static limitation of our concepts of "real" and "symbol"; for in worship especially the *symbols* are often symbolic actions, or even symbolic or mystery dramas in which the "primal deeds" or saving events can begin to realize themselves in the present.

In any case the Bible has a realistic conception of symbol; it recognizes the fact of the pure real symbol, and this not just as a meaningless survival from a heathen cult, but as a God-given means for communicating with him. The uniqueness of the means can be appreciated from the fact that the term *symbolon* is used only twice in the Greek Bible and on both occasions in a derogatory sense (Hos. 4, 12; Wis. 2, 9). Yet the Bible contains clear references to the symbolical and to the fact of the symbolical function. . . .

THE TRANSFORMATION AT THE CONSECRATION

The real symbol, whose roots in sacred history we have indicated, leads us to a greater understanding of the mystery of the eucharist. Not only the eucharistic gifts but also the sacred actions are symbols in the strict sense, for the reality symbolized is actually present in both.

If we start with the eucharistic event we can see there, as in all cultic sacrifices, a process that has three phases: gifts are brought or offered, they are set apart for God and they are consecrated for his acceptance. Corresponding to these three cult acts there are the three existential "moments": the self-offering (renunciation), the transformation (movement from the profane to the sacred realm), and the union with God (communion). The bread and wine in the eucharist are offered, therefore, as signs of our own self-offering. As such they already have a symbolic value in their own right, if only in a very preliminary sense. The sacrifice of the Mass does not really consist of our gifts or self-offering; rather both are symbols through which the sacrifice of Christ accomplishes itself. What we have to offer, however valuable and noble, can never effect salvation and sanctification. We are expected to offer gifts and, above all, ourselves, but these are useless if they do not become part of Christ's sacrifice. Though it is God who invites us to offer gifts, it is he alone who, through the Spirit of Christ, sanctifies and consecrates them. Our offerings are themselves God's gift to us and so must always become thanksgiving (*eucharistia*) for these offerings and for all the works of creation and salvation.

This thanksgiving "in the name of Jesus" is the efficacious word which transforms and consecrates the offerings—it "eucharistizes" them as Justin said. They then become *symbola*, visible manifestations of the sanctified body and blood of the crucified Christ. The unique saving sacrifice becomes a saving and sanctifying presence among us.

The Mass is not *just* a sacrificial action, it is also a sacrificial *meal*. That is why we offer food. But this food now has a very different meaning. It functions not just to nourish and strengthen man's body so that he can prolong his earthly life, but principally to feed the "inner man," not just his "soul" but the whole of his human nature so as to prepare him for the "other" true eternal life with God.

There is therefore at least a threefold change in the fundamental significance of the bread and wine: (1) prior to the consecration they function as signs of our self-offering; after it they realize the presence in a symbol of Christ's sacrifice on the cross; (2) bread and wine become more than purely natural nourishment; they are "spiritual food" (1 Cor. 10, 3); (3) as part of a meal they constitute a table-fellowship among those present, but in communion the eucharistic gifts unite us first to Christ, then through him with one another in the one spiritual body of the Church. . . .

If we try to situate the eucharist within saving history we perceive that it is the meeting place of the descent (*katabasis*) of the self-emptying (*kenosis*) and the ascent (*anabasis*) to glorification (*doxa*). To be more precise: the paschal mystery is realized in the eucharist to the extent that it also contains that unique *kairos*, that irrevocable all-embracing turning point in Christ's course through his sacrificial death to a new life. The path which stretches from his incarnation to the criminal's death on a cross is expressed in the sacrament by him, emptying himself under the forms of bread and wine, so that the eucharist can be valued as a new incarnation of Christ. Its meaning stems from the "perpetuation" of his unique sacrifice and from the fellowship (*koinonia*) of the sacred meal.

The natural creative power of selfless love changes the earthly materials of bread and wine in their innermost being, making them like a window through which shines the self-offering and glorification of the dying and risen Lord—visible to those with faith. Just as Jesus' visible body was his historical and personal manifestation (*species*) in his temporal existence, so the eucharistic gifts are the manifestation (*species*) of Christ in his transition to the world of God. We, too, must share in this unique transition if we wish to be saved.

Although we can parallel the "form" of bread and wine and the human form of the "fleshly body" (Col. 1, 22), there are nevertheless essential differences between the historical and the sacramental manifestations of Christ: (1) the body which the *Logos* took from the Virgin is only a "symbol" for the present Lord in a derivative sense, whereas the bread and wine, because of their institution and consecration, are proper cult symbols and consequently make him present; (2) the presence of Christ in the sacrament is not historical or spatio-temporal but real and "substantial" (or better, personal) which as sacramental or pneumatic is beyond space and time, as the encyclical *Mysterium Fidei* emphasized. This spiritual or pneumatic form of existence is not less real but rather more fully real. In contrast to an impoverished and empty idea of reality to be found in positivism, Christian realism has always seen in spiritual being its highest and richest form, positively surpassing space and time by overflowing their boundaries. Matter is not thereby denied value or turned into spirit. It is illumined and made radiant through the spirit, brought to its true fulfillment in the unity and completeness (*pleroma*) of Christ's spiritual body. So our sacrificial gifts undergo a radical (ontological) transformation which leaves their form (species) unaltered as the manifesting medium, while radically altering their being, giving them totally new relationships and connections.

What we mean can be clarified and to some extent justified by a short consideration of the fundamental ontological structure of things. Modern science and scientifically orientated philosophy considers bread and wine to be a mixture of organic and inorganic materials which cannot properly speaking be called "substances" (that is, entities relatively independent in their own being but not their origin). The true substance of bread and wine is rather the cosmos "not yet as" a system of purely physical forces and fields but as the nature (*physis*) transformed by man.

Bread and wine represent together, in a picture, a world fashioned by human resources. They are especially suitable therefore to symbolize (in a broad sense) human self-offering. They are the principal materials by which men are nourished and they imply man's limitation to this world. Naturally they are typical of human offerings since Melchizedek's time, if not long before that.

In the present saving order our human offerings become meaningless unless they are part of the one saving sacrifice of Christ. He has therefore taken our useless gifts and made them his own, his own sacrifice of body and blood, thus linking them with his very being which is by nature one of sacrificial love. In this way they are changed ontologically and become the "species" of a different "substance." The ground and the meaning of their being, that is, their "substance" is no longer the cosmos; it is Christ himself, the Lord of the cosmos, who makes these "forms" (*species*) into a self-manifestation. Bread and wine, therefore, become his body and blood; through them he really and sacramentally "appears," offering himself here and now. The cult-symbol finds in this rite its highest realization. In this sense one can really speak of "transubstantiation," meaning that instead of the substance of the cosmos Christ himself bears bread and wine as his "species," so that they express him and he becomes their "substance." ["Symbol and Reality in the Eucharist"]

22. Prayer as encounter with the divine

Prayer is the most common form of religious experience, argues **Nels Ferré (1908–1971),** the way in which most people actually encounter the Holy in their lives. The widely respected Protestant theologian states below that "unless we meet God in prayer, we never meet him." What does this form of religious experience have in common with the ways of mysticism (St. Teresa, #18) and of intellectual conversion (St. Augustine, #15)? How is it different? Why does Ferré hold that prayer is more essential to religion than good works?

Prayer is the main highway to making religion real. Unless we meet God in prayer we never meet Him, for prayer is meeting God. Unless we meet Him, He can never become real to us. A person can be fully real to us only as we get to know him personally. No amount of mere talking or thinking about him can take the place of knowing face to face. Not even the most intimate correspondence with a "pen pal" can substitute for knowing him in person. To learn to know God, then, we must learn to pray. If we have prayed and still do not know Him, we need to learn to pray aright.

Long ago Descartes uttered the famous words, "I think, therefore I am." Even though he might doubt everything else, he felt sure of being the one thinking. Today, however, the existentialists tell us that Descartes was too intellectual. Life, they say, is more a matter of decisions. According to this approach Descartes should have written, "I decide, therefore I am!" Nathaniel Micklem, the renowned Oxford scholar, has pointed out, nevertheless, that since prayer is man's main relation to

God, he who prays knows the deepest truth; that is to say, "I pray, therefore I am." We are real in proportion to our right relation with God; and we are in right relation to Him in accordance with our praying.

The great men of God have been examples of prayer. They moved the world nearer to God mostly by the way they prayed. They came to be near God by the way they prayed and praying, they took the world part way with them. A young man who was writing his doctoral dissertation on the work of an illustrious preacher recounted that on passing through the preacher's city, he decided on the spur of the moment to call on him between trains. The visit was in vain, however, for the minister's secretary had orders to admit no one during his hour of prayer. His congregation may never have seen him on his knees, but they none the less felt his power. The saints of God have always been giants of prayer.

Peter Taylor Forsyth, one of the most eminent among recent Christian thinkers, suggested that the "priestliness of Christ was a priestliness of prayer" and that even "the atoning death of his deity" was "prayer and complete self-renunciation." On all the great occasions of his life Jesus is reported to have prayed. At the end of his ministry Gethsemane could become a victory of prayer because in the wilderness at the beginning of his mission he had prayed down his basic temptations. Jesus entered his ministry praying and he died praying. Gandhi died on his way to prayer. St. Francis developed a prayer life so real that when one of his followers eavesdropped on him, he heard the saint say nothing all night except "my God, my God." Life can offer no higher reward or usefulness than having religion become real through prayer.

People have a right to know why there is need for prayer. If God both knows our needs and wants to meet them, what real use can there be for prayer?

We should pray because God Himself has made prayer the way to His own presence. God does not force fellowship on us. He loves us enough to respect our freedom. Companionship is not consummated except by mutual free will. God longs to be loved because He is our Father; to help us He waits only for our willingness to receive. The heart of prayer is communion with God. Such communion requires that we accept God in the same way that He is ever ready to accept us.

We need to pray too because God respects our privacy. For our sake God hides Himself. Sometimes we think that God is merely hidden to our blind eyes. We believe that if we could see things as they really are we should find God everywhere. God, however, is not only hidden because of our imperfect sight; He also cannot be found precisely because He is not there. He hides Himself for the very purpose that we might become real. God does not want us to be puppets; He creates us to become living children. Our own children sometimes need to be free from parental participation. God never becomes guilty of "mom-ism," a selfish mother's refusing to let the child think or act by himself. Some people, to be sure, who pray "Father" really mean "Mamma"! But God never stoops to encouraging apron-string prayers!

We often think of God's presence as operating like atmospheric pressure, equally present everywhere. Is not God, we say, on the golf course as well as in the prayer meeting? But if He were, why should we pray for His holy presence? Why, if such were the case, should the Bible urge us, "Call upon me and I will be near"? Why should Jesus then have promised that where two or three should be gathered in his name he would himself be with them? No! God is personally present only to praying people. God is present only in the Spirit. When we are in the Spirit we are in a state of prayer.

To be in the Spirit is to be in communion with God regardless of how we have that communion, whether in words or silence, in worship or work. To be sure, God is always and everywhere present as the one who creates, sustains and controls the world. But as such He is not *personally* present. We can meet God personally only in communion with Him *and such communion is prayer.*

We also need to pray for the sake of finding light on our way. How we need light! I have heard a friend tell unforgettably a boyhood experience of cruising with his father off the rocky coast of Maine. Night had closed in as they approached the particularly treacherous reef that guarded the harbor's mouth. To their horror no light burned in the little lighthouse that should have given them their direction. Fuel was running low; they could hardly put out to sea again. Death waited in the darkness of the unseen, jagged rocks. Then a light! The smallest beam, perhaps a temporary lantern, but enough to give direction and to guide them safely into harbor.

But light seems hard to get. The difficulty, strangely enough, is because we are afraid of it. When we were children we were afraid of the dark. As we grow up we become afraid of the light, for the light shows us up. We want to fool ourselves. We want to believe that there are easier ways than his whose life was the light of men. The light shows that the way of love is the way of God. The way of God is the narrow path of truth. To follow it would cost all we have and all that we want to keep away from God and others.

Light seems hard to obtain because the kind of light we are seeking is light on how to get, to keep and to enjoy things for ourselves. Between us and the true light we puff up a smokescreen of anxiety as a protection of all that we hold dear. How can light pierce so dense a cloud of fear? Only an acceptance of God's love, that perfect love which casts out fear, can dissolve our inner anxieties and deliver us from outer pressures. True prayer gives us the fearlessness that brings rightness and brightness of heart. When we pray, we see things as they are, in their true light. The most objective person in the world is the one who has learned to pray, "Thy will be done."

Another reason for prayer is our need to receive power for good. Much of what we take for goodness is merely our foolish attempts to set things straight; meddling with God's order. Since we feel guilty within, we want to please God and, so to speak, to earn credit with Him. Therefore, we strive to outdo one another in good works. To be sure, God sees our intention; He knows how complicated our motives are. While most of do-gooding, however, never amounts to much, prayer, if it be genuine, makes the difference. How then does prayer give us power for good?

No one has ever seen power as such. We have seen the display of power in mighty waves that toss huge ocean liners like a ship—or in the little woman who runs the church. Power is not a thing. Power is the expression of some process or person. It is the ability to do something, to control something, or to direct something. While all power is ultimately from God, He shares some of it with us in order that we might become responsibly free. Besides, inasmuch as we need to do things together, having power also teaches us community concern.

We are free, of course, to go contrary to God's intention in using our power. We may become irresponsible and careless, or we may become concerned mostly about our own ease or pleasure. Irresponsible use of power, however, increases the world's problems and sufferings. Darting about doing good in our own way, apart from God's design for the common good, we introduce more trouble than we solve. When, on the contrary, in prayer we learn of God's way and therefore direct our small decisions in line with His large ones, we work according to God's real intention for the world and obtain power for lasting good. Prayer is opening our little lives to the power of God that we might gain and use more of it for the common good.

We should also pray to get love. To pray for love is to pray for God since God is love. At the outset we saw that we should pray in order to find God personally present. He is so present only in love. God is love and we are made for love. When we pray, therefore, if we pray for love, we find both God and ourselves. . . . [from *Making Religion Real*]

B. Theology

23. *"Faith seeking understanding"*

The term "theology" derives from the Greek words "theos" ("God") and "logos" ("reason" or "word"). It thus signifies a rational discourse about God. Theology attempts to provide a critical understanding of the encounter with the Holy experienced in the depths of life, personally confronted in prayer, and expressed in symbols. **St. Anselm of Canterbury (1033–1109)**—also known as Anselm of Aosta, from his place of birth in Italy—was successively a monk, abbot of the monastery of Bec in Normandy, and bishop of the primatial see of England. He was one of the first great Christian thinkers of the middle ages and gave impetus to the intellectual movement which would become scholasticism. In the spirit of St. Augustine, Anselm insists that faith must come before rational understanding of the mystery of the self-revealing God. He argues that there can be no knowledge without experience; but without faith —a personal relationship with God and acceptance of his revelation—we would not have the relevant experience. (On the so-called "natural" knowledge of God, see below, section *III A*.) Thus faith has an absolute priority for theology. Nevertheless, Anselm holds that faith would be lacking if it did not use human reason to explore the mysteries of revelation. In this brief and famous passage from his book *Why God Became Human* (*Cur Deus Homo*) Anselm succinctly states the function of theology: "to understand what we believe." This idea is the source of the classical definition of theology as "faith seeking understanding."

Just as the right order of things demands that we first believe in the mysteries of Christian faith before daring to examine them rationally, so likewise it seems to me that, once we have been confirmed in faith, we would be neglectful if we did not then attempt to understand what we believe.   [from *Cur Deus Homo*, I, c.2; trans. R. Viladesau]

24. Theology as the *"science of God"*

The Dominican friar **St. Thomas Aquinas (1224–1274)** is widely regarded as the preeminent Christian theologian of the middle ages, and his influence continues to the present. St. Thomas attempted to synthesize Christian faith with human reason, as represented especially by the newly recovered philosophy of Aristotle. In the first of the following passages, St. Thomas describes theology as a "science" in the sense defined by Aristotle. (How does this sense differ from the modern notion of "science"?) In the second, he explains in what sense this study can bring us to the knowledge of God, and acknowledges important limitations: the human mind can never fully grasp the nature of God, so that God's essence always remains beyond whatever we can say of him. Note how St. Thomas' method involves a "dialectic" of contrasting opinions: he first examines the objections against the thesis proposed, then a contrasting argument in favor; he then gives his solution to the question and replies to the objections.

Article 2: Whether Christian theology ("sacred doctrine") is a science.

On the point of the article: It would seem that Christian theology is not a science. For:

1. Every science takes its start from self-evident principles. But theology starts from the articles of faith, which are not self-evident, since they are not admitted by everyone; as it says in the second epistle to the Thessalonians "not all have faith." Therefore theology is not a science.

2. Furthermore, science does not deal with individual cases. But theology does: think, for example, of the deeds of Abraham, Isaac, and Jacob, and other such matters. Therefore theology is not a science.

On the other hand: Augustine says (in Book XIV of his *On the Trinity*): "This science alone is responsible for the arising, the nourishment, the defense, and the strengthening of the healthiest faith." This applies to no other science than to theology. Therefore theology is a science.

I reply: Theology is a science. But it must be noted that there are two kinds of science. Some sciences take as their starting point principles that are known directly by the natural light of human reason—for example, arithmetic, geometry, and other such sciences. But other sciences begin from premises accepted from a superior body of knowledge—as, for example, the science of perspective gets its start from principles known from geometry, and music takes its principles from arithmetic. Theology is a science in this second sense: for it takes as its starting point principles that are known in the light of a higher body of knowledge—namely, God's own knowledge and the knowledge of those who have the vision of God. Thus, just as music accepts on faith its principles taken from arithmetic, so theology takes on faith its starting point, the basic knowledge revealed by God.

In response to the first point raised: the premises of any science are either self-evident [within the realm of that science] or are derived from what is recognized in a superior science or body of knowledge. The latter is the case of theology.

In response to the second point raised: individual cases are dealt with in theology, not because it is principally concerned with them, but because they serve as examples for our lives (as in moral science) or because they proclaim the authority of those from whom we receive the divine revelation on which sacred Scripture and doctrine are based.   [*Summa Theologiae*, Part I, question 1, article 2]

Article 7: Whether God is the subject of this science.

On the point of the article: It would seem that God is not the subject of this science. For:

1. In any science, it is necessary to know the essence [i.e., "what it is"] of its subject—as Aristotle says (in the first book of the Posterior Analytics). But the science of theology cannot know the essence of God; as St. John Damascene says, "it is impossible to know what God is [i.e., his essence]." Therefore God cannot be the subject of this science.

2. Furthermore, everything that is treated in a particular science should be included in the subject of that science. But in the sacred Scriptures many things are treated besides God; for example, they teach about creatures and human behavior. Therefore God is not the subject of this science.

On the other hand: the subject of a science is what is spoken of in that science. But in this science, we speak about God; indeed, it is called "theology," that is, "speech about God." Therefore God is the subject of this science.

I reply: God is the subject of this science. . . . For every topic of theology has to do with God: either because it is God himself, or because it is related to God as the origin and goal of all things. Hence it follows that God really is the subject of this science. This becomes clear if we consider the premises of this science, namely the articles of faith, which are about God; for the subject of the principles of a science is the subject of the whole science, since the latter is virtually contained in its premises.[1]

1. In the Aristotelian notion of "science," all conclusions are deduced from the premises; hence the whole science is implicitly "contained" in the science's principles [ed.].

Some people, however, paying attention to the topics dealt with in theology rather than the reason why they are treated, have considered something else the subject of this science: for example, signs and reality, or the work of redemption, or the total Christ, i.e., the "head" and "members" of Christ's body. It is true that all these things are dealt with in theology; but they are treated because they are related to God.

In response to the first point raised: it is true that we cannot know the essence of God. But in theology we use God's created effects—whether on the level of nature or grace—in place of a definition of what God is, in order to speak about God; just as in philosophy, one can show something about a cause from a consideration of its effects, accepting the effect in place of a definition of the cause.

In response to the second point raised: every thing that is treated in theology is included under the subject, God; not as though they were parts or forms or qualities of God, but insofar as they are related in some way to him. [*Summa Theologiae*, Part I, question 1, article 7; trans. R. Viladesau]

25. Theology and the human situation

Paul Tillich [see above, #5] insists that theology, in order to reflect on God's revelation, must at the same time consider the human situation to which God's word is addressed. In order to preach the "kerygma" ("proclamation"; the word used for the basic message of the New Testament about Jesus), theology must also include an aspect of "apologetics"—i.e., of "giving answer" for faith, explaining and justifying its claims in terms understandable to the human circumstances and thought of each age. For Tillich, every human situation is in need of God, and can be seen as a "question" whose answer is to be found in God's self-revelation in Christ. Tillich's "method of correlation" consists in bringing these two elements together.

1. MESSAGE AND SITUATION

Theology, as a function of the Christian church, must serve the needs of the church. A theological system is supposed to satisfy two basic needs: the statement of the truth of the Christian message and the interpretation of this truth for every new generation. Theology moves back and forth between two poles, the eternal truth of its foundation and the temporal situation in which the eternal truth must be received. Not many theological systems have been able to balance these two demands perfectly. Most of them either sacrifice elements of the truth or are not able to speak to the situation. Some of them combine both shortcomings. Afraid of missing the eternal truth, they identify it with some previous theological work, with traditional concepts and solutions, and try to impose these on a new, different situation. They confuse eternal truth with a temporal expression of this truth. This is evident in European theological orthodoxy, which in America is known as fundamentalism. When fundamentalism is combined with an antitheological bias, as it is, for instance, in its biblicistic-evangelical form, the theological truth of yesterday is defended as an unchangeable message against the theological truth of today and tomorrow. Fundamentalism fails to make contact with the present situation, not because it speaks from beyond every situation, but because it speaks from a situation of the past. It elevates something finite and transitory to infinite and eternal validity. In this respect fundamentalism has demonic traits. It destroys the humble honesty of the search for truth, it splits the conscience of its thoughtful adherents, and it makes them fanatical because they are forced to suppress elements of truth of which they are dimly aware.

Fundamentalists in America and orthodox theologians in Europe can point to the fact that their theology is eagerly received and held by many people just because of the historical or biographical situation in which men find themselves today. The fact is obvious, but the interpretation is wrong. "Situation," as one pole of all theological work, does not refer to the psychological or sociological state in which individuals or groups live. It refers to the scientific and artistic, the economic, political, and ethical forms in which they express their interpretation of existence. The "situation" to which theology must speak relevantly is not the situation of the individual as individual and not the situation of the group as group. Theology is neither preaching nor counseling; therefore, the success of a theology when it is applied to preaching or to the care of souls is not necessarily a criterion of its truth. The fact that fundamentalist ideas are eagerly grasped in a period of personal or communal disintegration does not prove their theological validity, just as the success of a liberal theology in periods of personal or communal integration is no certification of its truth. The "situation" theology must consider is the creative interpretation of existence, an interpretation which is carried on in every period of history under all kinds of psychological and sociological condi-

tions. The "situation" certainly is not independent of these factors. However, theology deals with the cultural expression they have found in
practice as well as in theory and not with these conditioning factors as
such. Thus theology is not concerned with the political split between
East and West, but it *is* concerned with the political interpretation of this
split. Theology is not concerned with the spread of mental diseases or
with our increasing awareness of them, but it *is* concerned with the
psychiatric interpretation of these trends. The "situation" to which theology must respond is the totality of man's creative self-interpretation in a
special period. Fundamentalism and orthodoxy reject this task, and, in
doing so, they miss the meaning of theology. . . .

2. APOLOGETIC THEOLOGY AND THE KERYGMA

Apologetic theology is "answering theology." It answers the questions
implied in the "situation" in the power of the eternal message and with
the means provided by the situation whose questions it answers.

The term "apologetic," which had such a high standing in the early
church, has fallen into disrepute because of the methods employed in
the abortive attempts to defend Christianity against attacks from modern humanism, naturalism, and historism. An especially weak and dis-
gusting form of apologetics used the *argumentum ex ignorantia*,[2] that is, it
tried to discover gaps in our scientific and historical knowledge in order
to find a place for God and his actions within an otherwise completely
calculable and "immanent" world. Whenever our knowledge advanced,
another defense position had to be given up; but eager apologetes were
not dissuaded by this continuous retreat from finding in the most recent
developments of physics and historiography new occasions to establish
God's activity in new gaps of scientific knowledge. This undignified
procedure has discredited everything which is called "apologetics."

There is, however, a more profound reason for the distrust of apologetic methods, especially on the part of the kerygmatic theologians. In
order to answer a question, one must have something in common with
the person who asks it. Apologetics presupposes common ground, however vague it may be. But kerygmatic theologians are inclined to deny
any common ground with those outside the "theological circle." They
are afraid that the common ground will destroy the uniqueness of the
message. They point to the early Christian Apologists who saw a com-

2. "argument from ignorance" [ed.].

mon ground in the acceptance of the Logos; they point to the Alexandrian school which found a common ground in Platonism; they point to Thomas Aquinas' use of Aristotle; above all, they point to the common ground which apologetic theology believed itself to have found with the philosophy of the Enlightenment, with Romanticism, with Hegelianism and Kantianism, with humanism and naturalism. They try to demonstrate that in each case what was assumed to be common ground actually was the ground of the "situation"; that theology lost its own ground when it entered the situation. Apologetic theology in all these forms—and that means practically all nonfundamentalist theology since the beginning of the eighteenth century—is, from the point of view of recent kerygmatic theologians, a surrender of the kerygma, of the immovable truth. If this is an accurate reading of theological history, then the only real theology is kerygmatic theology. The "situation" cannot be entered; no answer to the questions implied in it can be given, at least not in terms which are felt to be an answer. The message must be thrown at those in the situation—thrown like a stone. This certainly can be an effective method of preaching under special psychological conditions, for instance, in revivals; it can even be effective if expressed in aggressive theological terms; but it does not fulfil the aim of the theological function of the church. And, beyond all this, it is impossible. Even kerygmatic theology must use the conceptual tools of its period. It cannot simply repeat biblical passages. Even when it does, it cannot escape the conceptual situation of the different biblical writers. Since language is the basic and all-pervasive expression of every situation, theology cannot escape the problem of the "situation." Kerygmatic theology must give up its exclusive transcendence and take seriously the attempt of apologetic theology to answer the questions put before it by the contemporary situation.

On the other hand, apologetic theology must heed the warning implied in the existence and the claim of kerygmatic theology. It loses itself if it is not based on the kerygma as the substance and criterion of each of its statements. More than two centuries of theological work have been determined by the apologetic problem. "The Christian message and the modern mind" has been the dominating theme since the end of classical orthodoxy. The perennial question has been: Can the Christian message be adapted to the modern mind without losing its essential and unique character? Most theologians have believed that it is possible; some have deemed it impossible either in the name of the Christian message or in the name of the modern mind. No doubt the voices of those who have emphasized the contrast, the *diastasis*, have been louder and more impressive—men usually are more powerful in their negations than in their affirmations. But the continuous toil of those who have tried to find a union, a "synthesis," has kept theology alive. Without them traditional Christianity would have become narrow and superstitious, and the general cultural movement would have proceeded without the "thorn in the flesh" which it needed, namely, an honest theology of cultural high standing. The wholesale condemnations of theology during the last two centuries of theology which are fashionable in traditional and neo-orthodox groups are profoundly wrong (as Barth himself has acknowledged in his *Die protestantische Theologie im neunzehnten Jahrhundert*). Yet certainly it is necessary to ask in every special case whether or not the apologetic bias has dissolved the Christian message. And it is further necessary to seek a theological method in which message and situation are related in such a way that neither of them is obliterated. If such a method is found, the two centuries' old question of "Christianity and the modern mind" can be attacked more successfully. The following system is an attempt to use the "method of correlation" as a way of uniting message and situation. It tries to correlate the questions implied in the situation with the answers implied in the message. It does not derive the answers from the questions as a self-defying apologetic theology does. Nor does it elaborate answers without relating them to the questions as a self-defying kerygmatic theology does. It correlates questions and answers, situation and message, human existence and divine manifestation.

Obviously, such a method is not a tool to be handled at will. It is neither a trick nor a mechanical device. It is itself a theological assertion, and, like all theological assertions, it is made with passion and risk; and ultimately it is not different from the system which is built upon it. System and method belong to each other and are to be judged with each other. It will be a positive judgment if the theologians of the coming generations acknowledge that it has helped them, and nontheological thinkers as well, to understand the Christian message as the answer to the questions implied in their own and in every human situation. [from *Systematic Theology*, vol. 1]

Chapter Three

Revelation and Faith

A. General Revelation: The Knowledge of God Through Reason

A strong part of the Christian tradition holds that God is revealed not only in his salvific acts in the history of Israel and in Christ, recorded in the scriptures ("special" revelation), but also in his creation, so that he may in principle be known—albeit obscurely—by all people, through the use of reason ("general" revelation).[1]

The First Vatican Council in 1870 officially defined the proposition that "God, the source and goal of all things, can be known with certitude from creation by the natural light of human reason" (session III). The council purposely refrained from considering whether anyone actually attains knowledge of God without his grace, but it considered the essential capacity of human beings for such knowledge to be a necessary presupposition of our ability to be addressed by God at all. In this it echoes the thought of St. Thomas Aquinas (below, #27) that "grace presupposes nature": there is a continuity between the "levels" of creation and grace. While most contemporary theologians hold that the distinction between the levels of nature and grace is a purely abstract one—we never encounter "pure" human nature; every human being exists in a "supernatural" situation of the offer of God's grace—nevertheless the principle represented by the idea of "natural" revelation remains

---

1. Note that this does not imply that "general revelation" is *restricted* to what is knowable by "natural reason" reflecting on creation, but only that it includes it. Contemporary theologians hold that "supernatural" grace, revelation, and faith are also found outside scriptural revelation.

important: it means that while faith goes "beyond" reason, it is not unreasonable, but in continuity with our rationality. Moreover, it represents the conviction that God can only be revealed in a "supernatural" way because by creation itself, by the very essence of being human, there is already a "natural" capacity, openness and desire for him. This idea reflects the famous saying of St. Augustine (above, #15): "Thou hast made us for Thyself, and our hearts are restless until they rest in Thee."

26. God's revelation through creation in the scriptures

The abstract theological idea of the "natural" knowledge of God does not occur in the Bible; but the idea that God can be known by all people through his creation is found in several places—even though it is also stated that the "pagans" have in fact rejected this knowledge of the real God and turned instead to idols. But they can only be held guilty of sin precisely because they had the ability to know the true God.

Romans 1:18–23—God's eternal power and divinity are recognizable in his creation.

Wisdom 13:1–9—From the greatness and beauty of created things their author is seen.

Acts 17:24–29—Paul's discourse on the Areopagus: the "unknown God" of the pagans now revealed.

1 Corinthians 1:21—The world did not come to know God through "wisdom."

27. Knowledge of God and belief in God

For **St. Thomas Aquinas** (see above, #24) the existence of God is knowable by human reason. That is, we can know by reason that the world must have a cause which is an absolute being that we call "God" (see below, #30); but the nature of God remains a mystery. Our "natural" knowledge is limited to saying what God is not; we can know that God is, but we cannot know what God is.

According to St. Thomas, then, the existence of God should not ordinarily be a matter of faith; it should be a matter of knowledge. Thus for him there is a difference between believing *in* God and believing *that there is a God*. Only the person who is incapable of exercising reason to arrive at God's existence will believe "that there is" a God; but even the person who knows the existence of God by reason must believe *in* God. Hence for St. Thomas belief "in" God is more than the intellectual affirmation of his existence: it implies a personal relation of trust and acceptance of the God whose existence is known by reason, and who reveals himself in history to faith.

QUESTION 2, ARTICLE 2: WHETHER GOD'S EXISTENCE CAN BE DEMONSTRATED

It would seem that God's existence cannot be demonstrated. For the existence of God is an article of faith. But matters of faith cannot be demonstrated by reason, since rational proof gives knowledge, while faith is concerned with what is not apparent, as is clear from the Apostle (in the Epistle to the Hebrews, 11:1). Therefore it cannot be demonstrated that God exists. . . .

In response to this objection it should be stated that the existence of God, and other things that can be known about God by natural reason, as is said in Rom. 1, are not articles of faith. They are rather "preambles" to faith: just as grace presupposes nature, and perfection presupposes a capacity to be perfected, so faith presupposes natural knowledge of God. However, it is possible that something which is in itself knowable and provable may be accepted by a particular person on faith, if that person does not grasp the rational demonstration. [from the *Summa Theologiae*, Part I, question 2, article 2] [Trans. R. Viladesau]

28. The "ontological" argument

St. Anselm of Canterbury (see above, #23) was convinced that his prayer and meditation on the meaning of God had yielded him an infallible argument for God's existence, one that depended solely on understanding what we mean when we say "God." God's existence, according to Anselm, is unique, because he is the only being whose existence is necessary; he cannot not exist. This argument is *a priori* because it depends only on the process of thinking, without any appeal to external experience. This line of thought was named the "ontological argument" by the philosopher Emmanuel Kant, who rejected it on the grounds that actual existence can never be known simply from an idea. It is to be noted, however, that St. Anselm himself develops the argument not as a purely philosophical exercise, but in a context of faith; it is presented as part of a long prayer addressed to God, in which Anselm states explicitly: "I do not seek to understand in order to believe; rather, I believe in order to understand. For I also believe this: that unless I believed, I would not understand."

Therefore, O Lord, you who give understanding to our faith, grant me, insofar as you deem it helpful to me, that I may understand that you exist as we believe, and that you are what we believe you to be. We believe that you are something than which no greater thing can be thought. But is there such a Being—since "the fool says in his heart, 'there is no God' " [Ps. 13:1]? . . . But even the fool must admit that something than which no greater can be thought exists at least in the mind, since he understands the words when he hears them; and whatever is understood exists in the mind [as an idea]. But it is clear that "that than which no greater can be thought" cannot exist only in the mind. For if it were only an idea in the mind, we could think of it as existing also in reality—which would be greater. Therefore, if "that than which no greater can be thought" were only an idea, then something greater than it *could* be thought [namely, an actually existing being "than which no greater can be thought"]. Thus [we must conclude, in order to avoid self-contradiction] something than which no greater can be thought certainly exists, not only as an idea, but as an actual being.

So truly does this Being exist, that its non-existence is unthinkable. For we can think of the existence of something whose non-existence is inconceivable; and this is greater than anything whose non-existence can be conceived. So, if "that than which no greater can be thought" could be conceived not to exist—then it would not be "that than which no greater can be thought"; which would be self-contradictory. Hence something "than which no greater can be thought" so truly exists, that it cannot even be thought not to exist; and you are this Being, O Lord our God. So truly do you exist, Lord my God, that your non-existence is inconceivable. . . . And yet everything else, apart from you, can be thought not to be. . . .

What, therefore, are you, Lord God, than whom nothing greater can be thought? What can you be but the One existing by its own nature, above all things, who made everything from nothing? For anything less than this would not be "that than which no greater can be thought," and hence would not be you. Then, what good quality could be lacking to this greatest Good, the source of all other good? Therefore you must be just, truthful, joyous, and everything else that it is better to be than not be. . . .   [*Proslogion*, II–III, V] [Trans. R. Viladesau]

29. *The evidence of the idea of God*

The scientist, mathematician, and philosopher **René Descartes (1596–1650)** is renowned as the inventor of analytic geometry, and is considered by many to be the father of modern philosophy. While St. Anselm developed his thoughts on God's existence in the context of prayer, Descartes presents his version of the "ontological argument" in the thoroughly rationalist setting of his universal "methodical doubt"—a determination not to accept anything as true unless it can be founded on rational evidence. Descartes holds that we can know certain things to be true simply from having "clear and distinct ideas" of them; for example, if I conceive of a geometrical figure with three angles, I can know with certitude that it can only have three sides, because this property is "clearly and distinctly" conceived when I think of a triangle. The same is true of analytic mathematical truths. Descartes believes that the idea of God is also of this kind; the idea provides evidence of his existence, since existence belongs to the very concept of God. This part of the argument is similar to St. Anselm's. In the first part of the following selection, however, Descartes proposes a different kind of a priori argument. For him the idea of God is not the product of the human mind, but is "innate." (By this he does not mean that human beings are actually born with this idea in their minds, or even that they will necessarily come to it; but that it is given as an inborn potentiality with the capacity of thinking itself.) Descartes holds, contrary to the notion that God is merely a "projection" of the human mind (a critique later to be developed by Feuerbach, Marx, Freud), that we could not conceive of a truly infinite being at all unless we had received the idea from God. Finally, for Descartes the knowledge of the existence of God is the guarantee for the possibility of knowing anything with certitude; for God is seen as the source of all "clear and distinct" perceptions, on which knowledge is based.

By the word "God" I mean an infinite, eternal, changeless, independent, omniscient, omnipotent substance, by which I and all other things that exist (if they exist) were created or produced. Now, these qualities are so great and eminent that, the more I think about them, the less I can believe that my idea of them can have originated from myself alone. . . . I can have the idea of a "substance" from the very fact that I am a substance; but I, a finite being, could never have the idea of an infinite substance unless that idea was placed in my mind by a real infinite substance.

And I should not imagine that I really do not really conceive the infinite through a true idea, but only through the negation of what is finite . . . since, on the contrary, I see clearly that there is more reality in the infinite substance than in finite substance, and that, in a certain sense, I have the notion of the infinite before I have that of the finite; that is, I have the idea of God before the idea of myself. For how could I know that I doubt and that I desire—that is, that I am lacking something, and that I am not totally perfect—unless I had in myself some idea of a being more perfect than my own, in comparison to which I know the faults of my nature? . . .

But perhaps I am really more than I imagine, and all the perfections that I attribute to the nature of a God are in some way my own potentialities, even though they have not yet manifested themselves or become actual. . . . However, when I look at this idea more closely, I see that it cannot be so; for, first of all, although it is true that my knowledge acquires every day new degrees of perfection, and that there are many potentialities in my nature that have not been actualized, nevertheless these qualities do not in any way belong to or even approach the idea that I have of the Divinity, in which there is no potentiality, but only pure actuality. . . .

It remains only to examine how I acquired this idea [of God]; for I did not receive it through my senses . . . nor is it a pure product or invention of my mind, since it is not in my power to add to or subtract from it. . . . Consequently, there is no alternative but to say that this idea was born and produced with me when I was created, just as was the idea of my "self." And, indeed, it should not be thought strange that God, in creating me, should have placed this idea in me like the mark of the workman imprinted on his work. . . .

... Now, if it follows from the mere fact that I can conceive the idea of something, that everything that I recognize clearly and distinctly as a property of that thing is in fact its property—can I not from this construct an argument and a demonstrative proof for the existence of God? It is certain that the idea of God—that is, the idea of a supremely perfect being—is no less present in me than the idea of any geometrical or mathematical reality; and my knowledge that an actual and eternal existence belongs to his nature is no less clear and distinct than my knowledge that anything that I can rationally demonstrate concerning geometrical or mathematical realities is really true of them. . . . Hence, I should consider the existence of God to be no less certain to me than I have heretofore considered the truths of geometry and mathematics. The reasoning behind this, however, may not at first appear totally clear, but may seem to be based on a certain sophistry. For, since I am accustomed in every other case to make a distinction between existence and essence, I can easily think that existence can be separated from the essence of God, and therefore that one could conceive of God as not actually existing. Nevertheless, when I consider the matter more attentively, I find that it is obvious that God's existence cannot be separated from his essence—any more than the essence of a right triangle can be separated from having three angles adding up to 180 degrees, or than the idea of a mountain can be separated from that of a valley. So, it is just as impossible to conceive of God—that is, a supremely perfect being—lacking existence (which would mean lacking in a perfection), as it is to conceive a mountain which has no valley.

But even though I can no more conceive of God not existing than I can conceive a mountain without a valley, nevertheless, from the fact that I think of a mountain with a valley, it does not follow that any mountain exists in the world. Likewise, it would seem that from the fact that I conceive of God as existing, it does not follow that God really does exist; for my thought does not make things real. I can imagine a horse with wings; but this does not mean there are any winged horses. So perhaps I attribute existence to God, even though no God actually exists. But it is here that there is a sophism, hidden in this apparent objection. From the fact that I cannot conceive of a mountain without a valley it does not follow that any mountain or valley exists in the world, but only that mountain and valley—whether they exist or not—are inseparable from each other. Similarly, from the very fact that I cannot conceive of God except as existing, it follows that existence is inseparable from him, and therefore that he really does exist. It is not that my idea makes it true, or that thinking makes things real; on the contrary, it is the necessity of

God's existence that forces me to have this idea. For I am not free to conceive of a God without existence—that is, to conceive of a supremely perfect Being without supreme perfection—as I am free to imagine a horse, with or without wings.

And one should not say at this point that I must indeed admit the existence of God once I have supposed that he possesses every kind of perfection, since existence is a perfection—but that my original supposition was not necessary. . . . For, even though it is not necessary that I should ever have an idea of God, nevertheless, whenever I do in fact think of a first and supreme Being, it is necessary that I attribute to him every kind of profection, even though I cannot enumerate them all or apply my attention to every one of them individually. And this necessity is sufficient for me to conclude that this first and supreme Being does exist, as soon as I recognize that existence is a perfection. In the same way, it is not necessary for me ever to think of a triangle; but any time I do want to consider a rectilinear figure composed of only three angles, it is absolutely necessary that I attribute to it all the properties that lead to the conclusion that the three angles cannot exceed a total of 180 degrees, even though I may not think of that conclusion in particular at the time. On the other hand, if I examine all the figures that can be inscribed within a circle, it is by no means necessary for me to think that all four-sided figures will be among them; on the contrary, I cannot even suppose that such would be the case, since I do not wish to receive in my thought anything except what I can conceive clearly and distinctly. Consequently, there is a great difference between false suppositions, like that about the four-sided figures, and real ideas, which are innate, and of which the first and foremost is the idea of God. For I recognize, in fact, in several ways, that this idea is by no means something invented or thought up by me, depending on my thought alone, but is the image of a real and immutable nature. . . . And even though I have had to go through much mental labor in order to conceive the truth of God's existence accurately, now I am not only as sure of it as I am of the most profound certitudes, but I would also remark that the certitude of all other things absolutely depends on it: without the knowledge of God's existence, it is impossible ever to be sure of anything.   [from *Méditations Métaphysiques*, III, V], [Trans. R. Viladesau]

30. The five ways

St. Thomas Aquinas agrees with St. Anselm that God is the necessary being who cannot not exist; God's essence is his existence.

Nevertheless, he rejects the ontological argument: for even if we understand "God" to mean "that than which no greater can be thought," and admit that it is "greater" to be than not to be, it only follows from this that we must *think* of God as existing; it does not follow that what we think actually exists. Moreover, God's essence so transcends the human mind that no concept of ours can grasp or comprehend it. Therefore, "because we do not know God's essence, his existence is not self-evident to us, but needs to be demonstrated through those things that are more known to us . . . namely, God's created effects."

All our knowledge, says St. Thomas, proceeds from experience. Even our knowledge of God must start from the world. He gives five famous "ways" of the mind from the world to God. In each, the essence of the reasoning is the same: the finite world cannot explain its own existence, order, or dynamism; hence we must posit a self-existing, absolute cause. (Note that for St. Thomas, to say that the world needs a "cause" is not the same as saying that the world must have a "beginning": when he speaks of God as the "first" mover, etc., the reference is metaphysical, not temporal. He explicitly holds that God could make a world that had no beginning in time; but it would always be created, i.e. totally dependent for its existence on God.)

I reply that God's existence can be proven by five ways.

The first and clearest way is from motion. For it is certain, and apparent to our senses, that there is movement (change) in this world; but everything that moves is moved by another. For nothing can be moved, except insofar as it is in potency toward that toward which it is moved; while that which performs the motion does so insofar as it is in act. For movement or change is nothing but the reduction of potency to act. But nothing can be brought from potency to act except by the agency of something that is already in act. . . . It is impossible that a thing be both mover and moved in the same regard and in the same way; that is, it is impossible for anything to move or change itself. Therefore anything that moves is moved by something else. Now, if that thing by which it is moved is itself moved, it also must be moved by another; and that other by yet another. But this cannot go on to infinity, because then there would be no first mover, and consequently no motion at all; for the secondary causes of motion only move insofar as they are themselves moved by the first mover. . . . Therefore, it is necessary to arrive at a first mover of some kind, which is not moved by any other; and this is what everyone understands by God.

The second way is from the nature of efficient causality. We find that there is in the sensible world an order of efficient causes. We do not find (and it is not possible) that any thing is the efficient cause of itself; for in order to be so, it would have to be prior to itself, which is impossible. Now, it is not possible to have an infinite series of efficient causes: for in every series of efficient causes, the first is the cause of the intermediate cause, and the intermediate is the cause of the last cause, whether the intermediate be a plurality of causes or a single one. If, however, one takes away the cause, one removes the effect as well. Therefore, if there were no first cause among efficient causes, neither would there be an intermediate or a last. But if there were an infinite procession of efficient causes, there would be no first efficient cause; and thus there would be no ultimate effect, nor any intermediate causes. But this is plainly false. Therefore, it is necessary to posit some first efficient cause: which is what all call God.

The third way is taken from the possible and the necessary, and it states the following: we encounter among things some which have the possibility of being or of not being; for things are found to be generated and to be corrupted, and therefore it is possible for them to be or not to be. But it is impossible for such things always to exist; for if it is possible for something not to be, then at some time it is not. It follows then that if everything had the possibility of not being, there would have been a time when nothing existed at all. But if this were so, then there would still be nothing in existence; for what does not exist can only come into being by means of something already existing. Therefore, if at one time there was nothing at all, it would have been impossible for anything to come into being; and thus there would now be nothing in existence. But this is plainly false. Therefore not all beings are merely possible; there must be something whose existence is necessary. But every necessary being either has its necessity caused by another, or does not. It is not possible, however, to proceed to infinity in necessary things that have their necessity caused by another, just as it is not possible to have an infinite procession of efficient causes, as we have shown. Therefore it is necessary to posit some being which is necessary in and of itself, and which does not have the cause of its necessity from another, but is rather the cause of the necessity of other things. And this is what all call God.

The fourth way is taken from the degrees which are found in things.

For we find among things some which are more or which are less good, true, noble, and so forth. But "more" and "less" signify that things to different degrees approach something which is the maximum; so, for example, something is "more hot" when it more greatly approaches the hottest. There exists, therefore, something which is the truest, and the best, and the most noble, and, consequently, something which is most in being; for those things which are most true, are the greatest in being (as is said in *Metaphys. ii*). Now, the greatest in any genus is the cause of all others which are of the same genus; just as fire, which is the maximum of heat, is the cause of all other things which are hot (as is stated in the same book). Therefore there exists something which is for all things the cause of their being, and goodness, and of every perfection; and this is what we call God.

The fifth way is taken from the ordering of things. For we see that certain things which lack knowledge, such as natural bodies, act for an end; and this is clear from the fact that they always (or at least nearly always) act in the same way, so as to obtain the best result; and this shows that they attain their end not by accident, but by intention. But things which have no faculty of knowledge cannot move toward an end unless they are directed by some intelligent and knowing being—as an arrow is directed by an archer. Therefore there exists some intelligent being, by whom all natural objects are directed to their end; and this being we call God.   [from the *Summa Theologiae*, Part I, question 2, article 3], [Trans. R. Viladesau]

31. The "ontological wager"

Like his contemporary Descartes, **Blaise Pascal (1623–1662)** was a great mathematician, as well as a man of letters, a physicist, and an inventor (his mechanical calculator is considered a forerunner of the modern computer). Unlike Descartes or Aquinas, Pascal had little trust in human reason's capacity to lead us to God; for him, faith alone was of value. But why should one take the risk of faith? In an imaginary dialogue, Pascal compares believing in God to a wager that is worth making because one loses nothing if one is wrong, and gains everything if one is right. Commentators are divided on how this passage should be taken. For some, it is an accurate portrayal of the existential human situation with regard to belief and unbelief. Others consider the presuppositions of the argument questionable;

and some even think that Pascal merely meant it as an intellectual game, not to be taken in earnest. The passage is fragmentary, but its dramatic power is undiminished by the incompleteness and ambiguity of some of its expressions.

If there is a God, he is infinitely incomprehensible since, having no parts and no limits, he has no relationship to us. We are therefore incapable of knowing either what he is, or whether he exists. This being the case, who will undertake to resolve this question? Not we, who have no relation to him. . . .

Let us then examine this point, and let us say: "Either God exists, or he does not." But which side should we incline to? Reason can determine nothing; there is an infinite chaos that separates us. A game is being played, at the end of this infinite distance: heads or tails. Which will you bet on? Reason cannot bring you to choose one or the other; reason cannot defend either choice. Therefore do not blame as wrong those who have made a choice; for you know nothing about it.

"No; but I will say they are wrong, not for having made this or that particular choice, but for having chosen at all; whether one chooses heads or tails, one is equally wrong; the right course would be not to bet at all."

Yes; but you have to bet. There is no option; you are in the game. Which side will you take, then? Let us see. . . . Your reason is no more harmed one way than the other, since you must necessarily choose. . . . But your happiness? Let us weigh the gain and the loss if you take "heads": that God exists. Let us examine the two possibilities. If you win, you win everything; if you lose, you lose nothing. So bet on God's existence, without hesitation.

"Wonderful! Yes, I must bet; but perhaps the stakes are too high."

Let us see. Since there is an equal chance of winning or losing, if you could win only two lifetimes by risking one, you could still be ahead; but if you could win three . . . you would be imprudent, since you are forced to play, not to risk your life in order to gain three lives, in a game where the chances of winning and losing are equal. . . . But in this case there is an infinity of infinitely happy life to be won. . . . That decides it; where something infinite [to gain] is involved, and where the risks of loss are not infinite, there is no equality of choice; you must give all. . . .

So our proposition has an infinite force, since there is only something finite at risk, and something infinite to be gained, in a game where there are equal chances of winning and losing. This is proven; and, if human beings are capable of attaining any truth, this is it.   [from *Pensées*, no. 233], [Trans. R. Viladesau]

32. *"Fundamental trust" and the existence of God*

Swiss theologian **Hans Küng** argues that every human being, faced with uncertain reality, must opt for a positive or negative basic attitude toward life: a fundamental trust or mistrust in existence. Fundamental trust is the only rational and psychologically healthy stance, but it is not forced on us; we must choose it. Belief in God means that fundamental trust has an ultimate rational ground; for the unbeliever, on the other hand, fundamental trust can have no final rational justification.

Küng's reasoning bears a certain resemblance to the "moral argument" of Emmanuel Kant. Kant held that the human mind is not capable of knowing metaphysical truths like the existence of God. Thus for him there can be no "proof" of God's existence in "speculative" reason. Nevertheless, Kant thought that there are good grounds to *believe* in God's existence; for without God, there can be no final basis for the absoluteness of morality, which Kant took to be a given of human existence (the "categorical imperative"). Hence God's existence for Kant is a necessary "postulate" of "practical reason." Similarly for Küng, the existence of God cannot be strictly proven; but the affirmation of God is a necessary condition for a rationally justified fundamental trust.

THE HYPOTHESIS

The ultimate questions, which—according to Kant—combine all the interests of human reason, are also the first questions, the commonplace questions. "What can I know?" sums up questions about truth. "What ought I to do?" questions about the norm. "What may I hope?" questions about meaning. "Functional" and "essential" questions, technical-rational and total-personal questions, can all be distinguished, but are linked together in concrete life. "Calculating" thought, which—in Heidegger's sense—is concerned with what is feasible, computable, accurate, cannot be separated in ordinary life from "meditative" thought, which is concerned with meaning and truth. But the essential questions about meaning and truth, norms and values can be covered up and suppressed—more than ever under the soporific influence of the welfare society—until they emerge again as a result of reflection or even more as a result of "fate" in great things or in small.

In order to answer the question of the existence of God, it must be assumed that man accepts in principle his own existence and reality as a whole: that he therefore does not regard this undoubtedly profoundly uncertain reality and particularly his own profoundly uncertain existence *a priori* as meaningless, worthless, vain, as nihilism asserts; that he regards this reality, despite its uncertainty, as in principle meaningful, valuable, actual. Thus he brings to reality—as he is free to do—not a fundamental mistrust, a basic lack of confidence, but a *fundamental trust*, a basic confidence.

Even for someone who so accepts in basic trust the reality of the world and man, the complete uncertainty of reality of course still persists in its ontic, noetic and ethical aspects. Trust in uncertain reality does not eliminate its radical uncertainty. And it is here that the question of God arises: reality, which can justify a basic trust, seems itself to be mysteriously unsubstantiated, sustaining though not itself sustained, evolving but without aim. Reality is there as a fact, yet remains enigmatic, without any manifest ground, support or purpose. Thus at any time the question can arise again of reality and unreality, being or not being, basic trust or nihilism.

Fundamentally, it amounts to the question: *where* is the explanation to be found of utterly uncertain reality? What makes it possible? What then is the *condition of the possibility* of this uncertain *reality?* The question therefore is not merely: what is the condition of the possibility of this utter *uncertainty?* This way of stating the question neglects the reality which persists in all uncertainty.

If man is not to abandon any attempt to understand himself and reality, then these ultimate questions—which are likewise primary and which call inescapably for an answer—must be answered. At the same time the believer is in competition with the unbeliever, as to who can interpret more convincingly the basic human experiences.

A. From the quite concrete experience of life's insecurity, the uncertainty of knowledge and man's manifold fear and disorientation, which does not have to be set out in detail here, there arises the irrecusable question: what is the *source* of this radically *uncertain reality,* suspended between being and not being, meaning and meaninglessness, supporting without support, evolving without aim?

Even someone who does not think *that* God exists could at least agree with the *hypothesis* (which of course does not as such decide his existence or non-existence) that, *if* God existed, then a fundamental solution *would be* provided of the enigma of permanently uncertain reality, a fundamental answer—which would emerge naturally and would need interpretation—to the question of the source. The hypothesis may be set out in a succinct form:

> If God existed, then the substantiating reality itself would not ultimately be unsubstantiated. God would be the *primal reason* of all reality.
> If God existed, then the supporting reality itself would not ultimately be unsupported. God would be the *primal support* of all reality.
> If God existed, then evolving reality would not ultimately be without aim. God would be the *primal goal* of all reality.
> If God existed, then there would be no suspicion that reality, suspended between being and not being, might ultimately be void. God would be the *being itself* of all reality.

This hypothesis may be given more exact expression, positively and negatively:

a. *positively:* If God existed, then it could be understood why ultimately in all the disruption a hidden unity can be confidently assumed, in all the meaninglessness a hidden significance, in all the worthlessness a hidden value: God would be the *primal source, primal meaning, primal value* of all that is; why ultimately in all the emptiness a hidden being of reality can be confidently assumed: God would be the *being* of all that is.

b. *negatively:* If God existed, then on the other hand it could also be understood why ultimately substantiating reality seems to be without substantiation from itself, supporting reality without support in itself, evolving reality without aim for itself; why its unity is threatened by disruption, its significance by meaninglessness, its value by worthlessness; why reality, suspended between being and not being, is suspected of being ultimately unreal and void.

The basic answer is always the same: because uncertain reality is itself *not God;* because the self, society, the world, cannot be identified with their primal reason, primal support and primal goal, with their primal source, primal meaning and primal value, with being itself.

B. In view of the particular uncertainty of *human existence,* a hypothetical answer might be formulated in this way: if God existed, then the enigma also of the permanent uncertainty of human existence *would be* solved in principle. It can be stated more exactly as follows: if God existed, then, against all threats of fate and death, I could justifiably affirm the unity and identity of my human existence: for God would be the first ground also of my life;

then, against all threats of emptiness and meaninglessness, I could justifiably affirm the truth and significance of my existence: for God would be the ultimate meaning also of my life;

then, against all threats of sin and rejection, I could justifiably affirm the goodness and value of my existence: for then God would also be the comprehensive hope of my life;

then, against all threats of nothingness, I could justifiably affirm with confidence the being of my human existence: for God would then be the being itself particularly of human life.

This hypothetical answer too can be negatively tested. *If* God existed, then it would be understood also in relation to my existence why the unity and identity, truth and significance, goodness and value of human existence remain threatened by fate and death, emptiness and meaninglessness, sin and damnation, why the being of my existence remains threatened by nothingness. The fundamental answer would always be one and the same: because man is *not God,* because my human self cannot be identified with its primal reason, primal meaning, primal goal, with being itself.

In sum: If God existed, then the condition of the possibility of this uncertain reality would exist, its "whence" (in the widest sense) would be indicated. If! But from the hypothesis of God we cannot conclude to the reality of God.

REALITY

If we are not to be rushed into a premature conclusion, we must again proceed step by step. How are the alternatives to be judged and how can we reach a solution?

a. One thing must be conceded to atheism from the very beginning: it is *possible to deny God.* Atheism cannot be eliminated rationally. It is unproved, but it is also irrefutable. Why?

It is the experience of the radical *uncertainty* of every reality which provides atheism with sufficient grounds for maintaining that reality has absolutely no primal reason, primal support or primal goal. Any talk of primal source, primal meaning, primal value, must be rejected. We simply cannot know any of these things (agnosticism). Indeed, reality is perhaps ultimately chaos, absurdity, illusion, appearance and not being, just nothing (atheism tending to nihilism).

Hence there are in fact no positive arguments against the *impossibility* of atheism. If someone says that there is no God, his claim cannot be positively refuted. In the last resort neither a strict proof nor a demonstration of God is of any avail against such an assertion. This unproved assertion rests ultimately on a *decision* which is connected with the basic decision for reality as a whole. The denial of God cannot be refuted purely rationally.

b. On the other hand, atheism is also incapable of positively excluding the other alternative: as it is possible to deny him, so also it is *possible to affirm God*. Why?

It is *reality* in all its uncertainty which provides sufficient grounds for venturing not only a confident assent to this reality, its identity, significance and value, but also an assent to that without which reality ultimately seems unsubstantiated in all substantiation, unsupported in all support, aimless in all its evolving: a confident assent therefore to a primal reason, primal support and primal goal of uncertain reality.

Hence there is no conclusive argument for the *necessity* of atheism. If someone says that there is a God, his claim too cannot be positively refuted. Atheism for its own part is ultimately of no avail against such confidence imposed by reality itself. The irrefutable affirmation of God also rests ultimately on a *decision* which here too is connected with the basic decision for reality as a whole. For this reason it is also rationally irrefutable. And of course the affirmation of God is also impossible to prove by purely rational arguments. Stalemate?

c. The alternatives have become clear. And it is just here—beyond "natural," "dialectical" or "morally postulating" theology—that the essential difficulty lies in solving the question of the existence of God:

> *If* God is, he is the answer to the radical uncertainty of reality.
>
> *That* God is, can however be accepted neither stringently in virtue of a proof or demonstration of pure reason nor absolutely in virtue of a moral postulate of practical reason, still less solely in virtue of the biblical testimony.
>
> *That* God is, can ultimately be accepted only in a confidence founded on reality itself.

This trusting commitment to an ultimate reason, support and meaning of reality is itself rightly designated in general usage as "belief" in God ("faith in God," "trust in God"). This is belief in a very broad sense, insofar as it does not necessarily have to be prompted by Christian proclamation but is also possible for non-Christians. People who profess this faith—whether Christians or not—are rightly called "believers in God." On the other hand, atheism as a refusal to trust in God is again quite rightly described in general usage as "unbelief."

Hence man simply cannot avoid a *decision*—free but not arbitrary—both with reference to reality as such and also with reference to its primal reason, primal support and primal meaning. Since reality and its primal reason, primal support and primal meaning are not imposed on us with conclusive evidence, there remains scope for human freedom. Man is expected to decide, without intellectual constraint. Both atheism and belief in God are ventures, they are also risks. Any criticism of proofs of God is aimed at showing that belief in God has the character of a decision and—on the other hand—that a decision for God has the character of belief.

The question of God therefore involves a decision which must in fact be faced on a deeper level than the decision—necessary in view of nihilism—for or against reality as such. As soon as the individual becomes aware of this ultimate depth and the question arises, the decision becomes unavoidable. In the question of God too, not to choose is in fact a choice: the person has *chosen* not to choose. To abstain from voting in a vote of confidence in regard to the question of God means a refusal of confidence.

Yet unfortunately the "depth" (or "height") of a truth and man's certainty in accepting it are in inverse ratio. The more banal the truth ("truism," "platitude"), the greater the certainty. The more significant the truth (for instance, aesthetic, moral and religious truth by comparison with arithmetical), the slighter the certainty. For the "deeper" the truth is for me, the more must I first lay myself open to it, inwardly prepare myself, attune myself to it intellectually, willingly, emotionally, in order to reach that genuine "certainty" which is somewhat different from assured "security." A *deep* truth, for me outwardly uncertain, threatened by doubts, which presupposes a generous commitment on my part, can possess much more cognitive value than a certain—or even an "absolutely certain"—*banal* truth.

Yet here too it does not follow from the possibility of affirming or denying God that the choice is immaterial. Denial of God implies an ultimately *unsubstantiated* basic trust in reality (if not an absolutely basic mistrust). But acceptance of God implies an ultimately *substantiated* basic trust in reality. A person who affirms God knows *why* he trusts reality. There can be no talk therefore, as will soon be made clear, of a stalemate.

d. If *atheism* is not nourished simply by a nihilistic basic mistrust, it must be nourished by a basic trust—but one that is ultimately *unsubstantiated*. By denying God, man decides against an ultimate reason, support, an ultimate end of reality. In agnostic atheism the assent to reality proves to be ultimately unsubstantiated and inconsistent: a free-wheeling, nowhere anchored and therefore paradoxical basic trust. In less superficial, more consistent nihilistic atheism, radical mistrust makes an assent to reality quite impossible. Atheism anyway is unable to suggest *any condition for the possibility* of uncertain reality. For this reason it lacks a radical rationality, although this is often concealed by a rationalistic but fundamentally irrational trust in human reason.

The price paid by atheism for its denial is obvious. It is exposed to the danger of an ultimate lack of reason, of support, of purpose: to possible futility, worthlessness, emptiness of reality as a whole. If he becomes aware of it, the atheist is also exposed quite personally to the danger of an ultimate abandonment, menace and decay, resulting in doubt, fear, even despair. All this is true of course only if atheism is quite serious and not an intellectual pose, snobbish caprice or thoughtless superficiality.

For the atheist there is no answer to those ultimate and yet immediate, perennial questions of human life, which are not to be suppressed by simply being prohibited: questions which arise not merely in borderline situations, but in the very midst of man's personal and social life. Keeping to Kant's formulation of them:

> What can we *know*? Why is there anything at all? Why not nothing? Where does man come from and where does he go to? Why is the world as it is? What is the ultimate reason and meaning of all reality?
>
> What ought we *to do*? Why do what we do? Why and to whom are we finally responsible? What deserves forthright contempt and what love? What is the point of loyalty and friendship, but also what is the point of suffering and sin? What really matters for man?
>
> What may we *hope*? Why are we here? What is it all about? What is there left for us: death, making everything pointless at the end? What will give us courage for life and what courage for death?

In all these questions it is all or nothing. They are questions not only for the dying, but for the living. They are not for weaklings and uninformed people, but precisely for the informed and committed. They are not excuses for not acting, but incentives to action. Is there something which sustains us in all this, which never permits us to despair? Is there something stable in all change, something unconditioned in all that is conditioned, something absolute in the relativizing experienced everywhere? Atheism leaves all these questions without a final answer.

e. Belief in God is nourished by an ultimately substantiated basic trust: when he assents to God, man opts for an ultimate reason, support, meaning of reality. In belief in God assent to reality turns out to be ultimately substantiated and consistent: a basic trust anchored in the ultimate depth, in the reason of reasons. Belief in God as radical basic trust can therefore point also to the *condition of the possibility* of uncertain reality. In this sense it displays a radical rationality—which is not the same thing as rationalism.

The price received by belief in God for its yes is likewise obvious. Since I confidently decide for a primal reason instead of groundlessness, for a primal support instead of unsupportedness, for a primal goal instead of aimlessness, I have now reason to recognize a unity of the reality of world and man despite all disruption, a meaning despite all meaninglessness, a value despite all worthlessness. And, despite all the uncertainty and insecurity, abandonment and exposure, menace and decay of my own existence, I am *granted* in the light of the ultimate primal source, primal meaning and primal value an ultimate certainty, assurance and stability. This is no mere abstract security, isolating me from my fellow men, but always involves a concrete reference to the human "Thou": how is man to learn what it means to be accepted by God, if he is not accepted by any single human being? I cannot simply take or create for myself ultimate certainty, assurance and stability. It is ultimate reality itself in a variety of ways which challenges me to accept it, with which—so to speak—the "initiative" lies. Ultimate reality itself enables me to see that patience in regard to the present, gratitude in regard to the past and hope in regard to the future are ultimately substantiated, despite all doubt, all fear and despair.

Thus those ultimate and yet immediate religio-social questions of man, not to be suppressed by simply being prohibited, which we summed up under Kant's leading questions, receive in principle at least an answer with which man can live in the world of today: an answer from the reality of God.

f. How far then is belief in God *rationally justified?* Faced with the decision between atheism and belief in God, man cannot be indifferent. He approaches this decision with a mind already burdened. Essentially he would like to understand the world and himself, to respond to the uncertainty of reality, to perceive the condition of the possibility of uncertain reality: he would like to know of an ultimate reason, an ultimate support and an ultimate goal of reality.

Yet here too man remains free. He can say "No." He can adopt a skeptical attitude and ignore or even stifle any dawning confidence in an ultimate reason, support and goal. He can, perhaps utterly honestly and truthfully, declare his inability to know (agnostic atheism) or even assert that reality—uncertain anyway—is completely void, without reason or goal, without meaning or value (nihilistic atheism). Unless a person is prepared for a confident acknowledgment of God, with its practical consequences, he will never reach a rationally meaningful knowledge of God. And even when someone has given his assent to God, he is continually faced with the temptation to deny him.

If however man does not isolate himself, but remains completely open to reality as it is revealed to him; if he does not try to get away from the ultimate reason, support and goal of reality, but ventures to apply himself and give himself up to it: then he knows that—*by the very fact* of doing this—he is doing the right thing, in fact the most sensible thing of all. For in the very act of acknowledging what he perceives (in carrying out his *rationabile obsequium*) he experiences that which cannot be stringently proved or demonstrated in advance. Reality is manifested in its ultimate depth. Its ultimate reason, support, goal, its primal source, primal meaning and primal value are laid open to him as soon as he lays himself open. And at the same time, despite all uncertainty, he experiences an ultimate rationality of his own reason: in the light of this, an ultimate confidence in reason appears not as irrational but as rationally substantiated.

There is nothing in all this of an *external rationality*, which could not produce an assured *certainty*. The existence of God is not first rationally and stringently proved or demonstrated and then believed, as if the rationality of belief in God were thus guaranteed. There is not first rational knowledge of God and then confident acknowledgment. The hidden reality of God is not forced on reason.

What is implied is *an intrinsic rationality* which can produce a basic certainty. Despite all temptations to doubt, in the practical realization of this venturesome trust in God's reality man experiences the rationality of his trust: based on the perceptible ultimate identity, significance and value of reality; on its primal reason, primal meaning and primal value now becoming apparent. This then is the rationally justified venture of belief in God through which—despite all doubts—man reaches and must constantly maintain—despite all doubts—an ultimate certainty: a certainty from which no fear, no despair, no agnostic or nihilistic atheism can drive him, even in borderline situations, without his consent.

g. The *connection between basic trust and belief in God* is now obvious. From a material standpoint basic trust relates to reality as such and to one's own existence, while belief in God relates to the primal reason, primal support and primal meaning of reality; but, from a formal standpoint, basic trust and belief in God ("trust in God") have an analogous structure which is based on the material connection (despite the difference) between the two. Like basic trust, belief in God is a matter not only of human reason, but of the whole, concrete, living man: with mind and body, reason and instinct, in his quite definite historical situation, in his dependence on traditions, authorities, habits of thought, scales of values, with his personal interest and his social involvement. Man cannot speak of this "matter" while remaining outside the "matter";

therefore super-rational: as there is no logically stringent proof that reality is real, neither is there such a proof of God. The proof of God is no more logically stringent than is love. The relationship to God is one of trust;

not however irrational: there is a reflection on the reality of God emerging from human experience and calling for man's free decision. Belief in God can be justified in face of a rational critique. It is rooted in the experience of the uncertainty of reality, which raises ultimate questions about the condition of its possibility;

thus not a blind decision, devoid of reality, but one that is substantiated, related to reality and therefore rationally justified in concrete existence. Its relevance to both existential needs and social conditions becomes apparent from the reality of the world and of man;

realized in a concrete relationship with our fellow man. Without the experience of being accepted by men, it seems difficult to experience acceptance by God;

not taken once and for all, for every case, but constantly to be freshly realized. Rational arguments never render belief in God unassailable and immune from crises in face of atheism. Belief in God is continually threatened and—under pressure of doubts—must constantly be realized, upheld, lived, regained in a new decision. Even in regard to God, man remains in insoluble conflict between trust and mistrust, belief and unbelief.

h. Looking back then on our reflections, what "help" can be given to the atheist? Not a rationally stringent proof of God, not an appeal to an unconditional "thou shalt," not an apologetic intended to be intellectually coercive, not a dogmatic theology decreeing from above. But:

First of all—at least where an appeal to the biblical message is not directly fruitful—*joint reflection* on the reality of the world and of men, aided by common experiences in regard to those ultimate and primary questions: that is, not simply getting people away from the point where they are standing, but staying with them and first considering and opening up their world, discovering the great questions of life in the everyday questions—all this, not in instruction, but in conversation.

At the same time—and perhaps more important—*trust shown in practice*, which elicits trust, a living venture as an invitation to the same venture: a leap into the water which "proves" in practice the possibility of being sustained and at the same time calls on the other to make a similar leap, that is, a testimony of belief in God confirmed by practice.

Finally—and really this is all that can help—*our own venture of trust.*

We can learn to swim only by swimming ourselves. Like other experiences, this basic experience is brought to light only in its realization. [from *On Being a Christian*, A II]

33. *The unity of the ways of the mind to God*

For theologian **Karl Rahner** (see above, #12), all arguments for God's existence are actually different ways of clarifying the one fundamental "proof," which is found in humanity's "transcendental experience": the fact that every conscious act takes place within the horizon of an absolute being, or "holy mystery." The dynamism of our spirit always implicitly contains a reference to and anticipation of this horizon, even if we do not advert to it. Thus the existence of God is always implicitly and non-conceptually "known" as the "condition of possibility" for our actual acts of transcendence in knowledge and love. The process by which Rahner and others (Emerich Coreth, Bernard Lonergan, José Gómez Caffarena) attempt to establish this is called the "transcendental method."

The point of the reflexive proofs for the existence of God is to indicate that all knowledge, even in the form of a doubt or a question or even a refusal to raise the metaphysical question, takes place against the background of an affirmation of the holy mystery, or of absolute being, as the horizon of the asymptotic term and of the questioning ground of the act of knowledge and of its "object." It is a relatively secondary question what this nameless and distant presence is called, whether the "holy mystery" or "absolute being," or, bringing into the foreground the freedom aspect of this transcendence and the personal structure of the act, the "absolute good," the "personal and absolute Thou," the "ground of absolute responsibility," the "ultimate horizon of hope," and so on. In all the so-called proofs for the existence of God the one and only thing which is being presented and represented in a reflexive and systematic conceptualization is something which has already taken place: in the fact that a person comes to the objective reality of his everyday life both in the involvement of action and in the intellectual activity of thought and comprehension, he is actualizing, as the condition which makes possible such involvement and comprehension, an unthematic and nonobjective pre-apprehension of the inconceivable and incomprehensible single fullness of reality. This fullness in its original unity is at once the condition of possibility both for knowledge and for the individual thing known objectively. As such a condition of possibility it is always affirmed unthematically, even in an act which denies it thematically.

The individual person, of course, experiences this fundamental and inescapable structure best in that basic situation of his own existence which occurs with special intensity for him as an individual. If, therefore, he is really to understand this reflection on "proofs" for God's existence, the individual person must reflect precisely upon whatever is the clearest experience *for him:* on the luminous and incomprehensible light of his spirit; on the capacity for absolute questioning which a person directs against himself and which seemingly reduces him to nothing, but in which he reaches radically beyond himself; on annihilating anxiety, which is something quite different from fear of a definite object and is prior to the latter as the condition of its possibility; on that joy which surpasses all understanding; on an absolute moral obligation in which a person really goes beyond himself; on the experience of death in which he faces himself in his absolute powerlessness. Man reflects upon these and many other modes of the basic and transcendental experience of human existence. Because he experiences himself as finite in his self-questioning, he is not able to identify himself with the ground which discloses itself in this experience as what is innermost and at the same time what is absolutely different. The explicit proofs for God's existence only make thematic this fundamental structure and its term.

The experience that every act of judgment takes place as an act which is borne by and is moved by absolute being, which does not live by the grace of our thought, but is present as that by which thought is borne and not as something produced by thought, this experience is made thematic in the metaphysical principle of causality. This must not be confused with the functional law of causality in the natural sciences. According to this law, for every phenomenon as "effect" there is coordinated another phenomenon of quantitative equality as "cause." When understood correctly the metaphysical principle of causality is not an extrapolation from the scientific law of nature, nor is it an extrapolation from the causal thinking that we use in everyday affairs. It is grounded rather in the transcendental experience of the relationship between transcendence and its term. The metaphysical principle of causality, which is applied in the traditional proofs for the existence of God, is not a universal principle which is applied in these proofs to a particular, individual instance alongside of others, although even many scholastic philosophers understand it this way. Rather it only points to the transcendental experience in which the relationship between something conditioned and finite and its incomprehensible source is immediately present, and through its presence is experienced. [from *Foundations of Christian Faith*]

B. Special Revelation

34. *Revelation and its transmission*

The Second Vatican Council sees revelation as an interplay of words and deeds of God in history. It recognizes a "natural" revelation through creation, as well as a "general" revelation to all people; but it emphasizes above all the supernatural and "special" revelation that takes place through God's call to Israel and that culminates in Christ. This revelation is transmitted through the community that receives it in faith; the sacred scriptures, inspired by God's Spirit and accepted and interpreted by the church, have a special place in this transmission.

The scriptures themselves do not so much give a theory of revelation as a recounting of its occurrence. In the following selection the document refers to a number of important passages that illustrate the scriptural notion of how God's word is addressed to his people.

CHAPTER I

Revelation Itself

2. In His goodness and wisdom, God chose to reveal Himself and to make known to us the hidden purpose of His will (cf. Eph. 1:9) by which through Christ, the Word made flesh, man has access to the Father in the Holy Spirit and comes to share in the divine nature (cf. Eph. 2:18; 2 Pet. 1:4). Through this revelation, therefore, the invisible God (cf. Col. 1:15; 1 Tim. 1:17) out of the abundance of His love speaks to men as friends (cf. Ex. 33:11; Jn. 15:14–15) and lives among them (cf. Bar. 3:38), so that He may invite and take them into fellowship with Himself. This plan of revelation is realized by deeds and words having an inner unity: the

deeds wrought by God in the history of salvation manifest and confirm the teaching and realities signified by the words, while the words proclaim the deeds and clarify the mystery contained in them. By this revelation then, the deepest truth about God and the salvation of man is made clear to us in Christ, who is the Mediator and at the same time the fullness of all revelation.

3. God, who through the Word creates all things (cf. Jn. 1:3) and keeps them in existence, gives men an enduring witness to Himself in created realities (cf. Rom. 1:19–20). Planning to make known the way of heavenly salvation, He went further and from the start manifested Himself to our first parents. Then after their fall His promise of redemption aroused in them the hope of being saved (cf. Gen. 3:15), and from that time on He ceaselessly kept the human race in His care, in order to give eternal life to those who perseveringly do good in search of salvation (cf. Rom. 2:6–7). Then, at the time He had appointed, He called Abraham in order to make of him a great nation (cf. Gen. 12:2). Through the patriarchs, and after them through Moses and the prophets, He taught this nation to acknowledge Himself as the one living and true God, provident Father and just Judge, and to wait for the Savior promised by Him. In this manner He prepared the way for the gospel down through the centuries.

4. Then, after speaking in many places and varied ways through the prophets, God "last of all in these days has spoken to us by his son" (Heb. 1:1–2). For he sent His Son, the eternal Word, who enlightens all men, so that He might dwell among men and tell them the innermost realities about God (cf. Jn. 1:1–18). Jesus Christ, therefore, the Word made flesh, sent as "a man to men," "speaks the words of God" (Jn. 3:34), and completes the work of salvation which His Father gave Him to do (cf. Jn. 5:36, 17:4). To see Jesus is to see His Father (Jn. 14:9). For this reason Jesus perfected revelation by fulfilling it through His whole work of making Himself present and manifesting Himself: through His words and deeds, His signs and wonders, but especially through His death and glorious resurrection from the dead and final sending of the Spirit of truth. Moreover, He confirmed with divine testimony what revelation proclaimed: that God is with us to free us from the darkness of sin and death, and to raise us up to life eternal.

The Christian dispensation, therefore, as the new and definitive covenant, will never pass away, and we now await no further new public revelation before the glorious manifestation of our Lord Jesus Christ (cf. 1 Tim. 6:14 and Tit. 2:13).

5. "The obedience of faith" (Rom. 16:26; cf. 1:5; 2 Cor. 10:5–6) must

be given to God who reveals, an obedience by which man entrusts his whole self freely to God, offering "the full submission of intellect and will to God who reveals," and freely assenting to the truth revealed by Him. If this faith is to be shown, the grace of God and the interior help of the Holy Spirit must precede and assist, moving the heart and turning it to God, opening the eyes of the mind, and giving "joy and ease to everyone in assenting to the truth and believing it." To bring about an ever deeper understanding of revelation, the same Holy Spirit constantly brings faith to completion by His gifts.

6. Through divine revelation, God chose to show forth and communicate Himself and the eternal decisions of His will regarding the salvation of men. That is to say, He chose "to share those divine treasures which totally transcend the understanding of the human mind."

This sacred Synod affirms, "God, the beginning and end of all things, can be known with certainty from created reality by the light of human reason" (cf. Rom. 1:20); but the Synod teaches that it is through His revelation "that those divine realities which are by their nature accessible to human reason can be known by all men with ease, with solid certitude, and with no trace of error, even in the present state of the human race."

CHAPTER II

The Transmission of Divine Revelation

7. In His gracious goodness, God has seen to it that what He had revealed for the salvation of all nations would abide perpetually in its full integrity and be handed on to all generations. Therefore Christ the Lord, in whom the full revelation of the supreme God is brought to completion (cf. 2 Cor. 1:20; 3:16; 4:6), commissioned the apostles to preach to all men that gospel which is the source of all saving truth and moral teaching, and thus to impart to them divine gifts. This gospel had been promised in former times through the prophets, and Christ Himself fulfilled it and promulgated it with His own lips. This commission was faithfully fulfilled by the apostles who, by their oral preaching, by example, and by ordinances, handed on what they had received from the lips of Christ, from living with Him, and from what He did, or what they had learned through the prompting of the Holy Spirit. The commission was fulfilled, too, by those apostles and apostolic men who under the inspiration of the same Holy Spirit committed the message of salvation to writing.

But in order to keep the gospel forever whole and alive within the Church, the apostles left bishops as their successors, "handing over their own teaching role" to them. This sacred tradition, therefore, and sacred Scripture of both the Old and the New Testament are like a mirror in which the pilgrim Church on earth looks at God, from whom she has received everything, until she is brought finally to see Him as He is, face to face (cf. 1 Jn. 3:2).

8. And so the apostolic preaching, which is expressed in a special way in the inspired books, was to be preserved by a continuous succession of preachers until the end of time. Therefore the apostles, handing on what they themselves had received, warn the faithful to hold fast to the traditions which they have learned either by word of mouth or by letter (cf. 2 Th. 2:15), and to fight in defense of the faith handed on once and for all (cf. Jude 3). Now what was handed on by the apostles includes everything which contributes to the holiness of life, and the increase in faith of the People of God; and so the Church, in her teaching, life, and worship, perpetuates and hands on to all generations all that she herself is, all that she believes.

This tradition which comes from the apostles develops in the Church with the help of the Holy Spirit. For there is a growth in the understanding of the realities and the words which have been handed down. This happens through the contemplation and study made by believers, who treasure these things in their hearts (cf. Lk. 2:19, 51), through the intimate understanding of spiritual things they experience, and through the preaching of those who have received through episcopal succession the sure gift of truth. For, as the centuries succeed one another, the Church constantly moves forward toward the fullness of divine truth until the words of God reach their complete fulfillment in her.

The words of the holy Fathers witness to the living presence of this tradition, whose wealth is poured into the practice and life of the believing and praying Church. Through the same tradition the full canon of the sacred books becomes known to the Church, and the sacred writings themselves are more profoundly understood and unceasingly made active in her; and thus God, who spoke of old, uninterruptedly converses with the Bride of His beloved Son; and the Holy Spirit, through whom the living voice of the gospel resounds in the Church, and through her, in the world, leads unto all truth those who believe and makes the word of Christ dwell abundantly in them (cf. Col. 3:16).

9. Hence there exist a close connection and communication between sacred tradition and sacred Scripture. For both of them, flowing from the same divine wellspring, in a certain way merge into a unity and tend

toward the same end. For sacred Scripture is the word of God inasmuch as it is consigned to writing under the inspiration of the divine Spirit. To the successors of the apostles, sacred tradition hands on in its full purity God's word, which was entrusted to the apostles by Christ the Lord and the Holy Spirit. Thus, led by the light of the Spirit of truth, these successors can in their preaching preserve this word of God faithfully, explain it, and make it more widely known. Consequently, it is not from sacred Scripture alone that the Church draws her certainty about everything which has been revealed. Therefore both sacred tradition and sacred Scripture are to be accepted and venerated with the same sense of devotion and reverence.

10. Sacred tradition and sacred Scripture form one sacred deposit of the word of God, which is committed to the Church. Holding fast to this deposit, the entire holy people united with their shepherds remain always steadfast in the teaching of the apostles, in the common life, in the breaking of the bread, and in prayers (cf. Acts 2, 42, Greek text), so that in holding to, practicing, and professing the heritage of the faith, there results on the part of the bishops and faithful a remarkable common effort.

The task of authentically interpreting the word of God, whether written or handed on, has been entrusted exclusively to the living teaching office of the Church, whose authority is exercised in the name of Jesus Christ. This teaching office is not above the word of God, but serves it, teaching only what has been handed on, listening to it devoutly, guarding it scrupulously, and explaining it faithfully by divine commission and with the help of the Holy Spirit; it draws from this one deposit of faith everything which it presents for belief as divinely revealed.

It is clear, therefore, that sacred tradition, sacred Scripture, and the teaching authority of the Church, in accord with God's most wise design, are so linked and joined together that one cannot stand without the others, and that all together and each in its own way under the action of the one Holy Spirit contribute effectively to the salvation of souls. [from the Dogmatic Constitution on Divine Revelation (*Dei Verbum*)]

35. Preaching the gospel: St. Paul and the beginnings of Christian theology

St. Paul's epistles—letters written to early Christian communities to offer advice and counsel on the faith—represent the oldest written records in what is today the New Testament. **Karl Barth (1886–**

1968) here offers a commentary on the opening verses of Paul's epistle to the early Christian community in Rome in order to uncover Paul's understanding of the message he was preaching. According to Barth, how does Paul separate his message from that of all other ideologies and creeds? On what authority does he base his preaching of the gospel? What is that gospel?

THE FIRST CHAPTER

Introduction

The Author to His Readers

I. 1–7

Paul, a servant of Jesus Christ, called to be an apostle, separated unto the gospel of God, which he promised afore by his prophets in the holy scriptures, concerning his Son, who was born of the seed of David according to the flesh, and declared to be the Son of God with power, according to the Holy Spirit, through his resurrection from the dead— even Jesus Christ our Lord, through whom we received grace and apostleship to bring into being obedience to the faithfulness of God which is confirmed in the gospel among all nations, for his name's sake: among whom are ye also the called of Jesus Christ: To all that are in Rome, beloved of God, called to be saints: Grace to you and peace from God our Father and the Lord Jesus Christ.

Paul, a servant of Jesus Christ, called to be an apostle. Here is no 'genius rejoicing in his own creative ability' (Zündel). The man who is now speaking is an emissary, bound to perform his duty; the minister of his King; a servant, not a master. However great and important a man Paul may have been, the essential theme of his mission is not within him but above him—unapproachably distant and unutterably strange. His call to apostleship is not a familiar episode in his own personal history: 'The call to be an apostle is a paradoxical occurrence, lying always beyond his personal self-identity' (Kierkegaard). Paul, it is true, is always himself, and moves essentially on the same plane as all other men. But, in contradiction to himself and in distinction from all others, he is—called by God and sent forth. Are we then to name him a Pharisee? Yes, a Pharisee—'separated', isolated, and distinct. But he is a Pharisee of a higher order. Fashioned of the same stuff as all other men, a stone differing in no way from other stones, yet in his relation to God—and in this only—he is unique. As an apostle—and only as an apostle—he stands in no organic relationship with human society as it exists in history: seen from the point of view of human society, he can be regarded only as an exception, nay, rather, as an impossibility. Paul's position can be justified only as resting in God, and so only can his words be regarded as at all credible, for they are as incapable of direct apprehension as is God Himself. For this reason he dares to approach others and to demand a hearing without fear either of exalting himself or of approximating too closely to his audience. He appeals only to the authority of God. This is the ground of his authority. There is no other.

Paul is authorized to deliver—**the Gospel of God.** He is commissioned to hand over to men something quite new and unprecedented, joyful and good,—the truth of God. Yes, precisely—*of God!* The Gospel is not a religious message to inform mankind of their divinity or to tell them how they may become divine. The Gospel proclaims a God utterly distinct from men. Salvation comes to them from Him, because they are, as men, incapable of knowing Him, and because they have no right to claim anything from Him. The Gospel is not one thing in the midst of other things, to be directly apprehended and comprehended. The Gospel is the Word of the Primal Origin of all things, the Word which, since it is ever new, must ever be received with renewed fear and trembling. The Gospel is therefore not an event, nor an experience, nor an emotion—however delicate! Rather, it is the clear and objective perception of what eye hath not seen nor ear heard. Moreover, what it demands of men is more than notice, or understanding, or sympathy. It demands participation, comprehension, co-operation; for it is a communication which presumes faith in the living God, and which creates that which it presumes.

Being the Gospel of God it was—**promised afore.** The Gospel is no intrusion of to-day. As the seed of eternity it is the fruit of time, the meaning and maturity of history—the fulfilment of prophecy. The Gospel is the word spoken by the prophets from time immemorial, the word which can now be received and has now been accepted. Such is the Gospel with which the apostle has been entrusted. By it his speech is authorized, but by it also that which he says is judged. The words of the prophets, long fastened under lock and key, are now set free. Now it is possible to hear what Jeremiah and Job and the preacher Solomon had proclaimed long ago. Now we can see and understand what is written, for we have an 'entrance into the Old Testament' (Luther). Therefore the man who now speaks, stands firmly upon a history which has been expounded and veritably understood: 'From the outset he disclaims the honour due to an innovator' (Schlatter).

Jesus Christ our Lord. This is the Gospel and the meaning of history. In this name two worlds meet and go apart, two planes intersect, the one known and the other unknown. The known plane is God's creation, fallen out of its union with Him, and therefore the world of the 'flesh' needing redemption, the world of men, and of time, and of things—our world. This known plane is intersected by another plane that is unknown—the world of the Father, of the Primal Creation, and of the final Redemption. The relation between us and God, between this world and His world, presses for recognition; but the line of intersection is not self-evident. The point on the line of intersection at which the relation becomes observable and observed is Jesus, Jesus of Nazareth, the historical Jesus,—**born of the seed of David according to the flesh.** The name Jesus defines an historical occurrence and marks the point where the unknown world cuts the known world. This does not mean that, at this point, time and things and men are in themselves exalted above other time and things and other men, but that they are exalted inasmuch as they serve to define the neighbourhood of the point at which the hidden line, intersecting time and eternity, concrete occurrence and primal origin, men and God, becomes visible. The years A.D. 1–30 are the era of revelation and disclosure; the era which, as is shown by the reference to David, sets forth the new and strange and divine definition of all time. The particularity of the years A.D. 1–30 is dissolved by this divine definition, because it makes every epoch a potential field of revelation and disclosure. The point on the line of intersection is no more extended onto the known plane than is the unknown plane of which it proclaims the existence. The effulgence, or, rather, the crater made at the percussion point of an exploding shell, the void by which the point on the line of intersection makes itself known in the concrete world of history, is not— even though it be named the Life of Jesus—that other world which touches our world in Him. In so far as our world is touched in Jesus by the other world, it ceases to be capable of direct observation as history, time, or thing. Jesus has been—**declared to be the Son of God with power, according to the Holy Spirit, through his resurrection from the dead.** In this declaration and appointment—which are beyond historical definition—lies the true significance of Jesus. Jesus as the Christ, as the Messiah, is the End of History; and He can be comprehended only as Paradox (Kierkegaard), as Victor (Blumhardt), as Primal History (Overbeck). As Christ, Jesus is the plane which lies beyond our comprehension. The plane which is known to us, He intersects vertically, from above. Within history, Jesus as the Christ can be understood only as Problem or Myth. As the Christ, He brings the world of the Father. But we who stand in this concrete world know nothing, and are incapable of knowing anything, of that other world. The Resurrection from the dead is, however, the transformation: the establishing or *declaration* of that point from above, and the corresponding discerning of it from below. The Resurrection is the revelation: the disclosing of Jesus as the Christ, the appearing of God, and the apprehending of God in Jesus. The Resurrection is the emergence of the necessity of giving glory to God: the reckoning with what is unknown and unobservable in Jesus, the recognition of Him as Paradox, Victor, and Primal History. In the Resurrection the new world of the Holy Spirit touches the old world of the flesh, but touches it as a tangent touches a circle, that is, without touching it. And, precisely because it does not touch it, it touches it as its frontier—as the new world. The Resurrection is therefore an occurrence in history, which took place outside the gates of Jerusalem in the year A.D. 30, inasmuch as it there 'came to pass', was discovered and recognized. But inasmuch as the occurrence was conditioned by the Resurrection, in so far, that is, as it was not the 'coming to pass', or the discovery, or the recognition, which conditioned its necessity and appearance and revelation, the Resurrection is not an event in history at all. Jesus is *declared to be the Son of God* wherever He reveals Himself and is recognized as the Messiah, before the first Easter Day and, most assuredly, after it. This declaration of the Son of man to be the Son of God is the significance of Jesus, and, apart from this, Jesus has no more significance or insignificance than may be attached to any man or thing or period of history in itself.—*Even though we have known Christ after the flesh, yet now we know him so no longer.* What He was, He is. But what He is underlies what He was. There is here no merging or fusion of God and man, no exaltation of humanity to divinity, no overflowing of God into human nature. What touches us—and yet does not touch us—in Jesus the Christ, is the Kingdom of God who is both Creator and Redeemer. The Kingdom of God has become actual, is nigh at hand (iii. 21, 22). And this Jesus Christ is—our Lord. Through His presence in the world and in our life we have been dissolved as men and established in God. By directing our eyes to Him our advance is stopped—and we are set in motion. We tarry and—hurry. Because Jesus is Lord over Paul and over the Roman Christians, the word 'God' is no empty word in the Epistle to the Romans.

From Jesus Christ Paul has received—grace and apostleship. Grace is the incomprehensible fact that God is well pleased with a man, and that a man can rejoice in God. Only when grace is recognized to be incomprehensible is it grace. Grace exists, therefore, only where the Resurrection is reflected. Grace is the gift of Christ, who exposes the gulf which separates God and man, and, by exposing it, bridges it. But inasmuch as God knows men from afar and is known by them in His undiscoverable majesty, the man of God must inevitably approach his fellow men as an 'emissary': *Necessity is laid upon me; yea, woe is unto me, if I preach not the gospel* (I Cor. ix.16). And yet the distinction between Paul and other Christians can be a matter of degree only. For, where the grace of God is, men participate in proclaiming the transformation of time and of things, the Resurrection—however reservedly and with whatever scepticism they proclaim it. Where the grace of God is, the very existence of the world and the very existence of God become a question and a hope with which and for which men must wrestle. For we are not now concerned with the propaganda of a conviction or with its imposition on others; grace means bearing witness to the faithfulness of God which a man has encountered in Christ, and which, when it is encountered and recognized, requires a corresponding fidelity towards God. The fidelity of a man to the faithfulness of God—the faith, that is, which accepts grace—is itself the demand for obedience and itself demands obedience from others. Hence the demand is a call which enlightens and rouses to action; it carries with it mission, beside which no other mission is possible. For the name of Him in whom the two worlds meet and are separated must be honoured, and for this mission grace provides full authority, since men are shattered by it (v. 2).

The Gospel of the Resurrection is the—**power of God,** His virtus (Vulgate), the disclosing and apprehending of His meaning, His effective pre-eminence over all gods. The Gospel of the Resurrection is the action, the supreme miracle, by which God, the unknown God dwelling in light unapproachable, the Holy One, Creator, and Redeemer, makes Himself known: *What therefore ye worship in ignorance, this set I forth unto you* (Acts xvii. 23). No divinity remaining on this side the line of resurrection; no divinity which dwells in temples made with hands or which is served by the hand of man; no divinity which NEEDS ANYTHING, any human propaganda (Acts xvii. 24, 25),—can be God. God is the unknown God, and, precisely because He is unknown, He bestows life and breath and all things. Therefore the power of God can be detected neither in the world of nature nor in the souls of men. It must not be confounded with any high, exalted force, known or knowable. The power of God is not the most exalted of observable forces, nor is it either their sum or their fount. Being completely different, it is the KRISIS of all power, that by which all power is measured, and by which it is pronounced to be both something and—nothing, nothing and—something. It is that which sets all these powers in motion and fashions their eternal rest. It is the Primal Origin by which they all are dissolved, the consummation by which they all are established. The power of God stands neither at the side of nor above–supernatural!—these limited and limiting powers. It is pure and pre-eminent and—beyond them all. It can neither be substituted for them nor ranged with them, and, save with the greatest caution, it cannot even be compared with them. The assumption that Jesus is the Christ (i. 4) is, in the strictest sense of the word, an assumption, void of any content that can be comprehended by us. The appointment of Jesus to be the Christ takes place in the Spirit and must be apprehended in the Spirit. It is self-sufficient, unlimited, and in itself true. And moreover, it is what is altogether new, the decisive factor and turning-point in man's consideration of God. This it is which is communicated between Paul and his hearers. To the proclamation and receiving of this Gospel the whole activity of the Christian community—its teaching, ethics, and worship—is strictly related. But the activity of the community is related to the Gospel only in so far as it is no more than a crater formed by the explosion of a shell and seeks to be no more than a void in which the Gospel reveals itself. The people of Christ, His community, know that no sacred word or work or thing exists in its own right: they know only those words and works and things which by their negation are sign-posts to the Holy One. If anything Christian(!) be unrelated to the Gospel, it is a human by-product, a dangerous religious survival, a regrettable misunderstanding. For in this case content would be substituted for a void, convex for concave, positive for negative, and the characteristic marks of Christianity would be possession and self-sufficiency rather than deprivation and hope. If this be persisted in, there emerges, instead of the community of Christ, Christendom, an ineffective peacepact or compromise with that existence which, moving with its own momentum, lies on this side resurrection. Christianity would then have lost all relation to the power of God. Now, whenever this occurs, the Gospel, so far from being removed from all rivalry, stands hard pressed in the midst of other religions and philosophies of this world. Hard pressed, because, if men must have their religious needs satisfied, if they must surround themselves with comfortable illusions about their knowledge of God and particularly about their union with Him,—well, the world penetrates far deeper into such matters than does a Christianity which misunderstands itself, and of such a 'gospel' we have good cause to be ashamed. Paul, however, is speaking of the power of the UN-KNOWN God, of—*Things which eye saw not and ear heard not, and which entered not into the heart of man.* Of such a Gospel he has no cause to be ashamed.   [Karl Barth: from *The Epistle to the Romans*]

36. Contemporary theologies of revelation

Jesuit theologian **Avery Dulles** discerns five basic "models" or types of theological understanding of revelation in contemporary theology. While these types are only intended as schematic generalizations, they uncover the principal issues debated in current thought about revelation. After examining each in detail, Dulles draws upon all of them to suggest a contemporary theology of revelation based on the concept of symbol.

The great Western religions—Judaism, Christianity, and Islam—are based on the conviction that the existence of the world and the final meaning and value of all that it contains ultimately depend on a personal God who, while distinct from the world and everything in it, is absolute in terms of reality, goodness, and power. These religions profess to derive their fundamental vision not from mere human speculation, which would be tentative and uncertain, but from God's own testimony—that is to say, from a historically given divine revelation.

Christian faith and theology, for nearly two thousand years, have been predicated on the conviction that God gave a permanently valid revelation concerning himself in biblical times—a revelation that deepened progressively with the patriarchs, Moses, and the prophets, until it reached its unsurpassable climax in Jesus Christ. The Christian Church down through the centuries has been committed to this revelation and has sought to propagate it, defend it, and explain its implications.

Contemporary systems, in my opinion, may be divided into five major classes according to their central vision of how and where revelation occurs. These five types, to be studied in more detail in the next five chapters, may here be set forth in summary fashion.

1. *Revelation as Doctrine.* According to this view revelation is principally found in clear propositional statements attributed to God as authoritative teacher. For Protestants who accept this approach, revelation is generally identified with the Bible, viewed as a collection of inspired and inerrant teachings. For Catholic representatives of this approach, revelation is to be found, at least most accessibly, in the official teaching of the Church, viewed as God's infallible oracle. The truth of the teach-

ing is held to be recognizable by external signs (miracles and the like), but some proponents of this position, both Protestant and Catholic, regard interior grace as a necessary precondition not only for the response of faith but even for perceiving the force of the evidence.

2. *Revelation as History.* This type of theory, proposed in conscious opposition to the preceding, maintains that God reveals himself primarily in his great deeds, especially those which form the major themes of biblical history. The Bible and the official teaching of the Church are considered to embody revelation only to the extent that they are reliable reports about what God has done. Although some adherents of this approach look upon biblical and ecclesiastical teaching as revelation in a derivative sense, most prefer to say that the Bible and church teaching are rather *witnesses* to revelation.

3. *Revelation as Inner Experience.* For some modern theologians, both Protestant and Catholic, revelation is neither an impersonal body of objective truths nor a series of external, historical events. Rather it is a privileged interior experience of grace or communion with God. Although this perception of the divine is held to be immediate to each individual, some proponents of this position say that the experience of grace depends on the mediation of Christ, who experienced the Father's presence in a unique and exemplary way.

4. *Revelation as Dialectical Presence.* A number of European theologians, especially in the years following World War I, repudiated both the objectivism of the first two types of revelation theology and the subjectivism of the third. God, they insisted, could never be an object known either by inference from nature or history, by propositional teaching, or by direct perception of a mystical kind. Utterly transcendent, God encounters the human subject when it pleases him by means of a word in which faith recognizes him to be present. The word of God simultaneously reveals and conceals the divine presence.

5. *Revelation as New Awareness.* Especially since the middle of the twentieth century, an increasing number of theologians have felt that the prevalent theories of revelation were too authoritarian, and that the "inner experience" model, which tries to corect this, is too individualist and unworldly. These thinkers hold that revelation takes place as an expansion of consciousness or shift of perspective when people join in the movements of secular history. God, for them, is not a direct object of experience but is mysteriously present as the transcendent dimension of human engagement in creative tasks.

Each of these five typical positions situates the crucial moment of revelation at a different point. For the doctrinal type, the pivotal moment is the formulation of teaching in clear conceptual form. For the historical type, the decisive point is the occurrence of a historical event through which God signifies his intentions. For the experiential type (i.e., the type emphasizing *inner* experience), the crux is an immediate, interior perception of the divine presence. For the dialectical type, the key element is God's utterance of a word charged with divine power. For the awareness type, the decisive moment is the stimulation of the human imagination to restructure experience in a new framework.

After surveying five models of revelation theology we resolved to correct the specific weaknesses of each model while seeking to preserve their valid insights. Such a critical retrieval did not seem possible without recourse to a dialectical tool that would help to identify what was sound and what deficient in the rival models. As a dialectical tool we selected the concept of symbolic mediation. Without contending that revelation is the same as symbol, we described revelation as the self-manifestation of God through a form of communications that could be termed, at least in a broad sense, symbolic.

Our understanding of symbol was not a purely generic one, but was itself shaped by Christian conviction and refined in dialogue with the five models. In light of this procedure, we adopted a position that may be called symbolic realism. Five important points regarding symbol are characteristic of this position.

First, revelatory symbols are not pure creations of the human imagination. The basic symbols of Christian revelation, we maintained, are the persons, events, and other realities whereby God brings into existence the community of faith we call the Christian Church. On the basis of this self-manifestation, God may inspire believers to construct images that are helpful for understanding and communicating what has been given, but the figures of speech and the literary imagery are secondary to the real symbols out of which they emerge.

Secondly, Christian revelation is not simply the product of human interpretation of the natural symbols contained in cosmic nature. Through specific actions at definite points in time and place, the universal symbolism of nature is taken up into the biblical and Christian tradition and thereby given added depth and significance. . . .

Thirdly, symbols do not necessarily point to things strictly other than themselves. Although there must be at least a formal distinction between the symbol and what it points to, the symbol and the symbolized may constitute "a single interlocked reality," as Vatican Council II said of the two natures of Christ and of the two aspects of the Church. Just as the human body is really one with the spiritual person who comes to expression through it, so according to Christian theology, the man Jesus Christ is one with the Word of God. So, likewise, with differing modes of union, the Church is one with the Spirit of Christ, and the sacraments are, in still another way, one with the divine persons present and active in them. Jesus in his human nature, the Church in its social structure, and the sacraments in their visible aspect may all be described, in their several ways, as "realizing symbols"—symbols that contain and mediate the reality they signify.

Fourthly, revelatory symbols do not simply arouse emotions, strivings, fantasies, and ideals. They point to, and provide insight into, realities inaccessible to direct human experience. Although they are not scale models, pictures, or descriptions of what they signify, such symbols denote and disclose what is ontologically real.

Revelatory symbols, fifthly, have a twofold truth. They have "symbolic truth" insofar as they express, communicate, or produce a transformed consciousness. But the truth of the symbol is not merely its symbolic truth. In reflection, symbols give rise to true affirmations about what is antecedently real. Revelatory symbols, being dense and concrete, can generate an inexhaustible brood of affirmations. Yet the symbols are not indefinitely malleable. Only some statements can claim to be grounded in the symbols; certain others are excluded by the symbols, rightly understood.

With the help of symbolic realism we may at this point formulate certain conclusions about revelation. . . . Our first set of conclusions will be negative, our second set positive, with reference to the five models. Negatively, then:

1. Revelation does not initially occur in the form of propositions, still less that of prefabricated propositions miraculously inserted into the human mind. Nor can revelation be adequately transposed into any determinate set of propositions. The statements in Scripture and tradition represent valid though limited aspects of revelation as seen from particular points of view.

2. Revelation is not a series of events in the remote past, recoverable only through historical-critical method. While historical investigation can always be useful, it does not by itself yield revelation. Granted the nature of the biblical materials, and the antiquity of the events, dispassionate, academic history is rarely capable of reconstructing the revela-

tory events in detail. The process whereby revelatory meaning is discerned in the events is not a matter of formal inference, but a synthesis of subsidiarily known clues. The events of biblical history, as seen in the framework of Scripture and Christian tradition, are disclosive of God.

3. Revelation is not an ineffable mystical encounter between God and the individual soul. While mystical experiences of union may sometimes be authentic, they do not by themselves yield a determinate revelation. For them to be interpreted in a theistic or Christian sense, one must rely on the mediation of Christian symbols, traditions, and doctrines.

4. Revelation is not an unintelligible word or an absurd message to be accepted in a blind leap of faith. It has a content beyond the mere fact of revelation itself. It does not occur in a time wholly incommensurable with chronological time nor without continuity with other events in history.

5. Revelation is not a mere invitation or impulse to adapt one's attitudes and behavior to the needs of a particular phase of the evolutionary process. The meaning of revelation does not change so radically from one age to another as to contradict the previous meaning.

These negative conclusions may be balanced by the following positive statements, embodying themes from each of the five models.

1. Revelation has cognitive value that can be expressed, to some extent, in true propositions. The truth of these propositions is permanent and universal in the sense that, if they are ever authorized by revelation, they at no time or place become false in their own terms. The propositions help to establish the context in which the symbols yield their revelatory meaning.

2. The chief symbols of biblical and Christian revelation are given in a specific history mediated to every generation through the canonical Scriptures, read in the light of living and ongoing tradition. The events, attributable in their specificity to God as agent, convey a divinely intended meaning, discernible with particular clarity and assurance by prophetically endowed interpreters.

3. By evoking participation, the revelatory symbols mediate a lived, personal communion with God, which is, in its way, immediate. This may be described as an experience of God or of grace, provided that God or grace is not depicted as an object to be encountered but as a horizon within which inner-wordly objects are encountered.

4. The words of Scripture and Christian proclamation are dynamic. They are, under favorable circumstances, imbued with the power of God who speaks and acts through them. The word is an event as well as a

content, and the word-event exceeds all that can be said about it in clear propositional speech. Especially when the revelatory events are seen as visible words, the word takes on characteristics like those we have attributed to symbol.

5. Revelation is not merely speculative truth. It has implications for human existence and conduct. Demanding obedience, it brings with it a new horizon, a new consciousness. The full significance of revelation can be perceived only by those who respond, with personal commitment, within a community of faith.   [from *Models of Revelation*]

C. Faith: Response to Revelation

37. *Faith in the scriptures*

The idea of "faith" in the Judeo-Christian scriptures presents two distinct but complementary aspects. On the one hand, faith is seen as a personal relationship of trust and confidence in God, implying humble acceptance of God's gracious covenant, hope in God's promises, and living in accord with God's will. On the other hand, faith also has the character of belief, or intellectual conviction of and commitment to certain realities on the basis of God's revelation. While the aspect of relationship is always presupposed, the element of belief comes to have a certain predominance in the New Testament because of the conviction that God's revelation reaches its culmination in the historical person of Jesus; hence acceptance of the "kerygma" or proclamation about Jesus as real is crucial to entering into the "new covenant" which he brings about.

Genesis 12:1-4—Abram called to a journey of faith

Genesis 15:1-6—Abram put faith in the Lord's promise

Deuteronomy 6:20-25; 26:5-9—faith as remembrance of God's saving deeds and observance of his covenant

Joshua 24:2-28—the covenant of God with Israel

Psalm 91—taking refuge in the Lord

Psalm 105—God's fidelity

Psalm 146—trust in God

Mark 4:35-41 [Matthew 8:23-26; Luke 8:22-25]—the disciples lack faith

Mark 5:25-34 [Matthew 9:20-22]—a story of healing by faith: a woman with a hemorrhage

Mark 9:14-29—"I do believe; help my unbelief!"

Mark 10:46-52—healing by faith: a blind man

Mark 11:20-24—all things are possible for faith

Matthew 6:25-34—faith removes anxiety

Matthew 8:5-12 [Luke 7:1-10]—faith of a pagan centurion

Matthew 14:22-33—a parable of faith: Peter walks on water

Matthew 15:21-28—faith outside Israel: a Canaanite woman

Matthew 17:19 [Luke 17:5-6]—"if you had faith as a mustard seed . . ."

Matthew 21:21—have faith and do not doubt

Romans 4:9-5:1—the example of Abraham's faith

Romans 10:8-17—salvation through faith in Jesus; faith comes through hearing the message

1 Corinthians 15:14-17—the resurrection of Jesus: center of Christian faith

Galatians 3:2-14—faith versus works

John 3:11-21, 31-36—whoever believes in the Son will have eternal life

John 5:36-47—the Father testifies to Jesus

John 6:41-47—the Father interiorly inspires faith in Jesus

John 17:1-8—belief in Jesus as the messenger of the Father

Hebrews 11:1-12:1—faith is the assurance of things hoped for; examples of faith

James 2:14-26—faith without works is dead

38. *The classical definition of faith*

For **St. Thomas Aquinas** (see #24, 27, 30, 43, 58) faith is defined as an assent of the intellect to revealed truth. Nevertheless, the relational aspect of faith is very much present, for the "truths" of faith are beyond the natural capacity of the human mind; we can only assent to them because we are internally "drawn" to do so by the presence of God's own life within us. Thus faith is not merely a matter of believing certain things about God, but of believing God himself as the one who internally "testifies" to the truths of faith, and of believing "toward" God as the goal of the dynamism of faith. Furthermore, for St. Thomas it is love that ultimately moves faith in this dynamism. Hence faith as intellectual assent must be rooted in the experience and the love of God, which are possible because of his gracious gift of his life to us.

In the first of the following passages, St. Thomas is commenting on the description of faith in the letter to the Hebrews 11:1. Note that the Latin translation used by St. Thomas ("faith is the substance of things hoped for, and proof of things we do not see") somewhat obscures the meaning of the original. What is significant, however, is how St. Thomas uses these ideas to formulate his own definition of faith.

The relationship of the act of faith to its goal, which is the object of the will, is signified in the words, "faith is the substance of things hoped for." "Substance" means the first beginnings of some reality, especially when the total reality is dynamically implied in its beginnings (for example, we could say that the axioms of a deductive system of knowledge are its "substance," since they are what we first know of the system, and all the rest is dynamically contained in them). In this sense faith is called the "substance of things hoped for": because the beginning of what we hope for is present in us through the assent of faith, which dynamically contains everything that we hope. For we hope to attain our complete happiness in the clear vision of what we now adhere to by faith [i.e., in the vision of God].

The relationship of the act of faith to the object of the intellect, insofar as it is the object of faith, is signified in the words, "proof of things we do not see." "Proof" here means the effect of proof; for by means of proof the intellect is brought to assent to some truth. Hence, the firm assent of the intellect to a truth not apparent to faith is called here "proof." Therefore other translations say "conviction," rather than "proof," since through the divine authority the intellect of the believer is brought to the conviction that it should assent to things that it cannot know by its own power.

If one wished to put these phrases into the form of a definition, one could say: faith is a dynamic state of mind [habitus mentis] through which eternal life is begun in us, making the intellect assent to things that are not evident to it.   (Summa Theologiae II, II, q. IV, a. 1)

If we look at faith from the point of view of the intellect, we can consider two aspects of the object of faith. First there is the "material" object of faith [i.e., the content that is believed]. In this sense, the act of faith is *believing in God*, since everything that we believe in faith has a relationship to God. Second, there is the "formal" nature of the object of faith, which is the reason why we assent to what we believe. In this sense, the act of faith is *believing God:* for (as was shown above), the formal object of faith is the primordial Truth [i.e., God], to which we adhere, and because of which we assent to what we believe. If we look at the object of faith in yet a third way, that is, insofar as the intellect is moved by the will, then we can say that the act of faith is *believing toward God:* for the primordial Truth is the goal of the will.   [II, II, q. II, a. 2]

It is clear that the act of faith is directed toward the object of the will, i.e. the good, as its goal. But this good that is the goal of faith, namely the divine Goodness, is the proper object of love. And therefore love is called the "form" of faith, insofar as the act of faith is perfected and given its full reality by love. . . . Faith which is given its form by love is a virtue; but faith which is not formed by love is not a virtue.   (q. IV, a. 3, 5)

39. Can we still believe?

Theologian **Karl Rahner** (#12, 33, 44) examines honestly the difficulty of belief in today's world. Doubts and difficulties of faith, for Rahner, may have a positive function: they may lead to a more mature faith in the genuine, mysterious and incomprehensible reality of God and his love. Even the explicit unbeliever, Rahner says, may in an "anonymous" way be responding to that reality; but the person of explicit Christian faith has in Jesus a sign and assurance of the ultimate meaningfulness of life because of God's victorious love made manifest in our history.

We speak of believing in the infinite mystery that we call God. We believe—try to believe—in this deepest of mysteries, which as *our* mystery has drawn near to us in Jesus Christ and his grace: a grace even when it is not recognized as such and where a man seems to be plunging into the black abyss of emptiness and nothingness.

Is it possible to profess this faith even today? It is not possible without dreading that one will fail to say the very thing which would have tipped the balance, giving a particular reader or hearer the courage to believe. All I can do is try to speak honestly.

The faith I am talking about is faith in the real sense of the word, faith that is rooted in personal decision, not simply in middle-class habit and the conventions of society. And therefore, nothing sound can be said about the future there is likely to be for faith unless one asks what influence faith has in our personal existence today. The future of faith will arise out of the personal decisions made by each one of us. Today we must answer for our existence.

Let me try to put the matter quite simply. I begin with the fact that I find myself a believer and have not come upon any good reason for not believing. I was baptized and brought up in the faith, and so the faith that is my inheritance has also become the faith of my own deliberate choice, a real, personal faith. God knows that is how matters stand; his mystery sees into the depths of my being, depths that are impenetrable to me. And at all events I can say: "I have not come upon any good reason to stop believing in God—to stop being the person I am."

Before a man changes himself he ought to have good reasons for doing so. If a man tried to change without having such reasons, to give up this fulfillment of his spiritual person, he would drop into the void; for him there would be no escape from *disintegration*. A datum must be accepted and upheld until it is disproved. One's life and growth can spring only from a root that is already alive, from one's own beginning, from the gift of primordial trust in the meaningfulness of life.

When tradition has bestowed high and holy things on a man and confronted him with an absolute summons, then his critical conscience and probing reason may accept this mere fact as sufficient evidence— both as unthematic experience and as logical justification—for the truth of the tradition. But whatever doubts may have assailed me, one thing has always stood out in my mind, sustaining me as I clung to it: the conviction that the experience handed down to me must not yield to empty routine. Spiritual dullness and benighted skepticism must yield to nothing less than that mightier being who calls me into a more remorse-less light.

Of course the inherited faith was always a faith under assault, but it was always experienced as the faith which asked: "Will you also go away?" and to which one could only say: "Lord, to whom shall we go?" (Jn. 6, 67f.). It was experienced as the faith that was mighty and kindly, that a man therefore would not have been justified in giving up unless, at least, its contrary had been proven true. But nobody has presented me with such proof, nor does it emerge from the experience of my own life.

Certainly there are many difficulties and many sources of bitterness in my mind and in my life. And yet it is plain that any difficulty which I am to entertain as a serious objection to my faith must correspond to the dignity and depth of what it would attack and alter. Intellectual difficulties may abound in the field of this science or that; they may arise from the history of religions, from biblical criticism, from the history of the early Church—difficulties to which I have no direct, pat answer. But these difficulties are too nice and too flimsy, compared with the gravity of existence, for me to let them decide ultimate issues and shape my whole life in its unutterable depths. For example, my faith does not depend on whether the right exegetical and Catholic interpretation of the first chapters of Genesis has been found or not, whether a decree of the Biblical Commission or the Congregation for the Doctrine of the Faith is eminently wise or not. Such arguments are ruled out from the start.

True, there are other and more profound trials. But when these are faced with honesty and courage, they bring out one's true Christianity for the first time. They affect the heart, the inmost core of existence. They place it in jeopardy and thrust it into the ultimate dubiousness of man—but precisely by so doing they may be the birth pangs of true Christian life.

Simply experiencing life isolates a man; it leaves him in a kind of void, exposed to his freedom and yet not assured of it; he finds himself lost in an unending sea of darkness, in a monstrous night where one only staggers from one makeshift to the next, frail, poverty-stricken, throbbing with the pain of finite existence, ever and again thrown back to one's dependence on the merely biological, on stupid institutions, on inherited ways (even when one resists them). A man feels death there inside him, in the midst of his life; he senses how death is the frontier that no one can cross of his own strength, how the ideals of life lose their youthful splendor and droop, how one wearies of clever talk at the annual fair of life and learning—yes, even learning.

The real argument against Christianity is the experience of life, this experience of darkness. And I have always observed that the elemental force and the arbitrary prejudgment which lie behind the technical arguments of the learned—or rather of individual learned men—against Christianity always spring from these ultimate experiences of existence which plunge mind and heart into darkness, fatigue and despair. These experiences seek utterance in the doubts of learned men—carefully as their doubts need to be weighed.

But the experience we are speaking of is also the argument *for* Christianity. For what does Christianity say? What does it preach? Despite an apparently complicated system of dogma and morals, it says something quite simple, nothing else but this: mystery always remains mystery, but this mystery wills to disclose itself as the infinite, the incomprehensible, the unutterable being that is called God, as intimacy that gives itself in an absolute self-communication in the midst of the experience of human emptiness. This intimacy has not only occurred in what we call grace; it has also become historically tangible in him whom we call the God-Man. Both these modes of divine self-communication—that of God "in himself" and that of God "for us"—involve what we call the threefold divine personality: three relations of God's one being and working: as the creator, as the sanctifier and as the inward guide and principle of unity.

Man finds it difficult to believe that this utter mystery is close to us and not remote, is love and not a spurning judgment. It is a light that may seem darker to us than our own darkness. But does it not bestow so much light, so much joy, so much love, so much glory in the world of faith as to cause us to say that all this can come only from an absolute light, an absolute love and glory, from an absolute being—even if we do not understand how this our darkness and nothingness can exist when infinite fullness exists, albeit as a mystery? Can I not say that I am right in clinging to light, be it ever so feeble, instead of darkness—to beatitude instead of the hellish torment of my existence?

Suppose I accepted the arguments which existence raises against Christianity. What would they offer me to live by? The courage of an honest man, perhaps—the nobility of one who resolutely faces an absurd existence? But then can this be accepted as something manly, binding and exalted unless again one has said that something honorable and glorious exists—and how can such a thing exist in the abyss of utter absurdity?

Now here we have said something significant. A man who boldly accepts life, even if he be a myopic positivist, has already accepted God as he is in himself, as what he wills to be for us in love and freedom, which means the God of eternal life in his divine self-communication. For anyone who really accepts *himself* accepts mystery as the infinite emptiness that man is and thereby tacitly accepts him who has decided to fill this emptiness that is the mystery of man with the infinite mystery that is God.

Christianity can be regarded as the clear affirmation of what man obscurely experiences in his concrete existence. Man, after all, is not only superior to animals as a spiritual nature; he is also a spirit inwardly alight with love by God's grace. And if man, being such, really and totally accepts *himself* as he is, mutely accepts himself in this light, then that is faith, and Christianity is essentially the affirmation in utter trust of this mystery, man, in the spirit of Christ. If I acknowledge and affirm this fact, what reason can I then have not to be a Christian? I know of only one compelling reason: the weariness, sin and despair that I experience in myself; the crumbling of existence by a dreary skepticism which can no longer even summon up a protest against existence; slothful evasion of the unspoken but eternal question that we ourselves are not facing or seeking to answer but from which we are rather taking refuge in the wretchedness of daily routine.

We would not deny that silent, patient uprightness in attending to one's daily duties can also be a form of "anonymous Christianity," a form in which many a man (if he does not turn stubborn skepticism into an absolute system) may be able to practice Christianity genuinely— perhaps more genuinely than in certain more explicit forms which are often lived so vacuously as a flight from mystery instead of a real confrontation with it.

Experience of such anonymous Christianity, unexplicit but genuinely lived, might undermine one's Christian confidence that man is the finitude endowed with God's infinitude. But if I should yield to this doubt, what would I then have in exchange for Christianity? Emptiness, despair, night, death.

And what reason have I to regard *that* abyss as truer than the abyss of God? It is easier to drop into one's own emptiness than into the abyss of God's blessed mystery—but it is not braver, and it is not wiser. Of course this truth only emerges if it is lived and accepted as "the truth that makes men free" and dares all things which lead us upward.

St. Augustine prays: "O God, the Father of truth . . . I call upon thee, wellspring, ground and author of the truth of all that is true" (*Soliloquies* I). I have called upon it and it attests itself to me and gives me what I must give it, so as to be and remain the blessed strength of life in me. It gives me the courage to believe in it and call upon it when dark night would swallow me up.

I see thousands upon thousands of men about me, whole cultures and eras that are explicitly non-Christian, and I see times coming when Christianity will no longer be taken for granted in Europe and the world at large. But when all is said and done, that cannot unsettle me. Why not? Because everywhere I see a Christianity that does not call itself Christian, because my explicit Christianity is not, for me, one opinion among others that gainsay it but the homecoming and flowering of what I can live elsewhere, too, as love and truth. I do not consider non-Christians to be people with less wit or less good will than I have. But were I to subside into a hollow, craven skepticism because there are many different views of the world, would I stand a better chance of reaching the truth than if I remained a Christian? No, for skepticism and agnosticism are themselves only opinions among other opinions, and the hollowest and most craven of opinions at that. This is no escape from the multitude of world views. Even refraining from any decision about them is a decision—the worst decision.

Besides, I have no reason at all to consider Christianity one world view among others. Let us understand exactly what Christianity is; let us listen carefully to what it really says and compare it, listen to its message with the utmost care but also with the utmost receptivity of mind and heart. Then we shall never hear anything good, true and redemptive illuminating our lives and opening up vistas of eternity that exists in another world view but is missing in Christianity. Elsewhere, indeed, we may hear things to rouse us, spur us on, widen our mind's horizon and enrich us. But all this is either something tentative which neither solves nor attempts to solve the ultimate problem of existence in the face of death—and then it can perfectly well be taken into the breadth of Christian living—or else it is something which we will recognize as a part of genuine Christianity if we but explore Christianity with more care, more courage and sharper eyes. Perhaps we shall observe that we never quite achieve a complete integration of this knowledge, these experiences, these realities of art, philosophy and poetry, with our Christianity as we have thought it out. But between any legitimate experience and knowledge on the one hand, and genuine Christianity on the other, we shall never discover any ultimate, irreconcilable contradiction. And that is enough.

Thus we have a right and duty to listen to Christianity as the *universal* message of truth which nothing can limit, and which rejects only the negations of other world views, but no real affirmation that they have to offer. Let us listen to Christianity as the universal message which embraces and thus preserves everything else, which forbids man nothing except to lock himself inside his finitude, except to disbelieve that he is endowed with God's infinitude and that as "finite he is receptive to the infinite."

Therefore we Christians do not look on non-Christians as people who have mistaken error for truth because they are more stupid, more wicked and more unfortunate than we, but as people who in the depths of their being are already pardoned, or can be pardoned, by God's infinite grace in virtue of his universal salvific will and are on the road toward perfection, as people who have simply not yet come to an explicit awareness of what they already are: men called by God. If we know this, it is a grace which we cannot yet attribute to those others; it is also a fearful responsibility weighing upon us, who now must be of our own accord what they are necessarily as men summoned by God. But the fact that others are only anonymous Christians is no reason for us not to be Christians explicitly.

We know full well that Jesus of Nazareth is *the* great sign that God himself has radically intervened in the world. This fact cannot be arrived at by logic; it is God's saving gift to mankind, no matter of course but an historical reality. It is not difficult to believe in Jesus Christ, the Son of God, on the basis of what he says of himself and the signs that mark his life and death. It is easy for a man who has been given love, which makes the hardest things easy.

For in the first place there is nothing mythological about this doctrine of the God-Man (the divine nature and the human nature, inseparable and unconfused in the one Person of the incarnate God). It is not mythology to say that in my mind's absolute transcendence (when my mind rises above immediate data) God's infinitude is given to me. And no more is it mythology to say that in one particular human being the transcendence of self (which otherwise is always a mere becoming) reached an absolute acme, because here God's self-communication to the created mind and spirit happened in a unique way. Now if one can really grasp *this* proposition in all its weight, one has affirmed God's incarnation as a *possible* embodiment of what it is to be man.

We must always bear in mind that, according to the Christian doctrine of the relation between the world and God, the more creatures belong to God the more independent they become; therefore, precisely because Jesus' humanity belongs to the eternal Word of God in the most radical way, he is man in the truest sense; he descended deepest of all into the abysses of human things and experienced the truest death of all. It does seem that people first arrived at the idea of the God-Man through God's actual incarnation. But once that event has taken place there is not much difficulty about identifying the biblical Jesus with it. Who but Jesus could give me the courage to believe such a thing? If, as Teilhard de Chardin says, there must be a point omega toward which all the history of man's world is headed, and if experience of my own grace-given closeness to God entitles me to expect that acme really exists, then why must I feel sheepish about finding it in Jesus of Nazareth—in him who, even as he was dying, commended his soul into the Father's hands, in him who knew the mystery of man, the devouring judgment, death and abysmal guilt through and through and yet called the supreme mystery "my Father" and called us his "brethren"?

Argument will force no one to believe in Jesus of Nazareth as God's absolute presence. That faith is a voluntary thing, if only because its object is something historical, which therefore does not exist necessarily. But anyone who considers that ideas only become living truth in earnest when they stand forth in flesh and blood can more readily believe in the theandric idea if he believes in Jesus of Nazareth.

Something further must be said about the idea of the God-Man and its embodiment in Jesus. Because he is God's assent to the world and the acceptance of the world into God, he is the eschatological event that will never be superseded. After him no prophet can appear who will displace him. For there are two words and things, each ordered to the other, which cannot be superseded: man as infinite questioning, and God as the absolute answer which necessarily remains mysterious because it is *God's* answer. That is why the God-Man cannot be superseded. Through him the world and history have found their own meaning—but not as though now the world could no longer have any history worthy to be enacted and pondered. Quite the contrary: now human history, which takes place in knowledge and freedom, has caught up with its true principle, can perceive its true destiny to be a *partaking* (2 Pet. 1, 4) in the God-Man Jesus Christ. And so with him history only begins on its proper level: the obscure and incalculable history of a mankind that knows it is hidden away in the love of God.

Human history, of course, still stands, as it has ever stood, in the sign of *conflict* between man and the mystery of God. But it may now be interpreted as the history of God's revealed love in spite of all the horrible things that have happened and are still to happen, perhaps even swelling to apocalyptic proportions. The meaning, the goal of history is the intimacy with God (an intimacy resting upon the God-Man) of all who are called and saved—an immediacy with God which by its nature is grounded and embodied in the God-Man Jesus Christ. From the very beginning we have been regarded as the brethren of the God-Man, so that it is possible to say with Soloviev that all mankind is truly theandric.

Now there is yet another hindrance and menace to faith: the very community of believers, *the Church*. To one who scans history with an unprejudiced eye, no doubt, she is holy Church, the sign raised among the nations; for as the fruitful mother of saints she bears witness that God is at work in her. But she is also the Church of sinners and to that extent a sinful Church, because we, the members of the Church, are sinners. This fact makes itself felt in what the Church herself does and refrains from doing. Sinful humanness, inadequacy, short-sightedness, falling short of what the hour demands, failure to understand the needs of the age, the tasks she assigns us and the direction in which she is heading—all these very human traits are also the traits of the Church's office-bearers and of all her members. It would be arrant self-delusion and a clerical arrogance ill becoming the Church as Jesus' community were one to deny or gloss over this sinfulness or pretend that it was rampant only in the Church of former ages. That sort of thing is an assault on faith which may practically suffocate the individual.

And yet, are we not ourselves part of this burden that weighs upon us and jeopardizes our faith? And if we know that truth can be fulfilled on earth, in the flesh, and not in a hollow idealism, if today we know better than ever that man can find himself only in a community which makes clear-cut demands, that any withdrawal of the individual into isolation is a fossilized ideal that was always wrong anyhow, then there can be only one course for the man of today: to put up with the burden of community as the one means to the freedom of the person.

And finally, we are baptized into the death of the Lord and receive his body, and we wish to be included in the community of saints. Now all that is possible only if we live in the Church and help bear her burden, which is also our own. The concrete Church may be a trial to our faith, but may also mature it, and need not be the cause of its death if we have not first let faith die in our own hearts.

Though it is no easy matter to judge one's own era, I do think that *young* minds have rather a hard time of it these days. It is especially difficult for them—and yet how necessary—to distinguish faith in Jesus Christ and his kingdom from matters on which opinions may differ widely. Society must be organized to a certain extent, but no clear-cut imperative as to world order can be deduced from the Christian message *alone*; this means that Christians, too, may hold different opinions about the dosage of order and freedom and therefore even about the suitability of man-made Church ordinances. Disagreement over such matters must be borne with sobriety and patience, in a spirit of love for the Church and the Church's people; a responsible attitude toward our own duties must be combined with obedience, longanimity and an ability to wait. A man who discharges his responsibilities toward the future by living this way in the Church will accept the Church's historical aspect and will not permit it to become a grave threat to his faith that God and Christ are present in the Church.

Here again it behooves us to have a sense of fraternal solidarity with those who do not outwardly belong to the Church. They are not free, either, to do whatever they choose; their road, too, has been marked out for them and they must keep to it in their concrete living—in their home life, in their career, in their social activities. To the extent that they make an effort to do so, they are *unconsciously* what the Christian is consciously and explicitly—and, Jesus would say, "not far from the kingdom of God" (Mk. 12, 34). Such a man may assume he is an atheist; he may grieve at the thought that he does not believe; concrete Christian doctrine may seem outlandish to him. Let him but press on, following the light there in his heart of hearts, and he is on the right road; and the Christian has no fear that such a man will not reach the goal, even though he has not managed to turn his anonymous Christianity into explicit Christianity.

It is a Christian truth that a man who seeks has already been found by the One he is honestly looking for, albeit anonymously. All roads lead to him. "In him we live and move and have our being" (Acts 17, 28). Comprehending all things, he is comprehended by none. And therefore Christianity, faith in God through Christ in *one* Spirit, is child's play, because all it says is that we are called into the immediate mystery of God, waiting for the revelation of that which already is so—"that God [is] everything to everyone."   [from *Do You Believe in God?*]

Chapter Four

The Nature of God

40. The biblical idea of God

The Judeo-Christian scriptures were written and compiled over the course of many centuries. It is not surprising, then, that they contain a number of different and sometimes antithetical ideas about God: from the powerful and warlike leader of the Israelite tribes, who demands the slaughter of his people's enemies (Deut 7:1–4; 20:12–18) to the God who is love (1 Jn 4:8) and wills the salvation of all (1 Tim 2:3–6). The Bible does not present a systematic or comprehensive doctrine of God, but describes his relationship to us. The following passages are suggested as representing some of the most significant features of God as implied in his saving acts.

Genesis 1:1–2:4a—God as creator of all

Exodus 3:1–14—"I am who I am"

Deuteronomy 10:12–22—the majesty and goodness of God

1 Samuel 2:1–10—the prayer of Hannah: God is all-knowing, all-powerful, and aids the humble

Job 40:6–41:26—God speaks to Job from the whirlwind and manifests his unquestionable power

Psalm 23—the Lord is my shepherd

Psalm 103—the divine goodness

Psalm 104—God as creator

Psalm 115—the true God contrasted with idols

Psalm 145—the goodness of God

Sirach 18:1–13—the eternity and mercy of God

Isaiah 6:1-7—the vision of Isaiah: the thrice-holy God

Isaiah 25:1-12—the Lord destroys and saves

Isaiah 40:12-41:21—God's power to save; his uniqueness

Isaiah 55:1-11—Gods ways and thoughts are above ours

Ezekiel 1:1-28—the vision of Ezekiel: the glory of God

Zephaniah 1:2-18—God's anger and punishment of those who are unfaithful to him

Matthew 11:25-27—God reveals through Jesus, his Son

Luke 6:35-37—love and compassion are the imitation of God

Luke 15:11-32—parable of the loving father and his two sons

John 3:16-17—God so loved the world

John 4:24—God is Spirit

John 5:19-26—the Father gives life through the Son

Acts 17:22-31—Paul's discourse on the Areopagus: "in him we live and
move and have our being"

Romans 8:28-39—God's love triumphs over all things

1 John 4:7-21—God is love

41. God as the ineffable

The anonymous author of this Greek hymn from the patristic era
emphasizes the absoluteness and transcendence of God, who is
beyond all words and thought. At the same time, God is intimately
present to all things. In the line of the philosophies of Plato and
Aristotle, the author thinks of God as the goal of all that exists, the
object of their desire (even if unknown to them), and hence the
cause of their motion. It is this absolutely transcendent and immanent being who freely enters into relation with human beings; the
hymn ends with a prayer for his mercy.

A Hymn to God

O You beyond all things!—for how else can I proclaim You?

What word can I use to sing of You? for no word can express You.

By what thought should I contemplate You? for no thought can
apprehend You.

You alone are beyond speech; for you produce all things that speak.

You alone are beyond thought; for you produce all things that think.

All things—both those that speak and those that do not—proclaim You;

All things—both those that think and those that do not—glorify You.

The common yearnings and anguish of all things

Are for You. To You all things pray.

To You all thinking beings raise together a silent hymn.

In You alone all things remain; toward You all things together hasten.

You are the goal of all things; You are One, and All, and None;

You are neither one nor all. How shall I call You, You of all names,

Who alone cannot be limited? What heavenly mind can enter into

The veil beyond the clouds? Be gracious,

O You beyond all things; for how else can I proclaim You?
[from the Patrologia Graeca] [Trans. R. Viladesau]

42. The transcendence of God

For **St. Augustine** (see above, #15) God's nature is totally spiritual, and is therefore beyond the apprehension of the human mind and human words. Even after God's self-revelation, he remains a mystery. What we can most truly say about God is that he "is"—and in an absolute way. Contrast Augustine's philosophical discourse with the images used by the Bible to speak of God. Can the two approaches be reconciled?

We shall more easily be mutually forgiving [in theological disputes] if we know, or at least firmly believe and hold, that anything we can say about a nature that is invisible and immutable, self-sufficient and alive in an absolute way [i.e. God], cannot be grasped in the same way as things that are visible and changeable, finite and mortal. Despite all our labor, we fail to grasp and know even sensible, bodily things; yet piety, filled with faith, is not ashamed to yearn after the divine and inneffable realities that are above. And this yearning does not come from arrogance, but is inspired by the grace of our Creator and Savior himself. How can we hope to understand God, when we do not understand our own minds, by which we desire to grasp Him? And if one does understand one's own mind, one should carefully consider the fact that it is the highest thing in our nature. . . . Certainly, we find nothing of a material nature in what is highest in ourselves, namely, in our intellect, through which we are wise, according to our ability. Therefore, we should not expect to find in God what we do not find in our own best part, since he is far better than what is best in us. So, we should understand God, if we can, and insofar as we can, as being good, but without having any qualities; as being great, but without quantity; as creator, although he lacks nothing; as ruling, but from no position; as sustaining all things, without having them; as being, in his entirety, everywhere, and yet not being in any place; as being eternal, without time; as making things that change, without himself being changeable or being subject to any external influence at all. If one thinks in this way about God, one still has not grasped in every way what he is; but at least one is respectfully careful, as much as possible, not to think of him falsely. . . .

God is, however, without doubt a "substance" or, if you prefer, an "essence"—what the Greeks call "ousia." For just as the word "wisdom" refers to being wise, and "knowledge" refers to knowing, so "essence" comes from being [esse]. And who is there that IS, more than the One who said to his servant Moses, "I am who am," and "Say to the children of Israel, 'He Who Is' has sent me to you"? [Ex. 3:14] But other things that we call "essences" or "substances" can have non-essential qualities ["accidents"], through which changes great or small occur in them. But there can be no such changeable qualities in God; and therefore God is the only unchangeable substance or essence. To him most especially and properly belongs the name BEING [esse] (from which the term "essence" comes). For what changes, does not retain its own being; and what can be changed, even if it does not actually change, is able not to be what it had been. Therefore, only that which not only is not in fact changed, but actually cannot be changed in any way, can most truly and unhesitatingly be called BEING. . . .

. . . God is more truly thought than He can be spoken of; and he exists more truly than he can be thought.   [from On the Trinity, V, VII]

43. The attributes of God

St. Thomas Aquinas (see above, #24, 27, 30), like St. Augustine, holds that God's nature transcends anything that we can grasp or say about it. Nevertheless, we can by analogy affirm certain perfections of God, because he creates us in his image. We must always remember, however, that we are speaking analogously; any perfection that we affirm of him does not exist in God in the same way as we know it in ourselves or in other creatures. Hence, if we say that God is "good," we must also say that God is not good (in the limited way in which we know "goodness" from finite things), but that God is "eminently" good—i.e., is the supreme good, the cause of good, in a way that surpasses the content of our minds.

After showing that God exists, and is the cause of all things, St. Thomas proceeds to examine the "attributes" of God.

God is not a body . . . for it is necessary that the primary being [i.e., the "first mover" or cause of all things] should be totally actual, and not in any way potential. But every body is in potency . . . hence it is impossible for God to be bodily. [ST I, 3, a.1]

God not only is identical with his essence, but is also identical with his act of existing. . . . Since in God there is no potentiality, it follows that there is nothing in his essence other than his act of existing. Hence his essence is his existence. [ST I, 3, a.4]

There can be no changeable qualities [accidents] in God. For the relationship between a subject and its changeable qualities is that of potency to act; for these changeable qualities make the subject actually exist in some particular way. But there can be no potentiality in God. [ST I, 3, a.6]

God's being is totally simple; for every being that has parts must be in some way potential—the parts must be in potency with regard to each other, or at least with regard to the whole—and this is not true of God. [ST I, 3, a.7]

God contains the perfections of all beings; he is not lacking any noble quality . . . for any perfection that is found in an effect, must also be found—either in the same way, or in an eminent way—in its cause. . . . But since God is the first cause of all things, it is necessary that the perfections of all things preexist in him, in an eminent way. [ST I, 4, a.2]

Furthermore, because (as has been shown) God is self-subsistent Being itself, it follows that he has the total perfection of being. . . . All perfections whatsoever have to do with being; every perfection is a perfection of existing. Hence it follows that no perfection that is in any thing can be lacking to God. [ST I, 6, a.1]

Since God is the first efficient cause of all things, it is clear that he is good and desirable. . . . All things, when they desire their own perfections, desire God, insofar as the perfections of all things are images of the divine being. . . . God and he alone is good by his very essence. . . . He is not directed toward any other being as his goal; but he himself is the goal of all beings. Hence it is clear that God alone has every perfection by his very essence. [ST I, 6, a.3]

Because God is himself subsistent Being, his being is not received in any limited way . . . hence God is infinite and perfect. [ST I, 7, a.1]

God is in all things, not as a part, or as a quality of things, but in the way that an agent is present in what it acts upon. . . . Since God is subsistent Being, the being of creatures is his effect. . . . God causes things not only when they begin to exist, but at every moment that they are preserved in existence. . . . So, as long as a thing exists, God is present to it, giving it existence. But existence is what is most intimate to any being, and what is most interior to it, since it actually makes things to be whatever they are; hence it follows that God is intimately present in all things. [ST I, 7, a.2]

God is entirely changeless. For the primary being must be pure act, without admixture of potency . . . but anything that changes, must in some way be in potency. Hence it is clearly impossible for God to change in any way. [ST I, 9, a.1]

Eternity can mean two things: first, having no beginning or end; second, having no succession, but existing all at once. [ST I, 10, a.1] Eternity follows from immutability, because time is a measure of change. Since God is totally changeless, he is also eternal. [ST I, 10, a.2]

That God is one is shown in three ways: first, from his simplicity . . . second, from the infinity of his perfection; for if there were more than one god, they would be different; some would have different qualities from others. But this would mean the privation of some perfection . . . hence there cannot be more than one God . . . third, from the oneness of the world; things that are different would not come together into an ordered whole unless they were ordered by one principle. . . . [ST I, 11, a.3]

God necessarily knows things other than himself. It is clear that he knows himself perfectly; otherwise he would not be perfect, since his being is his knowledge. But to know something perfectly is also to know its power; and the power of something cannot be known without also knowing its effects. Hence, since the divine power extends to things outside God, and since he is the first efficient cause of all beings, it is necessary that he knows them. [ST I, 14, a.5] God causes things through his intellect, since God's intellect is the same as his being. Therefore God's knowledge, united with his will, is the cause of things. [ST I, 14, a.8]

God loves all existing things. For everything that exists, insofar as it exists, is good; the very being of any thing is a good; and the same is true of every perfection that it has. It has been shown, however, that God's will is the cause of all things; and hence it follows that, insofar as anything exists, or is good, to that extent it is willed by God. Thus God wills some good to every existing being. Since love is nothing other than willing the good to someone, it is clear that God loves everything that exists. Not, indeed, in the same way that we love; for our will is not the cause of the goodness of things; on the contrary, the goodness of things (whether real or imagined) provokes our love; we wish to preserve the good that they have, and add to it; and we act accordingly. But God's love is what infuses and creates goodness in things. [ST I, 20, a.2]   [from the *Summa Theologiae*, Part I], [trans. R. Viladesau]

44. God as the "holy mystery"

According to **Karl Rahner,** (see above, #12, 33) we experience God first of all as the implicit goal of our transcendence, i.e. our spiritual dynamism toward knowledge and love. Rahner calls this non-conceptual experience a "pre-apprehension" of God as the "holy mystery."

THE TERM OF TRANSCENDENCE AS THE "HOLY MYSTERY"

We have already and by way of anticipation called the term of transcendence the *holy* mystery. The reason why we had to call it "mystery" consisted ultimately in the fact that we experience it as that which cannot be encompassed by a pre-apprehension which reaches beyond it, and hence it cannot be defined. But why do we characterize it as the "holy" mystery?

We have already emphasized in the first chapter that when we speak of transcendence we do not mean only and exclusively the transcendence which is the condition of possibility for categorical knowledge as such. We mean also and just as much the *transcendence of freedom, of willing,* and *of love.* This transcendence, which is constitutive of the subject as a free and personal subject of action within an unlimited realm of action, is just as important, and is basically just another aspect of the transcendence of a spiritual, and therefore knowing, and precisely for this reason free subject. Freedom is always the freedom of a subject who exists in interpersonal communication with other subjects. Therefore it is necessarily freedom vis-à-vis another subject of transcendence, and this transcendence is not primarily the condition of possibility for knowing *things,* but is the condition of possibility for a subject being present to himself and just as basically and originally being present to another *subject.* But for a subject who is present to himself to affirm freely vis-à-vis another subject means ultimately to love.

Hence when we reflect here upon transcendence as will and as freedom, we must also take into account the character of the term and source of transcendence as love. It is a term which possesses absolute freedom, and this term is at work in freedom and in love as that which is nameless and which is not at our disposal, for we are completely at its disposal. It is what opens up my own transcendence as freedom and as love. But the term of transcendence is always and originally the source of the mystery which offers itself. This term itself opens our transcendence; it is not established by us and by our own power as though we were absolute subjects. Hence if transcendence moves in freedom and in love towards a term which itself opens this transcendence, then we can say that that which is nameless and which is not at our disposal, and at whose complete disposal we exist, that this very thing is present in loving freedom, and this is what we mean when we say "holy mystery."

For what else would we call that which is nameless, that at whose disposal we exist and from which we are distanced in our finiteness, but which nevertheless we affirm in our transcendence through freedom and love, what else would we call this if not "holy"? And what could we call "holy" if not this, or to whom would the name "holy" belong more basically and more originally than to this infinite term of love, which love in the presence of the incomprehensible and the ineffable necessarily becomes worship.

In transcendence, therefore, dwells the holy, nameless and infinite, disposing but not being disposed, forbidding and distant. And this we call mystery, or somewhat more explicitly, the holy mystery, lest in focusing upon the knowledge element we overlook the transcendentality of freedom and love, and so that both elements remain present in their original and personal unity. The two words "holy mystery," which are understood as a unity, but between which nevertheless there is an intrinsic difference, express equally the transcendentality both of knowledge and of freedom and love.

Every experience of transcendence is a basic and original experience which is not derived from something prior, and it receives this character of being underived and irreducible from what is encountered and becomes manifest in it. The designation of this term of transcendence as the "holy mystery," therefore, does not employ concepts derived from elsewhere and applied extrinsically to this term. It derives them rather from this original "object," which is its own ground and the ground and horizon of the knowledge of it, and which discloses itself in and through transcendental experience itself.

If we have arrived in this way at the basic and original idea of mystery and of the holy, and if it is correct to designate the term of transcendence by this name, there can be no question, of course, of giving a *definition* of the essence of this holy mystery. Mystery is as indefinable as every other transcendental "concept." They do not admit of definition because what is expressed in them is known only in transcendental experience, and transcendental experience, as always and everywhere given antecedently, has nothing outside of itself by which it and its term could be defined.   [from *Foundations of Christian Faith*]

Chapter Five

The Message and Meaning of Jesus

A. The Judaic Background

45. *Understanding the written tradition*

Biblical criticism, the collection of critical methods and linguistic tools applied to scripture by theologians, seeks to uncover and clarify the full meaning of the written record of revelation. Biblical scholars use a variety of literary tools—form, source, and redaction criticism, among others—in studying and interpreting scripture. **Daniel Harrington** reviews the purpose and approaches of each of these methods of biblical criticism in a selection from his lucid "practical guide" to interpreting the Old Testament.

1. BASIC LITERARY CRITICISM

A. The Old Testament as Literature

A browser, who enters the religion section in a bookstore or library and pages through the various editions of the Bible, will probably come away confused by the experience. If the browser first picks up a translation of the Bible prepared under Jewish auspices or even a copy of the Hebrew Bible, there will be twenty-four books separated into three major divisions. The Torah or Law consists of the books of Genesis, Exodus, Leviticus, Numbers, and Deuteronomy. The Prophets contain Joshua, Judges, 1–2 Samuel, 1–2 Kings, Isaiah, Jeremiah, Ezekiel, and the Twelve Minor Prophets. The Writings include Psalms, Job, Proverbs, Ruth, Song of

Songs, Ecclesiastes, Lamentations, Esther, Daniel, Ezra-Nehemiah, and 1–2 Chronicles.

Bibles produced under Protestant sponsorship like the *Revised Standard Version* or the *New International Version* contain the same material as the Hebrew Bible, but it is divided into thirty-nine books and arranged in quite a different order. A Catholic Bible such as the *New American Bible* or the *Jerusalem Bible* will contain seven more books (Tobit, Judith, 1 Maccabees, 2 Maccabees, Wisdom, Sirach, and Baruch) and somewhat larger editions of Daniel and Esther. Since the additional books in the Catholic canon are interspersed among the historical, wisdom, and prophetic books of the Hebrew Bible, the result is a third order of biblical books.

The book that Christians traditionally call the Old Testament and Jews know as the Hebrew Bible or "Tanak" (from the initial letters of the Hebrew words for Law, Prophets, and Writings) is really a collection of books, something like an anthology or a portable library. Even the individual books within the collection have an anthological character. For example, the book of Exodus is made up of narratives, an ancient song (15:1–18), and various kinds of laws and cultic regulations. The book of Jeremiah blends prose narratives and poetic oracles, and Proverbs consists of blocks of wisdom sayings attributed to Solomon, the sages, Agur, and Lemuel. Within the covers of the Old Testament there is material as early as the twelfth century B.C. (especially hymns) and as late as the second century B.C. (Daniel) or the first century B.C. (Wisdom). Most of the books were composed in Palestine (though Wisdom probably came from Alexandria in Egypt), but they show influences from Egypt, Syria, Persia, Greece, and the other lands of the ancient Near East.

If our browser persists and begins to read parts of the Old Testament, he or she will find more surprises. Some parts of the Bible do not seem very "religious" in the conventional understanding of that term. The Song of Songs appears to be love poetry, and the Psalms are full of talk about vengeance against enemies. The historical books are largely concerned with victories and defeats in battle, and the prophets stand right in the middle of the political affairs of their people. The great ancestors of Israel like Jacob and David perform questionable or even reprehensible actions. The browser's understanding of religion may begin to undergo some necessary adjustments at this point.

What holds together this collection of many writings from over a thousand years of time and from various theological perspectives? It is the conviction that the Bible is the record of God's dealings with his chosen people. God relates to his people in story and song, in proverb and prophecy, in vision and law. God is involved in every aspect of his people's life—in its loves and hates, triumphs and defeats, history and imaginings. God remains faithful to his people in its rebellions, its exiles, and its sufferings. Since it tells the story of God's relationship with his people, the Old Testament promotes a historical and communal religious stance. Christian faith sees in Jesus of Nazareth the culmination of God's relationship to his people and the means by which those not born Jewish may become part of God's people. See my *God's People in Christ: New Testament Perspectives on the Church and Judaism* (Philadelphia: Fortress, 1980).

The documents that make up the Old Testament are pieces of literature, and our understanding and appreciation of them grows when we study them with the basic techniques of literary analysis. These techniques are not very complicated. They demand only that we look seriously at a text and ask ourselves some simple questions. In the effort to answer these questions we begin to penetrate beneath the surface and allow ourselves to be drawn into the dynamic of the text. The Old Testament is never abstract and seldom relies on theological theses or propositions to communicate its religious message. Because the Bible is the record of God's dealings with his people, it communicates in literary forms that touch all the aspects of human life—stories, laws, poems, proverbs, and so forth. The basic techniques of literary analysis are necessary for understanding the Old Testament message.

B. Literary Analysis

What are the basic concerns of literary analysis? What questions does one ask of a text in order to grasp it more surely and to let oneself be grasped by it? The first concern of literary analysis is the words and images of the text, the materials from which any piece of literature is constructed. Most of the Old Testament is written in ancient Hebrew. Aramaic[1] passages occur in a few places (Ezra 4:8–6:18; 7:12–26; Dan 2:4–7:28; Jer 10:11; and Gen 31:47). The additional material in the Roman Catholic canon is based on Greek texts, though some of those books were surely composed in Hebrew (e.g., Sirach). Hebrew and Aramaic are

---

1. Aramaic was a widely-used language in the Middle East, especially from about 700 B.C. onwards. It was an official language in the Persian empire and in later Old Testament times was the language spoken by at least a good portion of the Jews.

closely related Semitic languages, and even the Greek books of the Old Testament were strongly influenced by Semitic patterns of thought and expression. The words and images of the Old Testament reflect the life of a particular people in the ancient Near East. If we are to understand the record of God's dealings with this people, we need first of all to understand the words and images in which that record is expressed.

During the past hundred years or so, the task of analyzing the words and images has been greatly facilitated by the discovery of ancient texts from the Near East. Some of the texts were written in Hebrew, and many more of them are in related Semitic languages like Ugaritic, Akkadian, Aramaic, and now Eblaite. These firsthand witnesses to antiquity frequently shed a penetrating light on the meaning of words in the Old Testament, and sometimes they even make matters more complicated than scholars had previously imagined. Texts in non-Semitic languages like Sumerian, Hittite, and Egyptian can illuminate the meaning of foreign words in the Hebrew texts of the Bible and, most importantly, give valuable information about the customs and social realities that prevailed in the ancient Near East. The point is that words and images in the literature of the Old Testament must be read first and foremost on their own historical terms, and those terms are the languages and customs of a people that lived in the ancient Near East more than two thousand years ago.

The second concern in the literary analysis of the Old Testament is the characters and the movement of the text. Who says or does what to whom? What happens? How have things changed when the text is finished? In some texts there is very little movement. The poetry and proverbs of the Old Testament luxuriate in parallelisms in which the same point is made twice. For example, Psalm 32:1 pronounces blessed one "whose transgression is forgiven, whose sin is covered." In a largely oral culture where traditions were memorized and recited, this device of parallelism was necessary to make sure that the hearers understood the one point. The modern reader who assumes that two points are necessarily being made by the two statements or that there is some gradation between forgiving transgressions and covering sins, fails to take the text on its own terms. On the other hand, the stories of the book of Genesis or the accounts about King David's court show a great deal of movement. In analyzing them we need to focus on the various characters and their relations with one another: Who is the focus of attention or the main characters? How do others relate to them? In what situation were these characters at the beginning of the story, and where do they find themselves at the end?

A third and related concern of literary analysis is the form of the text. How the author has chosen to communicate is intimately related to what is communicated. Wisdom derived from long experience is best presented in a proverb. Direction for a people in crisis is properly cast in a prophetic oracle. Cultic regulations are customarily stated as directives, and laws specify the case and the punishment. The exploits of kings and warriors take the form of a story. The attentive reader, after trying to understand the words and images in the text and to follow the logical flow, will then stand back and ask: What kind of text is this? The twentieth century has it stock of literary forms—the novel, the editorial, the question-and-answer, the free-verse poem, and so on. The people that produced the Scriptures and their neighbors had their own favorite modes of literary communication. To ignore this fact is to guarantee that the Old Testament texts will be misunderstood.

The final concern of literary analysis is the message of the text. The present volume has been written as the introduction to a series of commentaries entitled the *Old Testament Message*. The use of the term "message" may mislead people into thinking that the ultimate goal of biblical study is the theological proposition (e.g., "God is faithful"). It may seem that the analysis of the text's language, movement, and literary form are useful only to isolate the abstract message expressed in general terms. Not so! If the Bible teaches us anything about God's dealings with his people, it is that this relationship touches all aspects of human existence. The "message" of a biblical text is so closely connected with the words and form in which it is expressed that the very medium of communication provides much of the message. Literary form and theological content are intimately related; the former is not simply the means to arrive at the latter.

With these cautions about the "message" in mind, the question of significance remains necessary and valid. The reflective reader wants to know what this text says about God and human existence, what implications it may have today for the life of individuals or communities, and what transfer value it can have. There are people who are satisfied to study the Old Testament simply as an important document for understanding ancient Near Eastern history and culture. They are content to defer the question of religious truth or have already come to a negative decision about it. But most readers of the Bible come to it as a source of religious insight. Although they often ask the question about the message of the text and its application far too early in the process of interpre-

tation, their basic instinct of asking religious questions of religious literature is sound.

2. FORM CRITICISM

A. Form Criticism in General

The term "form criticism" can seem quite mysterious to beginners in
biblical studies until they recognize how much a part of their everyday
experience this operation is. A daily newspaper contains a variety of
literary forms: news story, editorial, obituary, recipe, box-score, book
review, and so forth. These different items follow relatively fixed formal
patterns, and anyone with some experience and intelligence can immediately distinguish one from another. The very form in which the various
items are presented already communicates a good deal of information.

In biblical studies, form criticism concerns itself with the formal devices of communication in the traditions or sources used by the biblical
writers. It seeks to discover the units of tradition, to describe their formal
characteristics, to determine their intent, and to offer some clues to the
setting in which the form was used (e.g., worship, school). Form criticism has a literary dimension (the isolation and description of the modes
of communication) and a historical dimension (the determination of the
form's setting in the life of the community). The historical dimension is
not always a possibility for the form critic.

Were the units of tradition oral or written? In any given case that
question is not easy to answer, and it is wise always to reckon with both
possibilities. The claims of some Scandinavian scholars that practically
everything was in oral form until Israel's return from the Babylonian
exile are accepted by very few Old Testament specialists. The extreme
character of these claims, however, does bring out the point that the
milieu that produced the Bible was very much an oral culture. Writing
materials were crude and cumbersome by today's standards, and there
were no printing presses or copying machines.

An oral culture is a traditional culture, one in which compositions in
oral form can be handed on from generation to generation with great
accuracy. There are certainly oral elements in the biblical tradition. But it
seems just as likely that there are written elements also. Inscriptions
from pre-exilic times have been found in Palestine, and there is no reason to believe that writing and reading were very unusual. Oral traditions and written traditions most likely existed side by side. For example,

those who recited the Psalms probably did so from memory, but this does not exclude the existence of a written text also.

B. Narrative Forms

The Old Testament is full of good stories—good not only in their power for religious inspiration but also in the artistic skill with which they are told. There are stories about the beginning of the world and the human race, the great ancestors of Israel, the escape from slavery in Egypt, the conquest of the land of Canaan, the exploits of judges and kings, the destruction of Jerusalem, the restoration of the temple, and the triumphs of Daniel and Esther in the courts of foreign kings. Rather than talking about the forms of all these stories, I prefer to focus on one kind of narrative—the call—in the hope of illustrating the values and limitations of form criticism. This discussion will prepare for more general remarks on legal, poetic, wisdom, and prophetic forms of speech.

When the Midianites were causing great trouble for the people of Israel after the entrance into the land of Canaan, the task of defending and rescuing the people fell to the judge named Gideon. The story of Gideon's call to deliver Israel is told to Judges 6:11–18:

> [11]Now the angel of the Lord came and sat under the oak at Ophrah, which belonged to Joash the Abiezrite, as his son Gideon was beating out wheat in the wine press, to hide it from the Midianites. [12]And the angel of the Lord appeared to him and said to him, "The Lord is with you, you mighty man of valor." [13]And Gideon said to him, "Pray, sir, if the Lord is with us, why then has all this befallen us? And where are all his wonderful deeds which our fathers recounted to us, saying, 'Did not the Lord bring us up from Egypt?' But now the Lord has cast us off, and given us into the hand of Midian." [14]And the Lord turned to him and said, "Go in this might of yours and deliver Israel from the hand of Midian; do not I send you?" [15]And he said to him, "Pray, Lord, how can I deliver Israel? Behold, my clan is the weakest in Manasseh, and I am the least in my family." [16]And the Lord said to him, "But I will be with you, and you shall smite the Midianites as one man." [17]And he said to him, "If now I have found favor with thee, then show me a sign that it is thou who speakest with me. [18]Do not depart from here, I pray thee, until I come to thee, and bring out my present, and set it before thee." And he said, "I will stay till you return."

The story has a clear progression of action. The messenger of the Lord appears to Gideon and tells him by way of greeting that the Lord is with him (vv. 11–12). After an initial objection from Gideon (v. 13), the Lord gives Gideon a commission to deliver Israel from the hand of Midian (v. 14). When Gideon objects that he is from a weak clan and that he is the least in his family (v. 15), the Lord reassures him that he will be with him in battle (v. 16) and accedes to Gideon's request for a sign (v. 17–18). The outline of the story begins with the divine or angelic encounter with the person to be called and consists of (a) the greeting, (b) the commission, (c) the objection, (d) the divine reassurance, and (e) the sign.

Discerning the outline of the call of Gideon in Judges 6:11–18 would be simply the literary-critical task of charting the progress of the story, if the same pattern did not occur elsewhere in the Bible. But the call pattern is repeated in connection with Moses in Exod 3:1–12 and Jeremiah in Jer 1:4–10. In the book of Exodus the angel of the Lord appears to Moses on Horeb, the mountain of God, and calls to him from the burning bush (3:1–5). The angel is suddenly changed into the Lord, who greets Moses by identifying himself with the God of Abraham, Isaac, and Jacob (3:6). After the encounter and the greetings comes the commission that Moses is to go to Pharaoh and bring forth the children of Israel from Egypt (3:7–9). Moses objects: "Who am I . . . (v. 10)?" But God reassures him that "I will be with you" (v. 11) and promises as a sign that Moses and the people will serve God on this same mountain (v. 12). The other elements in the call pattern have been placed before us: commission, objection, reassurance, and sign.

The call pattern occurs also in the story of Jeremiah as it is told in Jer 1:4–10. The encounter and greeting are somewhat truncated, but the story leaves no doubt that Jeremiah engages in conversation with God. He is appointed to be a prophet to the nations (v. 5), but he objects that he does not know how to speak because he is only a youth (v. 6). The Lord breaks down his objections and reassures Jeremiah that "I am with you to deliver you" (v. 8). As a sign, the Lord touches Jeremiah's mouth and interprets the sign by saying that he has put his words in the prophet's mouth (v. 9). The story of Jeremiah's call shows the same pattern as the calls of Gideon and Moses: encounter, greeting, commission, objection, reassurance, and sign.

What are we to make of the fact that the calls of Israel's liberator and lawgiver, a famous judge, and a great prophet are told in very much the same way? There are no clear indications that Gideon and Jeremiah modelled the stories of their calls on the call of Moses, and the contents of the three stories do not force one to suppose that two authors were copying from a third author. Rather, it seems that this is the way in which the calls of famous religious characters were told in ancient Israel and handed on from generation to generation. It is appropriate to speak of a call or commissioning form that contains the six elements present in the stories of Moses, Gideon, and Jeremiah.

Analysis of the three call-stories represents the first step in form criticism—the isolation of the literary pattern. The second step—determining the setting in life—is not so easy. The call pattern occurs in connection with characters hundreds of years apart, who exercised very different functions under very different social and political conditions. Relating the call narrative to the temple or the prophetic guild or to local shrines lacks solid foundation. Explaining the stories as based on the everyday experience of a superior's commissioning of a servant or subject helps us to understand the dynamics of the dialogue, but touches only a part of the account.

The more satisfactory explanation is that this call pattern corresponds to the nature of religious experience in ancient Israel. As people in ancient Israel tried to articulate what remains ultimately beyond human speech, they struck upon this call or commissioning form as a good way of expressing the dynamics involved in encounter with God. The lordship of God, his entrance into our lives for specific purposes, the acknowledgement of human weaknesses and limitations, and the assurance that God is with us—all these dimensions of the human encounter with God are expressed in these call stories. In this instance the form critic is hard put to come up with a specific setting in life, and it is preferable to look to everyday experience and the dynamics of religious experience in ancient Israel to get behind the written text.

C. Legal Forms

The material in the legal sections of the Old Testament is customarily divided into two major types: apodictic and casuistic. An apodictic law is an absolute statement. No circumstances and no motives are supplied. The classic examples of apodictic law are found in the Ten Commandments: "You shall not kill. You shall not commit adultery. You shall not steal . . ." (Exod 20:13–17; Deut 5:17–21). Another form of apodictic law is represented by passages like Exod 21:15: "Whoever strikes his father or his mother shall be put to death." A third formula in which apodictic law is expressed is represented by Deut 27:16: "Cursed be he who dishonors his father or his mother." The claim is sometimes made that apodictic law is unique to Israel's religious tradition and that this kind of ruling reflects faith in the absolute authority of Yahweh. But instances of apodictic law are found in ancient Near Eastern documents, though not in such numbers as in the Old Testament.

The more widespread legal form is casuistic law. The term "casuistic" refers to the cases or legal precedents on which the laws are based, not to the lawmaker's interest in fine distinctions. Casuistic law has a two-part structure: *if/whenever* the circumstances are such and such, *then* the punishment shall be so and so. This form of law has countless parallels in antiquity and is still used today. Indeed it reflects the essence of the law in that it deals with specific cases and relates the punishment to the case.

An example of casuistic law is Exod 21:18–19: "When men quarrel and one strikes the other with a stone or with his fist and the man does not die but keeps to his bed, if the man rises again and walks abroad with his staff, then he that struck him shall be clear; only he shall pay for the loss of time, and shall have him thoroughly healed." The case involves a fight between two men in which one of them is injured. If the injured man recovers, the aggressor is liable only for the injured party's loss of pay and medical expenses. The case has been stated, and the punishment is specified. No one claims that casuistic law is unique to Israel. Its prominence in the Old Testament shows how much the Jewish legal system shares with the legal systems of its neighbors.

D. Psalms

In the study of the Psalms form criticism has been particularly effective in distinguishing the various literary types and in determining their settings in the life of the community. The result has been to relate the Psalms closely to the worship services carried on in the temple at Jerusalem.

The largest class of Psalms is the *individual lament* in which the speaker in a difficult situation complains about his enemies. The psalms belonging to this category are Psalms 3; 5; 6; 7; 13; 17; 22; 25; 26; 27:7–14; 28; 31; 35; 38; 39; 42; 43; 51; 53; 55; 56; 57; 61; 63; 64; 69; 70; 71; 86; 88; 102; 109; 120; 130; 140; 141; 142; 143. The elements present in this kind of psalm are the address to God, the complaint describing the situation, the request for help, the reasons why God should intervene, the expression of confidence in God's ability to help, the affirmation of innocence or confession of sin, and the conclusion.

The so-called psalms of confidence (Psalms 4; 11; 16; 23; 27:1–6; 63; 131) are sometimes associated with the expression of confidence in God's ability to help that occurs in the individual laments. The liturgical setting of these psalms is not entirely obvious, but the *communal laments* (Psalms 44; 58; 74; 79; 80; 83; 106; 125) seem to have been used on fast days and in times when there was a threat of natural or military catastrophe. The components of the communal lament are the lament designed to move God to be compassionate, the prayer to avert the calamity, and the certainty that the prayer will be heard.

A third major class of psalms is the *individual thanksgiving* (Psalms 18; 30; 32; 40:2–12; 41; 66; 92; 116; 118; 138) consisting of the introductory expression of praise or thanks, the description of the distress and rescue from it, confession of God as redeemer, proclamation of the thanksgiving sacrifice, and the conclusion. This kind of psalm probably accompanied the offering of thanksgiving sacrifices in the temple.

The *hymns* (Psalms 8; 19; 29; 33; 46; 48; 65; 67; 68; 76; 84; 96; 98; 100; 103; 104; 105; 111; 113; 114; 117; 122; 135; 136; 145; 146; 147; 148; 149; 150) were apparently used at the temple on the great holy days. They contain a call to praise or an affirmation of praise, the body of the hymn in which God's attributes and actions are praised, and the conclusion. A subcategory of the hymn is the enthronement song (Psalms 47; 93; 96:10–13; 97; 99) in which the enthronement of God as king is celebrated. The fifth class of psalms is the *royal psalm* (Psalms 2; 18; 20; 21; 45; 72; 101; 110; 132; 144:1–11) in which the king is a major figure. Besides the five major forms there are wisdom songs, victory songs, communal thanksgivings, etc.

Not every psalm assigned to the five major classes contains all the elements, but in most cases there are enough common elements to know that we are dealing with five distinct ways of expressing prayer to God. The components provide a broad outline in which the content of the particular psalm is expressed, but the discovery of the outline should not distract from what is contained within it. Nevertheless, the recognition that most of the material in the book of Psalms conforms to a limited number of literary patterns is an important achievement toward understanding the content. Furthermore, the recognition that these psalms by and large were used in worship services at the Jerusalem temple supplies more help and direction in efforts at using them today in worship.

E. Wisdom Forms

The basic form for expressing wisdom teachings in the Old Testament is the proverb—a brief statement expressing in general terms the results of long human experience. In keeping with the conventions of ancient Near Eastern poetry, many proverbs consist of two parallel phrases. When the phrases say pretty much the same thing, it is synonymous parallelism: "He who corrects a scoffer gets himself abuse, and he who reproves a wicked man incurs injury" (Prov 9:7). When opposite things are said, it is antithetical parallelism: "Do not reprove a scoffer, or he will hate you; reprove a wise man, and he will love you" (Prov 9:8). Sometimes a reason is given as in Prov 26:4: "Answer not a fool according to his folly, lest you be like him yourself." There are only a few appeals to the nature of God or to Israel's history. The primary concern seems to be getting along successfully in everyday life, with enlightened self-interest as the major motivation.

Wisdom teachings are frequently expressed in comparisons taken over from everyday life: "Like a madman who throws firebrands, arrows, and death, is the man who deceives his neighbor and says, 'I am only joking!' " (Prov 26:18–19). The list is another common form: "Three things are never satisfied; four never say 'Enough': Sheol, the barren womb, the earth ever thirsty for water, and the fire which never says, 'Enough' " (Prov 30:15–16). Besides these more obvious forms, wisdom teachings can be expressed in riddles (see Judges 14:14), in psalms (Psalms 1; 37; 49; 73; 112; 127; 128), and in narratives (Prov 4:1–9; 7:6–23).

The settings in life offered for wisdom teaching cover a wide spread: the family or clan, the schools, and the royal court. Given the international character of most of the wisdom material and the breadth of its concerns, it is difficult to point to a single setting as primary. The wisdom sayings are expressed in a way that made memorization easy, and clearly—as we shall later discuss under the rubric of "source criticism" —they circulated in small units before being collected into whole books like Proverbs, Ecclesiastes, and Sirach.

F. Prophetic Forms

The Old Testament prophets used the wide range of rhetorical devices found in the Wisdom books—songs, questions, similitudes, narratives, etc. But the most distinctive and best-known form of prophetic speech is the prophetic oracle spoken in the name of the Lord: "Thus says the Lord . . ." This form captures the prophet's identity as one who speaks on God's behalf to the people and makes known his will. Most prophetic oracles are short, poetic pieces, full of passion, looking toward the future, and somewhat mysterious. The prophetic books gather together these brief units into anthologies bearing the name of a single prophet. But the prophets did not set out to write books. Rather, their oracles were delivered orally and were memorized by disciples and admirers who eventually produced written collections. This process of transmission was surely accompanied by adaptation and interpretation on the part of the disciples and admirers.

Among the most important forms of prophetic speech are the threat and the reproach, and these two forms frequently appear together as in Amos 2:6–8:

> [6]Thus says the Lord:
> "For three transgressions of Israel,
> and for four, I will not revoke the punishment."

The oracle is introduced as the word of the Lord and contains a threat that God will indeed punish the people of the northern kingdom for their sins. Then Israel is reproached:

> because they sell the righteous for silver, and the needy for a pair of shoes—[7]they that trample the head of the poor into the dust of the earth, and turn aside the way of the afflicted; a man and his father go in to the same maiden, so that my holy name is profaned; [8]they lay themselves down beside every altar upon garments taken in pledge; and in the house of their God they drink the wine of those who have been fined.

The reproach contains the reasons why the threat will be brought to fulfillment. The order may be reversed so that the reproach precedes the threat as in Amos 3:10–11:

> [10]"They do not know how to do right," says the Lord, "those who store up violence and robbery in their strongholds." [11]Therefore thus says the Lord God: "An adversary shall surround the land, and bring down your defenses from you, and your strongholds shall be plundered."

Instead of a threat there may be a promise as in Amos 9:11–12:

> [11]"In that day I will raise up the booth of David that is fallen and repair its breaches, and raise up its ruins, and rebuild it as in the days of old; [12]that they may possess the remnant of Edom and all the nations who are called by my name," says the Lord who does this.

The few examples of prophetic speech from the book of Amos illustrate the most important formal features. The units are short and fairly simple. Parallel phrases are used to make the same points in slightly different ways. The threats and the promises will be carried out in the future. The speech is passionate and poetic, and it is not entirely clear when or how these things are to come to pass.

Attention to the reproach, the threat, and the promise as the most distinctive forms of prophetic speech should not obscure the fact that the prophets used many other forms of communication. These other forms included the dispute in which God lays out his case against his people

(Isa 40:12–13), the lament in which the prophet bewails the destruction and suffering (Isa 1:4–9; 5:8–25), the exhortation in which the prophet urges conversion and better conduct (Amos 5:4–6), and symbolic actions in which the prophet acts out the prophecy (Isa 20).

Summary. Form criticism considers the range of devices used to communicate and seeks to determine the settings in which the literary forms were used in ancient Israel before they became part of the biblical books. In addition to narrative forms (the call), there are legal (apodictic and casuistic), poetic (the various classes of psalms), wisdom (proverb), and prophetic (threat, reproach, promise) forms of speech. The isolation of the individual literary forms is an important step in understanding the content of the Old Testament. It is not always possible to connect the literary forms with specific settings in Israel's life.

3. SOURCE CRITICISM AND REDACTION CRITICISM

A. Their Relationship

Just as the recognition of literary forms is part of everyday experience, so are the use of sources and the task of editing or redacting sources into final form. Suppose that you have been appointed to be recording secretary of a committee or social organization. The group wishes to make a proposal to someone in authority. A meeting of your organization has been called, and you have the responsibility to make a report on the issue to those in authority. Obviously you are not going to write the report on your own and entirely out of your own head. Otherwise, you need not bother to go to the meeting. If you want to write a good report, you will gather whatever material exists in writing and take notes on what is said at the meeting. If the written and oral material represents a clear and acceptable position, your task of editing will be easy. If not, then your own intelligence and creativity will have to go to work. Your contribution is as an editor or redactor.

The present forms of nearly all the books of the Old Testament reflect a complicated combination of tradition and redaction. The biblical writers lived in a traditional society, with a great respect for the past. Originality of authorship was not an important value, and the use of existing sources was a very common procedure.

Source criticism tries to detect where sources were used in the book. Redaction criticism pays attention to how the sources were used and what the adaptation of the sources tells us about the editor's theological interests. They are really two aspects of one operation. Once the source has been isolated on external grounds (we are told that a source has been used) or internal grounds (the vocabulary and literary style mark the passage off from surrounding material), then it is often possible to see what the biblical writer has done with it (redaction criticism).

B. Source Criticism

Source criticism aims to show the extent to which the present forms of our biblical books reflect the reliance on or incorporation of already existing written or fixed oral material. At some points the biblical writers tell us that they used written sources. In Num 21:14–15 there is a quotation from the "Book of the Wars of the Lord," and in Josh 10:13 and 2 Sam 1:18 there are citations from the "Book of Jashar." Apart from these references, nothing is known of the now-lost books. In 1 Kings there are mentions of the "Book of the Acts of Solomon" (11:41), the "Book of the Chronicles of the Kings of Israel" (14:19), and the "Book of the Chronicles of the Kings of Judah" (14:29). 2 Chr 25:26 refers to the "Book of the Kings of Judah and Israel," probably identical with the books of Samuel and Kings in the canon of Scripture. In the book of Nehemiah the autobiographical memoirs of the central character are introduced with the phrase "the Words of Nehemiah the son of Hacaliah" (1:1).

The few stray references to written sources in the Old Testament are far from exhausting the subject of the use of existing material by the biblical writers. Our analysis of the legal forms into apodictic and casuistic established the existence of individual units at the disposal of ancient authors. When the legal material is treated from the perspective of source criticism, the question arises as to whether the biblical writer simply put together these individual legal rulings or had access to already formed blocks of laws.

When there is no explicit notice that a source is used, how can one detect the presence of an already existing source in a book of the Old Testament? There are several indicators: a vocabulary that differs greatly from everything else in the book, a sudden shift in literary style or tone, an unexpected interruption of the context and an awkward resumption of it a little later, the appearance of the same story twice in slightly different forms (a doublet), and theological or ideological contradictions within the same book.

It is possible to point to several passages in the Pentateuch that appear to incorporate large sections of legal source material. For example, in the so-called Holiness Code of Leviticus 17–26 there are two blocks of regulations about marriage and sexual relationships (18:6–30 and 20:10–26). The content of these laws is basically the same, and apparently the two sections represent collections taken over almost verbatim by the editor of the Holiness Code. In the Book of the Covenant (Exod 20:22–23:33) the "ordinances" beginning in Exod 21:1 and ending in 22:17 form a separate unit and probably existed as such prior to their uses in the larger portion. The block of case laws in Deuteronomy 21–25 probably also existed before the book as a whole was formed. These examples indicate that some written sources were used in the legal books of the Old Testament.

That the narrative books of the Old Testament utilized existing sources is easy to see. The vocabulary, literary style, and content of 2 Sam 9–20 and 1 Kings 1–2 suggest that an early account of events connected with King David's court has been incorporated into the larger story of the monarchy. The colorful exploits of the prophets Elijah and Elisha in 1 Kings 17–2 Kings 10 bear the mark of already existing material. For the Chronicler, the books of Samuel and Kings were written sources to be shaped in accordance with the realities and hopes of Jewish life in Jerusalem around 400 B.C. The book of Ezra cites official Aramaic documents in chaps. 4–7, and the book of Nehemiah incorporates the memoirs of Nehemiah. Surely the many lists in Ezra-Nehemiah also reflect the reliance upon written sources.

The narrative parts of the Pentateuch involve some special source-critical problems. The first five books of the Old Testament were most likely put in final form around 550 B.C. during the period of the Babylonian exile. This so-called Priestly edition incorporated older sources and provided a framework that expressed the interests and concerns of the priests. The material added to the older sources in this edition is designated by the symbol P for "Priestly." The book of Deuteronomy, which is the fifth book of the Pentateuch, was probably designed as an introduction to the history of the conquest and the monarchy. It has been given the sign D. The Priestly editors apparently had access to at least two extensive written sources. The earlier source used the name "Yahweh" for God, and so it won the designation J for "Jahwist." This source took shape around 950 B.C., perhaps at the court of King Solomon. The later source called God "Elohim" (the Hebrew word for "gods") and thus is designated as E for "Elohist." The Elohist source was formed around 900 B.C., probably in the court of the king of the northern branch of the divided monarchy. Sometime after the fall of the northern kingdom in 722 B.C. the Yahwist source and the Elohist source were combined into a single narrative. The Priestly editors had access to the combined narrative as a source.

According to the documentary hypothesis outlined in the preceding paragraph, the Pentateuch consists of four major sources: Yahwist (J), Elohist (E), Priestly (P), and Deuteronomist (D). The time-span from the earliest of the four documents (J) to the final form incorporating the Priestly material (P) is about four-hundred years.

The neatness of this documentary hypothesis can mask the fact that the composition of the Pentateuch was probably even more complicated. Surely the Yahwist and the Elohist writers used sources going well back into the second millennium. Efforts at isolating such sources and placing them under a single designation have not won universal approval, but the persistence of such attempts bears witness to the recognition that not everything is explained by the classic documentary hypothesis.

Furthermore, there have been serious attempts at distinguishing strata or levels within the individual sources (J^1, J^2, E^1, E^2, etc.). The main outlines of the documentary hypothesis for the composition of the Pentateuch are fairly well established, but these outlines represent only the general framework in which a much more complex process of tradition is to be located.

The other books of the Old Testament provide even clearer indications that they incorporate blocks of already formed material. The collection of hymns that is called the book of Psalms contains several groups of songs: the songs of ascents or pilgrimage songs (Psalms 120–134), the psalms attributed to Korah (Psalms 42; 44–49; 84–85; 87–88) and Asaph (Psalms 50; 73–83), and the many psalms of David. The present Psalter emerges as a collection of several existing collections.

A similar situation is supposed by the book of Proverbs, where the various collections of sayings are marked off by headings: the proverbs of Solomon (1:1), the proverbs of Solomon (10:1), the words of the wise (22:17), the sayings of the wise (24:23), the proverbs of Solomon which the men of Hezekiah king of Judah copied (25:1), the words of Agur son of Jakeh of Massa (30:1), and the words of Lemuel, king of Massa, which his mother taught him (31:1).

Likewise, the books of the prophets feature collections of oracles spoken in God's name or about God, autobiographical reminiscences about the prophet, and narratives about him as told by disciples. Almost every book in the Old Testament presupposes the use of written sources. [from *Interpreting the Old Testament*]

46. *The Holy in Jewish myth and ritual*

For **Jacob Neusner,** one of the foremost contemporary scholars of
Jewish thought, the "Holy" is revealed most clearly to Jews in Hebrew myth, rather than in philosophical or theological writings.
These myths, acted out in ritual ("the most widely present and
meaningful" elements of Judaism), reveal the true nature of Jewish
belief—how Jews understand and experience God. Neusner here
examines two Jewish rituals (the marriage ceremony and Passover)
in order to uncover the "mythic structure" that lies at the heart of
Judaism. How is the author using the word "myth" in this selection?
According to Neusner, how are myth and ritual related in Judaism?

In a history of nearly forty centuries, the Jews have produced rich and
complex religious phenomena. Indeed, Judaic religious and historical
data, like those of other religions, may seem at the outset to defy adequate description. The varieties of historical setting, ritual, intellectual
and religious expression, literary and theological literature—these can
scarcely be satisfactorily apprehended in the modest framework of a
lifetime of study. In working toward a definition of any religion, one
must confront the same formidable complexities.

Our operative criteria of selection ought to be, What phenomena are
most widely present and meaningful? What, further, is important as a
representation of the reality both viewed and shaped by "Judaism"? The
answers surely cannot be found only in philosophical, legal, mystical, or
theological literature produced by and for a religious elite. We cannot
suppose sophisticated conceptions of extraordinary men were fully
grasped by common folk. Theological writings, while important, testify
to the conceptions of reality held by only a tiny minority. The legal ideals
and values of Judaism were first shaped by the rabbis, a class of religious
virtuosi, then imposed upon the life of ordinary people. Excluding
learned theological and legal writings, the religious materials best conforming to our criteria are liturgical. The myths conveyed by prayer and
associated rituals were universal, everywhere present and meaningful in
the history of Judaism. Of greatest importance, they provide the clearest
picture of how Jews in archaic times envisioned the meaning of life and
of themselves.

Before proceeding, we had best clarify the meaning of "mythic structure." By myth, historians of religion do *not* mean, "something which is

not true." They mean, in Streng's words, "that the essential structure of reality manifests itself in particular moments that are remembered and repeated from generation to generation." These moments are preserved in myths. This meaning is wholly congruent to the Judaic data we shall now consider. If, in general, myth has the power to transform life because "it reveals the truth of life," as Streng says, then what is the nature of Judaic myth?

If a myth is present, it must be everywhere present, somehow hidden in every ceremony and rite, every liturgy, every sacred gesture and taboo. We must be able to locate it in commonplace, not merely extraordinary, events of piety. Liturgy provides the clearest and, at the same time, the most reliable evidence of the structure of Judaic myth. . . .

. . . For the Jew the most intimate occasion is the marriage ceremony. Here a new family begins. Individual lover and beloved celebrate the uniqueness, the privacy of their love. One should, therefore, expect the nuptial prayer to speak of him and her, natural man and natural woman. Yet the blessings that are said over the cup of wine of sanctification are as follows:

> Praised are You, O Lord our God, King of the universe, Creator of the fruit of the vine.
> Praised are You, O Lord our God, King of the universe, who created all things for Your glory.
> Praised are You, O Lord our God, King of the universe, Creator of man.
> Praised are You, O Lord our God, King of the universe, who created man and woman in his image, fashioning woman from man as his mate, that together they might perpetuate life. Praised are You, O Lord, Creator of man.
> May Zion rejoice as her children are restored to her in joy. Praised are You, O Lord, who causes Zion to rejoice at her children's return.
> Grant perfect joy to these loving companions, as You did to the first man and woman in the Garden of Eden. Praised are You, O Lord, who grants the joy of bride and groom.
> Praised are You, O Lord, our God, King of the universe, who created joy and gladness, bride and groom, mirth, song, delight and rejoicing, love and harmony, peace and companionship. O Lord our God, may there ever be heard in the cities of Judah and in the streets of Jerusalem voices of joy and gladness, voices of bride and groom, the jubilant voices of those joined in marriage under the bridal canopy, the voices of young people feasting and singing. Praised are You, O Lord, who causes the groom to rejoice with his bride.

These seven blessings say nothing of private people and of their anonymously falling in love. Nor do they speak of the community of Israel, as one might expect on a public occasion. In them are no hidden sermons, "to be loyal to the community and faithful in raising up new generations in it." Lover and beloved rather are transformed from natural to mythical figures. The blessings speak of archetypical Israel, represented here and now by the bride and groom.

Israel's history begins with creation, first, the creation of the vine, creature present in the place of the natural world. Creation is for God's glory. All things speak to nature, to the physical as much as the spiritual, for all things were made by God, and the Hebrew ends, "who formed the *Adam.*" All things glorify God; above all creation is man. The theme of ancient paradise is introduced by the simple choice of the word "Adam," so heavy with meaning. The myth of man's creation is rehearsed: man and woman are in God's image, together complete and whole, creators of life, "like God." Woman was fashioned from man, together with him to perpetuate life. And again, "blessed is the creator of man." We have moved, therefore, from the natural world to the archetypical realm of paradise. Before us we see not merely a man and a woman, but Adam and Eve.

But this Adam and this Eve also are Israel, children of Zion the mother, as expressed in the fifth blessing. Zion lies in ruins, her children scattered:

> If I forget you, O Jerusalem, may my right hand forget its skill . . . if I do not place Jerusalem above my greatest joy.

Adam and Eve cannot celebrate together without thought to the condition of the mother, Jerusalem. The children will one day come home. The mood is hopeful, yet sad as it was meant to be, for archaic Israel mourns as it rejoices, and rejoices as it mourns. Quickly, then, back to the happy occasion, for we do not let mourning lead to melancholy: "Grant perfect joy to the loving companions," for they are creators of a new line in mankind, the new Adam, the new Eve, and their home—may it be the garden of Eden. And if joy is there, then "praised are you for the joy of bride and groom."

The concluding blessing returns to the theme of Jerusalem. This time it evokes the tragic hour of Jerusalem's first destruction. When everyone had given up hope, supposing with the end of Jerusalem had come the end of time, only Jeremiah counseled renewed hope. With the enemy at the gate, he sang of coming gladness:

> Thus says the Lord:
> In this place of which you say, "It is a waste, without man or beast," in the

cities of Judah and the streets of Jerusalem that are desolate, without man or inhabitant or beast,

There shall be heard again the voice of mirth and the voice of gladness, the voice of the bridegroom and the voice of the bride, the voice of those who sing as they bring thank-offerings to the house of the Lord . . .

For I shall restore the fortunes of the land as first, says the Lord.
—*Jeremiah 33:10–11*

The closing blessing is not merely a literary artifice or a learned allusion to the ancient prophet. It is rather the exultant, jubilant climax of this acted-out myth: Just as here and now there stand before us Adam and Eve, so here and now in this wedding, the olden sorrow having been rehearsed, we listen to the voice of gladness that is coming. The joy of this new creation prefigures the joy of the Messiah's coming, hope for which is very present in this hour. And when he comes, the joy then will echo the joy of bride and groom before us. Zion the bride, Israel the groom, united now as they will be reunited by the compassionate God— these stand under the marriage canopy.

In classical Judaism, who is Jewish man? He is an ordinary, natural man who lives within a mythic structure, who thereby holds a view of history centered upon Israel from the creation of the world to its final redemption. Political defeats of this world are by myth transformed into eternal sorrow. The natural events of human life, here the marriage of ordinary folk, are by myth heightened into a reenactment of Israel's life as a people. In marriage, individuals stand in the place of mythic figures, yet remain, after all, a boy and a girl. What gives their love its true meaning is the myth of creation, destruction, and redemption, here and now embodied in that love. But in the end, the couple goes to bed: the sacred and secular are in most profane, physical love united.

The wedding of symbol and reality, the fusion and confusion of the two—these mark the classical Judaic experience, shaped by myths of creation, Adam and Eve, the Garden of Eden, the equally mythic memory of the this-worldly destruction of an old, unexceptional temple. Ordinary events, such as a political and military defeat or success, are changed into theological categories such as divine punishment and heavenly compassion. If religion is a "means of ultimate transformation," rendering the commonplace into the paradigmatic, changing the here and now into a moment of eternity and of eternal return, then the marriage liturgy serves to exemplify what is *religious* in Judaic existence.

. . . At the festival of Passover, in the spring, Jewish families gather around their tables for a holy meal. There they retell the story of the Exodus from Egypt in times long past. With unleavened bread and sanctified wine, they celebrate the liberation of slaves from Pharaoh's bondage. How do they see themselves?

> *We* were the slaves of Pharaoh in Egypt; and the Lord our God brought us forth from there with a mighty hand and an outstretched arm. And if the Holy One, blessed be He, had not brought our fathers forth from Egypt, then surely we, and our children, and our children's children, would be enslaved to Pharaoh in Egypt. And so, even if all of us were full of wisdom and understanding, well along in years and deeply versed in the tradition, we should still be bidden to repeat once more the story of the exodus from Egypt; and he who delights to dwell on the liberation is a man to be praised.

Through the natural eye, one sees ordinary folk, not much different from their neighbors in dress, language, or aspirations. The words they speak do not describe reality and are not meant to. When Jewish people say of themselves, "We were the slaves of Pharaoh in Egypt," they know they never felt the lash; but through the eye of faith that is just what they have done. It is *their* liberation, not merely that of long-dead forebears, they now celebrate.

To be a Jew means to be a slave who has been liberated by God. To be Israel means to give eternal thanks for God's deliverance. And that deliverance is not at a single moment in historical time. It comes in every generation, is always celebrated. Here again, events of natural, ordinary life are transformed through myth into paradigmatic, eternal, and ever-recurrent sacred moments. Jews think of themselves as having gone forth from Egypt, and Scripture so instructs them. God did not redeem the dead generation of the Exodus alone, but the living too—especially the living. Thus the family states:

> Again and again, in double and redoubled measure, are we beholden to God the All-Present: that He freed us from the Egyptians and wrought His judgment on them; that He sentenced all their idols and slaughtered all their first-born; that He gave their treasure to us and split the Red Sea for us; that He led us through it dry-shod and drowned the tyrants in it; that He helped us through the desert and fed us with the manna; that He gave the Sabbath to us and brought us to Mount Sinai; that He gave the Torah to us and brought us to our homeland there to build the Temple for us, for atonement of our sins.
>
> This is the promise which has stood by our forefathers and stands by us. For neither once, nor twice, nor three times was our destruction planned; in every generation they rise against us, and in every generation God delivers us from their hands into freedom, out of anguish into joy, out of mourning into festivity, out of darkness into light, out of bondage into redemption.
>
> For ever after, in every generation, *every man must think of himself as*

having gone forth from Egypt [italics mine]. For we read in the Torah: "In that day thou shalt teach thy son, saying: All this is because of what God did for me when I went forth from Egypt." It was not only our forefathers that the Holy One, blessed be He, redeemed; us, too, the living, He redeemed together with them, as we learn from the verse in the Torah: "And He brought us out from thence, so that He might bring us home, and give us the land which he pledged to our forefathers."

Israel was born in historical time. Historians, biblical scholars, archaeologists have much to say about that event. But to the classical Jew, their findings, while interesting, have little bearing on the meaning of reality. The redemptive promise that stood by the forefathers and *stands by us* is not a mundane historical event, but a mythic interpretation of historical, natural events. Oppression, homelessness, extermination, like salvation, homecoming, renaissance—these are this-worldly and profane, supplying headlines for newspapers. The myth that a man must think of himself as having gone forth from Egypt (or, as we shall see, from Auschwitz) and as being redeemed by God renders ordinary experience into a moment of celebration. If "we, too, the living, have been redeemed," then the observer no longer witnesses only historical men in historical time, but an eternal return to sacred time.

The "going forth" of Passover is one sort of exodus. Another comes morning and night when Jews complete their service of worship. Every synagogue service concludes with a prayer prior to going forth, called *Alenu*, from its first word in Hebrew. Like the Exodus, the moment of the congregation's departure becomes a celebration of Israel's God, a self-conscious, articulated rehearsal of Israel's peoplehood. But now it is the end, rather than the beginning, of time that is important. When Jews go forth, they look forward:

> Let us praise Him, Lord over all the world;
> Let us acclaim Him, Author of all creation.
> He made our lot unlike that of other peoples;
> He assigned to us a unique destiny.
> We bend the knee, worship, and acknowledge
> The King of kings, the Holy One, praised is He.
> He unrolled the heavens and established the earth;
> His throne of glory is in the heavens above;
> His majestic Presence is in the loftiest heights.
> He and no other is God and faithful King,
> Even as we are told in His Torah:
> Remember, now and always, that the Lord is God;
> Remember, no other is Lord of heaven and earth.
> We, therefore, hope in You, O Lord our God,

That we shall soon see the triumph of Your might,
That idolatry shall be removed from the earth,
And false gods shall be utterly destroyed.
Then will the world be a true kingdom of God,
When all mankind will invoke Your name,
And all the earth's wicked will return to You.
Then all the inhabitants of the world will surely know
That to You every knee must bend,
Every tongue must pledge loyalty.
Before You, O Lord, let them bow in worship,
Let them give honor to Your glory.
May they all accept the rule of Your kingdom.
May you reign over them soon through all time.
Sovereignty is Yours in glory, now and forever.
So it is written in Your Torah:
The Lord shall reign for ever and ever.

In secular terms, Jews know that in some ways they form a separate, distinct group. In mythical reality, they thank God they enjoy a unique destiny. They do not conclude with thanks for their particular "being," but sing a hymn of hope that he who made their lot unlike that of all others will soon rule as sovereign over all. The secular difference, the unique destiny, is for the time being only. When the destiny is fulfilled, there will be no further difference. The natural eye beholds a social group, with some particular cultural characteristics defining that group. The myth of peoplehood transforms *difference* into *destiny*.

The existence of the natural group means little, except as testimony to the sovereignty of the God who shaped the group and rules its life. The unique, the particular, the private—these now are no longer profane matters of culture, but become testimonies of divine sovereignty, pertinent to all men, all groups. The particularism of the group is for the moment alone; the will of God is for eternity. When that will be done, then all men will recognize that the unique destiny of Israel was intended for everyone. The ordinary facts of sociology no longer predominate. The myth of Israel has changed the secular and commonplace into a paradigm of true being.   [from *The Way of the Torah*]

47. The covenant made present: the Passover

Passover, the annual celebration of God's deliverance of Israel in the exodus event, is both a family meal and the central Jewish religious rite. During the course of the meal, the story of the exodus unfolds in present-tense language—God did this for us, and not just for our ancestors. The meal is thus far more than a simple recital of a past event: it is both a memorial and a pledge, an historical account and a contemporary religious experience. Comparing the order of a Passover meal below with the account of the exodus in the Bible (Ex 12–14), what would you say is the relationship of sacred event to worship—that is, how is the historical account of the exodus in scripture related to the religious ritual of a Passover meal? What kind of experience does the Passover meal seek to foster in its participants? How is this religious?

THE SEDER TRAY

The candles have been lit and are in the center of the table. There are also wine, goblets or cups for all participants, and a pillow for the leader to lean on. At the head of the table there is a platter or tray on which the following are arranged:

A roasted bone, usually a shank bone but often the neck of a chicken or some other fowl. Originally the most important part of the Passover celebration was offering and eating a special sacrifice of a lamb. When the Temple in Jerusalem was destroyed and sacrifices were no longer possible, the Z'roa became the symbol or reminder of the celebration in days of old when the ceremony as described in the Bible was performed.

A roasted egg. Passover is one of the three major Jewish festivals of the year. In Temple days, a sacrifice was offered on each of these holidays. The egg on the Seder tray recalls the general sacrifice for all three festivals.

The bitter herb. Slavery in Egypt was a life of hardship and bitterness. The Maror (from the Hebrew root מַר, bitter) brings to mind the bitterness of bondage in Egypt. Most Jews use horse-radish. Some use another vegetable.

Many Seder trays have two places for bitter herb. One is for the herb used for the "Hillel sandwich."

A mixture of chopped or grated apple and nuts, flavored with cinnamon and colored with red wine. Haroset looks like the clay used by the Israelites to mix the mortar and form the bricks that went into the cities and pyramids they built for Pharaoh.

Vegetable greens, usually parsley. Karpas is the symbol of spring when nature blooms after the long, cold winter. Passover is the festival of spring. *Karpas* also recalls the relish or appetizer eaten at festive meals long ago.

THE MATZOT

The *Seder* Tray rests on a dish containing three whole *Matzot*. Each is separately covered by a napkin, or fits into a separate section of a special *Matzah* cloth. The uppermost of the *Matzot* is called *Kohen*, the middle *Levi*, and the bottom one *Yisrael*. These are the names of the three classes into which our people have been divided: Kohen (*Priest*), Levi (*Levite*), and Israel (*all other Jews*).

SALT WATER

The salt water represents the tears shed by our people in Egypt. The *Karpas* will be dipped into it. In some communities the dish of salt water is placed right on the *Seder* tray instead of next to it.

THE CUP OF ELIJAH

A good-sized goblet or cup is kept ready for the point in the *Seder* when the door is opened. The cup is filled with wine and set in the middle of the table immediately after the third of the four cups of wine is drunk, and the fourth filled. Elijah, the prophet, is the symbol of our people's hope for a time when there will be an end to slavery, suspicion, and war. Elijah is held to be the protector of the poor and unfortunate, and the messenger who will announce the coming of the days of perfect peace and goodness.

CANDLE LIGHTING

The candles are lit before sunset. When the *Seder* eve falls on the Sabbath, the words in parentheses are included.
Dear God,
　　We prepare to celebrate (the Sabbath and) the festival of Passover. We pray that the lights we kindle may add brightness and hope to our

lives and to the lives of our family and friends. May they inspire us always to walk in the way of the righteous.

We praise You, O Lord our God, Ruler of the universe, for giving us commandments that make us holy and for instructing us to light the (Sabbath and) Festival candles.

We praise You, O Lord our God, Ruler of the universe, for keeping us alive and in good health so that we might reach this day and be privileged to celebrate it.

ORDER OF THE SEDER

The *Seder* consists of 15 steps or actions following a definite order. To help remember the sequence, a Hebrew rhyme has been memorized by many generations of Jews:

Chant the *Kiddush* and wash your hands

Eat the greens and divide the middle *Matzah* in two

Read the *Haggadah*—then wash your hands again

Recite the blessing for bread and one for *Matzah*

Eat the bitter herb and then the sandwich as Hillel did

Enjoy the meal

Have the *Afikoman,* then say Grace

Chant the *Hallel* and conclude the *Seder*

CHANT THE KIDDUSH

We praise You, O Lord our God, Ruler of the universe, Creator of the fruit of the vine.

We praise You for having called upon us to serve You. By giving us Your Torah and its commandments, You have shown us Your love.

In Your kindness, You have instructed us to keep this joyous festival of *Pesah,* as a reminder of our liberation from Egypt. All Your holy days are dear to us. They bring us gladness and peace and a feeling of Your nearness.

We praise You, O Lord our God, Ruler of the universe, for keeping us alive and in good health so we might reach this day and be privileged to celebrate it.

WASH YOUR HANDS

We wash our hands but do not recite the usual blessing.

If we were about to begin our meal, we would recite the *b'rakhah* for washing. At this point, however, we are merely going to eat *Karpas*.

EAT THE GREENS

We dip the Karpas into the salt water and eat it after reciting:
"Blessed are You, O Lord our God, Creator of the fruit of the earth."

DIVIDE THE MIDDLE MATZAH IN TWO

The leader breaks the middle Matzah in two. He leaves one piece in the Matzah cloth or platter. The other piece, which is to be the Afikoman, is removed and hidden. It will be eaten at the end of the meal.

READ THE HAGGADAH

The leader raises the Seder plate so that all may see. He also uncovers the Matzot. This is the humble bread our fathers ate as slaves in the land of Egypt. Let all who are hungry come and eat with us. Let them observe Passover with us as our guests. This year we celebrate Passover here. Next year may we celebrate it in the land of Israel. This year, many of our people still are not free. Next year, at this time, may they and all men everywhere be free.

The Wine Glasses Are Filled a Second Time
The Following Is Then Recited:

THE FOUR QUESTIONS

Why is this night different from all other nights? On all other nights, we eat either bread or *Matzah*; why on this night only *Matzah*?

On all other nights, we eat any vegetable we wish; why on this night do we make a special point of eating bitter herbs?

On all other nights, it is not necessary to dip one food into another even once; why on this night twice—the greens into salt water and the bitter herbs into *Haroset?*

On all other nights, we have our meal in a sitting or reclining position; why on this night do we recline?

All Join the Leader In Reciting:

WHY WE CELEBRATE

This night *is* different from all other nights. For it is given over to recalling the most important event in the history of our people—our liberation from Pharaoh. All that we do and say here tonight brings that event to life for us. It is as if we ourselves share in the liberation that came to our fathers.

We were once slaves in Egypt, but the Lord our God rescued us by His power and might. Had God not brought our forefathers out of Egypt, we might still be Pharaoh's slaves!

Therefore, regardless of how well we know the story, how wise or old we are, or how learned in the Torah, it is still our duty each year to repeat the tale of the exodus from Egypt. And the more time and attention we devote to repeating it, the more we deserve to be praised.

THE THREE MAJOR PASSOVER SYMBOLS

In the *Seder* there are many interesting and important symbols. But three are of utmost importance. Without them the celebration has no meaning. Rabban Gamliel used to say: He who does not discuss these three symbols at the *Seder* has not fulfilled his duty. They are: PESAH, MAT-ZAH, MAROR.

Point to the Roasted-Bone On the *Seder* Tray.

The roasted bone is called PESAH. For it recalls the Passover lamb our fathers ate in the days of the Temple. It takes us back to the original lamb which the Israelites in Egypt sacrificed for their households on the fourteenth day of *Nissan.* That night the Holy One, blessed be He, spared our ancestors when He passed over their houses and struck the Egyptians.

Point to the Top *Matzah* On the Platter.

MATZAH brings to mind the bread our ancestors ate when they left Egypt: "And they baked the dough they had taken out of Egypt into cakes of *Matzah*. In their haste to leave Egypt, they did not wait for the dough to rise."

Point to the *Maror* On the *Seder* Tray.

MAROR means bitter. It is a reminder of how bitter the Egyptians made the lives of our ancestors: "The Egyptians embittered their life with hard labor, forcing them to make mortar and bricks and to do all kinds of work in the fields."

Based on Psalm 113

Halleluyah.
Praise the Lord, all who love Him;
Praise Him now and always.
   From the East, where the sun rises
   To the West, where it sets,
   The name of the Lord shall be praised.
For who can hope to do the many great things the Lord does?
   He is higher than the heavens,
   Yet everything on earth has His care.
He brings joy to those who are sad,
And help to the needy.
   He can change the fortune of a poor man,
   And raise him to a place of honor.
He blesses homes
With the gift of children.
   God alone has the power to do all this.
   Halleluyah.

The Second Cup of Wine

O Lord our God, it was You who saved our people from Pharaoh and made it possible for us to rejoice this night as free men. We pray that You will enable us to continue to observe holy days and festivals in the years ahead.

How great is our joy as we behold the redemption of Israel in our day. May we be privileged to see the dream of our fathers come true and to sing songs of thanksgiving to You in Zion.

Our Helper and Shield, we praise You.

All Wash Their Hands in Preparation for the Meal, and Say:

We praise You, O Lord our God, Ruler of the universe, for giving us commandments that make us holy and for instructing us to wash our hands.

Take a piece of the upper Matzah and a piece of the remainder of the middle Matzah, hold them together and recite these blessings:

We praise You, O Lord our God, Ruler of the universe, who brings forth bread from the earth. We also praise You for giving us commandments that make us holy and for instructing us to eat *Matzah* on Passover.

Dip some of the Maror in Haroset, and say:

Our forefathers survived the bitterness of slavery because it was sweetened by their faith that some day they would be free. In the end good must triumph over wickedness. This is part of God's plan for the world. And so we dip bitter herbs into sweet *Haroset* as a sign that we believe in God's goodness.

Break the bottom Matzah. Take two pieces and put Maror between them. Before eating the sandwich, say:

Now we do, as Hillel did, in the days of the Temple in Jerusalem. For it was the practice of that great sage to eat *Matzah* and *Maror* together with the Passover lamb. In this way, he observed the Torah's instructions: "They shall eat it on *Matzot* and bitter herbs."

Have the Afikoman

When the meal is over, the piece of Matzah which was put aside as Afikoman is divided among all present and eaten. Nothing more is eaten after this.

Say the Grace After Meals
Based on Psalm 126

When the Lord brought about our return to Zion,
We thought we were dreaming.

We laughed, and we sang with joy.
Other nations marveled and said:

"The Lord has done great things for them."
  The Lord has indeed done great things for us.
  We can truly rejoice.
O Lord, bring all our scattered people home.
  May all who sow in tears
  Reap in joy.

Drink the Fourth and Last Cup, Saying:

The Hallel

While ancient peoples worshipped idols,
  Made of brass or gold,
  Daily bought and sold;
Our people worshipped God alone,
  Whom man cannot touch or see,
  Who is and will always be.
While ancient peoples bowed to idols,
  Shaped by human hand,
  Built of metal, wood or sand;
Our people bowed to God alone,
  Whom Abraham revealed,
  A constant help and shield.
While ancient peoples prayed to idols,
  Which could not tell men that to live
  They must share and love and give;
Our people prayed to God alone,
  Whose Torah taught them to be good,
  And live in peace and brotherhood.

The Fourth Cup

As we drink the last cup of wine, we recall that the four cups represent
four promises of liberation God made to our ancestors:
  "I will bring you out of the house of bondage."
  "I will save you."
  "I will free you from slavery."
  "I will take you to be My people, to spread My word among the
nations."

It is also fitting that we remember a fifth promise, fulfilled in our time after nearly two thousand years of Jewish wandering:
"*I will bring you back* to the land of your fathers."

Conclude the Seder

We prepare to bring our *Seder* to a close, with a prayer for Israel:
Our God and God of our fathers, in Your great mercy protect the state of Israel and grant it peace. May it always be a fountain of hope for our people and a blessing to all mankind.

Speedily, O our Father, free those of our people who are still oppressed. Lead them and all our homeless brothers to Zion.

Next year, may we and our dear ones know the joy of celebrating the *Seder* in Jerusalem. Amen. [The Passover Haggadah, from Hyman Chanover: *A Haggadah for the School*]

B. The Person and Teaching of Jesus in the New Testament

48. *Jesus in the New Testament*

The reading of the New Testament itself is essential to an understanding of the person and teaching of Jesus. The following passages are meant only to suggest a few of the crucial aspects of its different theological perspectives.

Acts 2:14–39 (10:34–43; 13:16–41)—the kerygma

Mark 1:9–11 (Matthew 3:13–17; Luke 3:21–22)—the baptism of Jesus

Mark 1:14–15 (Matthew 4:17)—Jesus' message

Luke 4:16–30—Jesus as the eschatological prophet (the man of the Spirit)

Mark 1:32–34 (Matthew 8:16–17; Luke 4:40–41)—Jesus as healer and exorcist

Matthew 10:32–33; Luke 12:8–9—Jesus and the judgment by the Son of man

Mark 8:27–30; Matthew 16:13–20; Luke 9:18–21—the messiah

Mark 2:23-28 (Matthew 12:1-8; Luke 6:1-5)—the Son of man is lord of the sabbath

Matthew 11:25-27—Jesus as the Son; "Abba"

Matthew 5:1-7:29; Luke 6:17-49—the morality of the kingdom

Mark 4:1-34; Matthew 13:1-52—the parables of the kingdom

Luke 10:29-37—parable of the good Samaritan

Matthew 6:9-13; Luke 11:1-4—the Lord's prayer

Mark 8:34-9:1 (Matthew 16:24-28; Luke 9:23-27)—taking up the cross

Luke 14:25-33 (Matthew 10:37-38)—the cost of discipleship

Mark 2:16-17 (Matthew 9:11-13; Luke 5:30-32)—Jesus eats with sinners

Mark 14:1-15:41; Matthew 26:3-27:66; Luke 22:1-23:56; John 18:1-19:42—the passion

Mark 16:1-8; Matthew 28:1-20; Luke 24:1-53; John 20:1-30—the resurrection

1 Cor 15:1-49—the meaning of the resurrection

Philippians 2:1-11—the attitude of Christ

Colossians 1:15-20—the preeminence of Christ in all things

John 1:1-18—the Word made flesh

John 6:26-59—the bread of life

John 10:1-18—the good shepherd

1 John 5:1-13—the Son of God

Hebrews 7:18-8:6—the eternal priest and sacrifice of the new covenant

49. The search for the historical Jesus

Historical criticism—the application of critical principles and tools to the records of the past in order to understand as clearly as possible "what really happened"—seeks to uncover the immediacy and life of historical phenomena that tend to get buried or misunderstood in transmission. "Biblical criticism" is that discipline within theology that applies the tools of historical criticism to the central written record of Christianity, the Bible, studying the written accounts that have been transmitted to us in order that contemporary believers might understand them more clearly. Biblical criticism, as **John Meier** explains below, is an especially exciting but difficult theological discipline, as the written record that Christians call the "New Testament" emerged out of an oral tradition that was written at different places and for different audiences, being less a "history text" in the modern sense than a record of faith of various early Christian communities. Reconstructing the purposes for which the records were written and the audiences to which they were addressed gives biblical critics important insights into what the written record initially witnessed to. Meier, professor of New Testament at the Catholic University of America, offers an important overview of how Catholic and Protestant scholars have applied historical criticism to the New Testament record in this century, uncovering in the process an historical person in first century Palestine that Christians call "the Christ."

In his novel "Roger's Version," John Updike pits a skeptical theologian, desperately clinging to the distant God of Karl Barth, against a conservative and naive student in a fierce debate over whether the existence of God can be proved. As I sit at my desk, looking at a slender volume entitled "Jesus and the Word" (1926) by the skeptical and sometimes Barthian Rudolf Bultmann, and the much larger and more confident "Jesus and Judaism" (1985) by E. P. Sanders, I wonder whether the 20th century has not witnessed a similar debate over the historical Jesus.

The comparison is not quite apt. Mr. Sanders, neither conservative nor naive, does not represent the antithesis to Bultmann; that role belongs to the exegetical acrobats of an earlier generation, conservative Protestants and Roman Catholics who wrote lives of Jesus that desperately sought to harmonize the discordant testimony of the four Gospels. The Catholic lives seem especially poignant today, since often they were the result of official pressure. Many of their authors knew better, but they were subjected to censorship and silencing by the Vatican.

Mr. Sanders' book, by contrast, is an honest attempt to avoid both the minimalism of a Bultmann and the uncritical acceptance of the Gospels by fundamentalists who treat them like videotape replays. Whether one prefers the British Baptist, Norman Perrin, or the German Catholic, Anton Vögtle, the post-liberal American Protestant, Mr. Sanders, or Geza Vermes, the Jewish expert on the Dead Sea scrolls, one senses that the last 40 years have produced a rough consensus on valid sources, methods and criteria in the quest for the historical Jesus. Although opinions still vary greatly on the authenticity of individual sayings of Jesus, a surprising amount of agreement on His life has emerged since World War II.

Mr. Sanders represents the culmination of the post-World War II period in the quest for the Jesus of history. It is not that Mr. Sanders does not present new and debatable views; he does, from claiming that Jesus did not demand repentance to playing down the sayings of Jesus and totally ignoring the titles attributed to Him. Yet the greatest value of his "Jesus and Judaism" is that it embodies a generation's desire to avoid exaggerations from right or left, to stop portraying Jesus as a predecessor of Heidegger or Nicaragua's President Daniel Ortega, and to try to understand what He meant to say and accomplish.

That all this should have happened since 1945 is not totally accidental. Granted, popularizers have exaggerated the importance of the Jewish scrolls discovered at Qumran (the Jewish "monastery" at the northwest corner of the Dead Sea) and the Gnostic codices recovered at Nag Hammadi in Upper Egypt for research into the Jesus of history. One easily forgets that neither discovery tells us anything directly about the historical Jesus. Still, these finds have joined forces with Greek and Roman studies, research on the Talmud and the sociology of the New Testament to complement our picture of Jesus. They have helped keep professional flights of fancy within certain limits. As the quest in the 18th and 19th centuries shows, the historical Jesus can readily become the clear crystal pool into which scholars gaze to see themselves. The archeological finds since World War II have helped fend off this academic narcissism.

Still, no amount of archeology guarantees objectivity in interpretation of the data. In the quest for the historical Jesus, objectivity remains, to borrow a phrase from the Jesuit theologian Karl Rahner, an "asymptotic goal": we have to keep pressing toward it even though we never fully arrive. Seeking objectivity is what keeps one on target—along with an honest admission of one's own point of view.

For instance, as a Catholic, I have to beware of anachronistically reading back the expanded universe of church dogma into Jesus' earthly life. Nevertheless, vis-à-vis conservative Protestants, the Catholic approach has one advantage—the clear distinction between what is known through historical research and reason and what is affirmed in faith. The historical Jesus belongs solely to the former realm. Moreover, for a Catholic, what is affirmed in faith does not rest on the Bible alone; church tradition, official teaching and theological development all play a part. Consequently, my faith in Christ does not rise or fall on my fragmentary, hypothetical reconstruction of Jesus through historical research; the restricted nature of the enterprise is paradoxically liberating. Thus, on this Christmas 40 years after the Qumran discoveries, I can let the historical chips fall where they may as I ask what can "all reasonable people"—that Platonic will-o'-the-wisp—say with fair probability about the historical Jesus?

To begin with, the very notion that Jesus was born 1986 years ago on Dec. 25 is hopelessly wrong. A sixth-century monk named Dionysius Exiguus (Denny the Dwarf) is responsible for our present B.C.–A.D. system of dating; his mathematics was not as good as his piety. Jesus (Aramaic "Yeshu" or "Yeshua," a commonly used form of the Hebrew Joshua) was born toward the end of the reign of King Herod the Great around 6 B.C. to 4 B.C. His mother was Miriam (Mary), His putative father Joseph. That is all we can say for certain about His birth. Only one chapter each in the Gospels of Matthew and Luke speaks of a birth at Bethlehem. The rest of the New Testament knows only of Nazareth as Jesus' place of origin. Bethlehem may simply be symbolic of Jesus' status as the new David. I would not, however, be so quick to jettison some kind of Davidic descent for Jesus as certain critics are; many different and early streams of New Testament tradition affirm it.

Jesus spent about the first 30 years of His life at Nazareth in southern Galilee. We know almost nothing about this period. In the whole New Testament, only one verse tells us that Jesus was a *tekton*, most likely a carpenter, although the word can mean stonemason or smith. Jesus probably followed the trade of Joseph, although the matter is by no means as clear as most people think. Presumably Joseph died before Jesus began His ministry. At least Joseph is not mentioned during it, in contrast to Miriam, Jesus' mother, and His "brothers," Jacob (James), Joseph, Judah (Judas) and Simon. "Sisters" are also alluded to but not named.

Christian rhetoric about "Christ the high priest" has obscured the fact that Jesus the layman consorted almost entirely with other Jewish lay people, His few encounters with priests being invariably hostile. We miss the sharp barb in the parable of the good Samaritan if we forget it is an anticlerical joke. Since Jesus plied His ministry for the most part among the common people of Galilee and Judea, He presumably taught in Aramaic, the ordinary language of the lower classes. His reading of Scripture in the synagogue points to a knowledge of Hebrew, and commercial transactions in Galilee may have introduced Him to Greek (used perhaps with Pilate during His trial?). But there is no indication of higher education or rabbinic training (see John 7:15). Jesus, like John the Baptist, was addressed as "rabbi," but in the early first century that title was used widely and loosely.

Sometime around A.D. 28 or 29 (Luke 3:1), during the reign of the Emperor Tiberius (A.D. 14–37), Jesus journeyed to the Jordan River to receive a "baptism of repentance for the forgiveness of sins" from John the Baptist, a prophet described by the Jewish historian Josephus. (Josephus also seems to mention Jesus in two passages, but their authenticity is debated among specialists.) The embarrassing nature of Jesus' submission to a baptism of repentance, a point played down by the later Gospels, argues for the event's historicity and its pivotal place in the life of Jesus. By accepting John's baptism, Jesus indicated He accepted John's message of the imminent disaster that John thought was threatening Israel in the last days of its history. Mr. Sanders rightly takes to task recent literary critics who have sought to make Jesus relevant by ignoring His emphasis on an imminent and definitive intervention of God, bringing salvation or doom.

Although Jesus followed in the Baptist's footsteps, perhaps even baptizing for a while, there was a major shift in His message. While John emphasized judgment and punishment, Jesus proclaimed the good news that God, like a loving father, was seeking out and gathering in the poor, the marginalized, even the irreligious. Jesus was not concerned—as 19th-century liberal piety often portrayed Him—simply with touching individual souls. He sought to address all Israel. Seeing Himself as the final prophet sent to a sinful nation in its last hour, He aimed to gather the scattered people of God back into one, holy community. In this sense, Jesus could not have intended to found a church because He *found* a church already existing—the *qahal*, the *eda*, the *knesset* that Yahweh had once called together in the wilderness and was now calling together again. How the Gentiles fit into this vision is not clear. Positive encounters with individual Gentiles occurred, but they were exceptions.

Jesus concretely embodied His vision of an Israel restored in the last days by selecting from His followers an inner circle of 12 men, representing the patriarchs of the regathered 12 tribes. German scholars like Günter Klein ("The Twelve Apostles") and Walter Schmithals ("The Office of Apostles") have claimed that the Twelve are a retrojection of the early church's organization into the life of Jesus. As a matter of fact, the Twelve soon lost their prominence in the early church, which indeed had trouble even remembering all 12 names. Moreover, the Gospels' embarrassed acknowledgement that Judas the betrayer was one of the Twelve hardly sounds like an invention of church propaganda. That Jesus should choose 12 men to symbolize the restored Israel and not 11, with Himself as the 12th, indicates that He saw Himself standing over against and above the nucleus He was creating. The choice of the Twelve makes clear that Jesus did not intend to found a new sect separated from Israel.

Jesus' followers included the Twelve, other committed disciples who left family and employment to follow Him, and people who accepted Jesus' teaching but maintained their homes and jobs. The border between the latter two groups was no doubt fluid. Jesus' relation to His disciples differed from that of the later rabbis in a number of ways. He often took the initiative in calling people—including some not very promising candidates—to discipleship, even ordering them to forsake sacred duties to follow Him: "Let the dead bury their dead." At least in His inner group, He expected commitment to Himself to be a permanent affair; His disciples were not studying to be rabbis who would then leave Him and set up schools of their own. Especially striking was Jesus' inclusion of women in His traveling entourage and His willingness to teach them. They stood by Him—quite literally at the cross—when all the male disciples fled.

If we had only the Gospels of Mark, Matthew and Luke (the "Synoptic Gospels"), we would get the impression that almost all of Jesus' followers came from the countryside and towns of Galilee; indeed, some critics have referred to His supporters as "an agrarian reform movement." It is John's Gospel that reminds us that Jesus was also frequently active in and around Jerusalem; that helps explain how this supposedly agrarian movement suddenly became an urban phenomenon. John's Gospel is also correct, I think, in spreading Jesus' ministry over a number of years. Left with the Synoptic Gospels, we could easily compress it into a couple of months.

Jesus used the rich rhetorical traditions of Israel to hammer home His message. Oracles, woes, aphorisms, proverbs, and above all parables (*meshalim*) served to tease the minds of people, throw them off balance and challenge them to decide for or against His claim on their lives. The parables are troubling riddles, meant to create a fierce feeling of urgency. God is about to work His own kind of revelation—the poor will be exalted and the powerful dispossessed. For Jesus, the revolution would be God's doing, not man's. In this matter Bultmann's "Jesus and the Word" may have been correct—the historical Jesus seems to have had no interest in the great political and social questions of His day. He was not interested in the reform of the world because He was prophesying its end.

Jesus' impact did not come simply from powerful rhetoric. Like the Old Testament prophets, Jesus consciously willed His public activity to be a dramatic acting out of His message of God's welcome and forgiveness extended to prodigals. He insisted on associating and eating with the religious lowlifes of His day, "the toll collectors and sinners," Jews who in the eyes of the pious had apostatized and were no better than Gentiles. This practice of sharing meals (for Orientals, a serious and intimate form of solidarity) with the religiously "lost" put Jesus in a continual state of ritual impurity, as far as the stringently law-observant were concerned. As Mr. Sanders emphasizes, Jesus no doubt shocked the pious by offering salvation to these outcasts without demanding the usual Jewish mechanism of repentance. What Mr. Sanders does not sufficiently note is that in effect Jesus was making acceptance of Himself and His message the touchstone of true repentance. He proclaimed the joy of the heavenly banquet, a future event already anticipated in His table fellowship with those outside the pale.

There was, then, a conscious coherence between Jesus' words and deeds, His message and conduct. To the great discomfort of us moderns, part of His practice was His claim to perform healings and exorcisms. Many treatments of Jesus get bogged down in a discussion of the possibility of miracles; properly speaking, that is a philosophical rather than a historical or even a theological problem. From the perspective of religious history, it is simply a fact that faith healers and miracle workers are common phenomena in both ancient and modern religions. How one explains the phenomena varies with both the subject studied and the observer commenting. In the case of Jesus, all that need be noted is that ancient Christian, Jewish and pagan sources all agreed that Jesus did extraordinary things not easily explained by human means. While Jesus' disciples pointed to the Spirit of God as the source of His power, Jewish and pagan adversaries spoke of demonic or magical forces. It never occurred to any of the ancient polemicists to claim that nothing had happened.

For the modern interpreter, the key point is to situate Jesus' healings in the overall context of His message and practice (something Morton Smith does not do in his "Jesus the Magician"). Jesus saw His healings not simply as kind deeds done to help unfortunate individuals; the miracles were signs and partial realizations of what was about to be realized fully in the kingdom. An already/not-yet tension lay at the heart of Jesus' vision. Yet despite His stress on the imminent future of salvation, Jesus had no interest in detailed timetables. Indeed, to the great chagrin of Christian theologians, He even affirmed His ignorance of the date of the final judgment (Mark 13:32).

We must keep in mind this proclamation of the kingdom of God that was already present but yet to come when we try to understand Jesus' moral teaching. To put it in a paradox: Jesus exhorts His followers to live now by the power of a future event that has already touched and transformed their lives. This is not quite the same thing as Albert Schweitzer's "interim ethic"; Jesus gives no indication that His basic ethic is meant for only a short interval. The unrestricted love of God and neighbor that stands at the heart of Jesus' moral imperative is hardly a stopgap measure for the time being. Actually, the word "love" does not appear all that frequently in the authentic sayings of Jesus. Yet if we gather together all of His pronouncements and parables that deal with compassion and forgiveness, we find a stress on mercy without measure, love without limits—even love of one's enemies. To many of us, such ideals, however noble, seem simply unattainable. To Jesus, they were possible, but only for those who had experienced through Him God's incredible love changing their lives. Radical demand flowed from radical grace. If religion was grace, then ethics was gratitude—and not just for the interim.

Trying to formulate Jesus' moral teaching into some codified, rational system is futile, especially since it is in His attitude to morality and law that He proves Himself the true charismatic in the classical sense. Faced with a crisis of traditional authority, the charismatic claims direct authority and intuitive knowledge not mediated through the usual channels of law, custom or established institutions. That is a perfect description of Jesus' approach, and it led to a basic tension in His treatment of the Mosaic law.

Jesus fundamentally affirmed the Jewish law as God's will, though with a radicalizing thrust seen also at the Qumran community. At times, Jesus would engage in rabbinic-style debate to solve concrete problems. Yet on certain specific issues (divorce, oaths, unclean foods), He claimed to know intuitively and directly that Jewish law or custom was contrary to God's will. In such cases, the law had to give way to or be reinterpreted by the command of Jesus, simply because He said so ("but I say to you"). He made no attempt to ground or authenticate such teaching in the manner of the Old Testament prophets ("the word of the Lord came to me, saying") or the later rabbis ("Rabbi X said in the name of Rabbi Y"). His peculiar and solemn introduction to various pronouncements— "Amen, I say to you"—emphasized that He knew and taught God's will with absolute certitude. Hence, as people accepted or rejected His instruction, so they would be saved or condemned on the last day. It was perhaps this unheard-of claim to authority over the Mosaic law and people's lives, more than any title Jesus may or may not have used of Himself, that disturbed pious Jews and the Jewish authorities.

Jesus' exact relation to the various Jewish parties of His day is extremely difficult to fix, all the more so because our chief sources for Judaism, the Mishnah and the Talmud, were written down centuries after Jesus' death. In the early first century, Judaism was a richly variegated religion, spanning the spectrum from cultured "assimilationists" of the Diaspora to exclusivistic sectarians at Qumran. Scholars have identified Jesus with almost every Jewish movement of the time. Conservative Sadducee, strict Pharisee, liberal Pharisee, freewheeling holy man, Jewish magician, apocalyptic fanatic, prophet of the last days from Qumran—"Jesus the Jew" has been squeezed into each of these molds. Especially popular today is Jesus as Che Guevara, sympathetic to revolt against Rome. In "Jesus and the Zealots," the Anglican scholar S. G. F. Brandon used more than a dollop of imagination to find this liberationist Jesus between the lines of what he sees as the Gospels' cover-up. Recent essays by the Cambridge professors Ernst Bammel and C. F. D. Moule ("Jesus and the Politics of His Day") render the whole Jesus-as-Sandinista approach highly dubious. In fact, Jesus did not fit any pigeonhole, and that may be one reason He wound up deserted and crucified.

Who did Jesus claim to be? He apparently was quite sure of who He was, although no one since has been. The crux of the problem lies in the paradox that although Jesus rarely spoke about His own status, He implicitly made Himself the pivotal figure in the final drama He was announcing and inaugurating. The kingdom was somehow already present in His person and ministry, and on the last day He would be the criterion by which people would be judged.

He seems to have based such monumental claims at least in part on His special relationship with God. Following the argument of the German Lutheran scholar Joachim Jeremias in "The Proclamation of Jesus," the Dutch Dominican theologian Edward Schillebeeckx, in "Jesus: An Experiment in Christology," has focused on Jesus' use of the Aramaic word *abba* ("my own dear father") in His prayer to God, and on the whole relationship such prayer implies. The intimate address of *abba*, foreign to formal liturgy, expressed an extremely close, confident relation to God, Father Schillebeeckx says; it betokens the wellspring of Jesus' ministry. There is a danger here, however, of basing a great deal on very little. *Abba* occurs only once in the four Gospels and could be a retrojection of early Jewish Christian prayer, reflecting a popular Aramaic practice not recorded in formal liturgical documents. On balance, though, Father Schillebeeckx is probably correct.

Did Jesus go beyond this and actually apply any titles or categories to Himself? At the very least, it is safe to say He saw Himself as a prophet, indeed the final prophet sent to Israel in its last days. A similar figure appears in the Dead Sea scrolls. Jesus' reputation for performing miracles may have conjured up hopes that the wonderworking prophet Elijah had returned to prepare Israel for the end. Mr. Vermes even suggests that we see Jesus as standing in the tradition of the *hasid*, the charismatic holy man of Galilee, a product of popular folk religion rather than academic theology. However, in Jewish thought of the time the image of prophet was often connected with rejection and martyrdom; the title was much more ominous than it might at first appear to be.

The title Messiah ("the anointed one") is often presumed to be central to Jesus' identity, but that is to read later Christian concepts and definitions back into a much more confused situation. In the early first century there was no one doctrine on a Messiah or *the* Messiah, and some Jewish groups that looked for the imminent coming of God dispensed completely with any such intermediary figure. Qumran expected two Messiahs, one Davidic and royal, the other—who took precedence—Levitical and priestly. If Jesus was in fact of Davidic descent, it would not be surprising if some of His followers identified Him with the Davidic Messiah. That speculation about Jesus as the Davidic Messiah was well known, even to Jesus' enemies, is supported by the charge under which He was tried by Pilate and crucified—that He was called "King of the Jews."

As for the title "Son" or "Son of God," it is not inconceivable that a person who addressed God as "Abba" might understand Himself in some sense or other as God's son. As a matter of fact, the titles "Son of God" and "Son of the Most High" are applied to a mysterious royal figure of the final days in a fragmentary text from Qumran. Still, very few Gospel sayings in which Jesus calls Himself the "Son" have much chance of being authentic. The best candidate is Mark 13:32, which affirms that the Son (Jesus) does not know the time of the final judgment. It seems improbable that the early church went out of its way to make up sayings emphasizing the ignorance of its risen Lord.

Of all the titles, the most confusing is "Son of Man." As it now stands in the Gospels, it refers to the earthly ministry of Jesus, His death and resurrection and His coming as judge. The question whether Jesus ever used the title, and if so in what sense, has received every answer imaginable. Bultmann held that Jesus used "Son of Man" not of Himself but of some other figure still to come. Perrin came to believe that the title as applied to Jesus was totally a creation of the early church. The Anglican scholar Barnabas Lindars suggests that Jesus originally used "Son of Man" not as a title but simply as a modest circumlocution—"a man like myself"—and that it was the church that turned it into a title. I think it arguable that Jesus the parable maker did use "Son of Man" as an enigmatic designation of Himself during His ministry as the lowly yet powerful servant of God's kingdom.

As for the title "Lord," there is really no problem in its being applied to Jesus during His earthly life. As we now know from Qumran, the Aramaic *mare* could mean anything from a polite "sir" to a divine "Lord." No doubt different people gave the title to Jesus with varying degrees of reverence.

In the spring of the year 30 (or possibly 33), Jesus took the decisive action of going on pilgrimage to Jerusalem for Passover, apparently determined to engage the leadership of Israel in a once-for-all confrontation. Two symbolic acts were meant to press home the issue with the authorities—what are called the triumphal entry into Jerusalem and the cleansing of the temple. The historicity of both events has been called into question; but if we think of limited symbolic gestures rather than Hollywood-style riots, both acts fit in with the tradition of prophecy-by-action practiced by the Old Testament prophets. The entry into Jerusalem implied but did not define some sort of Messianic claim over the ancient Davidic capital. More crucial was the cleansing of the temple, which was not a call for reform but a prophecy that the temple would be destroyed. Various sayings of Jesus point in that direction and cohere with Jewish apocalyptic thought of the time.

As Father Schillebeeckx notes, given the challenge He put to the authorities on their home ground, Jesus would have had to be a simpleton not to realize the mortal danger in which He was placing Himself. Admittedly, most critics would agree that the explicit predictions of death and resurrection attributed to Him reflect the theology of the early church. Still, some sayings that speak of His death in general terms, often with no mention of resurrection or ultimate triumph, may come from the historical Jesus.

If Jesus ever gave a clearer explanation of how He viewed His approaching death, the most likely occasion would have been the last opportunity He had, at the last supper. The historicity of this final meal with His disciples is supported independently by Mark and John and by special traditions in Luke and an early formula preserved by Paul in I Corinthians 11. John is probably correct in dating the supper a day before Passover; for theological reasons, the Synoptic Gospels make it a Passover meal. During the supper, Jesus used bread and wine to represent graphically His coming death. The words He spoke over the bread and wine are recorded in four different versions, all influenced by Christian liturgy; many critics consider the original form irrecoverable. I would hazard as a guess: "This is my body [or flesh]. . . . This is the covenant [sealed] by my blood." With these words, Jesus interpreted His death as the (sacrifical?) means by which God would restore His covenant made with Israel at Sinai (Exodus 24:8) and bring it to fulfillment. The last supper was thus a pledge that, despite the apparent failure of Jesus' mission to Israel, God would vindicate Him even beyond death and bring Him and His followers to the final banquet in the kingdom. Hence Jesus insisted that His disciples all drink from the one cup, His cup, to emphasize their union with Him in imminent disaster and final triumph.

After the supper, Jesus led His disciples outside the city to a country estate on or at the foot of the Mount of Olives (Gethsemane means "oil press"). There He was apprehended by an armed band guided by Judas. The arresting police were in all likelihood controlled by the high priest, although John's Gospel gives indication of a Roman presence as well. The disciples abandoned Jesus and fled.

From this point until the trial before Pilate the succession of events is highly controverted, for three reasons: there are contradictions among the four Gospels; we are uncertain about Jewish and Roman law in Palestine before A.D. 70; and religious apologetics plague us still. Sifting through the vast literature, I find three major scenarios proposed, each of which is possible. In one, a night trial was held before the Sanhedrin, presided over by Caiaphas (high priest A.D. 18–36). This is the picture given by Mark and Matthew and is supported by the German Catholic Josef Blinzler and the German Protestant Otto Betz. In the second, the Sanhedrin held only an early morning session. This is the presentation of Luke and is supported by the British Protestant scholar David Catchpole. In the third, an informal hearing was held by some Jewish official, perhaps Annas, the father-in-law of Caiaphas, who had been high priest in A.D. 6–15; but no formal trial took place before the Sanhedrin. This scenario can be reconstructed from John's Gospel and is defended by the pioneering Jewish scholar Paul Winter.

Whether or not a trial or an informal hearing took place before Jewish authorities, some accusation against Jesus would have been considered. His threats against the temple, His teaching that rescinded commandments in the law, His claim to be a prophet and perhaps something more might all have been weighed; but once again we are in the dark. The ringing affirmations by Jesus that He was indeed "the Messiah," "Son of God" and "Son of Man" look like a Christological catechism drawn up by Christians.

What was no doubt *not* invented by Christians was Peter's cowardly denial of being Jesus' disciple, a denial that occurred sometime during the Jewish proceeding. This event, however embarrassing, is important, since it does place an eyewitness near the first stage of Jesus' passion. At the end of the process, the officials decided to charge Jesus before Pilate. Historians debate whether the Jewish authorities had to have recourse to Pilate for a death sentence to be executed. John 18:31 is probably correct in implying that the Sanhedrin no longer had the power to execute a death sentence.

From A.D. 26 to 36, Pontius Pilate was prefect of Judea—not procurator, as the Roman historian Tacitus thinks; an inscription discovered at Caesarea Maritima in Israel in 1961 confirms Pilate's lower title. Pilate would have been concerned only with accusations involving threats to Roman rule. Hence Jesus was brought before him charged with claiming to be King of the Jews. It was on this charge of kingship, understood no doubt in terms of being a revolutionary, that Jesus was tried and condemned by Pilate. The whole account of the freeing of Barabbas during the trial may be a later theological dramatization of what was at stake in the trial.

Roman crucifixion was usually preceded by scourging, which apparently so weakened Jesus that He could not carry the crossbeam (the upright stake remained in place at the site of execution). To aid Jesus, the soldiers pressed into service one Simon from Cyrene in Africa; his sons, Alexander and Rufus, must have been well-known members of Mark's church (see Mark 15:21). Once again, an eyewitness is present, this time for the whole process of carrying the cross and the crucifixion. Besides Simon, sympathetic witnesses included only a handful of female followers from Galilee. The placing of the mother of Jesus and the "beloved disciple" at the cross—present only in the Fourth Gospel—may reflect the symbolic mentality of John.

The crucifixion naturally took place outside the walls of the holy city, at a spot called Golgotha ("Skull Place"), possibly an abandoned quarry by the side of a road. None of the passion narratives specifies whether Jesus was tied or nailed to the cross, although nails are mentioned in accounts of His appearances after the resurrection. The use of nails does fit in with recent archeological discoveries of crucified bodies around Jerusalem. With regard to what Jesus may or may not have said from the cross, the historian can reach no certain conclusion. All of the "seven last words" (a later conflation, in any case) may come from subsequent Christian tradition.

Jesus died relatively quickly, and Jewish law required that the body not be left hanging overnight, especially when, as it did that year, Passover coincided with the Sabbath. Joseph of Arimathea, an influential Jew, interceded with Pilate in order to provide (temporary?) burial in a tomb he owned nearby. The actual tomb, long since destroyed, probably lay in a spot now enclosed by the Church of the Holy Sepulcher. The so-called Garden Tomb in East Jerusalem, beloved of tourists, is a product of 19th-century romanticism. The Galilean women at the cross also witnessed the preparations for burial, although the only name constant in all the traditions is Mary Magdalene. The story of setting a guard at the sealed tomb to prevent a grave robbery stems from later Jewish-Christian debates; it is intriguing, though, that neither side in later polemics thought to deny that the tomb was soon empty.

Since the Jesus of history is by definition open to empirical investigation by any and all observers, the resurrection of Jesus, of its very nature, lies outside the scope of this essay. This does not mean that the resurrection is not real, but simply that it is not an ordinary event of our time and space, verifiable in principle by believer and nonbeliever alike. All history can say is that, starting in the early 30's of the first century, people who had known Jesus during His earthly life and who had deserted Him out of fear did a remarkable about-face after His disgraceful death and affirmed that Jesus had risen and appeared to them. That these people were not raving lunatics is shown by their skillful organization and propagation of the new Christian movement. That they were sincere is demonstrated by their willingness to die for what they claimed.

How any of us reacts to all this is a question not only of historical investigation but also of existential decision. In the end, there is a hermeneutics of belief and a hermeneutics of unbelief. What is beyond dispute is that Jesus of Nazareth is one of those perennial questions in history with which mankind is never quite done. In a ministry of two or three years He attracted and infuriated His contemporaries, mesmerized and alienated the ancient world, unleashed a movement that has done the same ever since, and so changed the course of history forever. ["Jesus Among the Historians"]

50. Who was Jesus?

German theologian (and subsequently bishop) **Walter Kasper** examines the critical question posed by historical and scriptural studies: What can we know about who Jesus actually was? On the basis of contemporary scholarship, Kasper uncovers the essential elements of what can be known with security about Jesus' message and person, and from this draws important implications concerning the meaning of Jesus for modern persons of faith.

JESUS CHRIST: THE WITNESS TO FAITH

The Failure of the Quest for the Historical Jesus

All that I have said so far about the justification of faith has been confined to some extent to preliminary observations. I have spoken of various signs and indications that might lead to the situation in which faith is possible. The question concerning the meaning of the whole of our reality seemed, for example, to be a possible location of faith, but the signs pointing to such an ultimate meaning were vague and ambiguous. There were, however, signs pointing not to an unconditional meaning, but to the ultimate absurdity of reality, and I therefore concluded that an ultimate absence of ambiguity was not possible in this sphere. For Christians, the sign of God in this world, the sign that gives certainty to all other signs and deprives them of their ambiguity, is Jesus Christ. He is the sign of and the witness to faith. All attempts to justify faith must therefore be based on him. Christian faith stands or falls with him.

This argument gives rise to a number of questions. Have the historical figure of Jesus and the form of his message not, for example, been made extremely vague because of the historical and critical method of exegesis? Are there not so many different and even contradictory interpretations of the person and the work of Jesus that everything is fundamentally questionable? Has anything more than a heap of fragments been left behind by the historical and critical examination of the New Testament? How can such an uncertain basis be used as the point of departure for an attempt to justify faith?

Because of these and other related questions, we must go back to the sources before asking about the person of Jesus and his cause, and find out whether they can provide us with reliable information.

For centuries Christians were convinced that the four gospels should be read as faithful historical reports and testimonies of the Church's faith in Jesus Christ as true man and true God. One of the most important events in the whole history of theology was undoubtedly the emergence of the historical and critical method. According to Albert Schweitzer, in his history of the quest for the historical Jesus, it was the greatest event in German theology and represented 'the most tremendous aspect that has ever been undertaken in religious thought.' The point of departure in this historical research into the life of Jesus was not, Schweitzer was careful to point out, purely an interest in history. It was fundamentally an attempt to look for the Jesus of history as a helper in the struggle to become free from dogma.

According to Schweitzer, the Christology of Chalcedon had overlaid the historical figure of Jesus with the concepts of Greek philosophy and, in so doing, had alienated it from modern historical thought. The aim of the protagonists of the historical and critical method was therefore to remove the later layers of the painting and restore the original colour and lustre, in the conviction that the historical Jesus—Jesus as he really was—would be more in accordance with modern taste than the dogmatic Christ of the doctrine of the two natures. The result would be that each successive period of modern theology ought to be able to discover its ideal in Jesus. Schweitzer in fact sketched out such a long and changing history of research into the life of Jesus, from Hermann Samuel Reimarus in the eighteenth century, David Friedrich Strauss, Friedrich Schleiermacher, Ernest Renan and Adolf von Harnack until the present day. Since nothing is, in principle, impossible in science, Drews and others declared, at about the turn of the present century, that Jesus was not a historical figure at all and was purely mythical, a suggestion that is now only taken seriously in out-of-date Communist text-books.

The history of historical and critical research into the life of Jesus is also at an end now in any theological work that is to be taken seriously. Two data led to the breakdown of an entire period of theology. The first was the recognition that the Jesus of Nazareth, who appeared as the Messiah, proclaimed the morality of the kingdom of God, established the kingdom of heaven on earth and died, never in fact existed. Jesus was not a modern man and he cannot be modernized in any way at all. Anyone who comes closer to him is bound to discover a radical strangeness in him. The most important discovery made by Albert Schweitzer and Johannes Weiss in their historical and critical research into the New Testament was that eschatology was at the heart of Jesus' message.

This eschatology strikes us today as very strange. Schweitzer and Weiss were mistaken in believing that Jesus' eschatological teaching was apocalyptic in that it insisted that the existing world would be completely destroyed and that a new, heavenly world would miraculously descend to replace it. This background of apocalyptic ideas is now no longer attributed to Jesus himself, but is generally believed to go back to a later biblical tradition. Despite this, however, the discovery of the eschatological character of Jesus' message is still valid. This eschatological message of the future of God is nonetheless bound to strike us, whose historical thinking is purely immanent, as mythological, with the result that, for modern secularized man, the person of Jesus himself and his message are inevitably strange.

The second datum was even more important than the first. It is that the gospels do not allow us to write a life of Jesus. They do not provide a biography of Jesus or a psychology of Jesus. They are rather written in the form of historical reports of post-paschal proclamation. This datum is probably the most important insight gained by the leading representatives of the school of form criticism, Martin Dibelius and Rudolf Bultmann, whose methods and results were for a long time seriously criticized. In the case of Bultmann, the reason for this critical rejection is to be found in the Marburg professor's presentation of form criticism in close association with an existential interpretation of the New Testament and his demythologization of the gospels. Form criticism can, however, be practised without this existential interpretation and process of demythologization.

The methods and results of form criticism were also accepted, with some reservations, by the second Vatican Council. In the Council's *Constitution on Revelation,* a distinction was made between three stages of the gospel tradition. The first stage is what Jesus Christ himself did and taught during his earthly life. The second is what the apostles 'handed on . . . with that clearer understanding' after the Easter event in the light of the resurrection. The third stage recognized in the *Constitution on Revelation* is that of the editing of the gospels. The evangelists selected, summarized and clarified in accordance with the situation in which the Church was placed, but preserved the form of proclamation. It is clear, then, that the most fundamental insights of form criticism were officially recognized and accepted by the second Vatican Council.

These two data mark the end of theological research into the life of Jesus. From the point of view of systematic theology, however, a number of conclusions can be drawn from them. Many wonderful systematic Christ-roses have certainly been cultivated in the field of historical scepticism. One consequence that has been at least partly drawn from the failure of the quest for the historical Jesus is that we may now safely return to the old channel of dogmatic Christology. Many so-called conservative theologians have taken possession of the 'progressive' exegetical results and have decided to keep strictly to the post-paschal proclamation of the Church, since nothing can be known with historical certainty about Jesus himself. This led to the neo-orthodox movements in twentieth-century theology, in which a remarkable symbiosis between dogmatic theology and modern biblical exegesis has been

achieved. It also led to a widely discussed change of fronts, as represented in the theology of Ernst Käsemann. The more clearly certain
aspects of the new exegesis were revealed as negative, the more urgently
the conservative theologians, who had eventually taken over the liberal
theologians' research into the historical Jesus whom they had for so long
disputed, had to save what they could from the burning house.

Bultmann himself drew an entirely different conclusion. He made a
theological virtue out of the historical necessity. In his opinion, it was not
necessary to enquire about the historical Jesus behind the kerygma, since
this would be an attempt to make sure of faith by objective arguments
and therefore fundamentally a lack of faith. Bultmann declared that he
did not know and did not want to know what had gone on in Jesus'
heart. Only the fact that Jesus had come was important for him. He was
therefore able to combine a decidedly radical point of view with an
equally radical historical scepticism. The value of the figure of Jesus as a
sign, which is precisely what makes faith possible, was, however, destroyed in Bultmann's theology.

The New Quest for the Historical Jesus

Although Bultmann is already one of the classical theologians of the
twentieth century, he is certainly not the most modern. In their research
into the question of the historical Jesus, the theologians who have followed Bultmann have not in any way determined their position. The
advances made in this field by Ernst Käsemann led to a new quest for the
historical Jesus. In his research, Käsemann considered a legitimate concern of the liberal quest for the historical Jesus within the framework of
the changed theological climate of the second half of the twentieth century. There were two important reasons for this.

The first is this. Even though it may be impossible for us to reconstruct
a life of Jesus and many of Jesus' reported words and actions have to be
regarded as the products of post-paschal theology, editorial insertions
and so on, it is not true to say that no more than a heap of fragments has
been left by the earlier liberal research into the historical Jesus, with the
result that practically nothing more can be said with certainty. The situation is by no means so confused and hopeless as many popular publications often rather irresponsibly try to maintain. There is no reason at all
for us to give way to radical historical scepticism. As Günter Bornkamm
has rightly pointed out, the faith of the Christian community was 'not
simply the product of their imagination, but their response to Jesus'
figure and mission as a whole.' The gospels do not entitle us to be

resigned or sceptical. 'On the contrary, they make the historical figure of Jesus in its direct power visible to us, although they do not do this in the same way as chronicles or histories would do it. It is all too clear what the gospels report about Jesus' message, his actions and his history. They are still marked by authenticity and freshness and also by a special quality which is not dominated by the paschal faith of the early Christian community, but which points directly to the earthly figure of Jesus himself.' Bornkamm thought that the literary genre of the gospels was specific in that they proclaimed their message through history and that they proclaimed by reporting a history. 'It is the theologian's task to look for history in the kerygma of the gospels and also to look for the kerygma in that history.

This programme leads us to the second concern underlying the new quest for the historical Jesus. Käsemann was conscious of the danger of docetism, in other words, of underestimating and even suppressing Jesus' humanity and its saving significance in theology that neglected the earthly Jesus and placed a one-sided emphasis on the proclaimed Christ. One of the fundamental concerns of the Christology of the early Church was, of course, the human and historical nature of man's redemption. Another danger of which Käsemann was aware in Bultmann's theology was that of an enthusiasm that, in stressing the reality of salvation here and now, is forgetful of the fact that this salvation originated in the historical event of the crucifixion and that the Christian lives in the shadow of the cross until his redemption is fully brought about at the end of time. What is forgotten, then, in this new research into the life of Jesus is that, although Jesus is made present in the Church and its proclamation, Christ does not become merged into the Church, but remains Lord of that Church. The priority of Jesus Christ means that the Church's word cannot simply be identified with the word of Christ. The Church is rather tied to its criterion that has already been provided in Christ. The quest for the historical Jesus should express this priority of Christ over the Church. It should show that Jesus is the beginning, the constant ground and the norm of faith. The most important question that has to be answered, then, is: Who was this Jesus of Nazareth? Equally important questions are: What was the content of his message and what did he have to say about himself?

The Message of the Kingdom of God

Jesus can best be understood by considering his behaviour. There can be no doubt that he carried out all the duties of a pious Jew, praying and taking part in the services at the synagogue and the Temple. He was not, however, pious in the sense in which piety was then and is now generally understood. He was pious in an unprecedented and even revolutionary way, which pious men of his period found scandalizing and blasphemous. He was not ascetic. He shared the banquets of rich men and was therefore criticized as a glutton and a drinker (Mt 11:19). What is more, he did not observe the laws of cultic purity (Mk 7:1–23), he broke the commandment to keep the sabbath (Mk 2:23–28) and associated with tax-collectors, prostitutes and sinners (Mk 7:13–17), in other words, with all those who led a marginal existence. He broke the sacred conventions of religion and society. Man, not the law, was the norm of authentic piety for Jesus. 'The sabbath was made for man, not man for the sabbath' (Mk 2:27) sums up his attitude. He therefore provoked the representatives of the religious establishment of the time and goaded them into opposition.

On the other hand, it would be quite wrong to regard Jesus as a political revolutionary in the usual sense of the word. One of the most remarkable aspects of his whole attitude is revealed in the fact that he was never a zealot, opposing the established religious and political powers with force. At the very centre of Jesus' moral attitude and teaching was not violence of a kind that gave rise to further violence in return, but love. Jesus did not want to wound, but to heal wounds. He put an end to the unhappy circle of violence and counter-violence with his commandment to love one's enemies (Mt 5:38–48). He called for a renunciation of violence and his own way was one of suffering, from which violence was strikingly absent.

This attitude indirectly had social consequences, since Jesus was a revolutionary in a much deeper sense than that which is usually given to the word. He was in the last resort diametrically opposed to all existing norms. He called for nothing less than a total conversion, not only of external structures and forms of behaviour, but also of man's heart itself and his fundamental orientation.

The unprecedented freedom that appeared with Jesus gave rise to the question: 'By what authority are you doing these things?' (Mk 11:28). What was the ground and centre of Jesus' being? The only possible answer was and is that Jesus had the power and inspiration to act with such unprecedented freedom from what he proclaimed as the coming of the kingdom of God. According to Käsemann, 'fellow-humanity was the sphere in which his gospel lived, not its foundation or its objective'. The freedom with which Jesus promised salvation to sinners and outcasts calls for a justification and this can be found in the kingdom of God, which formed the centre of his message and the real content of his existence (Mk 1:14f).

Almost all biblical exegetes agree that the kingdom of God is not a kingdom or rule in the sense in which we usually understand the term. It is not a political order based on theocracy. On the contrary, it does away with all human claims to domination, because it is based on a concept of rule that is outside the reach of man and reserved for God alone (Mk 13:32). The kingdom of God cannot be reduced to an historical status. According to Jesus' message, it comes like lightning (Mt 24:27). We cannot know how it comes (Mk 4:26–29). It is the rule of God himself, the manifestation of his divinity, the establishment of his law and justice and at the same time the quintescence of man's deepest expectation of salvation.

Whenever man forgoes care for his own salvation and trusts in God, he escapes from the inhuman pressure of the need to achieve and from anxiety, and becomes joyful. That is why joy is an essential gift of the coming of the kingdom of God. Wholeness and salvation are only possible when man is set free from historical and other purposes. The manifestation of God's divinity and the gift of man's humanity are therefore two sides of the same coin. As the Roman Missal puts it, *Deo servire regnare est.*[1] The kingdom and rule of God mean that God makes his cause man's cause, and man's cause his own.

God's rule cannot be organized either in a revolutionary or in an evolutionary and conservative way. The only preparation that man can make for its coming is to give up his fundamental orientation towards ruling and possessing the world and finding security for himself, and in this way to create a space for God as the only reliable safeguard. What is required of him is a radically new orientation. He has to be converted. Conversion is the negative expression of what Jesus positively called faith. Faith implies a recognition of God's divinity. This recognition is practical and concrete whenever man builds on God as his foundation. Faith is not an achievement. On the contrary, it is a renunciation of all achievement, a state of being empty for God so that we can be completely filled with him. Faith, then, is the concrete way in which the kingdom of God can be present in man. God is Lord whenever he is believed in as Lord and obeyed as Lord. The kingdom of God and faith are therefore two sides of the same coin. The coming of the kingdom of God means that God makes himself valid in man's recognition and faith.

This concentration of Jesus' message on faith does not imply a reduc-

---

1. "To serve God is to reign" [ed.].

tion to a purely inner and spiritual message. All Jesus' miraculous actions bear witness to the fact that his message of the coming of the kingdom of God is concerned with man as a whole in all his physical and social relationships. Not only from the point of view of the natural sciences, but also in the historical sense, these actions undoubtedly present us with a very difficult problem today. There is, however, general agreement among exegetes in that they hardly dispute the historical existence of certain basic miraculous actions, especially the healings and the cases in which demons were driven out. In addition to this, these actions are also too closely associated with certain statements made by Jesus that are regarded as authentic. (An example of this is to be found in Lk 11:20). If it were not for this, it would hardly be possible to explain how the later tradition of miracles was possible. In any case, these actions are not strictly miraculous—they are signs. They had the aim of leading men to faith and can, moreover, only be recognized without ambiguity in faith as acts of God's sovereign power. They are above all signs of the coming kingdom of God. In them, God's kingdom is made proleptically present. The fact that the whole of mankind is brought to salvation and wholeness can be seen in these signs.

The Christological Question

On the basis of his behaviour, message and actions, we are bound to return to our original question, asked at the end of our second section above: Who was this Jesus of Nazareth? It is not an easy question to answer. In the first place, we must accept that almost all the Christological titles—Son of God, Son of Man, Messiah, Prophet, servant of God and so on—go back, not to the earthly Jesus, but to later proclamation in the early Church. Jesus did not proclaim himself. He proclaimed God and his kingdom. He did not teach any Christology, with the result that we can at the most only look for an indirect or implicit Christology of Jesus. Bultmann has already indicated the direction in which we should look, a way which has been followed by many subsequent theologians. This way has led in fact to much more convincing results than the rather precise apologetical approach in which an attempt is made to preserve individual sovereign titles as authentic words of Jesus himself.

It is also possible to take Jesus' behaviour as our point of departure, since a certain Christology is undoubtedly implied in the unusual aspect of his behaviour and the sovereign freedom that is expressed in it. Unlike the prophets, who simply proclaimed the kingdom of God, Jesus also brought it. It began here and now in his miraculous actions: 'If it is by the finger of God that I cast out demons, then the kingdom of God has come upon you' (Lk 11:20). The connection between Jesus' person and his cause is made clear in this logion, which is generally accepted as authentic. Jesus in fact included his person in his cause. His activity, which is in this case the driving out of demons, and the coming of the kingdom of God were directly connected with each other. The kingdom of God already came in Jesus' activity and appearance. The same also applies to his proclamation, which we must now briefly consider.

In the contrasts presented in the Sermon on the Mount—the first, second and fourth are usually regarded as authentic—what is clearly expressed is: 'It was said to the men of old . . . but I say to you' (Mt 5:21, 27, 33). In other words, Jesus ventures to call the authority of Moses, the highest authority in Judaism, into question and to place himself above the word of God in the Old Testament. He claimed to be the messenger of the definitive Word of God. For this reason, no confirmation was needed for what he said and he used the word 'amen', which was generally employed to confirm what another person had said, to confirm his own pronouncement: 'Amen, amen, I say to you. . . .' An entire Christology is in fact implied in this linguistic usage that is so characteristic of Jesus. He did not, in other words, do as the prophets had done in Israel and point from his word back to the Word of God: 'Thus says the Lord'. Jesus vouchsafed for his own word and spoke of his own authority, which was higher than that of the Old Testament. He was himself more than a prophet and we can only say that he himself speaks God's Word.

What was implicit and indirect in the sayings of the historical Jesus was made explicit and direct after the Easter event. The Christological titles of sovereignty and the whole Christology that followed the Easter event must be understood as the response made by the Christian community to Jesus' claim and his call to believers to come to a decision. These titles do not falsify Jesus' message in any way. On the contrary, they are fully in accordance with that message and make it more explicit. The unprecedented claim made by the earthly Jesus leads directly to the statement made in the fourth gospel: 'I and the Father are one' (Jn 10:30).

Even in the post-paschal levels of the New Testament, however, there are no really ontological statements that correspond to the later doctrine of the two natures of Christ. The Christology of the New Testament is rather functional, in other words, it contains statements that express Jesus' saving significance. It was less important for the New Testament authors to say who Jesus *was* than to say what he *meant* for us. If we were, however, to play one part of this statement off against the other, we would be seriously misunderstanding its significance, since it is very characteristic of Jesus that he completely identified himself with his function. He *was*, in other words, what he *meant*. His message and his person coincide and we are bound to say that his person is his function and that the two cannot be separated.

Jesus saw his whole life as obedience to the Father and service of his fellow men. He wanted nothing for himself. From the standpoint of this obedience to God, he was entirely the man for others. He was committed to this openness to God and to man and consumed by this commitment until he died. In this way, he was, in his person, the mode of existence of the rule of God's love. He *was* so radical in this that he was, in his free obedience as a man, the instrument for God's existence and activity in human history. In this sense, he was and *is* the Son of God. In his entirely human obedience Jesus *is* God's mode of existence. This way we can say that the later dogma of the Church, according to which Jesus is fully man and fully God, is quite right. It is, of course, historically conditioned, but it validly expresses, within the framework of that historically determined terminology, Jesus' cause, even though it now needs interpretation and can even be superseded.

Through this obedience, Jesus offers us a new possible human approach, because in his obedience to God he was totally committed to his fellow men. In that obedience, he also bore witness to a new mode of existence based on faith. Faith therefore means in the last resort being admitted to Jesus' innermost attitude. Jesus thus gives us the possibility of a new form of freedom, a freedom that is expressed in service to our fellow men. Within this outline of a new form of humanity everything that is great, noble and good in all other human norms is included. On the other hand, however, the Christian model of human behaviour is also in many ways the opposite of other norms. We can only learn how to live in faith in real life by studying Jesus' own behaviour. He is, in a word, the sign and the witness of faith.

What is the situation with regard to this claim made by Jesus? How can we know that he was right? It would be meaningless to try to find proof of this claim, but it can to some extent be verified. The inner truth of the reality and the possibility of a new form of humanity of the kind offered by Jesus can be established by the fact that this truth is confirmed in the phenomenon of human greatness and misery. Man wavers between greatness and misery. Should he acknowledge that the signs that encourage him to trust in his greatness are right or should he follow those that lead him to despair?

What is so convincing in Jesus' figure and message is that both do full justice to greatness and misery. Jesus points to man's greatness and reveals to him his mission and his vocation. At the same time, however, he also shows man his misery and that he is incapable of conforming to this greatness, at least of his own accord. In our knowledge of misery, we are preserved from pride and, in our knowledge of greatness, we are preserved from despair. Our true humanity is therefore revealed to us in Jesus Christ. This fact provides a certain inner evidence of Jesus' claim and message. Nowhere else can we find totally unambiguous statements, which do such full justice to the human situation, as we can in the life and message of Jesus Christ. We are therefore bound to ask where else we should and where else we might find such words of life.   [from *An Introduction to Christian Faith*]

51. The teaching of Jesus: the call to discipleship

Christian ethics—the application of Jesus' teaching to the concrete situations of daily life—is based on Jesus' own call to conversion and discipleship recorded in the gospels. **Richard McBrien** examines here how the moral message of Jesus, especially his commandment of love, provides the foundation for Christian morality and action. According to McBrien, what new emphases did Jesus give to the moral teaching of Judaism? How did Jesus' call to discipleship demand a radical break with some older conceptions of the Jewish law? What major themes in the teaching of Jesus form the foundation for judging Christian action? What is the relationship of conversion and discipleship in the teaching of Jesus?

THE MORAL MESSAGE OF JESUS

The Kingdom (Reign) of God

Although the idea of the Covenant is the axis around which the history of ancient Israel revolves, and although there was some expectation of a new covenant among the prophets (Jeremiah 31:31–34; Ezekiel 36:26–28), it was not central to the preaching of Jesus. As we have already noted in chapter 12, the *Kingdom* (or *reign*) *of God* was at the core of Jesus' proclamation and ministry, as it was, and must remain, at the heart of the Church's total mission (chapters 17 and 20). All else flows from that, including our understanding of Christian existence.

The whole of Jesus' preaching is summed up by Mark: "This is the time of fulfillment. The reign of God is at hand. Reform your lives and believe in the gospel" (1:15). Thus, his preaching is at once a proclamation and a warning, i.e., an announcement of a divine act and a demand for a response from men and women. Moral existence is always a response to a divine call. Nowhere in Jesus' preaching, nor in the New Testament at large, do we find an ethical system as such. On the other hand, neither do we find an existence devoid of obligation nor a faith divorced from action.

What Jesus announced was not only a renewal of the Covenant with the people of Israel. His message was even more comprehensive than that. It would embrace the whole world. Jesus returned to his home town of Nazareth to begin his preaching in the synagogue with these words from Isaiah (61:1–2): "The spirit of the Lord is upon me; therefore he has anointed me. He has sent me to bring glad tidings to the poor, to proclaim liberty to the captives, recovery of sight to the blind and release to prisoners, to announce a year of favor from the Lord" (Luke 4:18–19). Then he said, "Today this Scripture passage is fulfilled in your hearing." So obvious was his meaning that his fellow townspeople were filled with indignation and expelled him from Nazareth, attempting even to hurl him over the edge of a hill.

As we noted in chapter 12, Jesus' preaching of the reign of God was often couched in parables in which he often inverted his listeners' whole world view. Thus, the parable of the Good Samaritan (Luke 10:30–37) is not simply an example of neighborliness. If that is all Jesus wanted to communicate, he would have made the Samaritan the injured party and the Israelite the one who comes along to aid him. As it is, no Jew would ever have expected hospitality from a Samaritan (see Luke 9:52–56). Thus, the parable challenges the listener to conceive the inconceivable: The Samaritan is "good." The listener is thereby required to reexamine his or her most basic attitudes and values. The parable is no longer merely instruction; it is proclamation itself.

For Jesus nothing is more precious than the Kingdom of God (see chapter 20), i.e., the healing and renewing power and presence of God on our behalf. "Seek out his kingship over you, and the rest will follow in turn" (Luke 12:31). Like a person who finds a hidden treasure in a field, or a merchant who discovers a precious pearl, everyone must be prepared to give up everything else in order to possess the Kingdom (Matthew 13:44–46). But it is promised only to those with a certain outlook and way of life (see the Beatitudes in Matthew 5:3–12). One can inherit the Kingdom through love of one's neighbor (Matthew 5:38–48), and yet one must also accept it as a child (Mark 10:15). Jesus assured the

Scribe who grasped the meaning of the chief of the commandments (love of God and love of neighbor), "You are not far from the reign of God" (12:34). He also insisted to his disciples that their commitment to the Kingdom would make strong demands upon them (Mark 10:1; Luke 9:57–62; Matthew 19:12).

The Call to Conversion and Repentance

Jesus' fundamental though not ultimate demand was that they should *repent*. The Greek word *metanoia* suggests a "change of mind." To the Semite it suggested someone's turning away from his or her former consciousness, now recognized as wrong, and striking out in a completely new direction. Therefore, *metanoia*, or conversion and repentance, is not just sorrow for sin but a fundamental reorientation of one's whole life. Jesus demanded that his listeners not only repent but also believe the Gospel of forgiveness that he preached (Mark 2:10, 17). He drove home his point with various parables, especially those in Luke 15 and the parable of the Prodigal Son in particular. Jesus was so committed to the forgiveness of sins in the name of God that he made himself the friend of outcasts—e.g., publicans and sinners (Matthew 11:19)—and did not avoid their company (Mark 2:16). He rejoiced over their conversion (Luke 15:7–10; Matthew 18:13).

The antithesis of a repentant attitude is an attitude of self-righteousness and presumption. Jesus repudiates the proud Pharisee (Luke 18:10–14), the elder brother who resents his father's benevolent reaction to the prodigal son's return (Luke 15:25–30), and the discontented laborers in the vineyard (Matthew 20:1–15). To those who set themselves proudly above others, Jesus declared that publicans and harlots would enter the Kingdom before they would (Matthew 21:31–32). He condemned them for trying to shut the doors of the Kingdom (Matthew 23:13). All of us, he warned, are unprofitable servants (Luke 17:10), ever in God's debt (Matthew 6:12). God will exalt the humble and bring down the proud (Luke 14:11; 18:14). Each must pray that God forgives his or her trespasses. And whoever is without sin should cast the first stone (John 8:7). Repentance, therefore, remains a major requirement of Christian existence. The early Church would continue this message: "You must reform and be baptized . . ." (Acts of the Apostles 2:38).

The Demand for Faith

Jesus also demanded *faith*, which is the positive side of conversion (Mark 1:15). He says to the woman afflicted with a hemorrhage for a dozen years and who is cured by touching his clothing, "Daughter, it is your faith that has cured you" (Mark 5:34). From there he went to the official's house where the man's daughter was reported as being already dead. Jesus disregarded the report and said to the official, "Fear is useless. What is needed is trust" (5:36). It was the faith of the lame man's friends which called forth from Jesus the forgiveness of his sins and physical healing (2:5). Faith is central to the narrative of the cured boy (9:14–29). Jesus sighed over this unbelieving generation (9:19) and reminded the boy's father that all things are possible to him who believes (9:23). The great faith of the Syro-Phoenician woman moved Jesus to heal her daughter (7:30), and he drew attention to the faith of the pagan centurion who believed that a mere word from Jesus would heal his sick servant (Matthew 8:10; Luke 7:9). On the other hand, where Jesus encountered an obstinate lack of faith, he was not able to manifest the signs of salvation (Mark 6:5). (See chapter 2 for our fuller discussion of faith.)

The Call to Discipleship

Jesus also gathered disciples around him, a point that is not unrelated to the question of Jesus' intentions regarding the "founding" of the Church (see chapter 17). He encouraged people to leave home, take up their cross, and become his disciples (Luke 14:26–27). He advised the rich young man to sell all that he had, give the money to the poor, and then come follow him (Mark 10:21). To become his disciples meant leaving everything else behind (Luke 5:11; 9:58; 14:26; Mark 2:14). But this was consistent with the traditional Jewish notion of discipleship. *What was not traditional was his sending of disciples to act in his name* (Matthew 10). "Let the dead bury their dead," he chastized the man who wanted to bury his father first. "Come away and proclaim the kingdom of God" (Luke 9:59–60). To do so was to share in Jesus' own destiny. "Where I am, there will my servant be" (John 12:26). There would be an identification of the disciple with the suffering of the master (Mark 8:34–35), but also a participation in his triumph (Luke 22:28–30). *The call to discipleship is a call to the imitation of Christ* (John 13:15).

The Law

It was not Jesus' purpose simply to set aside the Law of the Old Testament. He was in the synagogue on the Sabbath (Mark 1:21; 6:2), went on pilgrimage during the festivals (Luke 2:41–52; John 2:13; 5:1; 7:14;

10:22; 12:12; Mark 11:1–11), taught in the synagogues and in the Temple (e.g., Mark 1:39; 14:49; John 6:59; 7:14; 8:20). He celebrated the paschal feast in the traditional way with his disciples (Mark 14:12–16; Luke 22:14–23), wore the prescribed tassels on his cloak (Mark 6:56; Luke 8:44), sent lepers to show themselves to the priests in accordance with the Law (Mark 1:44; Luke 17:14). He insisted that he had come not to destroy the Law but to fulfill it (Matthew 5:17).

On the other hand, Jesus also found himself at odds with Jewish teachers of the Law. He insisted that the Sabbath was made for men and women, not men and women for the Sabbath (Mark 2:27). He defended his disciples when they had neglected to perform the ritual hand-washing (Mark 7:1–23; Matthew 15:1–20). He argued that the tradition to which the teachers appealed was a merely human institution (Mark 7:8), and he gave a concrete example of what he meant (7:9–13): They neglected the duty of supporting parents (the fourth commandment of the Decalogue) because they permitted so-called *korban* oaths, even to the detriment of their parents' rights. These oaths expressed a son's intention to give money to the Temple, and the money, in turn, was no longer part of the support given to one's parents, even if later on the son decided not to give it to the Temple. *More fundamentally, Jesus attacked the traditional notion that every part of the Law was of equal importance and that the external observance is what finally counted.* For Jesus it is the inner disposition that determines an act's moral value (7:14–23).

But he did not ignore the external action itself (Luke 6:43–45). The final parable of the Sermon on the Mount, the house built on a rock (Matthew 7:24–27), is a call not only to listen to Jesus' words but to put them into action. "Treat others the way you would have them treat you: this sums up the law and the prophets" (7:12). And this must really be done, in deed and not only in word. "None of those who cry out, 'Lord, Lord,' will enter the kingdom of God but the only the one who does the will of my Father in heaven" (7:21). The same insistence on the connection between word and action is given in his indictment of the Scribes and Pharisees (23:1–36). He attacks them for straining at gnats and swallowing camels and for neglecting the weightier matters of the law: justice, mercy, and good faith (23:23). He is especially intolerant of their hypocrisy (23:4, 28). To return to the notion of *praxis* to which we referred at the beginning of this chapter: Jesus not only proclaimed the Kingdom of God; he practiced it, and he expected the same of others. God's will must be *done.*

The austere demands of Jesus are not to be explained away simply on the basis of his expectation of the coming of the Kingdom, but they are to be interpreted always in light of the coming Kingdom. Thus, it is clearly hyperbolic to say, as Jesus did, that it is easier for a camel to pass through the eye of a needle than for a rich man to enter into the Kingdom (Mark 10:25). The disciples expressed alarm: "Then who can be saved?" Jesus answered, "For man it is impossible but not for God. With God all things are possible" (10:27). But as severe as his ethical teaching may have been, his readiness to forgive was even stronger. Thus, a repentant Peter is singled out as the shepherd of the sheep despite his denial of Christ (Luke 22:32; John 21:15–17). Admonition and mercy are found together.

The Commandment of Love

All of Jesus' moral teaching is concentrated in the one commandment of love: the love of God and the love of neighbor (Mark 12:28–34; Matthew 22:34–40; Luke 10:25–28). On them all the Law and the prophets depend (Matthew 22:40). Apart from the great commandment, Jesus did not speak explicitly about loving God. He did say that we should not offer sacrifice to God unless and until we have been reconciled with our brother (Matthew 5:23–24) and that we cannot ask forgiveness for our sins unless we are also ready to forgive those who sin against us (6:12). But it would be wrong to equate love for God entirely with love for neighbor. Religious acts, such as prayer, also belong to the love of God (Matthew 6:1–15; 7:7–11; Mark 14:38). On the other hand, "religious" access to God through prayer cannot finally be divorced from the principal sacramental encounter with God in one's neighbor. The great picture of the Last Judgment in the parable of the Sheep and the Goats (Matthew 25:31–46) offers one of the classic illustrations of this principle.

According to John, Jesus gave himself as an example of unselfish love for others. He humbled himself to wash the feet of the disciples (13:4–15). He insisted that he was in their midst as one who serves (Luke 22:27), who gives his life as a ransom for many (Mark 10:45), and who thereby leaves a new commandment: "Love one another. Such as my love has been for you, so must your love be for each other. This is how all will know you for my disciples: your love for one another" (John 13:34–35). But such love is not to be reserved for one's friends. The disciple of Jesus is also commanded to love the enemy (Luke 6:27–28), to renounce revenge (6:29). We are to avoid judging and condemning others (6:37) and to be careful not to dwell on the speck in our brother's eye while missing the plank in our own (6:41–42). All of this is summed up in Paul's classic hymn to love: "There are in the end three things that last:

faith, hope, and love, and the greatest of these is love" (1 Corinthians 13).

Discipleship in the World

Jesus did not come to change the political order, but neither was he indifferent to it. What he preached was bound to affect the consciousness and behavior of those who heard and assimilated his words. The values he proclaimed would surely transform the world of those who shared them. But to make of him primarily a political figure is to put more into the New Testament than is there.

Jesus declared that he was sent to call sinners (Mark 2:17), to save the lost (Luke 19:10), to give his life for many (Mark 10:45). His kingdom was not of this world, he assured Pilate (John 18:36–37). He fled from the desire of his Galilean supporters to make him a political messianic king and national liberator (John 6:14–15). He rejected Peter's plea that he relinquish the path of suffering and death, just as he repelled the temptations of Satan to worldly power (Matthew 16:22–23). He maintained no contacts with the Zealot party. But all of this does not mean that Jesus' moral teaching had no bearing on political life.

He sent his disciples into the world (Matthew 10:16) and prayed, not that the Father would take his disciples out of the world, but that he would keep them safe in the world (John 17:15). He criticized contemporary institutions (Matthew 10). He saw what is dangerous and corrupting in political power as well as in riches: "You know how among the Gentiles those who seem to exercise authority lord it over them; their great ones make their importance felt. It cannot be like that with you" (Mark 10:42–43). When asked if he thought his fellow Jews should pay the tax to Caesar (Mark 12:13–37), he said they should, but he gave this answer only after asking about the image on the coin and pointing out to his interrogators that they already recognized Caesar's political authority over them by using his coinage. And then he added: "Give to Caesar what is Caesar's, but give to God what is God's" (12:17). Always it is the Kingdom which is supreme.

Jesus, of course, was a carpenter's son, and he himself labored for a time as a carpenter (Mark 6:3). His parables reflect his sense of identification with the poor and the workers: on the farm (Mark 4:3–8), in the vineyard (Matthew 20:1–15), on the sea (Matthew 13:47–50), in the home (Matthew 13:33; Luke 12:37–39; 17:7–10). But others also appear in his parables, without his passing judgment on their occupations or professions: e.g., merchants, traders, builders, soldiers, kings, judges, physicians, stewards. He did not attack the notion of private property, nor did he demand a redistribution of worldly goods. "The poor you will always have with you," he declared (Mark 14:7). Although he directed his severest warnings against the rich (Luke 6:24), he accepted hospitality from them (Luke 7:36; 10:38–42; 14:1, John 11:1–3; 12:1–3) and support from women of property (Luke 8:3). He certainly did not intend to exclude from the Kingdom such wealthy men as Nicodemus, Joseph of Arimathea, Zacchaeus the rich publican, and others like them (Luke 19:1–10).

The theme of wealth and property has an important place in the Gospel of Luke, so much so that some scholars have suggested that Luke deliberately intensified Jesus' sayings against the rich and riches. This may have been the case here and there (e.g., 5:11,28; 9:3; 10:4), but not as a general rule. As early as the Infancy Narrative Jesus' earthly origin is characterized as poverty-stricken (1:52–53; 2:7,24). The motif is sounded again in various discourses and parables (12:15–21; 14:12–14,33; 16). In Luke's version of the Beatitudes, Jesus first blesses the poor, for the reign of God is theirs (6:20)—not just the "poor" in the sense of the "poor in spirit" or the "just," but the economically poor. In the parable of the Rich Man and Lazarus (16:19–31), Lazarus, too, is literally poor. On the other hand, it is not poverty that entitles one to entrance into the Kingdom, but fidelity to the will of God (Matthew 7:21). In comparing the presentation of the Beatitudes in Matthew (5:3–12) and Luke (6:20–26), however, it is clear that Matthew emphasizes the religious and moral attitude of those who are called blessed and to whom the Kingdom of God is promised, whereas Luke stresses their social and economic position. Luke makes the same kind of modification in the parables of the Unfaithful Steward (16:1–7) and of the Rich Fool (12:16–20) and also in Jesus' attack on the Pharisees because of their greed (20:47).

Why do we find such a spirit in Luke? The evangelist had close contacts with certain circles in the original Jerusalem community who were literally poor and may have called themselves "the poor" in the religious sense (see Romans 15:26; Galatians 2:10). He praises the practice of sharing goods within the community of the first Christians (Acts of the Apostles 2:44–45; 4:32; 5:1–11). This contact undoubtedly shaped his own personal theology and piety.

What is of major, if not of revolutionary, significance in all of this is the assertion that *the poor have any place at all in the divine scheme of things*. Not only Luke but Matthew, too, removes the curse on poverty. Poverty is not by any means an obstacle to the Kingdom, as some apparently thought. Although other New Testament writings pay little attention to the poor and to poverty (it must have been discussed intensely in the Hellenistic communities for which Luke wrote), *the Christian movement itself was unique in the Roman world as one springing from the poor and lower classes.* [from *Catholicism*]

C. The Development of Christology

52. The Nicene Creed

The process by which the Christian community progressed from the New Testament faith to an explicit theological and dogmatic profession of the divinity of Christ and of the Trinity was long, complex and marked with dispute. From the earliest times, Christians worshiped Jesus and thought of him as "divine," but the exact nature of his relationship to the God whom he called "Father" was unclear. One explanation, put forth by the presbyter Arius, held that Christ was "divine" in a secondary sense as compared with the Father: he was the first and highest of all God's creatures, emanating from God as his "Word" and Son, a mediator between God and the world. For the Arians, therefore, Christ was a creature, although the highest of them; he had a "similar" nature to God's, but was not of the same essence (Greek "ousia") as God. At the same time, he was not completely human, but was a heavenly being who appeared in flesh on earth. The **Council of Nicaea (325 A.D.)** was called by the Roman emperor Constantine to settle the dispute caused by the conflict of interpretations of Christ's identity. It produced a "creed" (from the Latin "credo," meaning "I believe")—a formal statement of Christian belief used in worship and catechesis —which refutes the position of Arius and offers a concise guide to the content of faith in Christ.

We believe in one God, the Father almighty, creator of all things visible and invisible;

and in one Lord Jesus Christ, the son of God, born from the Father as his only begotten, that is, born from the substance [*ousia*] of the Father: God

from God, light from light, true God from true God; born, not made; of
the same substance [*ousia*] as the Father; through him all things in
heaven and on earth were made;

for us humans and for our salvation, he came down, was incarnated, and
became a human being; he suffered, and rose on the third day, ascended
into heaven, and will come to judge the living and the dead;

and in the Holy Spirit.

The Catholic Church excludes from its communion all those who say,
"there was a time when he did not exist," and "before his birth, he did
not exist," or that he was created, either from nothing or from some
other substance or essence, or that he was a creature, or a changeable or
mutable son of God.   [*Symbolum Nicaenum*, DS 125] /

53. The "exchange of attributes"

The doctrine of the divinity of Christ as proclaimed by the Council
of Nicaea was further developed and explained by the **Council of
Ephesus (431 A.D.),** called principally to condemn the position of
Nestorius, bishop of Constantinople. Nestorius held that in Christ
are both the divine Word and a full human being, but that these two
natures remain separate. To many of his contemporaries, Nestorius'
position seemed to posit two different subjects, joined only by a
moral union. In particular, they objected to Nestorius' statement
that one should not say that Mary is the mother of God, but only the
mother of the humanity of Christ. In refutation of this position, the
bishop **Cyril of Alexandria** wrote a letter and a series of "anathemas" (condemnations of exclusion from the church) which were
adopted by the council. Cyril enunciates the theological principle
that would be called the "communion" or "exchange" of attributes: whatever is said of one nature in Christ can be said of the
other, because of the unity of the one Christ; so that it is correct to
say that Mary is the mother of God, or that God died on the cross—
even though the divinity as such cannot be born or die—because
Christ, who is divine as well as human, was born and died.

The natures that were brought together [in the incarnation] to form a
true unity were different; but from both there is one Christ and one Son.
This does not mean that the difference between the natures was done

away with by their union; but rather that the divinity and humanity together constitute for us the one Lord and Son, Jesus Christ, by means of their hidden and ineffable conjoining. . . .

It was not that an ordinary human being was first born of the Virgin, and then the Word of God descended upon him; but rather, the Word is said to have been born in bodily fashion, having been united with the flesh in the womb itself. . . . Thus they [the holy Fathers of the church] did not hesitate to call the holy Virgin the God-bearer; not in the sense that the nature of God's Word or the divinity itself had its origin from the Virgin, but because the sacred body perfected by an intellectual soul— the body that he received from her, with which the Word of God is united in a substantial way ["according to *hypostasis*"]—is said to have been born bodily.   [from the Fourth Letter of Cyril of Alexandria, DS 250–251], [Trans. R. Viladesau]

If anyone does not profess that Emmanuel [= "God with us"—i.e., Christ] is truly God, and that therefore the holy Virgin is "Theotokos" [= "God-bearer," or "Mother of God"] (for she bore in bodily manner the Word of God made flesh), let that person be ananthema.

If anyone does not profess that the Word which comes from God the Father was substantially ["according to hypostasis"] united with flesh, and is one Christ in his own flesh, being one and the same God and man together, let that person be anathema.

If anyone divides the subsistences [hypostases] in Christ after their union, only joining them by a contiguity which relates them by dignity, or authority, or power, instead of recognizing a combining in a union of natures, let that person be ananthema.

If anyone divides the expressions used about Christ in the gospels . . . between two figures ["*prosopa*"] or subsistences ["*hypostases*"], applying some to the human being, conceived of as separate from God's Word, and applying others exclusively to the divine Word of the Father, let that person be anathema.

If anyone does not affirm that the Word of God suffered bodily and was bodily crucified, and tasted bodily death . . . let that person be anathema.   [from the *Anathemas of Cyril of Alexandria*, DS 252–263], [Trans. R. Viladesau]

54. The hypostatic union

Repeating the teachings of Nicaea and Ephesus, the **Council of Chalcedon** rejects the positions of those who deny either the divinity of Christ or his full humanity. Earlier discussion of the incarnation had been much hindered by the lack of equivalence between Greek and Latin concepts and by the ambiguity of the terms used by various theologians. This council marks the development of a technical theological language about Christ that could be accepted in both east and west. Chalcedon thus gave the church its classical christological formulation: in Christ there are two distinct natures, in the union of a single person or hypostasis (hence the term "hypostatic union").

Therefore, following the holy Fathers, we all in union teach that we must acknowledge one and the same Son, our Lord Jesus Christ, who is complete in divinity and complete in humanity, true God and true human being, having a body and a rational human soul; he is of the same substance [*homoousios*] as the Father in his divinity, and of the same substance [*homoousios*] as us in his humanity, like us in all things except sin; he was begotten by the Father before all ages in his divinity, and in the last times, for us humans and for our salvation, begotten of the Virgin Mary, mother of God, in his humanity. One and the same Christ, the Lord and only-begotten Son, is to be acknowledged in two natures, without mixture, without change, without division, without separation; the distinction of the natures is in no way abolished by the union; rather, the properties of each nature are preserved and come together to form one person [Greek *prosopon*] and one hypostasis [Latin *subsistentia*], not divided or separated into two persons, but one and the same only-begotten Son, God the Word, Our Lord Jesus Christ; just as the prophets in former times and Jesus Christ himself taught us, and as the Fathers passed down to us in the creed.   [The Symbol of the Council of Chalcedon, DS 301], [Trans. R. Viladesau]

55. Faith in the Trinity

Such was the emphasis on questions of christology in the early church that little explicit attention was paid in the definitions of the faith to the Holy Spirit. It was not until the **Council of Constantinople (381 A.D.)** that the doctrine of the Trinity was fully affirmed. The so-called **Athanasian Creed,** which is considered one of the three major professions of faith (the others being the Apostles' and Nicene Creeds), makes the Trinity the central focus of Christian belief. Attributed to St. Athanasius, the great defender of orthodoxy at the **Council of Nicaea (325),** this creed was probably actually composed some time in the fifth century.

Whoever wishes to be saved must first of all hold the catholic faith; for unless one maintains this faith in its entirety and without change, one will surely be lost eternally.

The catholic faith is this: that we worship one God in a Trinity, and the Trinity in unity, neither mixing the persons nor dividing the substance; for the Father is one person, the Son is another, and the Holy Spirit is another; but the divinity of the Father, the Son, and the Holy Spirit, is one, their glory is equal, and the majesty is co-eternal.

As the Father is, so is the Son, and so is the Holy Spirit: the Father is uncreated, the Son is uncreated, the Holy Spirit is uncreated; the Father is beyond measure, the Son is beyond measure, the Holy Spirit is beyond measure; the Father is eternal, the Son is eternal, the Holy Spirit is eternal; yet there are not three eternal beings, but one; just as there are not three uncreated nor three immeasurable, but one uncreated, one immeasurable. Likewise, the Father is omnipotent, the Son is imnipotent, the Holy Spirit is omnipotent; yet there are not three omnipotent beings, but one. So, the Father is God, the Son is God, the Holy Spirit is God; yet there are not three Gods, but one God. Thus the Father is Lord, the Son is Lord, the Holy Spirit is Lord; yet there are not three Lords, but one Lord; for as we are constrained by Christian truth to confess that each person individually is God and Lord, so we are forbidden by the catholic religion to speak of three Gods or Lords.

The Father was not made, nor created, nor begotten by anyone; the Son is from the Father alone, not made or created, but begotten; the Holy Spirit is from the Father and the Son, not made or created or begotten, but proceeding. Therefore there is one Father, not three; one Son, not three; one Holy Spirit, not three. In this Trinity, none is before or after another, none is more or less than another, but all three persons are co-eternal and co-equal. Thus in all things, as was said above, the Trinity in unity and the unity in Trinity is to be worshipped. Whoever wishes to be saved must believe this concerning the Trinity.

But it is also necessary to eternal salvation to believe faithfully in the incarnation of our Lord Jesus Christ. The right faith, therefore, is this: that we should believe and confess that our Lord Jesus Christ the Son of God is both God and a human: he is God, born from the substance of the

Father before the ages, and a human born in time from the substance of his mother; totally God, totally human, with a human rational soul and body; equal to the Father in his divinity, less than the Father in his humanity. Although he is God and a human, he is not two, but one Christ; not one by a changing of the godhead into flesh, but by the assumption of the humanity into God; altogether one, not by a mixture of substances, but by the unity of person. For just as a rational soul and a body are one human being, so God and humanity are one Christ. He suffered for our salvation, descended into hell, rose on the third day from the dead, ascended into the heavens, sits at the right hand of the Father, whence he will come to judge the living and the dead. At his coming, all humans will rise again bodily, and will have to give account of their own deeds; and those who have done good, will enter into eternal life, while those who have done evil, will enter into eternal fire.

This is the catholic faith; unless one faithfully and firmly believes it, one cannot be saved. [*Symbolum "Quicumque" pseudo-Athanasianum*, DS 75], [Trans. R. Viladesau]

Chapter Six

The Church

A. Historical Perspectives

56. *The earliest form of the eucharist*

The **Didache** is an early Christian manual on morals and worship, representing the earliest of the "church orders"—instructions on how to baptize and celebrate the eucharist. It is thought by some scholars to date from the first century. The selection below offers a description of how the early church prayed when it gathered for the eucharist. Compare this description of the eucharistic prayer with the contemporary form of the mass: What elements remain the same? How has the contemporary eucharist expanded on the form described in the *Didache?*

At the Eucharist, give thanks in this way. First for the chalice: "We give you thanks, our Father, for the holy vine of your servant David, which thou hast made known to us through your servant Jesus."

"Glory to you forever."

Then over the broken bread: "We give you thanks, our Father, for the life and knowledge that you have made known to us through your servant Jesus."

"Glory to you forever."

"As this broken bread was scattered on the hillsides, and was gathered together and made one, so may your church be gathered together from the ends of the earth into your Kingdom."

"Yours is the glory and the power through Jesus Christ forever."

Let no one eat or drink of your Eucharist except those that have been baptized in the name of the Lord. For about this the Lord has said, "Do not give what is holy to dogs."

When all have eaten enough, give thanks in this way: "We give you thanks, holy Father, for your sacred name, which you have made to dwell in our hearts, and for the knowledge and faith and everlasting life that you have revealed to us through your servant Jesus."

"Glory to you forever."

"You, almighty Lord, have created all things for your own name's sake; you gave food and drink to all people to enjoy, so that they might give you thanks; but to us you have granted spiritual food and drink, along with life eternal, through your servant. Above all we thank you for your mighty power."

"Glory to you forever."

"Remember, Lord, your church; deliver it from all evil, make it perfect in your love, and gather it, sanctified, from the four winds into the Kingdom which you have prepared for it."

"For yours is the power and the glory forever."

"Let his grace come, and let this world pass away."

"Hosanna to the God of David."

"Let those who are holy approach; those who are not, let them repent."

"O Lord, come [*Maranatha*]. Amen."

But let the prophets give thanks as they wish.   [from the *Didache*]

57. The eucharist in the second century

Justin Martyr, put to death for being a Christian in 165 A.D., was one of the most significant early Christian writers. His *First Apology,* addressed to the Roman emperor to refute charges that Christians were guilty of immorality, cannibalism, atheism, and theological absurdity, stands as one of the most important descriptions of Christian faith and practice in the second century. The three chapters below, taken from that work, describe how early Christian communities celebrated the eucharist, and offer some insight into the developing theological understanding about that rite. How does Justin's description of early Christian worship reveal his desire to correct popular misconceptions about his religion? In what ways do contemporary celebrations of the eucharist resemble the service described here? How are they different?

65. After having baptized the person who has been persuaded and has given consent, we bring that person to where those that are called "the brethren" are gathered, to offer communal prayers for themselves, for the one who has been enlightened, and for all people everywhere, with all our hearts, so that, having learned the truth, we may also be counted worthy to be esteemed as good citizens and keepers of the commandments, so that we may saved with an everlasting salvation. When our prayers are ended, we greet each other with a kiss. Then bread and a cup of water and wine are brought to the president of the brethren. He takes them, and offers up praise and glory to the Father of all, through the name of his Son and of the Holy Spirit, and gives thanks at length that we have been deemed worthy to receive these things at his hand. When the president has finished the prayers and thanksgiving, all the people present make assent by saying *Amen*. (*Amen* in Hebrew means "so be it.") When the president has given thanks and all the people have assented, those we call "deacons" give to those present a portion of the eucharistic bread and the mixed water and wine; and they also carry it to those who are absent.

66. We call this food "the Eucharist," and no one is allowed to partake of it except those convinced of the truth of our teachings, who have been washed with the washing for the forgiveness of sins and for regeneration, and who live as Christ has taught us. For we do not receive these things as ordinary food and drink; but as Jesus Christ our Savior took flesh and blood for our salvation by the word of God, so also, we are taught, the food blessed by the prayer which comes from him, and by which our flesh and blood is nourished by transformation, is the flesh and blood of the incarnate Jesus. For the Apostles, in the memoirs composed by them, called "gospels," have handed down the command that was given; that Jesus took bread, gave thanks, and said: "Do this in remembrance (*anamnesis*) of me; this is my body." And he took the cup likewise and said, "This is my blood," and gave it to them alone. The evil demons ordered the same thing to be done in imitation in the mysteries of Mithra; for as you know or may learn, bread and a cup of water are brought out, with the recitation of certain words, in their secret rites of initiation.

67. Thereafter we constantly remind each other of these things. The rich assist those that are needy; and we always stay together. At all our meals we bless the maker of all things through his son Jesus Christ and through the Holy Spirit. And on the day called "Sunday" all those who live either in the cities or the countryside gather together; and the memoirs of the Apostles or the writings of the prophets are read, for as long as

time permits. When the reader has finished, the president speaks, admonishing the people and exhorting them to imitate these examples of virtue. Then we arise together and offer prayers; and, as we said before, when we have concluded our prayer, bread is brought, and wine mixed with water, and the president likewise offers up prayers and thanksgivings according to his ability, and the people assent by saying *Amen;* the eucharistic elements are distributed and partaken by each person present, and they are sent to those who are absent by means of the deacons. Those who are prosperous, if they wish, contribute what they think fitting. The collection is deposited with the president, and he gives aid to the orphans and widows and to those that are in need because of sickness or some other reason, and to prisoners, and to strangers from abroad; in short, he is the protector of all the needy. We hold our assembly on Sunday because it is the first day, on which God, transforming the darkness and matter, made the world; and on the same day Jesus Christ our Savior rose from the dead; for he was crucified on the day before Saturn's day; and on the day after Saturday, which is the day of the Sun, he appeared to his Apostles and disciples and taught them these things which we have also transmitted to you for your consideration. [from the *First Apology*]

58. The law of worship

"*Lex orandi, lex credendi*" is an ancient saying theologians use to explain the relationship between how Christians worship and what they believe. Roughly translated, the phrase means that what the church says in prayer (*lex orandi*) guides what the church believes (*lex credendi*). The *Pange Lingua*—one of the most famous of all Christian hymns—was composed by **St. Thomas Aquinas** (see #24, 27, 30, 38, 43) in 1263 to celebrate Christ's presence in the eucharist, and is still sung on Holy Thursday and on the Feast of Corpus Christi. The power of the hymn, given below in the original highly poetic Latin and in a literal translation, lies in its clear theological expression of how the church prays when it celebrates the eucharist. St. Thomas was also the formulator of the theological idea of "transubstantiation" to explain how Christ was present in the eucharist. From your reading of the hymn, what does this theological concept mean? What does the hymn say about how Christ is pres-

ent in the bread and wine of the eucharist? What is the relationship
of faith and worship that the hymn celebrates?

Pange lingua gloriosi
Corporis mysterium,
Sanguinisque pretiosi,
Quem in mundi pretium
Fructus ventris generosi
Rex effudit gentium.

Sing, my tongue, of the mystery of the glorious Body and of the precious
Blood that the King of all nations, the fruit of a generous womb, poured
out as the price of the world's redemption.

Nobis datus, nobis natus
Ex intacta Virgine,
Et in mundo conversatus,
Sparso verbi semine,
Sui moras incolatus
Miro clausit ordine.

Given to us, born for us of an intact Virgin, he lived communing in the
world; having dwelt among us sowing the seed of the word, he wonder-
fully brought his life to its end.

In supremae nocte coenae
Recumbens cum fratribus,
Observata lege plene
Cibis in legalibus,
Cibum turbae duodenae
Se dat suis manibus.

On the night of his last supper, reclining with his brethren, having fully
observed the Law by the ritual meal [the Passover], with his own hands
he gave food to the group of Twelve.

Verbum caro, panem verum
Verbo carnem efficit:
Fitque sanquis Christi merum,
Et si sensus deficit,
Ad firmandum cor sincerum
Sola fides sufficit.

The Word made flesh by a word produces the true Bread; wine becomes the Blood of Christ; and, and although the senses are inadequate [to perceive this], faith alone suffices to strengthen the sincere heart.

Tantum ergo sacramentum
Veneremur cernui:
Et antinquum documentum
Novo cedat ritui:
Praestet fides supplementum
Sensuum defectui.

Let us therefore bowing down adore so great a sacrament; and let the old foreshadowing make way for a new rite. May faith make up for the inadequacy of the senses' perception.

Genitori, Genitoque
Laus et jubilatio,
Salus, honor, virtus quoque
Sit et benedictio:
Procedenti ab utroque
Compar sit laudatio. Amen.

To the Father and the Son be praise and rejoicing, salutation, honor, power and blessing; equal praise be given to the one proceeding from both [the Spirit]. [from the *Liber Usualis: Pange Lingua*], [Trans. R. Viladesau]

B. Modern Perspectives

59. The evolution of doctrine

John Henry Newman (1801–1890), perhaps the most famous Catholic convert in modern times, was also one of the most important and influential Catholic theologians of the nineteenth century. Newman, an influential Anglican priest, was received into the Catholic Church in 1845 at the end of a famous and tumultuous "intellectual conversion." Basic to his conversion was his growing belief, while still an Anglican, that Christian doctrine had "evolved" over history, and that there were definite "rules" governing that evolution. His magisterial *Essay on the Development of Christian Doctrine*, published in the same year as his conversion, offered his reasons for believing that ancient Christian beliefs underwent legitimate development over time; he thus argued that it was both unhistorical and untheological to expect modern doctrine simply to repeat the beliefs of the primitive Christian community recorded in scripture. Newman was made a cardinal in 1879, although his real influence occurred after his death, especially in the twentieth century, when Catholic theologians used his important concept of the "development of doctrine" to bring Catholic theology into conversation with modern culture. His *Essay,* excerpted below, remains one of the most important theological treatises for contemporary theology. What criteria does Newman offer to judge "legitimate development" of doctrine over time? Why does he think that such development is essential for true theological study?

3.

2. Again, if Christianity be an universal religion, suited not simply to one locality or period, but to all times and places, it cannot but vary in its relations and dealings towards the world around it, that is, it will develop. Principles require a very various application according as persons and circumstances vary, and must be thrown into new shapes according to the form of society which they are to influence. Hence all bodies of Christians, orthodox or not, develope the doctrines of Scripture. Few but will grant that Luther's view of justification had never been stated in words before his time: that his phraseology and his positions were novel, whether called for by circumstances or not. It is equally certain that the doctrine of justification defined at Trent was, in some sense, new also. The refutation and remedy of errors cannot precede their rise; and thus the fact of false developments or corruptions involves the correspondent manifestation of true ones. Moreover, all parties appeal to Scripture, that is, argue from Scripture; but argument implies deduction, that is, development. Here there is no difference between early times and late, between a Pope *ex cathedrá* and an individual Protestant, except that their authority is not on a par. On either side the claim of authority is the same, and the process of development.

Accordingly, the common complaint of Protestants against the Church of Rome is, not simply that she has added to the primitive or the Scriptural doctrine, (for this they do themselves,) but that she contradicts it, and moreover imposes her additions as fundamental truths under sanction of an anathema. For themselves they deduce by quite as subtle a method, and act upon doctrines as implicit and on reasons as little analyzed in time past, as Catholic schoolmen. What prominence has the Royal Supremacy in the New Testament, or the lawfulness of bearing arms, or the duty of public worship, or the substitution of the first day of the week for the seventh, or infant baptism, to say nothing of the fundamental principle that the Bible and the Bible only is the religion of Protestants? These doctrines and usages, true or not, which is not the question here, are surely not gained by the direct use and immediate application of Scripture, nor by a mere exercise of argument upon words and sentences placed before the eyes, but by the unconscious growth of ideas suggested by the letter and habitual to the mind.

4.

3. And, indeed, when we turn to the consideration of particular doctrines on which Scripture lays the greatest stress, we shall see that it is absolutely impossible for them to remain in the mere letter of Scripture, if they are to be more than mere words, and to convey a definite idea to the recipient. When it is declared that "the Word became flesh," three wide questions open upon us on the very announcement. What is meant by "the Word," what by "flesh," what by "became"? The answers to these involve a process of investigation, and are developments. Moreover, when they have been made, they will suggest a series of secondary questions; and thus at length a multitude of propositions is the result, which gather round the inspired sentence of which they come, giving it externally the form of a doctrine, and creating or deepening the idea of it in the mind.

It is true that, so far as such statements of Scripture are mysteries, they are relatively to us but words, and cannot be developed. But as a mystery implies in part what is incomprehensible or at least unknown, so does it in part imply what is not so; it implies a partial manifestation, or a representation by economy. Because then it is in a measure understood, it can so far be developed, though each result in the process will partake of the dimness and confusion of the original impression.

5.

4. This moreover should be considered,—that great questions exist in the subject-matter of which Scripture treats, which Scripture does not solve; questions too so real, so practical, that they must be answered,

and, unless we suppose a new revelation, answered by means of the revelation which we have, that is, by development. Such is the question of the Canon of Scripture and its inspiration: that is, whether Christianity depends upon a written document as Judaism;—if so, on what writings and how many;—whether that document is self-interpreting, or requires a comment, and whether any authoritative comment or commentator is provided;—whether the revelation and the document are commensurate, or the one outruns the other;—all these questions surely find no solution on the surface of Scripture, nor indeed under the surface in the case of most men, however long and diligent might be their study of it. Nor were these difficulties settled by authority, as far as we know, at the commencement of the religion; yet surely it is quite conceivable that an Apostle might have dissipated them all in a few words, had Divine Wisdom thought fit. But in matter of fact the decision has been left to time, to the slow process of thought, to the influence of mind upon mind, the issues of controversy, and the growth of opinion.

Thus developments of Christianity are proved to have been in the contemplation of its Divine Author, by an argument parallel to that by which we infer intelligence in the system of the physical world. In whatever sense the need and its supply are a proof of design in the visible creation, in the same do the gaps, if the word may be used, which occur in the structure of the original creed of the Church, make it probable that those developments, which grow out of the truths which lie around it, were intended to fill them up.

Nor can it be fairly objected that in thus arguing we are contradicting the great philosopher, who tells us, that "upon supposition of God affording us light and instruction by revelation, additional to what He has afforded us by reason and experience, we are in no sort judges by what methods, and in what proportion, it were to be expected that this supernatural light and instruction would be afforded us," because he is speaking of our judging before a revelation is given. He observes that "we have no principles of reason upon which to judge *beforehand*, how it were to be expected Revelation should have been left, or what was most suitable to the divine plan of government," in various respects; but the case is altogether altered when a Revelation is vouchsafed, for then a new precedent, or what he calls "principle of reason," is introduced, and from what is actually put into our hands we can form a judgment whether more is to be expected. Butler, indeed, as a well-known passage of his work shows, is far from denying the principle of progressive development.

9.

5. The method of revelation observed in Scripture abundantly confirms this anticipation. For instance, Prophecy, if it had so happened, need not have afforded a specimen of development; separate predictions might have been made to accumulate as time went on, prospects might have opened, definite knowledge might have been given, by communications independent of each other, as St. John's Gospel or the Epistles of St. Paul are unconnected with the first three Gospels, though the doctrine of each Apostle is a development of their matter. But the prophetic Revelation is, in matter of fact, not of this nature, but a process of development: the earlier prophecies are pregnant texts out of which the succeeding announcements grow; they are types. It is not that first one truth is told, then another; but the whole truth or large portions of it are told at once, yet only in their rudiments, or in miniature, and they are expanded and finished in their parts, as the course of revelation proceeds. The Seed of the woman was to bruise the serpent's head; the sceptre was not to depart from Judah till Shiloh came, to whom was to be the gathering of the people. He was to be Wonderful, Counsellor, the Prince of Peace. The question of the Ethiopian rises in the reader's mind, "Of whom speaketh the Prophet this?" Every word requires a comment. Accordingly, it is no uncommon theory with unbelievers, that the Messianic idea, as they call it, was gradually developed in the minds of the Jews by a continuous and traditional habit of contemplating it, and grew into its full proportions by a mere human process; and so far seems certain, without trenching on the doctrine of inspiration, that the books of Wisdom and Ecclesiasticus are developments of the writings of the Prophets, expressed or elicited by means of current ideas in the Greek philosophy, and ultimately adopted and ratified by the Apostle in his Epistle to the Hebrews.   [from *Essay on the Development of Dogma*, ch. 2]

60. The mystery of the Church

The **Second Vatican Council** (see above, #34) dramatically refocused Catholic energies in the second half of the twentieth century. Among the most important documents that emerged from its meetings between 1962 and 1965 was the *"Dogmatic Constitution on the Church"* (excerpted below). *Lumen Gentium* (the official Latin title of the Constitution) is considered by many theologians to be the most significant document to emerge from the council, as it uses biblical images and symbols to define more clearly the "mystery of the church" in history. What images and metaphors are emphasized in describing the church? What does the document say about the relationship of the Catholic Church to God's kingdom? According to the document, what is the relation between the Catholic Church and other Christian churches?

THE MYSTERY OF THE CHURCH

1. Christ is the light of all nations. Hence this most sacred Synod, which has been gathered in the Holy Spirit, eagerly desires to shed on all men that radiance of His which brightens the countenance of the Church. This it will do by proclaiming the gospel to every creature (cf. Mk. 16:15).

By her relationship with Christ, the Church is a kind of sacrament or sign of intimate union with God, and of the unity of all mankind. She is also an instrument for the achievement of such union and unity. For this reason, following in the path laid out by its predecessors, this Council wishes to set forth more precisely to the faithful and to the entire world the nature and encompassing mission of the Church. The conditions of this age lend special urgency to the Church's task of bringing all men to full union with Christ, since mankind today is joined together more closely than ever before by social, technical, and cultural bonds.

5. The mystery of the holy Church is manifest in her very foundation, for the Lord Jesus inaugurated her by preaching the good news, that is, the coming of God's Kingdom, which, for centuries, had been promised in the Scriptures: "The time is fulfilled, and the kingdom of God is at hand" (Mk. 1:15; cf. Mt. 4:17). In Christ's word, in His works, and in His presence this kingdom reveals itself to men. The word of the Lord is like a seed sown in a field (Mk. 4:14). Those who hear the word with faith and become part of the little flock of Christ (Lk. 12:32) have received the kingdom itself. Then, by its own power the seed sprouts and ripens until harvest time (cf. Mk. 4:26–29).

The miracles of Jesus also confirm that the kingdom has already arrived on earth: "If I cast out devils by the finger of God, then the kingdom of God has come upon you" (Lk. 11:20; cf. Mt. 12:28).

Before all things, however, the kingdom is clearly visible in the very person of Christ, Son of God and Son of Man, who came "to serve, and to give his life as a ransom for many" (Mk. 10:45).

When Jesus rose up again after suffering death on the cross for mankind, He manifested that He had been appointed Lord, Messiah, and

Priest forever (cf. Acts 2:36; Heb. 5:6; 7:17–21), and He poured out on His disciples the Spirit promised by the Father (cf. Acts 2:33). The Church, consequently, equipped with the gifts of her Founder and faithfully guarding His precepts of charity, humility, and self-sacrifice, receives the mission to proclaim and to establish among all peoples the kingdom of Christ and of God. She becomes on earth the initial budding forth of that kingdom. While she slowly grows, the Church strains toward the consummation of the kingdom and, with all her strength, hopes and desires to be united in glory with her King.

6. In the Old Testament the revelation of the kingdom had often been conveyed by figures of speech. In the same way the inner nature of the Church was now to be made known to us through various images. Drawn from pastoral life, agriculture, building construction, and even from family and married life, these images served a preparatory role in the writings of the prophets.

Thus, the Church is a sheepfold whose one and necessary door is Christ (Jn. 10:1–10). She is a flock of which God Himself foretold that He would be the Shepherd (cf. Is. 40:11; Ez. 34:11 ff.). Although guided by human shepherds, her sheep are nevertheless ceaselessly led and nourished by Christ Himself, the Good Shepherd and the Prince of Shepherds (cf. Jn. 10:11; 1 Pet. 5:4), who gave His life for the sheep (cf. Jn. 10:11–15).

The Church is a tract of land to be cultivated, the field of God (1 Cor. 3:9). On that land grows the ancient olive tree whose holy roots were the patriarchs and in which the reconciliation of Jew and Gentile has been brought about and will be brought about (Rom. 11:13–26). The Church has been cultivated by the heavenly Vinedresser as His choice vineyard (Mt. 21:33–43 par.; cf. Is. 5:1 ff.). The true Vine is Christ who gives life and fruitfulness to the branches, that is, to us. Through the Church, we abide in Christ, without whom we can do nothing (Jn. 15:1–5).

The Church has more often been called the edifice of God (1 Cor. 3:9). Even the Lord likened Himself to the stone which the builders rejected, but which became the cornerstone (Mt. 21:42 par.; cf. Acts 4:11; 1 Pet. 2:7; Ps. 117:22). On this foundation the Church is built by the apostles (cf. 1 Cor. 3:11), and from it the Church receives durability and solidity. This edifice is adorned by various names: the house of God (1 Tim. 3:15) in which dwells His family; the household of God in the Spirit (Eph. 2:19–22); the dwelling place of God among men (Apoc. 21:3); and, especially, the holy temple. This temple, symbolized by places of worship built out of stone, is praised by the holy Fathers and, not without reason, is compared in the liturgy to the Holy City, the New Jerusalem. As living stones we here on earth are being built up along with this City (1 Pet. 2:5). John contemplates this Holy City, coming down out of heaven from God when the world is made anew, and prepared like a bride adorned for her husband (Apoc. 21:1 f.).

The Church, "that Jerusalem which is above," is also called "our Mother" (Gal. 4:26; cf. Apoc. 12:17). She is described as the spotless spouse of the spotless Lamb (Apoc. 19:7; 21:2 and 9; 22:17). She it was whom Christ "loved and delivered himself up for her that he might sanctify her" (Eph. 5:26), whom He unites to Himself by an unbreakable covenant, and whom He unceasingly "nourishes and cherishes" (Eph. 5:29). Once she had been purified, He willed her to be joined unto Himself and to be subject to Him in love and fidelity (cf. Eph. 5:24). Finally, He filled her with heavenly gifts for all eternity, in order that we might know the love of God and of Christ for us, a love which surpasses all knowledge (cf. Eph. 3:19). The Church on earth, while journeying in a foreign land away from her Lord (cf. 2 Cor. 5:6), regards herself as an exile. Hence she seeks and experiences those things which are above, where Christ is seated at the right hand of God, where the life of the Church is hidden with Christ in God until she appears in glory with her Spouse (cf. Col. 3:1–4).

7. In the human nature which He united to Himself, the Son of God redeemed man and transformed him into a new creation (cf. Gal. 6:15; 2 Cor. 5:17) by overcoming death through His own death and resurrection. By communicating His Spirit to His brothers, called together from all peoples, Christ made them mystically into His own body.

In that body, the life of Christ is poured into the believers, who, through the sacraments, are united in a hidden and real way to Christ who suffered and was glorified. Through baptism we are formed in the likeness of Christ: "For in one Spirit we were all baptized into one body" (1 Cor. 12:13). In this sacred rite, a union with Christ's death and resurrection is both symbolized and brought about: "For we were buried with him by means of Baptism into death." And if "we have been united with him in the likeness of his death, we shall be so in the likeness of his resurrection also" (Rom. 6:4–5).

Truly partaking of the body of the Lord in the breaking of the Eucharistic bread, we are taken up into communion with Him and with one another. "Because the bread is one, we though many, are one body, all of us who partake of the one bread" (1 Cor. 10:17). In this way all of us are made members of His body (cf. 1 Cor. 12:27), "but severally members one of another" (Rom. 12:5).

As all the members of the human body, though they are many, form one body, so also are the faithful in Christ (cf. 1 Cor. 12:12). Also, in the building up of Christ's body there is a flourishing variety of members and functions. There is only one Spirit who, according to His own richness and the needs of the ministries, distributes His different gifts for the welfare of the Church (cf. 1 Cor. 12:1–11). Among these gifts stands out the grace given to the apostles. To their authority, the Spirit Himself subjected even those who were endowed with charisms (cf. 1 Cor. 14). Giving the body unity through Himself and through His power and through the internal cohesion of its members, this same Spirit produces and urges love among the believers. Consequently, if one member suffers anything, all the members suffer it too, and if one member is honored, all the members rejoice together (cf. 1 Cor. 12:26).

The Head of this body is Christ. He is the image of the invisible God and in Him all things came into being. He has priority over everyone and in Him all things hold together. He is the Head of that body which is the Church. He is the beginning, the firstborn from the dead, so that in all things He might have the first place (cf. Col. 1:15–18). By the greatness of His power He rules the things of heaven and the things of earth, and with His all-surpassing perfection and activity He fills the whole body with the riches of His glory (cf. Eph. 1:18–23).

All the members ought to be molded into Christ's image until He is formed in them (cf. Gal. 4:19). For this reason we who have been made like unto Him, who have died with Him and been raised up with Him, are taken up into the mysteries of His life, until we reign together with Him (cf. Phil. 3:21; 2 Tim. 2:11; Eph. 2:6; Col. 2:12; etc.). Still in pilgrimage upon the earth, we trace in trial and under oppression the paths He trod. Made one with His sufferings as the body is one with the head, we endure with Him, that with Him we may be glorified (cf. Rom. 8:17).

From Him, "the whole body, supplied and built up by joints and ligaments, attains a growth that is of God" (Col. 2:19). He continually distributes in His body, that is, in the Church, gifts of ministries through which, by His own power, we serve each other unto salvation so that, carrying out the truth in love, we may through all things grow up into Him who is our head (cf. Eph. 4:11–16, Greek text).

In order that we may be unceasingly renewed in Him (cf. Eph. 4:23), He has shared with us His Spirit who, existing as one and the same being in the head and in the members, vivifies, unifies, and moves the whole body. This He does in such a way that His work could be compared by the holy Fathers with the function which the soul fulfills in the human body, whose principle of life the soul is.

Having become the model of a man loving his wife as his own body,

Christ loves the Church as His bride (cf. Eph. 5:25–28). For her part, the Church is subject to her Head (cf. Eph. 5:22–23). "For in him dwells all the fullness of the Godhead bodily" (Col. 2:9). He fills the Church, which is His Body and His fullness, with His divine gifts (cf. Eph. 1:22–23) so that she may grow and reach all the fullness of God (cf. Eph. 3:19).

8. Christ, the one Mediator, established and ceaselessly sustains here on earth His holy Church, the community of faith, hope, and charity, as a visible structure. Through her He communicates truth and grace to all. But the society furnished with hierarchical agencies and the Mystical Body of Christ are not to be considered as two realities, nor are the visible assembly and the spiritual community, nor the earthly Church and the Church enriched with heavenly things. Rather they form one interlocked reality which is comprised of a divine and a human element. For this reason, by an excellent analogy, this reality is compared to the mystery of the incarnate Word. Just as the assumed nature inseparably united to the divine Word serves Him as a living instrument of salvation, so, in a similar way, does the communal structure of the Church serve Christ's Spirit, who vivifies it by way of building up the body (cf. Eph. 4:16).

This is the unique Church of Christ which in the Creed we avow as one, holy, catholic, and apostolic. After His Resurrection our Savior handed her over to Peter to be shepherded (Jn. 21:17), commissioning him and the other apostles to propagate and govern her (cf. Mt. 28:18 ff.). Her He erected for all ages as "the pillar and mainstay of the truth" (1 Tim. 3:15). This Church, constituted and organized in the world as a society, subsists in the Catholic Church, which is governed by the successor of Peter and by the bishops in union with that successor, although many elements of sanctification and of truth can be found outside of her visible structure. These elements, however, as gifts properly belonging to the Church of Christ, possess an inner dynamism toward Catholic unity.

Just as Christ carried out the work of redemption in poverty and under oppression, so the Church is called to follow the same path in communicating to men the fruits of salvation. Christ Jesus, "though He was by nature God . . . emptied himself, taking the nature of a slave" (Phil. 2:6), and "being rich, he became poor" (2 Cor. 8:9) for our sakes. Thus, although the Church needs human resources to carry out her mission, she is not set up to seek earthly glory, but to proclaim humility and self-sacrifice, even by her own example.

Christ was sent by the Father "to bring good news to the poor, to heal the contrite of heart" (Lk. 4:18), "to seek and to save what was lost" (Lk.

19:10). Similarly, the Church encompasses with love all those who are afflicted with human weakness. Indeed, she recognizes in the poor and the suffering the likeness of her poor and suffering Founder. She does all she can to relieve their need and in them she strives to serve Christ. While Christ, "holy, innocent, undefiled" (Heb. 7:26) knew nothing of sin (2 Cor. 5:21), but came to expiate only the sins of the people (cf. Heb. 2:17), the Church, embracing sinners in her bosom, is at the same time holy and always in need of being purified, and incessantly pursues the path of penance and renewal.

The Church, "like a pilgrim in a foreign land, presses forward amid the persecutions of the world and the consolations of God," announcing the cross and death of the Lord until He comes (cf. 1 Cor. 11:26). By the power of the risen Lord, she is given strength to overcome patiently and lovingly the afflictions and hardships which assail her from within and without, and to show forth in the world the mystery of the Lord in a faithful though shadowed way, until at the last it will be revealed in total splendor.

CHAPTER II

The People of God

9. At all times and among every people, God has given welcome to whosoever fears Him and does what is right (cf. Acts 10:35). It has pleased God, however, to make men holy and save them not merely as individuals without any mutual bonds, but by making them into a single people, a people which acknowledges Him in truth and serves Him in holiness. He therefore chose the race of Israel as a people unto Himself. With it He set up a covenant. Step by step He taught this people by manifesting in its history both Himself and the decree of His will, and by making it holy unto Himself. All these things, however, were done by way of preparation and as a figure of that new and perfect covenant which was to be ratified in Christ, and of that more luminous revelation which was to be given through God's very Word made flesh.

"Behold the days shall come, saith the Lord, and I will make a new covenant with the house of Israel, and with the house of Judah. . . . I will give my law in their bowels, and I will write it in their heart: and I will be their God, and they shall be my people. . . . For all shall know me, from the least of them even to the greatest, saith the Lord" (Jer. 31:31–34). Christ instituted this new covenant, that is to say, the new testament, in

His blood (cf. 1 Cor. 11:25), by calling together a people made up of Jew and Gentile, making them one, not according to the flesh but in the Spirit.

This was to be the new People of God. For, those who believe in Christ, who are reborn not from a perishable but from an imperishable seed through the Word of the living God (cf. 1 Pet. 1:23), not from the flesh but from water and the Holy Spirit (cf. Jn. 3:5–6), are finally established as "a chosen race, a royal priesthood, a holy nation, a purchased people. . . . You who in times past were not a people, but are now the people of God" (1 Pet. 2:9–10).

That messianic people has for its head Christ, "who was delivered up for our sins, and rose again for our justification" (Rom. 4:25), and who now, having won a name which is above all names, reigns in glory in heaven. The heritage of this people are the dignity and freedom of the sons of God, in whose hearts the Holy Spirit dwells as in His temple. Its law is the new commandment to love as Christ loved us (cf. Jn. 13:34). Its goal is the kingdom of God, which has been begun by God Himself on earth, and which is to be further extended until it is brought to perfection by Him at the end of time. Then Christ our life (cf. Col. 3:4), will appear, and "creation itself also will be delivered from its slavery to corruption into the freedom of the glory of the sons of God" (Rom. 8:21).

So it is that this messianic people, although it does not actually include all men, and may more than once look like a small flock, is nonetheless a lasting and sure seed of unity, hope, and salvation for the whole human race. Established by Christ as a fellowship of life, charity, and truth, it is also used by Him as an instrument for the redemption of all, and is sent forth into the whole world as the light of the world and the salt of the earth (cf. Mt. 5:13–16).

Israel according to the flesh, which wandered as an exile in the desert, was already called the Church of God (2 Esd. 13:1; cf. Num. 20:4; Dt. 23:1 ff). Likewise the new Israel which, while going forward in this present world, goes in search of a future and abiding city (cf. Heb. 13:14) is also called the Church of Christ (cf. Mt. 16:18). For He has bought it for Himself with His blood (cf. Acts 20:28), has filled it with His Spirit, and provided it with those means which befit it as a visible and social unity. God has gathered together as one all those who in faith look upon Jesus as the author of salvation and the source of unity and peace, and has established them as the Church, that for each and all she may be the visible sacrament of this saving unity.

While she transcends all limits of time and of race, the Church is destined to extend to all regions of the earth and so to enter into the history of mankind. Moving forward through trial and tribulation, the Church is strengthened by the power of God's grace promised to her by the Lord, so that in the weakness of the flesh she may not waver from perfect fidelity, but remain a bride worthy of her Lord; that moved by the Holy Spirit she may never cease to renew herself, until through the cross she arrives at the light which knows no setting.

10. Christ the Lord, High Priest taken from among men (cf. Heb. 5:1–5), "made a kingdom and priests to God his Father" (Apoc. 1:6; cf. 5:9–10) out of this new people. The baptized, by regeneration and the anointing of the Holy Spirit, are consecrated into a spiritual house and a holy priesthood. Thus through all those works befitting Christian men they can offer spiritual sacrifices and proclaim the power of Him who has called them out of darkness into His marvelous light (cf. 1 Pet. 2:4–10). Therefore all the disciples of Christ, persevering in prayer and praising God (cf. Acts 2:42–47), should present themselves as living sacrifices holy and pleasing to God (cf. Rom. 12:1). Everywhere on earth they must bear witness to Christ and give an answer to those who seek an account of that hope of eternal life which is in them (cf. 1 Pet. 3:15).

Though they differ from one another in essence and not only in degree, the common priesthood of the faithful and the ministerial or hierarchical priesthood are nonetheless interrelated. Each of them in its own special way is a participation in the one priesthood of Christ. The ministerial priest, by the sacred power he enjoys, molds and rules the priestly people. Acting in the person of Christ, he brings about the Eucharistic Sacrifice, and offers it to God in the name of all the people. For their part, the faithful join in the offering of the Eucharist by virtue of their royal priesthood. They likewise exercise that priesthood by receiving the sacraments, by prayer and thanksgiving, by the witness of a holy life, and by self-denial and active charity.

11. It is through the sacraments and the exercise of the virtues that the sacred nature and organic structure of the priestly community is brought into operation. Incorporated into the Church through baptism, the faithful are consecrated by the baptismal character to the exercise of the cult of the Christian religion. Reborn as sons of God, they must confess before men the faith which they have received from God through the Church. Bound more intimately to the Church by the sacrament of confirmation, they are endowed by the Holy Spirit with special strength. Hence they are more strictly obliged to spread and defend the faith both by word and by deed as true witnesses of Christ.

Taking part in the Eucharistic Sacrifice, which is the fount and apex of the whole Christian life, they offer the divine Victim to God, and offer themselves along with It. Thus, both by the act of oblation and through holy Communion, all perform their proper part in this liturgical service, not, indeed, all in the same way but each in that way which is appropriate to himself. Strengthened anew at the holy table by the Body of Christ, they manifest in a practical way that unity of God's People which is suitably signified and wondrously brought about by this most awesome sacrament.

Those who approach the sacrament of penance obtain pardon from the mercy of God for offenses committed against Him. They are at the same time reconciled with the Church, which they have wounded by their sins, and which by charity, example, and prayer seeks their conversion. By the sacred anointing of the sick and the prayer of her priests, the whole Church commends those who are ill to the suffering and glorified Lord, asking that He may lighten their suffering and save them (cf. Jas. 5:14–16). She exhorts them, moreover, to contribute to the welfare of the whole People of God by associating themselves freely with the passion and death of Christ (cf. Rom. 8:17; Col. 1:24; 2 Tim. 2:11–12; 1 Pet. 4:13). Those of the faithful who are consecrated by holy orders are appointed to feed the Church in Christ's name with the Word and the grace of God.

Finally, Christian spouses, in virtue of the sacrament of matrimony, signify and partake of the mystery of that unity and fruitful love which exists between Christ and His Church (cf. Eph. 5:32). The spouses thereby help each other to attain to holiness in their married life and by the rearing and education of their children. And so, in their state and way of life, they have their own special gift among the People of God (cf. 1 Cor. 7:7).

For from the wedlock of Christians there comes the family, in which new citizens of human society are born. By the grace of the Holy Spirit received in baptism these are made children of God, thus perpetuating the People of God through the centuries. The family is, so to speak, the domestic Church. In it parents should, by their word and example, be the first preachers of the faith to their children. They should encourage them in the vocation which is proper to each of them, fostering with special care any religious vocation.

Fortified by so many and such powerful means of salvation, all the faithful, whatever their condition or state, are called by the Lord, each in his own way, to that perfect holiness whereby the Father Himself is perfect.

12. The holy People of God shares also in Christ's prophetic office. It spreads abroad a living witness to Him, especially by means of a life of

faith and charity and by offering to God a sacrifice of praise, the tribute
of lips which give honor to His name (cf. Heb. 13:15). The body of the
faithful as a whole, anointed as they are by the Holy One (cf. Jn. 2:20,
27), cannot err in matters of belief. Thanks to a supernatural sense of the
faith which characterizes the People as a whole, it manifests this unerr-
ing quality when, "from the bishops down to the last member of the
laity," it shows universal agreement in matters of faith and morals.

For, by this sense of faith which is aroused and sustained by the Spirit
of truth, God's People accepts not the word of men but the very Word of
God (cf. 1 Th. 2:13). It clings without fail to the faith once delivered to
the saints (cf. Jude 3), penetrates it more deeply by accurate insights, and
applies it more thoroughly to life. All this it does under the lead of a
sacred teaching authority to which it loyally defers.

It is not only through the sacraments and Church ministries that the
same Holy Spirit sanctifies and leads the People of God and enriches it
with virtues. Allotting His gifts "to everyone according as he will" (1
Cor. 12:11), He distributes special graces among the faithful of every
rank. By these gifts He makes them fit and ready to undertake the
various tasks or offices advantageous for the renewal and upbuilding of
the Church, according to the words of the Apostle: "The manifestation
of the Spirit is given to everyone for profit" (1 Cor. 12:7). These charismatic gifts, whether they be the most outstanding or the more simple
and widely diffused, are to be received with thanksgiving and consolation, for they are exceedingly suitable and useful for the needs of the
Church.

Still, extraordinary gifts are not to be rashly sought after, nor are the
fruits of apostolic labor to be presumptuously expected from them. In
any case, judgment as to their genuineness and proper use belongs to
those who preside over the Church, and to whose special competence it
belongs, not indeed to extinguish the Spirit, but to test all things and
hold fast to that which is good (cf. 1 Th. 5:12, 19–21).

13. All men are called to belong to the new People of God. Wherefore this People, while remaining one and unique, is to be spread
throughout the whole world and must exist in all ages, so that the purpose of God's will may be fulfilled. In the beginning God made human
nature one. After His children were scattered, He decreed that they
should at length be unified again (cf. Jn. 11:52). It was for this reason
that God sent His Son, whom He appointed heir of all things (cf. Heb.
1:2), that He might be Teacher, King, and Priest of all, the Head of the
new and universal people of the sons of God. For this God finally sent
His Son's Spirit as Lord and Lifegiver. He it is who, on behalf of the

whole Church and each and every one of those who believe, is the principle of their coming together and remaining together in the teaching of the apostles and in fellowship, in the breaking of bread and in prayers (cf. Acts 2:42, Greek text).

It follows that among all the nations of earth there is but one People of God, which takes its citizens from every race, making them citizens of a kingdom which is of a heavenly and not an earthly nature. For all the faithful scattered throughout the world are in communion with each other in the Holy Spirit, so that "he who occupies the See of Rome knows the people of India are his members." Since the kingdom of Christ is not of this world (cf. Jn. 18:36), the Church or People of God takes nothing away from the temporal welfare of any people by establishing that kingdom. Rather does she foster and take to herself, insofar as they are good, the ability, resources, and customs of each people. Taking them to herself she purifies, strengthens, and ennobles them. The Church in this is mindful that she must harvest with that King to whom the nations were given for an inheritance (cf. Ps. 2:8) and into whose city they bring gifts and presents (cf. Ps. 71[72]:10; Is. 60:4–7; Apoc. 21:24). This characteristic of universality which adorns the People of God is a gift from the Lord Himself. By reason of it, the Catholic Church strives energetically and constantly to bring all humanity with all its riches back to Christ its Head in the unity of His Spirit.

In virtue of this catholicity each individual part of the Church contributes through its special gifts to the good of the other parts and of the whole Church. Thus through the common sharing of gifts and through the common effort to attain fullness in unity, the whole and each of the parts receive increase. Not only, then, is the People of God made up of different peoples but even in its inner structure it is composed of various ranks. This diversity among its members arises either by reason of their duties, as is the case with those who exercise the sacred ministry for the good of their brethren, or by reason of their situation and way of life, as is the case with those many who enter the religious state and, tending toward holiness by a narrower path, stimulate their brethren by their example.

Moreover, within the Church particular Churches hold a rightful place. These Churches retain their own traditions without in any way lessening the primacy of the Chair of Peter. This Chair presides over the whole assembly of charity and protects legitimate differences, while at the same time it sees that such differences do not hinder unity but rather contribute toward it. Finally, between all the parts of the Church there remains a bond of close communion with respect to spiritual riches, apostolic workers, and temporal resources. For the members of the People of God are called to share these goods, and to each of the Churches the words of the Apostle apply: "According to the gift that each has received, administer it to one another as good stewards of the manifold grace of God" (1 Pet. 4:10).

All men are called to be part of this catholic unity of the People of God, a unity which is harbinger of the universal peace it promotes. And there belong to it or are related to it in various ways, the Catholic faithful as well as all who believe in Christ, and indeed the whole of mankind. For all men are called to salvation by the grace of God.

14. This sacred Synod turns its attention first to the Catholic faithful. Basing itself upon sacred Scripture and tradition, it teaches that the Church, now sojourning on earth as an exile, is necessary for salvation. For Christ, made present to us in His Body, which is the Church, is the one Mediator and the unique Way of salvation. In explicit terms He Himself affirmed the necessity of faith and baptism (cf. Mk. 16:16; Jn. 3:5) and thereby affirmed also the necessity of the Church, for through baptism as through a door men enter the Church. Whosoever, therefore, knowing that the Catholic Church was made necessary by God through Jesus Christ, would refuse to enter her or to remain in her could not be saved.

They are fully incorporated into the society of the Church who, possessing the Spirit of Christ, accept her entire system and all the means of salvation given to her, and through union with her visible structure are joined to Christ, who rules her through the Supreme Pontiff and the bishops. This joining is effected by the bonds of professed faith, of the sacraments, of ecclesiastical government, and of communion. He is not saved, however, who, though he is part of the body of the Church, does not persevere in charity. He remains indeed in the bosom of the Church, but, as it were, only in a "bodily" manner and not "in his heart." All the sons of the Church should remember that their exalted status is to be attributed not to their own merits but to the special grace of Christ. If they fail moreover to respond to that grace in thought, word, and deed, not only will they not be saved but they will be the more severely judged.

Catechumens who, moved by the Holy Spirit, seek with explicit intention to be incorporated into the Church are by that very intention joined to her. With love and solicitude Mother Church already embraces them as her own. [from the Dogmatic Constitution on the Church (*Lumen Gentium*)]

61. Religious freedom

Perhaps the most significant specifically American contribution to contemporary Roman Catholic ecclesiology (the theology of the church) is represented in the **Second Vatican Council**'s "Declaration on Religious Freedom." In this document, the church officially accepts the idea of the separation of church and state and the right of individuals and groups to freedom of conscience in religious matters. The official declaration of these principles is particularly significant because it represents also an acceptance of the idea of the development of doctrine (see above, #59), since this document implicitly reverses certain ideas on the relation of church and state that had formerly been taught (for example in the 1864 "Syllabus of Errors" of Pope Pius IX).

DECLARATION ON RELIGIOUS FREEDOM

On the Right of the Person and of Communities to Social and Civil Freedom In Matters Religious

Paul, Bishop
Servant of the Servants of God
Together with the Fathers of the Sacred Council
For Everlasting Memory

1. A sense of the dignity of the human person has been impressing itself more and more deeply on the consciousness of contemporary man. And the demand is increasingly made that men should act on their own judgment, enjoying and making use of a responsible freedom, not driven by coercion but motivated by a sense of duty. The demand is also made that constitutional limits should be set to the powers of government, in order that there may be no encroachment on the rightful freedom of the person and of associations.

This demand for freedom in human society chiefly regards the quest for the values proper to the human spirit. It regards, in the first place, the free exercise of religion in society.

This Vatican Synod takes careful note of these desires in the minds of men. It proposes to declare them to be greatly in accord with truth and justice. To this end, it searches into the sacred tradition and doctrine of the Church—the treasury out of which the Church continually brings forth new things that are in harmony with the things that are old.

First, this sacred Synod professes its belief that God himself has made known to mankind the way in which men are to serve Him, and thus be saved in Christ and come to blessedness. We believe that this one true religion subsists in the catholic and apostolic Church, to which the Lord Jesus committed the duty of spreading it abroad among all men. Thus He spoke to the apostles: "Go, therefore, and make disciples of all nations, baptizing them in the name of the Father, and of the Son, and of the Holy Spirit, teaching them to observe all that I have commanded you" (Mt. 28:19–20). On their part, all men are bound to seek the truth, especially in what concerns God and His Church, and to embrace the truth they come to know, and to hold fast to it.

This sacred Synod likewise professes its belief that it is upon the human conscience that these obligations fall and exert their binding force. The truth cannot impose itself except by virtue of its own truth, as it makes its entrance into the mind at once quietly and with power. Religious freedom, in turn, which men demand as necessary to fulfill their duty to worship God, has to do with immunity from coercion in civil society. Therefore, it leaves untouched traditional Catholic doctrine on the moral duty of men and societies toward the true religion and toward the one Church of Christ.

Over and above all this, in taking up the matter of religious freedom this sacred Synod intends to develop the doctrine of recent Popes on the inviolable rights of the human person and on the constitutional order of society.

CHAPTER I

General Principle of Religious Freedom

2. This Vatican Synod declares that the human person has a right to religious freedom. This freedom means that all men are to be immune from coercion on the part of individuals or of social groups and of any human power, in such wise that in matters religious no one is to be forced to act in a manner contrary to his own beliefs. Nor is anyone to be

restrained from acting in accordance with his own beliefs, whether privately or publicly, whether alone or in association with others, within due limits.

The Synod further declares that the right to religious freedom has its foundation in the very dignity of the human person, as this dignity is known through the revealed Word of God and by reason itself. This right of the human person to religious freedom is to be recognized in the constitutional law whereby society is governed. Thus it is to become a civil right.

It is in accordance with their dignity as persons—that is, beings endowed with reason and free will and therefore privileged to bear personal responsibility—that all men should be at once impelled by nature and also bound by a moral obligation to seek the truth, especially religious truth. They are also bound to adhere to the truth, once it is known, and to order their whole lives in accord with the demands of truth.

However, men cannot discharge these obligations in a manner in keeping with their own nature unless they enjoy immunity from external coercion as well as psychological freedom. Therefore, the right to religious freedom has its foundation, not in the subjective disposition of the person, but in his very nature. In consequence, the right to this immunity continues to exist even in those who do not live up to their obligation of seeking the truth and adhering to it. Nor is the exercise of this right to be impeded, provided that the just requirements of public order are observed.

3. Further light is shed on the subject if one considers that the highest norm of human life is the divine law—eternal, objective, and universal —whereby God orders, directs, and governs the entire universe and all the ways of the human community, by a plan conceived in wisdom and love. Man has been made by God to participate in this law, with the result that, under the gentle disposition of divine Providence, he can come to perceive ever increasingly the unchanging truth. Hence every man has the duty, and therefore the right, to seek the truth in matters religious, in order that he may with prudence form for himself right and true judgments of conscience, with the use of all suitable means.

Truth, however, is to be sought after in a manner proper to the dignity of the human person and his social nature. The inquiry is to be free, carried on with the aid of teaching or instruction, communication, and dialogue. In the course of these, men explain to one another the truth they have discovered, or think they have discovered, in order thus to assist one another in the quest for truth. Moreover, as the truth is discovered, it is by a personal assent that men are to adhere to it.

On his part, man perceives and acknowledges the imperatives of the divine law through the mediation of conscience. In all his activity a man is bound to follow his conscience faithfully, in order that he may come to God, for whom he was created. It follows that he is not to be forced to act in a manner contrary to his conscience. Nor, on the other hand, is he to be restrained from acting in accordance with his conscience, especially in matters religious.

For, of its very nature, the exercise of religion consists before all else in those internal, voluntary, and free acts whereby man sets the course of his life directly toward God. No merely human power can either command or prohibit acts of this kind.

However, the social nature of man itself requires that he should give external expression to his internal acts of religion; that he should participate with others in matters religious; that he should profess his religion in community. Injury, therefore, is done to the human person and to the very order established by God for human life, if the free exercise of religion is denied in society when the just requirements of public order do not so require.

There is a further consideration. The religious acts whereby men, in private and in public and out of a sense of personal conviction, direct their lives to God transcend by their very nature the order of terrestrial and temporal affairs. Government, therefore, ought indeed to take account of the religious life of the people and show it favor, since the function of government is to make provision for the common welfare. However, it would clearly transgress the limits set to its power were it to presume to direct or inhibit acts that are religious.

4. The freedom or immunity from coercion in matters religious which is the endowment of persons as individuals is also to be recognized as their right when they act in community. Religious bodies are a requirement of the social nature both of man and of religion itself.

Provided the just requirements of public order are observed, religious bodies rightfully claim freedom in order that they may govern themselves according to their own norms, honor the Supreme Being in public worship, assist their members in the practice of the religious life, strengthen them by instruction, and promote institutions in which they may join together for the purpose of ordering their own lives in accordance with their religious principles.

Religious bodies also have the right not to be hindered, either by legal measures or by administrative action on the part of government, in the selection, training, appointment, and transferral of their own ministers, in communicating with religious authorities and communities abroad, in erecting buildings for religious purposes, and in the acquisition and use of suitable funds or properties.

Religious bodies also have the right not to be hindered in their public teaching and witness to their faith, whether by the spoken or by the written word. However, in spreading religious faith and in introducing religious practices, everyone ought at all times to refrain from any manner of action which might seem to carry a hint of coercion or of a kind of persuasion that would be dishonorable or unworthy, especially when dealing with poor or uneducated people. Such a manner of action would have to be considered an abuse of one's own right and a violation of the right of others.

In addition, it comes within the meaning of religious freedom that religious bodies should not be prohibited from freely undertaking to show the special value of their doctrine in what concerns the organization of society and the inspiration of the whole of human activity. Finally, the social nature of man and the very nature of religion afford the foundation of the right of men freely to hold meetings and to establish educational, cultural, charitable, and social organizations, under the impulse of their own religious sense.

5. Since the family is a society in its own original right, it has the right freely to live its own domestic religious life under the guidance of parents. Parents, moreover, have the right to determine, in accordance with their own religious beliefs, the kind of religious education that their children are to receive.

Government, in consequence, must acknowledge the right of parents to make a genuinely free choice of schools and of other means of education. The use of this freedom of choice is not to be made a reason for imposing unjust burdens on parents, whether directly or indirectly. Besides, the rights of parents are violated if their children are forced to attend lessons or instruction which are not in agreement with their religious beliefs. The same is true if a single system of education, from which all religious formation is excluded, is imposed upon all.

6. The common welfare of society consists in the entirety of those conditions of social life under which men enjoy the possibility of achieving their own perfection in a certain fullness of measure and also with some relative ease. Hence this welfare consists chiefly in the protection of the rights, and in the performance of the duties, of the human person. Therefore, the care of the right to religious freedom devolves upon the people as a whole, upon social groups, upon government, and upon the

Church and other religious Communities, in virtue of the duty of all toward the common welfare, and in the manner proper to each.

The protection and promotion of the inviolable rights of man ranks among the essential duties of government. Therefore, government is to assume the safeguard of the religious freedom of all its citizens, in an effective manner, by just laws and by other appropriate means. Government is also to help create conditions favorable to the fostering of religious life, in order that the people may be truly enabled to exercise their religious rights and to fulfill their religious duties, and also in order that society itself may profit by the moral qualities of justice and peace which have their origin in men's faithfulness to God and to His holy will.

If, in view of peculiar circumstances obtaining among certain peoples, special legal recognition is given in the constitutional order of society to one religious body, it is at the same time imperative that the right of all citizens and religious bodies to religious freedom should be recognized and made effective in practice.

Finally, government is to see to it that the equality of citizens before the law, which is itself an element of the common welfare, is never violated for religious reasons whether openly or covertly. Nor is there to be discrimination among citizens.

It follows that a wrong is done when government imposes upon its people, by force or fear or other means, the profession or repudiation of any religion, or when it hinders men from joining or leaving a religious body. All the more is it a violation of the will of God and of the sacred rights of the person and the family of nations, when force is brought to bear in any way in order to destroy or repress religion, either in the whole of mankind or in a particular country or in a specific community.

7. The right to religious freedom is exercised in human society; hence its exercise is subject to certain regulatory norms. In the use of all freedoms, the moral principle of personal and social responsibility is to be observed. In the exercise of their rights, individual men and social groups are bound by the moral law to have respect both for the rights of others and for their own duties toward others and for the common welfare of all. Men are to deal with their fellows in justice and civility.

Furthermore, society has the right to defend itself against possible abuses committed on pretext of freedom of religion. It is the special duty of government to provide this protection. However, government is not to act in arbitrary fashion or in an unfair spirit of partisanship. Its action is to be controlled by juridical norms which are in conformity with the objective moral order.

These norms arise out of the need for effective safeguard of the rights of all citizens and for peaceful settlement of conflicts of rights. They flow from the need for an adequate care of genuine public peace, which comes about when men live together in good order and in true justice. They come, finally, out of the need for a proper guardianship of public morality. These matters constitute the basic component of the common welfare: they are what is meant by public order.

For the rest, the usages of society are to be the usages of freedom in their full range. These require that the freedom of man be respected as far as possible, and curtailed only when and in so far as necessary.

8. Many pressures are brought to bear upon men of our day, to the point where the danger arises lest they lose the possibility of acting on their own judgment. On the other hand, not a few can be found who seem inclined to use the name of freedom as the pretext for refusing to submit to authority and for making light of the duty of obedience.

Therefore, this Vatican Synod urges everyone, especially those who are charged with the task of educating others, to do their utmost to form men who will respect the moral order and be obedient to lawful authority. Let them form men too who will be lovers of true freedom—men, in other words, who will come to decisions on their own judgment and in the light of truth, govern their activities with a sense of responsibility, and strive after what is true and right, willing always to join with others in cooperative effort.

Religious freedom, therefore, ought to have this further purpose and aim, namely, that men may come to act with greater responsibility in fulfilling their duties in community life.

CHAPTER II

Religious Freedom In the Light of Revelation

9. The declaration of this Vatican Synod on the right of man to religious freedom has its foundation in the dignity of the person. The requirements of this dignity have come to be more adequately known to human reason through centuries of experience. What is more, this doctrine of freedom has roots in divine revelation, and for this reason Christians are bound to respect it all the more conscientiously.

Revelation does not indeed affirm in so many words the right of man to immunity from external coercion in matters religious. It does, however, disclose the dignity of the human person in its full dimensions. It gives evidence of the respect which Christ showed toward the freedom with which man is to fulfill his duty of belief in the Word of God. It gives us lessons too in the spirit which disciples of such a Master ought to make their own and to follow in every situation.

Thus, further light is cast on the general principles upon which the doctrine of this Declaration on Religious Freedom is based. In particular, religious freedom in society is entirely consonant with the freedom of the act of Christian faith.

10. It is one of the major tenets of Catholic doctrine that man's response to God in faith must be free. Therefore no one is to be forced to embrace the Christian faith against his own will. This doctrine is contained in the Word of God and it was constantly proclaimed by the Fathers of the Church. The act of faith is of its very nature a free act. Man, redeemed by Christ the Savior and through Christ Jesus called to be God's adopted son, cannot give his adherence to God revealing Himself unless the Father draw him to offer to God the reasonable and free submission of faith.

It is therefore completely in accord with the nature of faith that in matters religious every manner of coercion on the part of men should be excluded. In consequence, the principle of religious freedom makes no small contribution to the creation of an environment in which men can without hindrance be invited to Christian faith, and embrace it of their own free will, and profess it effectively in their whole manner of life.

11. God calls men to serve Him in spirit and in truth. Hence they are bound in conscience but they stand under no compulsion. God has regard for the dignity of the human person whom He Himself created; man is to be guided by his own judgment and he is to enjoy freedom.

This truth appears at its height in Christ Jesus, in whom God perfectly manifested Himself and His ways with men. Christ is our Master and our Lord. He is also meek and humble of heart. And in attracting and inviting His disciples He acted patiently. He wrought miracles to shed light on His teaching and to establish its truth. But His intention was to rouse faith in His hearers and to confirm them in faith, not to exert coercion upon them.

He did indeed denounce the unbelief of some who listened to Him; but He left vengeance to God in expectation of the day of judgment. When He sent His apostles into the world, He said to them: "He who believes and is baptized shall be saved, but he who does not believe shall be condemned" (Mk. 16:16); but He Himself, noting that cockle had been sown amid the wheat, gave orders that both should be allowed to grow until the harvest time, which will come at the end of the world.

He refused to be a political Messiah, ruling by force; He preferred to call Himself the Son of Man, who came "to serve and to give his life as a ransom for many" (Mk. 10:45). He showed Himself the perfect Servant of God; "a bruised reed he will not break, and a smoking wick he will not quench" (Mt. 12:20).

He acknowledged the power of government and its rights, when He commanded that tribute be given to Caesar. But He gave clear warning that the higher rights of God are to be kept inviolate: "Render, therefore, to Caesar the things that are Caesar's, and to God the things that are God's" (Mt. 22:21).

In the end, when He completed on the cross the work of redemption whereby He achieved salvation and true freedom for men, He also brought His revelation to completion. He bore witness to the truth, but He refused to impose the truth by force on those who spoke against it. Not by force of blows does His rule assert its claims. Rather, it is established by witnessing to the truth and by hearing the truth, and it extends its dominion by the love whereby Christ, lifted up on the cross, draws all men to Himself.

Taught by the word and example of Christ, the apostles followed the same way. From the very origins of the Church the disciples of Christ strove to convert men to faith in Christ as the Lord—not, however, by the use of coercion or by devices unworthy of the gospel, but by the power, above all, of the Word of God. Steadfastly they proclaimed to all the plan of God our Savior, "who wishes all men to be saved and to come to the knowledge of the truth" (1 Tim. 2:4). At the same time, however, they showed respect for weaker souls even though these persons were in error. Thus they made it plain that "every one of us will render an account of himself to God" (Rom. 14:12), and for this reason is bound to obey his conscience.

Like Christ Himself, the apostles were unceasingly bent upon bearing witness to the truth of God. They showed special courage in speaking "the word of God with boldness" (Acts 4:31) before the people and their rulers. With a firm faith they held that the gospel is indeed the power of God unto salvation for all who believe. Therefore they rejected all "carnal weapons." They followed the example of the gentleness and respectfulness of Christ. And they preached the Word of God in the full confidence that there was resident in this Word itself a divine power able to destroy all the forces arrayed against God and to bring men to faith in

Christ and to His service. As the Master, so too the apostles recognized legitimate civil authority. "For there exists no authority except from God," the Apostle teaches, and therefore commands: "Let everyone be subject to the higher authorities . . . : he who resists the authority resists the ordinance of God" (Rom. 13:1–2).

At the same time, however, they did not hesitate to speak out against governing powers which set themselves in opposition to the holy will of God: "We must obey God rather than men" (Acts 5:29). This is the way along which countless martyrs and other believers have walked through all ages and over all the earth.

12. The Church therefore is being faithful to the truth of the gospel, and is following the way of Christ and the apostles when she recognizes, and gives support to, the principle of religious freedom as befitting the dignity of man and as being in accord with divine revelation. Throughout the ages, the Church has kept safe and handed on the doctrine received from the Master and from the apostles. In the life of the People of God as it has made its pilgrim way through the vicissitudes of human history, there have at times appeared ways of acting which were less in accord with the spirit of the gospel and even opposed to it. Nevertheless, the doctrine of the Church that no one is to be coerced into faith has always stood firm.

Thus the leaven of the gospel has long been about its quiet work in the minds of men. To it is due in great measure the fact that in the course of time men have come more widely to recognize their dignity as persons, and the conviction has grown stronger that in religious matters the person in society is to be kept free from all manner of human coercion.

13. Among the things which concern the good of the Church and indeed the welfare of society here on earth—things therefore which are always and everywhere to be kept secure and defended against all injury—this certainly is preeminent, namely, that the Church should enjoy that full measure of freedom which her care for the salvation of men requires. This freedom is sacred, because the only-begotten Son endowed with it the Church which He purchased with His blood. It is so much the property of the Church that to act against it is to act against the will of God. The freedom of the Church is the fundamental principle in what concerns the relations between the Church and governments and the whole civil order.

In human society and in the face of government, the Church claims freedom for herself in her character as a spiritual authority, established by Christ the Lord. Upon this authority there rests, by divine mandate, the duty of going out into the whole world and preaching the gospel to every creature. The Church also claims freedom for herself in her character as a society of men who have the right to live in society in accordance with the precepts of Christian faith.

In turn, where the principle of religious freedom is not only proclaimed in words or simply incorporated in law but also given sincere and practical application, there the Church succeeds in achieving a stable situation of right as well as of fact and the independence which is necessary for the fulfillment of her divine mission. This independence is precisely what the authorities of the Church claim in society.

At the same time, the Christian faithful, in common with all other men, possess the civil right not to be hindered in leading their lives in accordance with their conscience. Therefore, a harmony exists between the freedom of the Church and the religious freedom which is to be recognized as the right of all men and communities and sanctioned by constitutional law.

14. In order to be faithful to the divine command, "Make disciples of all nations" (Mt. 28:19), the Catholic Church must work with all urgency and concern "that the Word of God may run and be glorified" (2 Th. 3:1). Hence the Church earnestly begs of her children that, first of all, "supplications, prayers, intercessions, and thanksgivings be made for all men. . . . For this is good and agreeable in the sight of God our Savior, who wishes all men to be saved and to come to the knowledge of the truth" (1 Tim. 2:1–4).

In the formation of their consciences, the Christian faithful ought carefully to attend to the sacred and certain doctrine of the Church. The Church is, by the will of Christ, the teacher of the truth. It is her duty to give utterance to, and authoritatively to teach, that Truth which is Christ Himself, and also to declare and confirm by her authority those principles of the moral order which have their origin in human nature itself. Furthermore, let Christians walk in wisdom in the face of those outside, "in the Holy Spirit, in unaffected love, in the word of truth" (2 Cor. 6:6–7). Let them be about their task of spreading the light of life with all confidence and apostolic courage, even to the shedding of their blood.

The disciple is bound by a grave obligation toward Christ his Master ever more adequately to understand the truth received from Him, faithfully to proclaim it, and vigorously to defend it, never—be it understood—having recourse to means that are incompatible with the spirit of the gospel. At the same time, the charity of Christ urges him to act lovingly, prudently and patiently in his dealings with those who are in error or in ignorance with regard to the faith. All is to be taken into account—the Christian duty to Christ, the lifegiving Word which must be proclaimed, the rights of the human person, and the measure of grace granted by God through Christ to men, who are invited freely to accept and profess the faith.

15. The fact is that men of the present day want to be able freely to profess their religion in private and in public. Religious freedom has already been declared to be a civil right in most constitutions, and it is solemnly recognized in international documents. The further fact is that forms of government still exist under which, even though freedom of religious worship receives constitutional recognition, the powers of government are engaged in the effort to deter citizens from the profession of religion and to make life difficult and dangerous for religious Communities.

This sacred Synod greets with joy the first of these two facts, as among the signs of the times. With sorrow, however, it denounces the other fact, as only to be deplored. The Synod exhorts Catholics, and it directs a plea to all men, most carefully to consider how greatly necessary religious freedom is, especially in the present condition of the human family.

All nations are coming into even closer unity. Men of different cultures and religions are being brought together in closer relationships. There is a growing consciousness of the personal responsibility that weighs upon every man. All this is evident.

Consequently, in order that relationships of peace and harmony may be established and maintained within the whole of mankind, it is necessary that religious freedom be everywhere provided with an effective constitutional guarantee, and that respect be shown for the high duty and right of man freely to lead his religious life in society.

May the God and Father of all grant that the human family, through careful observance of the principle of religious freedom in society, may be brought by the grace of Christ and the power of the Holy Spirit to the sublime and unending "freedom of the glory of the sons of God" (Rom. 8:21).

Each and every one of the things set forth in this Declaration has won the consent of the Fathers of this most sacred Council. We too, by the apostolic authority conferred on us by Christ, join with the Venerable Fathers in approving, decreeing, and establishing these things in the Holy Spirit, and we direct that what has thus been enacted in synod be published to God's glory.

Rome, at St. Peter's, December 7, 1965

I, Paul, Bishop of the Catholic Church

There follow the signatures of the Fathers.   [Declaration on Religious Freedom (*Dignitatis Humanae*)]

C. Christian Life

62. Imitating Christ

The *Imitation of Christ,* a fifteenth century spiritual work generally attributed to **Thomas à Kempis,** is among the most widely read books in all of western literature, having been translated into fifty languages. The *Imitation* emphasizes a personal and heartfelt following of Christ in daily life, and exhorts the reader to be liberated from worldly concerns in order to prepare for conversation with God. What role does religious experience play in the author's call to a spiritual life? Why would this work speak so powerfully to millions of readers? What model of Christianity does the author hold up to the reader to emulate? How does its interior spirituality fit with the Christian call to social involvement and liberation (below, #65, 67)?

BOOK I

Reminders Useful for the Spiritual Life

1. Of the Imitation of Christ, and Indifference to All Earthly Vanities

He that follows me is not walking in the dark, says the Lord. These are the words of Christ by which we are reminded how we should imitate his life and ways if we wish to be truly illuminated and freed from all blindness of heart. Therefore let it be our chief duty to meditate on the life of Jesus Christ.

Christ's teaching excels all the instructions of the saints, and he who has the spirit will find hidden manna there. But it so happens that many through frequent hearing of the Gospel feel little moved because they have not the spirit of Christ. He who would fully and with relish understand the words of Christ must strive to fashion his life wholly to his.

What good is it to you to argue profoundly about the Trinity if you lack humility and so displease the Trinity? Fine words indeed do not make one holy and righteous, but a virtuous life makes one dear to God. I would rather feel compunction than know its definition. If you knew the whole Bible by heart, and the sayings of all the philosophers, what would it all be worth without the love and grace of God? Vanity of vanities and utter emptiness, except to love God and to serve him only.

The highest wisdom is this:—to aim for the heavenly kingdom through indifference to the world. Vanity it is therefore to strive for perishable riches and to rely on them. Vanity too it is to court honours and to set oneself out for lofty state. Vanity it is to go after fleshly desires and long for that by which you must presently be heavily punished. Vanity it is to wish for a long life and care little about a good life. Vanity it is to attend only to the life that is and not foresee the days that are ahead. Vanity it is to love what is passing at full speed and not hasten there where lasting joy awaits.

Frequently recall that saying:—the eye is not satisfied with the seen nor the ear filled with what is heard. Try then to draw your heart away from love of things visible and to bring yourself to the invisible. For by pursuing their sensual impulse men stain conscience and lose God's grace.

7. Of the Love of Jesus Beyond All

Blessed is he who realises what it can be to love Jesus, and to think nothing of himself compared with Jesus. He must leave the thing prized for the one beloved, since Jesus wishes to be loved alone beyond everything. Love of the created is deceptive and fickle: love of Jesus is faithful and steadfast. He who clings to the creature, falls with its falling: he that embraces Jesus grows stronger through all time.

Love him and retain him as friend who, when all things fade, will not leave you nor let you go to the end. From all else you must be parted, whether you will or no. Keep near to Jesus, living or dying, and entrust yourself to his safe keeping who, when all fail, alone can help you. Your beloved is of such a nature that he will not allow a rival, but alone will have your heart, and sit like a king on his own throne. If you could thoroughly free yourself from every creature, Jesus would gladly stay with you.

Whatever you have found in men, as separate from Jesus, you will discover to be almost total loss. Neither trust nor lean on the wind-blown reed: for all flesh is grass, and like the flower of grass all its glory will be shed. You will quickly be deceived if you have such regard for the outward appearance of men. For if you expect your own satisfaction and gain from others, you will often have a sense of loss. If you seek Jesus in everything, Jesus you will surely find. But if you seek self; self you will certainly find, but to your ruin. For if a man does not seek after Jesus, he does himself more harm than could the whole world and all his enemies.

8. *Of the Intimate Friendship of Jesus*

When Jesus is present all is well and nothing seems difficult. When Jesus is absent all is hard. When Jesus does not speak within, comfort is worthless. Yet if Jesus speaks but a single word, great comfort is felt. Did not Mary Magdalen rise at once from the place in which she was weeping when Martha said to her, "The Master is here and calls you"? Happy hour when Jesus calls the spirit from tears to gladness. How dry and hard you are without Jesus: how foolish and empty if you desire anything apart from Jesus. Is not this a greater loss than if you should lose the whole world? What can the world offer you without Jesus? To be without Jesus is a bitter underworld: and to be with Jesus, a sweet paradise. If Jesus were with you no foe could harm. He who finds Jesus finds good treasure, even a good beyond every good. And he who loses Jesus loses much indeed, even more than the whole world. Most poor is he who lives without Jesus, and most rich is he who stands well with Jesus.

It is a fine art to know how to live with Jesus, and a great wisdom to know how to retain Jesus. Be lowly and peace-making and Jesus will be with you. Be devout and quiet and Jesus will stay with you. You can soon drive Jesus away, and lose his influence, if you determine to turn towards external things. And if you drive him away and lose him, to whom will you fly, and whom will you then seek as a friend? You cannot very well live without a friend, and if Jesus is not your friend beyond all, you will be exceedingly sad and lonely. So you act like a fool if you trust or delight in any other. It were a better choice to have the whole world against us than to have Jesus hurt. Therefore of all dear ones let Jesus alone be specially loved.

Love all because of Jesus, but Jesus for himself. Jesus Christ alone is to be loved uniquely, he who before all friends is alone found good and faithful. Through him and in him let friends as well as foes be dear to you: and for all these he is to be entreated that they may all know and love him. Never wish to be singularly praised, for that alone is God's, who has none like himself. Nor wish that anyone should set his heart on you, nor that you should be possessed by a love for any other, but let it be Jesus in you, and in every good man.

Be pure and free throughout, not bound up with any other creature.

You must be stripped of all, and bring a clean heart to God, if you would be at leisure to see how sweet the Lord is. And truly you will not attain to this unless you are led and drawn by his grace, so that emptied and set free in all things you become at one with him, alone with the alone. For when God's grace comes to a man, then is he strong in every way: and when it withdraws then will he be poor and weak, and as one left only for the scourge. He should not be cast down at this, nor despair, but stand with a steady mind towards the will of God, and endure whatever comes to him for the glory of Jesus Christ: for after winter follows summer, after night the day returns, and after storm great calm.

BOOK III

Of Inward Consolation

1. Of Christ Speaking Inwardly to the Faithful Soul

I will listen to what the Lord God will say within me. Blessed is the soul that hears the Lord speaking within her, and receives a word of comfort from his mouth. Blessed are the ears which catch the pulsings of the divine whisper, and pay no heed to the murmurings of this world. Blessed indeed are the ears which heed no sound of voice outside, but truth teaching within. Blessed are the eyes which are closed to the outward, but are intent on the inward. Blessed are they who pass through to internal things, and by daily exercises strain to prepare themselves more and more to master heavenly secrets. Blessed are they who find time for God, and shake off every earthly impediment.

Mark these my soul, and shut the door of the senses so that you will hear what the Lord your God will speak within you. This thy beloved says: "I am thy safety, thy peace and thy life. Dwell with me and you will find peace." Put away all transitory things: seek those eternal. What are all temporal things, but deceitful? And what can all created things avail if you are left alone by the creator? Renounce all then, and make yourself pleasing and faithful to your creator so that you may be able to lay hold of true bliss.

3. That the Words of God Should Be Heard with Humility and that Many Do Not Weigh Them

Son, hear my words, sweetest of words, going beyond the knowledge of all the philosophers and wise men of this world. My words are spirit and life: not to be weighed by human reason. They are not to be brought out for mere pleasure, but to be heard in silence, and to be taken up with utter humility and great affection.

And I said: Blessed is he whom thou trainest, O Lord, and teachest him about thy law, that thou mayst make it easier for him in evil times, and he not feel alone on earth.

The Lord said: I taught the prophets from the beginning, and until now I cease not to speak to all, though many are deaf and yield not to my voice. Many listen more readily to the world than to God: they follow their fleshly desires more easily than God's good pleasure. The world offers petty and temporal things, and is served with great eagerness: I offer things high and eternal, and the hearts of mortals grow numb.

Who serves and obeys me with such care in everything as the world and its masters are served? "Blush, Sidon: says the sea." And if you ask the cause: hear why. For a modest living a long road is run: for living eternally scarce once will a foot be lifted from the ground by many. The paltriest wage is striven for, there is disgraceful quarrelling sometimes over a single coin: for a frivolous thing and a petty expectation they are not afraid to wear themselves out day and night: yet, Oh the shame of grudging the least fatigue for a changeless good, for a priceless gain, for highest honour, for endless glory.

Be heartily ashamed, you lazy and grumbling servant, that these are found readier for what must be lost than you for life. They are more joyful over an empty show, than you over reality. They indeed are sometimes disappointed in their hope, but my promise misleads no one, nor sends away empty him who trusts in me. What I have promised, I will give: what I have said, I will fulfill, if only anyone remains faithful in love of me right to the end. I am the rewarder of all the good, and the firm approver of all the devout.

Write my words on your heart, and earnestly dwell on them, for they will be very necessary in the hour of temptation. What you do not understand when you read, you will know at the time of my coming. I am wont to visit my chosen ones in two ways, namely by testing and by comforting. And I read two lessons to them daily: one, rebuking their faults, the other urging to growth in virtues. He who has heard my words, and despises them, has one who will judge him at the last day.

A prayer begging for the grace of devotion

O Lord my God, to me thou art all that is good. But who am I that I should dare to speak to thee? I am thy poorest little servant and a despicable little worm: far more poor and contemptible than I know and dare to say. Yet remember me O Lord, for I am nothing, have nothing, and can avail nothing. Thou alone art good, just and holy: thou canst do all, thou givest all, thou fillest all, leaving only the sinner empty.

Be mindful of thy mercies, and fill my heart with thy grace, thou who wouldst not have thy work be void. How can I sustain myself through this sad life unless thou fortify me with thy mercy and grace? Turn not thy face from me: delay not thy coming: withdraw not thy comfort: lest my soul become as unwatered land before thee.

O Lord teach me to do thy will: teach me to walk worthily and humbly before thee: for thou art my wisdom who truly knowest me, and knew me before the world was made, and before I was born into the world.   [from *The Imitation of Christ*, I, III]

63. *The dignity of human life*

One of the most important (and controversial) papal pronouncements of our century was the 1968 encyclical of **Pope Paul VI** entitled *Humanae Vitae*. This letter reflected the pope's concern that Christians always remember the dignity and importance of transmitting life through human sexuality. Why does the pope state that the church must guard the integrity of sexuality against biological, psychological, and sociological claims? What Christian principles form the "ends" of sexuality? Why is openness to having children considered one of the "ends of marriage"? Why did the pope's letter occasion so much controversy and dissent?

ENCYCLICAL LETTER OF POPE PAUL VI HUMANAE VITAE

To Our Dearest Sons and Brothers
Health and Apostolic Blessing

1

The most serious duty of transmitting human life, in which married people collaborate freely and responsibly with God the Creator, has always been a source of great joy to them even though sometimes not without considerable difficulties and distress.

The fulfilment of this duty has always posed problems to the conscience of married people, but the recent evolution in human society has resulted in changes which have provoked new questions which the Church could not ignore, for these concern matters intimately connected with the life and happiness of men.

7

The question of the birth of children, like every other question which touches human life, is too large to be resolved by limited criteria, such as are provided by biology, psychology, demography or sociology. It is the whole man and the whole complex of his responsibilities that must be considered, not only what is natural and limited to this earth, but also what is supernatural and eternal. And since in the attempt to justify artificial methods of birth control many appeal to the demands of married love or of 'responsible parenthood', these two important realities of married life must be accurately defined and analyzed. This is what We mean to do, with special reference to what the Second Vatican Council taught with the highest authority in its Pastoral Constitution *Gaudium et spes.*

8

Married love particularly reveals its true nature and nobility when we realize that it derives from God and finds its supreme origin in him who 'is Love', the Father 'from whom every family in heaven and on earth is named'.

Marriage, then, is far from being the effect of chance or the result of the blind evolution of natural forces. It is in reality the wise and provident institution of God the Creator, whose purpose was to establish in man his loving design. As a consequence, husband and wife, through that mutual gift of themselves, which is specific and exclusive to them alone, develop that union of two persons in which they perfect one another, in order to co-operate with God in the generation and education of new lives.

Furthermore, the marriage of those who have been baptized is invested with the dignity of a sacramental sign of grace, for it represents the union of Christ with his Church.

9

In the light of these facts the characteristic features and exigencies of married love are clearly indicated, and it is of the highest importance to evaluate them exactly.

This love is above all fully *human*, a compound of sense and spirit. It is not, then, merely a question of natural instinct or emotional drive. It is also, and above all, an act of the free will, whose dynamism ensures that not only does it endure through the joys and sorrows of daily life, but also that it grows, so that husband and wife become in a way one heart and one soul, and together attain their human fulfilment.

Then it is a love which is *total*—that very special form of personal friendship in which husband and wife generously share everything, allowing no unreasonable exceptions or thinking just of their own interests. Whoever really loves his partner loves not only for what he receives, but loves that partner for her own sake, content to be able to enrich the other with the gift of himself.

Again, married love is *faithful* and *exclusive* of all other, and this until death. This is how husband and wife understood it on the day on which, fully aware of what they were doing, they freely vowed themselves to one another in marriage. Though this fidelity of husband and wife sometimes presents difficulties, no one can assert that it is impossible, for it is always honourable and worthy of the highest esteem. The example of so many married persons down through the centuries shows not only that fidelity is conatural to marriage but also that it is the source of profound and enduring happiness.

And finally this love is *creative of life*, for it is not exhausted by the loving interchange of husband and wife, but also contrives to go beyond this to bring new life into being. 'Marriage and married love are by their character ordained to the procreation and bringing up of children. Children are the outstanding gift of marriage, and contribute in the highest degree to the parents' welfare.'

10

Married love, therefore, requires of husband and wife the full awareness of their obligations in the matter of responsible parenthood, which today, rightly enough, is much insisted upon, but which, at the same time, should be rightly understood. This, however, is to be studied in the light of various inter-related arguments which are its justification.

If first we consider it in relation to the biological processes involved, responsible parenthood is to be understood as the knowledge and observance of their specific functions. Human intelligence discovers in the faculty of procreative life the biological laws which relate to the human person.

If, on the other hand, we examine the innate drives and emotions of man, responsible parenthood expresses the domination which reason and will must exert over them.

But if we then attend to relevant physical, economic, psychological and social conditions, those are considered to exercise responsible parenthood who prudently and generously decide to have a large family, or who, for serious reasons and with due respect to the moral law, choose to have no more children for the time being or even for an indeterminate period.

Responsible parenthood, moreover, in the terms in which we use the phrase, retains a further and deeper significance of paramount importance which refers to the objective moral order instituted by God,—the order of which a right conscience is the true interpreter. As a consequence the commitment to responsible parenthood requires that husband and wife, keeping a right order of priorities, recognize their own duties towards God, themselves, their families and human society.

From this it follows that they are not free to act as they choose in the service of transmitting life, nor are they free to decide for themselves what is the right course to follow. On the contrary, they are bound to ensure that what they do corresponds to the will of God the Creator. The very nature of marriage and its use makes this clear, while the constant teaching of the Church affirms it.

11

The sexual activity, in which husband and wife are intimately and chastely united with one another, through which human life is transmitted, is, as the recent Council recalled, 'honourable and good'. It does not, moreover, cease to be legitimate even when, for reasons independent of their will, it is foreseen to be infertile. For its natural adaptation to the expression and strengthening of the union of husband and wife is not thereby suppressed. The facts are, as experience shows, that new life is not the result of each and every act of sexual intercourse. God has wisely ordered the laws of nature and the incidence of fertility in such a way that successive births are already naturally spaced through the inherent operation of these laws. The Church, nevertheless, in urging men to the observance of the precepts of the natural law, which it interprets by its constant doctrine, teaches as absolutely required that *any use whatever of marriage* must retain its natural potential to procreate human life.

12

This particular doctrine, often expounded by the Magisterium of the Church, is based on the inseparable connection, established by God, which man on his own initiative may not break, between the unitive significance and the procreative significance which are both inherent to the marriage act.

The reason is that the marriage act, because of its fundamental structure, while uniting husband and wife in the closest intimacy, actualizes their capacity to generate new life,—and this as a result of laws written into the actual nature of man and of woman. And if each of these essential qualities, the unitive and the procreative, is preserved, the use of marriage fully retains its sense of true mutual love and its ordination to the supreme responsibility of parenthood to which man is called. We believe that our contemporaries are particularly capable of seeing that this teaching is in harmony with human reason.   [from *Humanae Vitae*]

64. Catholic social teaching in the United States

An important part of "imitating Christ" is the application of gospel principles to the economic and social structures of our society. The United States Catholic bishops attempted to do this in 1986 when they published *Economic Justice for All,* a pastoral letter addressed to all American Catholics. Their letter applies the principles of Catholic social teaching to the U.S. economy in a sophisticated way, calling for Catholics to work for a society in which Christian values are reflected in economic structures. According to the bishops, what basic principles should guide economic decision making? What is the meaning of the distinction they make between "commutative" and "distributive" justice? What is the "moral significance of work"? What is the "fundamental option for the poor"?

Principal Themes of the Pastoral Letter

12. The pastoral letter is not a blueprint for the American economy. It does not embrace any particular theory of how the economy works, nor does it attempt to resolve the disputes between different schools of economic thought. Instead, our letter turns to Scripture and to the social teachings of the Church. There, we discover what our economic life must serve, what standards it must meet. Let us examine some of these basic moral principles.

13. *Every economic decision and institution must be judged in light of whether it protects or undermines, the dignity of the human person. The*

pastoral letter begins with the human person. We believe the person is sacred—the clearest reflection of God among us. Human dignity comes from God, not from nationality, race, sex, economic status, or any human accomplishment. We judge any economic system by what it does *for* and *to* people and by how it permits all to *participate* in it. The economy should serve people, not the other way around.

14. *Human dignity can be realized and protected only in community.* In our teaching, the human person is not only sacred but also social. How we organize our society—in economics and politics, in law and policy—directly affects human dignity and the capacity of individuals to grow in community. The obligation to "love our neighbor" has an individual dimension, but it also requires a broader social commitment to the common good. We have many partial ways to measure and debate the health of our economy: Gross National Product, per capita income, stock market prices, and so forth. The Christian vision of economic life looks beyond them all and asks, Does economic life enhance or threaten our life together as a community?

15. *All people have a right to participate in the economic life of society.* Basic justice demands that people be assured a minimum level of participation in the economy. It is wrong for a person or group to be excluded unfairly or to be unable to participate or contribute to the economy. For example, people who are both able and willing, but cannot get a job are deprived of the participation that is so vital to human development. For, it is through employment that most individuals and families meet their material needs, exercise their talents, and have an opportunity to contribute to the larger community. Such participation has a special significance in our tradition because we believe that it is a means by which we join in carrying forward God's creative activity.

16. *All members of society have a special obligation to the poor and vulnerable.* From the Scriptures and church teaching, we learn that the justice of a society is tested by the treatment of the poor. The justice that was the sign of God's covenant with Israel was measured by how the poor and unprotected—the widow, the orphan, and the stranger—were treated. The kingdom that Jesus proclaimed in his word and ministry excludes no one. Throughout Israel's history and in early Christianity, the poor are agents of God's transforming power. "The Spirit of the Lord is upon me, therefore he has anointed me. He has sent me to bring glad tidings to the poor" (Lk 4:18). This was Jesus' first public utterance. Jesus takes the side of those most in need. In the Last Judgment, so dramatically described in St. Matthew's Gospel, we are told that we will be judged according to how we respond to the hungry, the thirsty, the

naked, the stranger. As followers of Christ, we are challenged to make a fundamental "option for the poor"—to speak for the voiceless, to defend the defenseless, to assess life styles, policies, and social institutions in terms of their impact on the poor. This "option for the poor" does not mean pitting one group against another, but rather, strengthening the whole community by assisting those who are most vulnerable. As Christians, we are called to respond to the needs of *all* our brothers and sisters, but those with the greatest needs require the greatest response.

17. *Human rights are the minimum conditions for life in community.* In Catholic teaching, human rights include not only civil and political rights but also economic rights. As Pope John XXIII declared, "all people have a right to life, food, clothing, shelter, rest, medical care, education, and employment." This means that when people are without a chance to earn a living, and must go hungry and homeless, they are being denied basic rights. Society must ensure that these rights are protected. In this way, we will ensure that the minimum conditions of economic justice are met for all our sisters and brothers.

18. *Society as a whole, acting through public and private institutions, has the moral responsibility to enhance human dignity and protect human rights.* In addition to the clear responsibility of private institutions, government has an essential responsibility in this area. This does not mean that government has the primary or exclusive role, but it does have a positive moral responsibility in safeguarding human rights and ensuring that the minimum conditions of human dignity are met for all. In a democracy, government is a means by which we can act together to protect what is important to us and to promote our common values.

19. These six moral principles are not the only ones presented in the pastoral letter, but they give an overview of the moral vision that we are trying to share. This vision of economic life cannot exist in a vacuum; it must be translated into concrete measures. Our pastoral letter spells out some specific applications of Catholic moral principles. We call for a new national commitment to full employment. We say it is a social and moral scandal that one of every seven Americans is poor, and we call for concerted efforts to eradicate poverty. The fulfillment of the basic needs of the poor is of the highest priority. We urge that all economic policies be evaluated in light of their impact on the life and stability of the family. We support measures to halt the loss of family farms and to resist the growing concentration in the ownership of agricultural resources. We specify ways in which the United States can do far more to relieve the plight of poor nations and assist in their development. We also reaffirm

church teaching on the rights of workers, collective bargaining, private property, subsidiarity, and equal opportunity.

20. We believe that the recommendations in our letter are reasonable and balanced. In analyzing the economy, we reject ideological extremes and start from the fact that ours is a "mixed" economy, the product of a long history of reform and adjustment. We know that some of our specific recommendations are controversial. As bishops, we do not claim to make these prudential judgments with the same kind of authority that marks our declarations of principle. But, we feel obliged to teach by example how Christians can undertake concrete analysis and make specific judgments on economic issues. The Church's teachings cannot be left at the level of appealing generalities.

21. In the pastoral letter, we suggest that the time has come for a "New American Experiment"—to implement economic rights, to broaden the sharing of economic power, and to make economic decisions more accountable to the common good. This experiment can create new structures of economic partnership and participation within firms at the regional level, for the whole nation, and across borders.

22. Of course, there are many aspects of the economy the letter does not touch, and there are basic questions it leaves to further exploration. There are also many specific points on which men and women of good will may disagree. We look for a fruitful exchange among differing viewpoints. We pray only that all will take to heart the urgency of our concerns; that together we will test our views by the Gospel and the Church's teaching; and that we will listen to other voices in a spirit of mutual respect and open dialogue.

CHAPTER I

The Church and The Future of the U.S. Economy

1. Every perspective on economic life that is human, moral, and Christian must be shaped by three questions: What does the economy do *for* people? What does it do *to* people? And how do people *participate* in it? The economy is a human reality: men and women working together to develop and care for the whole of God's creation. All this work must serve the material and spiritual well-being of people. It influences what people hope for themselves and their loved ones. It affects the way they act together in society. It influences their very faith in God.

2. The Second Vatican Council declared that "the joys and hopes, the griefs and anxieties of the people of this age, especially those who are poor or in any way afflicted, these too are the joys and hopes, the griefs and anxieties of the followers of Christ." There are many signs of hope in U.S. economic life today:

- Many fathers and mothers skillfully balance the arduous responsibilities of work and family life. There are parents who pursue a purposeful and modest way of life and by their example encourage their children to follow a similar path. A large number of women and men, drawing on their religious tradition, recognize the challenging vocation of family life and child rearing in a culture that emphasizes material display and self-gratification.
- Conscientious business people seek new and more equitable ways to organize resources and the workplace. They face hard choices over expanding or retrenching, shifting investments, hiring or firing.
- Young people choosing their life's work ask whether success and security are compatible with service to others.
- Workers whose labor may be toilsome or repetitive try daily to ennoble their work with a spirit of solidarity and friendship.
- New immigrants brave dislocations while hoping for the opportunities realized by the millions who came before them.

3. These signs of hope are not the whole story. There have been failures—some of them massive and ugly:

- Poor and homeless people sleep in community shelters and in our church basements; the hungry line up in soup lines.
- Unemployment gnaws at the self-respect of both middle-aged persons who have lost jobs and the young who cannot find them.
- Hardworking men and women wonder if the system of enterprise that helped them yesterday might destroy their jobs and their communities tomorrow.
- Families confront major new challenges: dwindling social supports for family stability; economic pressures that force both parents of young children to work outside the home; a driven pace of life among the successful that can sap love and commitment; lack of hope among those who have less or nothing at all. Very different kinds of families bear different burdens of our economic system.
- Farmers face the loss of their land and way of life; young people find it difficult to choose farming as a vocation; farming communities are

threatened; migrant farmworkers break their backs in serf-like conditions for disgracefully low wages.

4. *And beyond our own shores, the reality of 800 million people living in absolute poverty and 450 million malnourished or facing starvation casts an ominous shadow over all these hopes and problems at home.*

5. Anyone who sees all this will understand our concern as pastors and bishops. People shape the economy and in turn are shaped by it. Economic arrangements can be sources of fulfillment, of hope, of community—or of frustration, isolation, and even despair. They teach virtues—or vices—and day by day help mold our characters. They affect the quality of people's lives; at the extreme even determining whether people live or die. Serious economic choices go beyond purely technical issues to fundamental questions of value and human purpose. We believe that in facing these questions the Christian religious and moral tradition can make an important contribution.

C. The Need for Moral Vision

22. Sustaining a common culture and a common commitment to moral values is not easy in our world. Modern economic life is based on a division of labor into specialized jobs and professions. Since the industrial revolution, people have had to define themselves and their work ever more narrowly to find a niche in the economy. The benefits of this are evident in the satisfaction many people derive from contributing their specialized skills to society. But the costs are social fragmentation, a decline in seeing how one's work serves the whole community, and an increased emphasis on personal goals and private interests. This is vividly clear in discussions of economic justice. Here it is often difficult to find a common ground among people with different backgrounds and concerns. One of our chief hopes in writing this letter is to encourage and contribute to the development of this common ground.

23. Strengthening common moral vision is essential if the economy is to serve all people more fairly. Many middle-class Americans feel themselves in the grip of economic demands and cultural pressures that go far beyond the individual family's capacity to cope. Without constructive guidance in making decisions with serious moral implications, men and women who hold positions of responsibility in corporations or government find their duties exacting a heavy price. We want these reflections to help them contribute to a more just economy.

24. The quality of the national discussion about our economic future will affect the poor most of all, in this country and throughout the world.

The life and dignity of millions of men, women, and children hang in the balance. Decisions must be judged in light of what they do *for* the poor, what they do *to* the poor, and what they enable the poor to do *for themselves.* The fundamental moral criterion for all economic decisions, policies, and institutions is this: They must be at the service of *all people, especially the poor.*

25. This letter is based on a long tradition of Catholic social thought, rooted in the Bible and developed over the past century by the popes and the Second Vatican Council in response to modern economic conditions. This tradition insists that human dignity, realized in community with others and with the whole of God's creation, is the norm against which every social institution must be measured.

26. This teaching has a rich history. It is also dynamic and growing. Pope Paul VI insisted that all Christian communities have the responsibility "to analyze with objectivity the situation which is proper to their own country, to shed on it the light of the Gospel's unalterable words and to draw principles of reflection, norms of judgment, and directives for action from the social teaching of the Church." Therefore, we build on the past work of our own bishops' conference, including the 1919 Program of Social Reconstruction and other pastoral letters. In addition many people from the Catholic, Protestant, and Jewish communities, in academic, business or political life, and from many different economic backgrounds have also provided guidance. We want to make the legacy of Christian social thought a living, growing resource that can inspire hope and help shape the future.

27. We write, then, first of all to provide guidance for members of our own Church as they seek to form their consciences about economic matters. No one may claim the name Christian and be comfortable in the face of the hunger, homelessness, insecurity, and injustice found in this country and the world. At the same time, we want to add our voice to the public debate about the directions in which the U.S. economy should be moving. We seek the cooperation and support of those who do not share our faith or tradition. The common bond of humanity that links all persons is the source of our belief that the country can attain a renewed public moral vision. The questions are basic and the answers are often elusive; they challenge us to serious and sustained attention to economic justice.

3. The Reign of God and Justice

41. Jesus enters human history as God's anointed son who announces the nearness of the reign of God (Mk 1:9–14). This proclamation sum-

mons us to acknowledge God as creator and covenant partner and challenges us to seek ways in which God's revelation of the dignity and destiny of all creation might become incarnate in history. It is not simply the promise of the future victory of God over sin and evil, but that this victory has already begun—in the life and teaching of Jesus.

42. What Jesus proclaims by word, he enacts in his ministry. He resists temptations of power and prestige, follows his Father's will, and teaches us to pray that it be accomplished on earth. He warns against attempts to "lay up treasures on earth" (Mt 6:19) and exhorts his followers not to be anxious about material goods but rather to seek first God's reign and God's justice (Mt 6:25–33). His mighty works symbolize that the reign of God is more powerful than evil, sickness, and the hardness of the human heart. He offers God's loving mercy to sinners (Mk 2:17), takes up the cause of those who suffered religious and social discrimination (Lk 7:36–50; 15:1–2), and attacks the use of religion to avoid the demands of charity and justice (Mk 7:9–13; Mt 23:23).

43. When asked what was the greatest commandment, Jesus quoted the age-old Jewish affirmation of faith that God alone is One and to be loved with the whole heart, mind, and soul (Dt 6:4–5) and immediately adds: "You shall love your neighbor as yourself" (Lv 19:18, Mk 12:28–34). This dual command of love that is at the basis of all Christian morality is illustrated in the Gospel of Luke by the parable of a Samaritan who interrupts his journey to come to the aid of a dying man (Lk 10:29–37). Unlike the other wayfarers who look on the man and pass by, the Samaritan "was moved with compassion at the sight"; he stops, tends the wounded man, and takes him to a place of safety. In this parable compassion is the bridge between mere seeing and action; love is made real through effective action.

44. Near the end of his life, Jesus offers a vivid picture of the last judgment (Mt 25:31–46). All the nations of the world will be assembled and will be divided into those blessed who are welcomed into God's kingdom or those cursed who are sent to eternal punishment. The blessed are those who fed the hungry, gave drink to the thirsty, welcomed the stranger, clothed the naked, and visited the sick and imprisoned; the cursed are those who neglected these works of mercy and love. Neither the blessed nor the cursed are astounded that they are judged by the Son of Man, nor that judgment is rendered according to works of charity. The shock comes when they find that in neglecting the poor, the outcast, and the oppressed, they were rejecting Jesus himself. Jesus who came as "Emmanuel" (God with us, Mt 1:23) and who promises to be with his people until the end of the age (Mt 28:20) is hidden in

those most in need; to reject them is to reject God made manifest in history.

4. Called To Be Disciples in Community

45. Jesus summoned his first followers to a change of heart and to take on the yoke of God's reign (Mk 1:14–15; Mt 11:29). They are to be the nucleus of that community which will continue the work of proclaiming and building God's kingdom through the centuries. As Jesus called the first disciples in the midst of their everyday occupations of fishing and tax collecting; so he again calls people in every age in the home, in the workplace, and in the marketplace.

46. The Church is, as Pope John Paul II reminded us, "a community of disciples" in which "we must see first and foremost Christ saying to each member of the community: follow me." To be a Christian is to join with others in responding to this personal call and in learning the meaning of Christ's life. It is to be sustained by that loving intimacy with the Father that Jesus experienced in his work, in his prayer, and in his suffering.

47. Discipleship involves imitating the pattern of Jesus' life by openness to God's will in the service of others (Mk 10:42–45). Disciples are also called to follow him on the way of the cross, and to heed his call that those who lose their lives for the sake of the Gospel will save them (Mk 8:34–35). Jesus' death is an example of that greater love which lays down one's life for others (cf. Jn 15:12–18). It is a model for those who suffer persecution for the sake of justice (Mt 5:10). The death of Jesus was not the end of his power and presence, for he was raised up by the power of God. Nor did it mark the end of the disciples' union with him. After Jesus had appeared to them and when they received the gift of the Spirit (Acts 2:1–12), they became apostles of the good news to the ends of the earth. In the face of poverty and persecution they transformed human lives and formed communities which became signs of the power and presence of God. Sharing in this same resurrection faith, contemporary followers of Christ can face the struggles and challenges that await those who bring the gospel vision to bear on our complex economic and social world.

5. Poverty, Riches, and the Challenge of Discipleship

48. The pattern of Christian life as presented in the Gospel of Luke has special relevance today. In her *Magnificat*, Mary rejoices in a God who scatters the proud, brings down the mighty, and raises up the poor and lowly (Lk 1:51–53). The first public utterance of Jesus is "The Spirit of

the Lord is upon me, because he has anointed me to preach the good news to the poor" (Lk 4:18 cf. Is 61:1–2). Jesus adds to the blessing on the poor a warning, "Woe to you who are rich, for you have received your consolation" (Lk 6:24). He warns his followers against greed and reliance on abundant possessions and underscores this by the parable of the man whose life is snatched away at the very moment he tries to secure his wealth (Lk 12:13–21). In Luke alone, Jesus tells the parable of the rich man who does not see the poor and suffering Lazarus at his gate (Lk 16:19–31). When the rich man finally "sees" Lazarus, it is from the place of torment and the opportunity for conversion has passed. Pope John Paul II has often recalled this parable to warn the prosperous not to be blind to the great poverty that exists beside great wealth.

49. Jesus, especially in Luke, lives as a poor man, like the prophets takes the side of the poor, and warns of the dangers of wealth. The terms used for poor, while primarily describing lack of material goods, also suggest dependence and powerlessness. The poor are also an exiled and oppressed people whom God will rescue (Is 51:21–23) as well as a faithful remnant who take refuge in God (Zep 3:12–13). Throughout the Bible, material poverty is a misfortune and a cause of sadness. A constant biblical refrain is that the poor must be cared for and protected and that when they are exploited, God hears their cries (Prv 22:22–23). Conversely, even though the goods of the earth are to be enjoyed and people are to thank God for material blessings, wealth is a constant danger. The rich are wise in their own eyes (Prv 28:11), and are prone to apostasy and idolatry (Am 5:4–13; Is 2:6–8), as well as to violence and oppression (Jas 2:6–7). Since they are neither blinded by wealth nor make it into an idol, the poor can be open to God's presence; throughout Israel's history and in early Christianity the poor are agents of God's transforming power.

50. The poor are often related to the lowly (Mt 5:3,5) to whom God reveals what was hidden from the wise (Mt 11:25–30). When Jesus calls the poor "blessed," he is not praising their condition of poverty, but their openness to God. When he states that the reign of God is theirs, he voices God's special concern for them, and promises that they are to be the beneficiaries of God's mercy and justice. When he summons disciples to leave all and follow him, he is calling them to share his own radical trust in the Father and his freedom from care and anxiety (cf. Mt 6:25–34). The practice of evangelical poverty in the Church has always been a living witness to the power of that trust and to the joy that comes with that freedom.

51. Early Christianity saw the poor as an object of God's special love, but it neither canonized material poverty nor accepted deprivation as an

inevitable fact of life. Though few early Christians possessed wealth or power (1 Cor 1:26–28; Jas 2:5), their communities had well-off members (Acts 16:14; 18:8). Jesus' concern for the poor was continued in different forms in the early Church. The early community at Jerusalem distributed its possessions so that "there was no needy person among them," and held "all things in common"—a phrase that suggests not only shared material possessions, but more fundamentally, friendship and mutual concern among all its members (Acts 4:32–34; 2:44). While recognizing the dangers of wealth, the early Church proposed the proper use of possessions to alleviate need and suffering, rather than universal dispossession. Beginning in the first century and throughout history, Christian communities have developed varied structures to support and sustain the weak and powerless in societies that were often brutally unconcerned about human suffering.

52. Such perspectives provide a basis today for what is called the "preferential option for the poor." Though in the Gospels and in the New Testament as a whole the offer of salvation is extended to all peoples, Jesus takes the side of those most in need, physically and spiritually. The example of Jesus poses a number of challenges to the contemporary Church. It imposes a prophetic mandate to speak for those who have no one to speak for them, to be a defender of the defenseless, who in biblical terms are the poor. It also demands a compassionate vision that enables the Church to see things from the side of the poor and powerless and to assess lifestyle, policies, and social institutions in terms of their impact on the poor. It summons the Church also to be an instrument in assisting people to experience the liberating power of God in their own lives so that they may respond to the Gospel in freedom and in dignity. Finally, and most radically, it calls for an emptying of self, both individually and corporately, that allows the Church to experience the power of God in the midst of poverty and powerlessness.

B. Ethical Norms for Economic Life

61. These biblical and theological themes shape the overall Christian perspective on economic ethics. This perspective is also subscribed to by many who do not share Christian religious convictions. Human understanding and religious belief are complementary, not contradictory. For human beings are created in God's image, and their dignity is manifest in the ability to reason and understand, in their freedom to shape their own lives and the life of their communities, and in the capacity for love and friendship. In proposing ethical norms, therefore, we appeal both to

Christians and to all in our pluralist society to show that respect and reverence owed to the dignity of every person. Intelligent reflection on the social and economic realities of today is also indispensible in the effort to respond to economic circumstances never envisioned in biblical times. Therefore, we now want to propose an ethical framework that can guide economic life today in ways that are both faithful to the Gospel and shaped by human experience and reason.

62. First we outline the *duties* all people have to each other and to the whole community: love of neighbor, the basic requirements of justice, and the special obligation to those who are poor or vulnerable. Corresponding to these duties are the *human rights* of every person; the obligation to protect the dignity of all demands respect for these rights. Finally these duties and rights entail several *priorities* that should guide the economic choices of individuals, communities, and the nation as a whole.

1. The Responsibilities of Social Living

63. Human life is life in community. Catholic social teaching proposes several complementary perspectives that show how moral responsibilities and duties in the economic sphere are rooted in this call to community.

a. Love and Solidarity

64. *The commandments to love God with all one's heart and to love one's neighbor as oneself are the heart and soul of Christian morality.* Jesus offers himself as the model of this all-inclusive love: "... love one another as I have loved you" (Jn 15:12). These commands point out the path toward true human fulfillment and happiness. They are not arbitrary restrictions on human freedom. Only active love of God and neighbor makes the fullness of community happen. Christians look forward in hope to a true communion among all persons with each other and with God. The Spirit of Christ labors in history to build up the bonds of solidarity among all persons until that day on which their union is brought to perfection in the Kingdom of God. Indeed Christian theological reflection on the very reality of God as a trinitarian unity of persons—Father, Son, and Holy Spirit—shows that being a person means being united to other persons in mutual love.

65. What the Bible and Christian tradition teach, human wisdom confirms. Centuries before Christ, the Greeks and Romans spoke of the

human person as a "social animal" made for friendship, community, and public life. These insights show that human beings achieve self-realization not in isolation, but in interaction with others.

66. The virtues of citizenship are an expression of Christian love more crucial in today's interdependent world than ever before. These virtues grow out of a lively sense of one's dependence on the common-weal and obligations to it. This civic commitment must also guide the economic institutions of society. In the absence of a vital sense of citizen-ship among the businesses, corporations, labor unions, and other groups that shape economic life, society as a whole is endangered. Solidarity is another name for this social friendship and civic commitment that make human moral and economic life possible.

67. The Christian tradition recognizes, of course, that the fullness of love and community will be achieved only when God's work in Christ comes to completion in the kingdom of God. This kingdom has been inaugurated among us, but God's redeeming and transforming work is not yet complete. Within history, knowledge of how to achieve the goal of social unity is limited. Human sin continues to wound the lives of both individuals and larger social bodies and places obstacles in the path toward greater social solidarity. If efforts to protect human dignity are to be effective, they must take these limits on knowledge and love into account. Nevertheless, sober realism should not be confused with re-signed or cynical pessimism. It is a challenge to develop a courageous hope that can sustain efforts that will sometimes be arduous and protracted.

b. Justice and Participation

68. Biblical justice is the goal we strive for. This rich biblical under-standing portrays a just society as one marked by the fullness of love, compassion, holiness, and peace. On their path through history, how-ever, sinful human beings need more specific guidance on how to move toward the realization of this great vision of God's Kingdom. This guid-ance is contained in the norms of basic or minimal justice. These norms state the *minimum* levels of mutual care and respect that all persons owe to each other in an imperfect world. Catholic social teaching, like much philosophical reflection, distinguishes three dimensions of basic justice: commutative justice, distributive justice, and social justice.

69. *Commutative justice calls for fundamental fairness in all agreements and exchanges between individuals or private social groups.* It demands respect for the equal human dignity of all persons in economic transac-

tions, contracts, or promises. For example, workers owe their employers diligent work in exchange for their wages. Employers are obligated to treat their employees as persons, paying them fair wages in exchange for the work done and establishing conditions and patterns of work that are truly human.

70. *Distributive justice requires that the allocation of income, wealth, and power in society be evaluated in light of its effects on persons whose basic material needs are unmet.* The Second Vatican Council stated: "The right to have a share of earthly goods sufficient for oneself and one's family belongs to everyone. The fathers and doctors of the Church held this view, teaching that we are obliged to come to the relief of the poor and to do so not merely out of our superfluous goods." Minimum material resources are an absolute necessity for human life. If persons are to be recognized as members of the human community, then the community has an obligation to help fulfill these basic needs unless an absolute scarcity of resources makes this strictly impossible. No such scarcity exists in the United States today.

71. Justice also has implications for the way the larger social, economic, and political institutions of society are organized. *Social justice implies that persons have an obligation to be active and productive participants in the life of society and that society has a duty to enable them to participate in this way.* This form of justice can also be called "contributive," for it stresses the duty of all who are able to help create the goods, services, and other nonmaterial or spiritual values necessary for the welfare of the whole community. In the words of Pius XI, "It is of the very essence of social justice to demand from each individual all that is necessary for the common good." Productivity is essential if the community is to have the resources to serve the well-being of all. Productivity, however, cannot be measured solely by its output in goods and services. Patterns of production must also be measured in light of their impact on the fulfillment of basic needs, employment levels, patterns of discrimination, environmental quality, and sense of community.

72. The meaning of social justice also includes a duty to organize economic and social institutions so that people can contribute to society in ways that respect their freedom and the dignity of their labor. Work should enable the working person to become "more a human being," more capable of acting intelligently, freely, and in ways that lead to self-realization.

73. Economic conditions that leave large numbers of able people unemployed, underemployed, or employed in dehumanizing conditions fail to meet the converging demands of these three forms of basic justice.

Work with adequate pay for all who seek it is the primary means for achieving basic justice in our society. Discrimination in job opportunities or income levels on the basis of race, sex, or other arbitrary standards can never be justified. It is a scandal that such discrimination continues in the United States today. Where the effects of past discrimination persist, society has the obligation to take positive steps to overcome the legacy of injustice. Judiciously administered affirmative action programs in education and employment can be important expressions of the drive for solidarity and participation that is at the heart of true justice. Social harm calls for social relief.

74. Basic justice also calls for the establishment of a floor of material well-being on which all can stand. This is a duty of the whole of society and it creates particular obligations for those with greater resources. This duty calls into question extreme inequalities of income and consumption when so many lack basic necessities. Catholic social teaching does not maintain that a flat, arithmetical equality of income and wealth is a demand of justice, but it does challenge economic arrangements that leave large numbers of people impoverished. Further, it sees extreme inequality as a threat to the solidarity of the human community, for great disparities lead to deep social divisions and conflict.

75. This means that all of us must examine our way of living in light of the needs of the poor. Christian faith and the norms of justice impose distinct limits on what we consume and how we view material goods. The great wealth of the United States can easily blind us to the poverty that exists in this nation and the destitution of hundreds of millions of people in other parts of the world. Americans are challenged today as never before to develop the inner freedom to resist the temptation constantly to seek more. Only in this way will the nation avoid what Paul VI called "the most evident form of moral underdevelopment," namely greed.

76. These duties call not only for individual charitable giving but also for a more systematic approach by businesses, labor unions, and the many other groups that shape economic life—as well as government. The concentration of privilege that exists today results far more from institutional relationships that distribute power and wealth inequitably than from differences in talent or lack of desire to work. These institutional patterns must be examined and revised if we are to meet the demands of basic justice. For example, a system of taxation based on assessment according to ability to pay is a prime necessity for the fulfillment of these social obligations.

c. Overcoming Marginalization and Powerlessness

77. These fundamental duties can be summarized this way: *Basic justice demands the establishment of minimum levels of participation in the life of the human community for all persons.* The ultimate injustice is for a person or group to be treated actively or abandoned passively as if they were nonmembers of the human race. To treat people this way is effectively to say that they simply do not count as human beings. This can take many forms, all of which can be described as varieties of marginalization, or exclusion from social life. This exclusion can occur in the political sphere: restriction of free speech, concentration of power in the hands of a few, or outright repression by the state. It can also take economic forms that are equally harmful. Within the United States, individuals, families, and local communities fall victim to a downward cycle of poverty generated by economic forces they are powerless to influence. The poor, the disabled, and the unemployed too often are simply left behind. This pattern is even more severe beyond our borders in the least-developed countries. Whole nations are prevented from fully participating in the international economic order because they lack the power to change their disadvantaged position. Many people within the less developed countries are excluded from sharing in the meager resources available in their homelands by unjust elites and unjust governments. These patterns of exclusion are created by free human beings. In this sense they can be called forms of social sin. Acquiescence in them or failure to correct them when it is possible to do so is a sinful dereliction of Christian duty.

78. Recent Catholic social thought regards the task of overcoming these patterns of exclusion and powerlessness as a most basic demand of justice. Stated positively, justice demands that social institutions be ordered in a way that guarantees all persons the ability to participate actively in the economic, political, and cultural life of society. The level of participation may legitimately be greater for some persons than for others, but there is a basic level of access that must be made available for all. Such participation is an essential expression of the social nature of human beings and of their communitarian vocation.

2. Human Rights: The Minimum Conditions for Life in Community

79. Catholic social teaching spells out the basic demands of justice in greater detail in the human rights of every person. These fundamental rights are prerequisites for a dignified life in community. The Bible vigor-

ously affirms the sacredness of every person as a creature formed in the image and likeness of God. The biblical emphasis on covenant and community also shows that human dignity can only be realized and protected in solidarity with others. In Catholic social thought, therefore, respect for human rights and a strong sense of both personal and community responsibility are linked, not opposed. Vatican II described the common good as "the sum of those conditions of social life which allow social groups and their individual members relatively thorough and ready access to their own fulfillment." These conditions include the rights to fulfillment of material needs, a guarantee of fundamental freedoms, and the protection of relationships that are essential to participation in the life of society. These rights are bestowed on human beings by God and grounded in the nature and dignity of human persons. They are not created by society. Indeed society has a duty to secure and protect them.

80. The full range of human rights has been systematically outlined by John XXIII in his encyclical *Peace on Earth*. His discussion echoes the United Nations Universal Declaration of Human Rights and implies that internationally accepted human rights standards are strongly supported by Catholic teaching. These rights include the civil and political rights to freedom of speech, worship, and assembly. A number of human rights also concern human welfare and are of a specifically economic nature. First among these are the rights to life, food, clothing, shelter, rest, medical care, and basic education. These are indispensable to the protection of human dignity. In order to ensure these necessities, all persons have a right to earn a living, which for most people in our economy is through remunerative employment. All persons also have a right to security in the event of sickness, unemployment, and old age. Participation in the life of the community calls for the protection of this same right to employment, as well as the right to healthful working conditions, to wages, and other benefits sufficient to provide individuals and their families with a standard of living in keeping with human dignity, and to the possibility of property ownership. These fundamental personal rights— civil and political as well as social and economic—state the minimum conditions for social institutions that respect human dignity, social solidarity, and justice. They are all essential to human dignity and to the integral development of both individuals and society, and are thus moral issues. Any denial of these rights harms persons and wounds the human community. Their serious and sustained denial violates individuals and destroys solidarity among persons.

81. Social and economic rights call for a mode of implementation

different from that required to secure civil and political rights. Freedom of worship and of speech imply immunity from interference on the part of both other persons and the government. The rights to education, employment, and social security, for example, are empowerments that call for positive action by individuals and society at large.

82. However, both kinds of rights call for positive action to create social and political institutions that enable all persons to become active members of society. Civil and political rights allow persons to participate freely in the public life of the community, for example, through free speech, assembly, and the vote. In democratic countries these rights have been secured through a long and vigorous history of creating the institutions of constitutional government. In seeking to secure the full range of social and economic rights today, a similar effort to shape new economic arrangements will be necessary.

83. The first step in such an effort is the development of a new cultural consensus that the basic economic conditions of human welfare are essential to human dignity and are due persons by right. Second, the securing of these rights will make demands on *all* members of society, on all private sector institutions, and on government. A concerted effort on all levels in our society is needed to meet these basic demands of justice and solidarity. Indeed political democracy and a commitment to secure economic rights are mutually reinforcing.

84. Securing economic rights for all will be an arduous task. There are a number of precedents in U.S. history, however, which show that the work has already begun. The country needs a serious dialogue about the appropriate levels of private and public sector involvement that are needed to move forward. There is certainly room for diversity of opinion in the Church and in U.S. society on *how* to protect the human dignity and economic rights of all our brothers and sisters. In our view, however, there can be no legitimate disagreement on the basic moral objectives.

3. Moral Priorities for the Nation

85. *The common good demands justice for all, the protection of the human rights of all.* Making cultural and economic institutions more supportive of the freedom, power, and security of individuals and families must be a central, long-range objective for the nation. Every person has a duty to contribute to building up the commonweal. All have a responsibility to develop their talents through education. Adults must contribute to society through their individual vocations and talents. Parents are called to guide their children to the maturity of Christian adulthood and responsi-

ble citizenship. Everyone has special duties toward the poor and the marginalized. Living up to these responsibilities, however, is often made difficult by the social and economic patterns of society. Schools and educational policies both public and private often serve the privileged exceedingly well, while the children of the poor are effectively abandoned as second-class citizens. Great stresses are created in family life by the way work is organized and scheduled, and by the social and cultural values communicated on TV. Many in the lower middle class are barely getting by and fear becoming victims of economic forces over which they have no control.

86. *The obligation to provide justice for all means that the poor have the single most urgent economic claim on the conscience of the nation.* Poverty can take many forms, spiritual as well as material. All people face struggles of the spirit as they ask deep questions about their purpose in life. Many have serious problems in marriage and family life at some time in their lives, and all of us face the certain reality of sickness and death. The Gospel of Christ proclaims that God's love is stronger than all these forms of diminishment. Material deprivation, however, seriously compounds such sufferings of the spirit and heart. To see a loved one sick is bad enough, but to have no possibility of obtaining health care is worse. To face family problems, such as the death of a spouse or a divorce, can be devastating, but to have these lead to the loss of one's home and end with living on the streets is something no one should have to endure in a country as rich as ours. In developing countries these human problems are even more greatly intensified by extreme material deprivation. This form of human suffering can be reduced if our own country, so rich in resources, chooses to increase its assistance.

87. As individuals and as a nation, therefore, we are called to make a fundamental "option for the poor." The obligation to evaluate social and economic activity from the viewpoint of the poor and the powerless arises from the radical command to love one's neighbor as one's self. Those who are marginalized and whose rights are denied have privileged claims if society is to provide justice for *all*. This obligation is deeply rooted in Christian belief. As Paul VI stated:

> In teaching us charity, the Gospel instructs us in the preferential respect due the poor and the special situation they have in society: the more fortunate should renounce some of their rights so as to place their goods more generously at the service of others.

John Paul II has described this special obligation to the poor as "a call to have a special openness with the small and the weak, those that suffer and weep, those that are humiliated and left on the margin of society, so as to help them win their dignity as human persons and children of God."

88. The prime purpose of this special commitment to the poor is to enable them to become active participants in the life of society. It is to enable *all* persons to share in and contribute to the common good. The "option for the poor," therefore, is not an adversarial slogan that pits one group or class against another. Rather it states that the deprivation and powerlessness of the poor wounds the whole community. The extent of their suffering is a measure of how far we are from being a true community of persons. These wounds will be healed only by greater solidarity with the poor and among the poor themselves.

89. In summary, the norms of love, basic justice, and human rights imply that personal decisions, social policies, and economic institutions should be governed by several key priorities. These priorities do not specify everything that must be considered in economic decision making. They do indicate the most fundamental and urgent objectives.

90. a. *The fulfillment of the basic needs of the poor is of the highest priority.* Personal decisions, policies of private and public bodies, and power relationships must all be evaluated by their effects on those who lack the minimum necessities of nutrition, housing, education, and health care. In particular, this principle recognizes that meeting fundamental human needs must come before the fulfillment of desires for luxury consumer goods, for profits not conducive to the common good, and for unnecessary military hardware.

91. b. *Increasing active participation in economic life by those who are presently excluded or vulnerable is a high social priority.* The human dignity of all is realized when people gain the power to work together to improve their lives, strengthen their families, and contribute to society. Basic justice calls for more than providing help to the poor and other vulnerable members of society. It recognizes the priority of policies and programs that support family life and enhance economic participation through employment and widespread ownership of property. It challenges privileged economic power in favor of the well-being of all. It points to the need to improve the present situation of those unjustly discriminated against in the past. And it has very important implications for both the domestic and the international distribution of power.

92. c. *The investment of wealth, talent, and human energy should be specially directed to benefit those who are poor or economically insecure.* Achieving a more just economy in the United States and the world depends in part on increasing economic resources and productivity. In

addition, the ways these resources are invested and managed must be scrutinized in light of their effects on non-monetary values. Investment and management decisions have crucial moral dimensions: they create jobs or eliminate them; they can push vulnerable families over the edge into poverty or give them new hope for the future; they help or hinder the building of a more equitable society. Indeed they can have either positive or negative influence on the fairness of the global economy. Therefore, this priority presents a strong moral challenge to policies that put large amounts of talent and capital into the production of luxury consumer goods and military technology while failing to invest sufficiently in education, health, the basic infrastructure of our society, and economic sectors that produce urgently needed jobs, goods, and services.

93. d. *Economic and social policies as well as the organization of the work world should be continually evaluated in light of their impact on the strength and stability of family life.* The long-range future of this nation is intimately linked with the well-being of families, for the family is the most basic form of human community. Efficiency and competition in the marketplace must be moderated by greater concern for the way work schedules and compensation support or threaten the bonds between spouses and between parents and children. Health, education, and social service programs should be scrutinized in light of how well they ensure both individual dignity and family integrity.

94. These priorities are not policies. They are norms that should guide the economic choices of all and shape economic institutions. They can help the United States move forward to fulfill the duties of justice and protect economic rights. They were strongly affirmed as implications of Catholic social teaching by Pope John Paul II during his visit to Canada in 1984: "The needs of the poor take priority over the desires of the rich; the rights of workers over the maximization of profits; the preservation of the environment over uncontrolled industrial expansion; production to meet social needs over production for military purposes." There will undoubtedly be disputes about the concrete applications of these priorities in our complex world. We do not seek to foreclose discussion about them. However, we believe that an effort to move in the direction they indicate is urgently needed.

95. The economic challenge of today has many parallels with the political challenge that confronted the founders of our nation. In order to create a new form of political democracy they were compelled to develop ways of thinking and political institutions that had never existed before. Their efforts were arduous and their goals imperfectly realized,

but they launched an experiment in the protection of civil and political rights that has prospered through the efforts of those who came after them. *We believe the time has come for a similar experiment in securing economic rights: the creation of an order that guarantees the minimum conditions of human dignity in the economic sphere for every person.* By drawing on the resources of the Catholic moral-religious tradition, we hope to make a contribution through this letter to such a new "American Experiment": a new venture to secure economic justice for all.

65. The faith that does justice

Dr. Martin Luther King (1929–1968), Baptist minister and leader of the civil rights movement during the 1960s, was arguably the most prophetic clerical voice in America at mid-century. King's passionate desire to wed Christian non-violent principles to the fight for political and social rights for the "poor" in America led to his reception of the Nobel Peace Prize, as well as to his assassination in 1968. In April 1963, King was arrested and imprisoned in Birmingham, Alabama, for "civil disobedience" against city laws that discriminated against people of color—city laws that King argued Christians had a duty in conscience to disobey. Below is the text of the now-famous public letter he sent from the Birmingham jail, in which he outlines his reasons—largely religious—for breaking the city laws. Like the Hebrew prophets and Jesus, King appeals to a "higher law" that Christians must use to judge human laws, and lays claim to a "faith that does justice" as the core of the prophetic impulse in the Judeo-Christian tradition. According to King, what social principles are the followers of Jesus obliged to follow? How is non-violence basic to these social principles? Why does King argue that Christianity supports the idea that some human laws *must* be disobeyed? How is the *manner* of such disobedience important in evaluating such action theologically?

My dear Fellow Clergymen,

While confined here in the Birmingham city jail, I came across your recent statement calling our present activities "unwise and untimely." Seldom, if ever, do I pause to answer criticism of my work and ideas. If I sought to answer all of the criticisms that cross my desk, my secretaries would be engaged in little else in the course of the day, and I would have no time for constructive work. But since I feel that you are men of genuine good will and your criticisms are sincerely set forth, I would like to answer your statement in what I hope will be patient and reasonable terms.

I think I should give the reason for my being in Birmingham, since you have been influenced by the argument of "outsiders coming in." I have the honor of serving as president of the Southern Christian Leadership Conference, an organization operating in every southern state, with headquarters in Atlanta, Georgia. We have some eighty-five affiliate organizations all across the South—one being the Alabama Christian Movement for Human Rights. Whenever necessary and possible we share staff, educational and financial resources with our affiliates. Several months ago our local affiliate here in Birmingham invited us to be on call to engage in a nonviolent direct-action program if such were deemed necessary. We readily consented and when the hour came we lived up to our promises. So I am here, along with several members of my staff, because we were invited here. I am here because I have basic organizational ties here.

Beyond this, I am in Birmingham because injustice is here. Just as the eighth century prophets left their little villages and carried their "thus saith the Lord" far beyond the boundaries of their hometowns; and just as the Apostle Paul left his little village of Tarsus and carried the gospel of Jesus Christ to practically every hamlet and city of the Graeco-Roman world, I too am compelled to carry the gospel of freedom beyond my particular hometown. Like Paul, I must constantly respond to the Macedonian call for aid.

Moreover, I am cognizant of the interrelatedness of all communities and states. I cannot sit idly by in Atlanta and not be concerned about what happens in Birmingham. Injustice anywhere is a threat to justice everywhere. We are caught in an inescapable network of mutuality, tied in a single garment of destiny. Whatever affects one directly affects all indirectly. Never again can we afford to live with the narrow, provincial "outside agitator" idea. Anyone who lives in the United States can never be considered an outsider anywhere in this country.

You deplore the demonstrations that are presently taking place in Birmingham. But I am sorry that your statement did not express a similar concern for the conditions that brought the demonstrations into being. I am sure that each of you would want to go beyond the superficial social analyst who looks merely at effects, and does not grapple with underlying causes. I would not hesitate to say that it is unfortunate that so-called demonstrations are taking place in Birmingham at this time, but I would say in more emphatic terms that it is even more unfortunate that the white power structure of this city left the Negro community with no other alternative.

In any nonviolent campaign there are four basic steps: (1) collection of the facts to determine whether injustices are alive, (2) negotiation, (3) self-purification, and (4) direct action. We have gone through all of these steps in Birmingham. There can be no gainsaying of the fact that racial injustice engulfs this community.

Birmingham is probably the most thoroughly segregated city in the United States. Its ugly record of police brutality is known in every section of this country. Its injust treatment of Negroes in the courts is a notorious reality. There have been more unsolved bombings of Negro homes and churches in Birmingham than any city in this nation. These are the hard, brutal and unbelievable facts. On the basis of these conditions Negro leaders sought to negotiate with the city fathers. But the political leaders consistently refused to engage in good faith negotiation.

Then came the opportunity last September to talk with some of the leaders of the economic community. In these negotiating sessions certain promises were made by the merchants—such as the promise to remove the humiliating racial signs from the stores. On the basis of these promises Rev. Shuttlesworth and the leaders of the Alabama Christian Movement for Human Rights agreed to call a moratorium on any type of demonstrations. As the weeks and months unfolded we realized that we were the victims of a broken promise. The signs remained. Like so many experiences of the past we were confronted with blasted hopes, and the dark shadow of a deep disappointment settled upon us. So we had no alternative except that of preparing for direct action, whereby we would present our very bodies as a means of laying our case before the conscience of the local and national community. We were not unmindful of the difficulties involved. So we decided to go through a process of self-purification. We started having workshops on nonviolence and repeatedly asked ourselves the questions, "Are you able to accept blows without retaliating?" "Are you able to endure the ordeals of jail?" We decided to set our direct-action program around the Easter season, realizing that with the exception of Christmas, this was the largest shopping period of the year. Knowing that a strong economic withdrawal program would be the by-product of direct action, we felt that this was the best time to bring pressure on the merchants for the needed changes. Then it occurred to us that the March election was ahead and so we speedily decided to postpone action until after election day. When we discovered that Mr. Connor was in the run-off, we decided again to postpone action so that the demonstrations could not be used to cloud the issues. At this time we agreed to begin our nonviolent witness the day after the run-off.

This reveals that we did not move irresponsibly into direct action. We too wanted to see Mr. Connor defeated; so we went through postponement after postponement to aid in this community need. After this we felt that direct action could be delayed no longer.

You may well ask, "Why direct action? Why sit-ins, marches, etc.? Isn't negotiation a better path?" You are exactly right in your call for negotiation. Indeed, this is the purpose of direct action. Nonviolent direct action seeks to create such a crisis and establish such creative tension that a community that has constantly refused to negotiate is forced to confront the issue. It seeks so to dramatize the issue that it can no longer be ignored. I just referred to the creation of tension as a part of the work of the nonviolent resister. This may sound rather shocking. But I must confess that I am not afraid of the word tension. I have earnestly worked and preached against violent tension, but there is a type of constructive nonviolent tension that is necessary for growth. Just as Socrates felt that it was necessary to create a tension in the mind so that individuals could rise from the bondage of myths and half-truths to the unfettered realm of creative analysis and objective appraisal, we must see the need of having nonviolent gadflies to create the kind of tension in society that will help men to rise from the dark depths of prejudice and racism to the majestic heights of understanding and brotherhood. So the purpose of the direct action is to create a situation so crisis-packed that it will inevitably open the door to negotiation. We, therefore, concur with you in your call for negotiation. Too long has our beloved Southland been bogged down in the tragic attempt to live in monologue rather than dialogue.

One of the basic points in your statement is that our acts are untimely. Some have asked, "Why didn't you give the new administration time to act?" The only answer that I can give to this inquiry is that the new administration must be prodded about as much as the outgoing one before it acts. We will be sadly mistaken if we feel that the election of Mr. Boutwell will bring the millennium to Birmingham. While Mr. Boutwell is much more articulate and gentle than Mr. Connor, they are both segregationists, dedicated to the task of maintaining the status quo. The hope I see in Mr. Boutwell is that he will be reasonable enough to see the futility of massive resistance to desegregation. But he will not see this without pressure from the devotees of civil rights. My friends, I must say to you that we have not made a single gain in civil rights without determined legal and nonviolent pressure. History is the long and tragic story of the fact that privileged groups seldom give up their privileges voluntarily. Individuals may see the moral light and voluntarily give up their unjust posture; but as Reinhold Niebuhr has reminded us, groups are more immoral than individuals.

We know through painful experience that freedom is never voluntarily given by the oppressor; it must be demanded by the oppressed. Frankly, I have never yet engaged in a direct action movement that was "well-timed," according to the timetable of those who have not suffered unduly from the disease of segregation. For years now I have heard the words "Wait!" It rings in the ear of every Negro with a piercing familiarity. This "Wait" has almost always meant "Never." It has been a tranquilizing thalidomide, relieving the emotional stress for a moment, only to give birth to an ill-formed infant of frustration. We must come to see with the distinguished jurist of yesterday that "justice too long delayed is justice denied." We have waited for more than 340 years for our constitutional and God-given rights. The nations of Asia and Africa are moving with jetlike speed toward the goal of political independence, and we still creep at horse and buggy pace toward the gaining of a cup of coffee at a lunch counter. I guess it is easy for those who have never felt the stinging darts of segregation to say, "Wait." But when you have seen vicious mobs lynch your mothers and fathers at will and drown your sisters and brothers at whim; when you have seen hate-filled policemen curse, kick, brutalize and even kill your black brothers and sisters with impunity; when you see the vast majority of your twenty million Negro brothers smothering in an airtight cage of poverty in the midst of an affluent society; when you suddenly find your tongue twisted and your speech stammering as you seek to explain to your six-year-old daughter why she can't go to the public amusement park that has just been advertised on television, and see tears welling up in her little eyes when she is told that Funtown is closed to colored children, and see the depressing clouds of inferiority begin to form in her little mental sky, and see her begin to distort her little personality by unconsciously developing a bitterness toward white people; when you have to concoct an answer for a five-year-old son asking in agonizing pathos: "Daddy, why do white people treat colored people so mean?"; when you take a cross-country drive and find it necessary to sleep night after night in the uncomfortable corners of your automobile because no motel will accept you; when you are humiliated day in and day out by nagging signs reading "white" and "colored"; when your first name becomes "nigger" and your middle name becomes "boy" (however old you are) and your last name becomes "John," and when your wife and mother are never given the respect title "Mrs."; when you are harried by day and haunted by night by the fact that you are a Negro, living constantly at tiptoe stance never quite knowing what to expect next, and plagued with inner fears and outer resentments; when you are forever fighting a degenerating sense of "nobodiness"; then you will understand why we find it difficult to wait. There comes a time when the cup of endurance runs over, and men are no longer willing to be plunged into an abyss of injustice where they experience the blackness of corroding despair. I hope, sirs, you can understand our legitimate and unavoidable impatience.

You express a great deal of anxiety over our willingness to break laws. This is certainly a legitimate concern. Since we so diligently urge people to obey the Supreme Court's decision of 1954 outlawing segregation in the public schools, it is rather strange and paradoxical to find us consciously breaking laws. One may well ask, "How can you advocate breaking some laws and obeying others?" The answer is found in the fact that there are two types of laws: there are *just* and there are *unjust* laws. I would agree with Saint Augustine that "An unjust law is no law at all."

Now what is the difference between the two? How does one determine when a law is just or unjust? A just law is a man-made code that squares with the moral law or the law of God. An unjust law is a code that is out of harmony with the moral law. To put it in the terms of Saint Thomas Aquinas, an unjust law is a human law that is not rooted in eternal and natural law. Any law that uplifts human personality is just. Any law that degrades human personality is unjust. All segregation statutes are unjust because segregation distorts the soul and damages the personality. It gives the segregator a false sense of superiority, and the segregated a false sense of inferiority. To use the words of Martin Buber, the great Jewish philosopher, segregation substitutes an "I-it" relationship for the "I-thou" relationship, and ends up relegating persons to the status of things. So segregation is not only politically, economically and sociologically unsound, but it is morally wrong and sinful. Paul Tillich has said that sin is separation. Isn't segregation an existential expression of man's tragic separation, an expression of his awful estrangement, his terrible sinfulness? So I can urge men to disobey segregation ordinances because they are morally wrong.

Let us turn to a more concrete example of just and unjust laws. An unjust law is a code that a majority inflicts on a minority that is not binding on itself. This is difference made legal. On the other hand a just law is a code that a majority compels a minority to follow that it is willing to follow itself. This is sameness made legal.

Let me give another explanation. An unjust law is a code inflicted upon a minority which that minority had no part in enacting or creating because they did not have the unhampered right to vote. Who can say that the legislature of Alabama which set up the segregation laws was democratically elected? Throughout the state of Alabama all types of conniving methods are used to prevent Negroes from becoming registered voters and there are some counties without a single Negro registered to vote despite the fact that the Negro constitutes a majority of the population. Can any law set up in such a state be considered democratically structured?

These are just a few examples of unjust and just laws. There are some instances when a law is just on its face and unjust in its application. For instance, I was arrested Friday on a charge of parading without a permit. Now there is nothing wrong with an ordinance which requires a permit for a parade, but when the ordinance is used to preserve segregation and to deny citizens the First Amendment privilege of peaceful assembly and peaceful protest, then it becomes unjust.

I hope you can see the distinction I am trying to point out. In no sense do I advocate evading or defying the law as the rabid segregationist would do. This would lead to anarchy. One who breaks an unjust law must do it *openly, lovingly* (not hatefully as the white mothers did in New Orleans when they were seen on television screaming, "nigger, nigger, nigger"), and with a willingness to accept the penalty. I submit that an individual who breaks a law that conscience tells him is unjust, and willingly accepts the penalty by staying in jail to arouse the conscience of the community over its injustice, is in reality expressing the very highest respect for law.

Of course, there is nothing new about this kind of civil disobedience. It was seen sublimely in the refusal of Shadrach, Meshach and Abednego to obey the laws of Nebuchadnezzar because a higher moral law was involved. It was practiced superbly by the early Christians who were willing to face hungry lions and the excruciating pain of chopping blocks, before submitting to certain unjust laws of the Roman Empire. To a degree academic freedom is a reality today because Socrates practiced civil disobedience.

We can never forget that everything Hitler did in Germany was "legal" and everything the Hungarian freedom fighters did in Hungary was "illegal." It was "illegal" to aid and comfort a Jew in Hitler's Germany.

But I am sure that if I had lived in Germany during that time I would have aided and comforted my Jewish brothers even though it was illegal. If I lived in a Communist country today where certain principles dear to the Christian faith are suppressed, I believe I would openly advocate disobeying these anti-religious laws. I must make two honest confessions to you, my Christian and Jewish brothers. First, I must confess that over the last few years I have been gravely disappointed with the white moderate. I have almost reached the regrettable conclusion that the Negro's great stumbling block in the stride toward freedom is not the White Citizen's Counciler or the Ku Klux Klanner, but the white moderate who is more devoted to "order" than to justice; who prefers a negative peace which is the absence of tension to a positive peace which is the presence of justice; who constantly says, "I agree with you in the goal you seek, but I can't agree with your methods of direct action"; who paternalistically feels that he can set the timetable for another man's freedom; who lives by the myth of time and who constantly advises the Negro to wait until a "more convenient season." Shallow understanding from people of good will is more frustrating than absolute misunderstanding from people of ill will. Lukewarm acceptance is much more bewildering than outright rejection.

I had hoped that the white moderate would understand that law and order exist for the purpose of establishing justice, and that when they fail to do this they become dangerously structured dams that block the flow of social progress. I had hoped that the white moderate would understand that the present tension of the South is merely a necessary phase of the transition from an obnoxious negative peace, where the Negro passively accepted his unjust plight, to a substance-filled positive peace, where all men will respect the dignity and worth of human personality. Actually, we who engage in nonviolent direct action are not the creators of tension. We merely bring to the surface the hidden tension that is already alive. We bring it out in the open where it can be seen and dealt with. Like a boil that can never be cured as long as it is covered up but must be opened with all its pus-flowing ugliness to the natural medicines of air and light, injustice must likewise be exposed, with all of the tension its exposing creates, to the light of human conscience and the air of national opinion before it can be cured.

In your statement you asserted that our actions, even though peaceful, must be condemned because they precipitate violence. But can this assertion be logically made? Isn't this like condemning the robbed man because his possession of money precipitated the evil act of robbery? Isn't this like condemning Socrates because his unswerving commitment to truth and his philosophical delvings precipitated the misguided popular mind to make him drink the hemlock? Isn't this like condemning Jesus because His unique God-consciousness and never-ceasing devotion to his will precipitated the evil act of crucifixion? We must come to see, as federal courts have consistently affirmed, that it is immoral to urge an individual to withdraw his efforts to gain his basic constitutional rights because the quest precipitates violence. Society must protect the robbed and punish the robber.

I had also hoped that the white moderate would reject the myth of time. I received a letter this morning from a white brother in Texas which said: "All Christians know that the colored people will receive equal rights eventually, but it is possible that you are in too great of a religious hurry. It has taken Christianity almost two thousand years to accomplish what it has. The teachings of Christ take time to come to earth." All that is said here grows out of a tragic misconception of time. It is the strangely irrational notion that there is something in the very flow of time that will inevitably cure all ills. Actually time is neutral. It can be used either destructively or constructively. I am coming to feel that the people of ill will have used time much more effectively than the people of good will. We will have to repent in this generation not merely for the vitriolic words and actions of the bad people, but for the appalling silence of the good people. We must come to see that human progress never rolls in on wheels of inevitability. It comes through the tireless efforts and persistent work of men willing to be co-workers with God, and without this hard work time itself becomes an ally of the forces of social stagnation. We must use time creatively, and forever realize that the time is always ripe to do right. Now is the time to make real the promise of democracy, and transform our pending national elegy into a creative psalm of brotherhood. Now is the time to lift our national policy from the quicksand of racial injustice to the solid rock of human dignity.

You spoke of our activity in Birmingham as extreme. At first I was rather disappointed that fellow clergymen would see my nonviolent efforts as those of the extremist. I started thinking about the fact that I stand in the middle of two opposing forces in the Negro community. One is a force of complacency made up of Negroes who, as a result of long years of oppression, have been so completely drained of self-respect and a sense of "somebodiness" that they have adjusted to segregation, and of a few Negroes in the middle class who, because of a degree of academic and economic security, and because at points they profit by segregation, have unconsciously become insensitive to the problems of the masses. The other force is one of bitterness and hatred, and comes perilously close to advocating violence. It is expressed in the various black nationalist groups that are springing up over the nation, the largest and best known being Elijah Muhammad's Muslim movement. This movement is nourished by the contemporary frustration over the continued existence of racial discrimination. It is made up of people who have lost faith in America, who have absolutely repudiated Christianity, and who have concluded that the white man is an incurable "devil." I have tried to stand between these two forces, saying that we need not follow the "do-nothingism" of the complacent or the hatred and despair of the black nationalist. There is the more excellent way of love and nonviolent protest. I'm grateful to God that, through the Negro church, the dimension of nonviolence entered our struggle. If this philosophy had not emerged, I am convinced that by now many streets of the South would be flowing with floods of blood. And I am further convinced that if our white brothers dismiss as "rabble-rousers" and "outside agitators" those of us who are working through the channels of nonviolent direct action and refuse to support our nonviolent efforts, millions of Negroes, out of frustration and despair, will seek solace and security in black nationalist ideologies, a development that will lead inevitably to a frightening racial nightmare.

Oppressed people cannot remain oppressed forever. The urge for freedom will eventually come. This is what happened to the American Negro. Something within has reminded him of his birthright of freedom; something without has reminded him that he can gain it. Consciously and unconsciously, he has been swept in by what the Germans call the *Zeitgeist,* and with his black brothers of Africa, and his brown and yellow brothers of Asia, South America and the Caribbean, he is moving with a sense of cosmic urgency toward the promised land of racial justice. Recognizing this vital urge that has engulfed the Negro community, one should readily understand public demonstrations. The Negro has many pent-up resentments and latent frustrations. He has to get them out. So let him march sometime; let him have his prayer pilgrimages to the city hall; understand why he must have sit-ins and freedom rides. If his repressed emotions do not come out in these nonviolent ways, they will come out in ominous expressions of violence. This is not a threat; it is a fact of history. So I have not said to my people "get rid of your discontent." But I have tried to say that this normal and healthy discontent can be channelized through the creative outlet of nonviolent direct action. Now this approach is being dismissed as extremist. I must admit that I was initially disappointed in being so categorized.

But as I continued to think about the matter I gradually gained a bit of satisfaction from being considered an extremist. Was not Jesus an extremist in love—"Love your enemies, bless them that curse you, pray for them that despitefully use you." Was not Amos an extremist for justice —"Let justice roll down like waters and righteousness like a mighty stream." Was not Paul an extremist for the gospel of Jesus Christ—"I bear in my body the marks of the Lord Jesus." Was not Martin Luther an extremist—"Here I stand; I can do none other so help me God." Was not John Bunyan an extremist—"I will stay in jail to the end of my days before I make a butchery of my conscience." Was not Abraham Lincoln an extremist—"This nation cannot survive half slave and half free." Was not Thomas Jefferson an extremist—"We hold these truths to be self-evident, that all men are created equal." So the question is not whether we will be extremist but what kind of extremist will we be. Will we be extremists for hate or will we be extremists for love? Will we be extremists for the preservation of injustice—or will we be extremists for the cause of justice? In that dramatic scene on Calvary's hill, three men were crucified. We must not forget that all three were crucified for the same crime—the crime of extremism. Two were extremists for immorality, and thusly fell below their environment. The other, Jesus Christ, was an extremist for love, truth and goodness, and thereby rose above his environment. So, after all, maybe the South, the nation and the world are in dire need of creative extremists.

I had hoped that the white moderate would see this. Maybe I was too optimistic. Maybe I expected too much. I guess I should have realized that few members of a race that has oppressed another race can understand or appreciate the deep groans and passionate yearnings of those that have been oppressed and still fewer have the vision to see that injustice must be rooted out by strong, persistent and determined action. I am thankful, however, that some of our white brothers have grasped the meaning of this social revolution and committed themselves to it. They are still all too small in quantity, but they are big in quality. Some like Ralph McGill, Lillian Smith, Harry Golden and James Dabbs have written about our struggle in eloquent, prophetic and understanding terms. Others have marched with us down nameless streets of the South. They have languished in filthy roach-infested jails, suffering the abuse and brutality of angry policemen who see them as "dirty niggerlovers." They, unlike so many of their moderate brothers and sisters, have recognized the urgency of the moment and sensed the need for powerful "action" antidotes to combat the disease of segregation.

Let me rush on to mention my other disappointment. I have been so greatly disappointed with the white church and its leadership. Of course, there are some notable exceptions. I am not unmindful of the fact that each of you has taken some significant stands on this issue. I commend you, Rev. Stallings, for your Christian stance on this past Sunday, in welcoming Negroes to your worship service on a nonsegregated basis. I commend the Catholic leaders of this state for integrating Springhill College several years ago.

But despite these notable exceptions I must honestly reiterate that I have been disappointed with the church. I do not say that as one of the negative critics who can always find something wrong with the church. I say it as a minister of the gospel, who loves the church; who was nurtured in its bosom; who has been sustained by its spiritual blessings and who will remain true to it as long as the cord of life shall lengthen.

I had the strange feeling when I was suddenly catapulted into the leadership of the bus protest in Montgomery several years ago that we would have the support of the white church. I felt that the white ministers, priests and rabbis of the South would be some of our strongest allies. Instead, some have been outright opponents, refusing to understand the freedom movement and misrepresenting its leaders; all too many others have been more cautious than courageous and have remained silent behind the anesthetizing security of the stained-glass windows.

In spite of my shattered dreams of the past, I came to Birmingham with the hope that the white religious leadership of this community would see the justice of our cause, and with deep moral concern, serve as the channel through which our just grievances would get to the power structure. I had hoped that each of you would understand. But again I have been disappointed. I have heard numerous religious leaders of the South call upon their worshippers to comply with a desegregation decision because it is the *law,* but I have longed to hear white ministers say, "Follow this decree because integration is morally *right* and the Negro is your brother." In the midst of blatant injustices inflicted upon the Negro, I have watched white churches stand on the sideline and merely mouth pious irrelevancies and sanctimonious trivialities. In the midst of a mighty struggle to rid our nation of racial and economic injustice, I have heard so many ministers say, "Those are social issues with which the gospel has no real concern," and I have watched so many churches commit themselves to a completely other-worldly religion which made a strange distinction between body and soul, the sacred and the secular.

So here we are moving toward the exit of the twentieth century with a religious community largely adjusted to the status quo, standing as a taillight behind other community agencies rather than a headlight leading men to higher levels of justice.

I have traveled the length and breadth of Alabama, Mississippi and all the other southern states. On sweltering summer days and crisp autumn mornings I have looked at her beautiful churches with their lofty spires pointing heavenward. I have beheld the impressive outlay of her massive religious education buildings. Over and over again I have found myself asking: "What kind of people worship here? Who is their God? Where were their voices when the lips of Governor Barnett dripped with words of interposition and nullification? Where were they when Governor Wallace gave the clarion call for defiance and hatred? Where were their voices of support when tired, bruised and weary Negro men and women decided to rise from the dark dungeons of complacency to the bright hills of creative protest?"

Yes, these questions are still in my mind. In deep disappointment, I have wept over the laxity of the church. But be assured that my tears have been tears of love. There can be no deep disappointment where there is not deep love. Yes, I love the church; I love her sacred walls. How could I do otherwise? I am in the rather unique position of being the son, the grandson and the great-grandson of preachers. Yes, I see the church as the body of Christ. But, oh! How we have blemished and scarred that body through social neglect and fear of being nonconformists.

There was a time when the church was very powerful. It was during that period when the early Christians rejoiced when they were deemed worthy to suffer for what they believed. In those days the church was not merely a thermometer that recorded the ideas and principles of popular opinion; it was a thermostat that transformed the mores of society. Wherever the early Christians entered a town the power structure got disturbed and immediately sought to convict them for being "disturbers of the peace" and "outside agitators." But they went on with the conviction that they were "a colony of heaven," and had to obey God rather than man. They were small in number but big in commitment. They were too God-intoxicated to be "astronomically intimidated." They brought an end to such ancient evils as infanticide and gladiatorial contest.

Things are different now. The contemporary church is often a weak, ineffectual voice with an uncertain sound. It is so often the arch-supporter of the status quo. Far from being disturbed by the presence of the church, the power structure of the average community is consoled by the church's silent and often vocal sanction of things as they are.

But the judgment of God is upon the church as never before. If the church of today does not recapture the sacrificial spirit of the early church, it will lose its authentic ring, forfeit the loyalty of millions, and be dismissed as an irrelevant social club with no meaning for the twentieth century. I am meeting young people every day whose disappointment with the church has risen to outright disgust.

Maybe again, I have been too optimistic. Is organized religion too inextricably bound to the status quo to save our nation and the world? Maybe I must turn my faith to the inner spiritual church, the church within the church, as the true *ecclesia* and the hope of the world. But again I am thankful to God that some noble souls from the ranks of organized religion have broken loose from the paralyzing chains of conformity and joined us as active partners in the struggle for freedom. They have left their secure congregations and walked the streets of Albany, Georgia, with us. They have gone through the highways of the South on tortuous rides for freedom. Yes, they have gone to jail with us. Some have been kicked out of their churches, and lost support of their bishops and fellow ministers. But they have gone with the faith that right defeated is stronger than evil triumphant. These men have been the leaven in the lump of the race. Their witness has been the spiritual salt that has preserved the true meaning of the gospel in these troubled times. They have carved a tunnel of hope through the dark mountain of disappointment.

I hope the church as a whole will meet the challenge of this decisive hour. But even if the church does not come to the aid of justice, I have no despair about the future. I have no fear about the outcome of our struggle in Birmingham, even if our motives are presently misunderstood. We will reach the goal of freedom in Birmingham and all over the nation, because the goal of America is freedom. Abused and scorned though we may be, our destiny is tied up with the destiny of America. Before the Pilgrims landed at Plymouth we were here. Before the pen of Jefferson etched across the pages of history the majestic words of the Declaration of Independence, we were here. For more than two centuries our foreparents labored in this country without wages; they made cotton king; and they built the homes of their masters in the midst of brutal injustice and shameful humiliation—and yet out of a bottomless vitality they continued to thrive and develop. If the inexpressible cruelties of slavery could not stop us, the opposition we now face will surely fail. We will win our freedom because the sacred heritage of our nation and the eternal will of God are embodied in our echoing demands.

I must close now. But before closing I am impelled to mention one other point in your statement that troubled me profoundly. You warmly commended the Birmingham police force for keeping "order" and "preventing violence." I don't believe you would have so warmly commended the police force if you had seen its angry violent dogs literally biting six unarmed, nonviolent Negroes. I don't believe you would so quickly commend the policemen if you would observe their ugly and inhuman treatment of Negroes here in the city jail; if you would watch them push and curse old Negro women and young Negro girls; if you would see them slap and kick old Negro men and young boys; if you will observe them, as they did on two occasions, refuse to give us food because we wanted to sing our grace together. I'm sorry that I can't join you in your praise for the police department.

It is true that they have been rather disciplined in their public handling of the demonstrators. In this sense they have been rather publicly "nonviolent." But for what purpose? To preserve the evil system of segregation. Over the last few years I have consistently preached that nonviolence demands that the means we use must be as pure as the ends we seek. So I have tried to make it clear that it is wrong to use immoral means to attain moral ends. But now I must affirm that it is just as wrong, or even more so, to use moral means to preserve immoral ends. Maybe Mr. Connor and his policemen have been rather publicly nonviolent, as Chief Pritchett was in Albany, Georgia, but they have used the moral means of nonviolence to maintain the immoral end of flagrant racial injustice. T. S. Eliot has said that there is no greater treason than to do the right deed for the wrong reason.

I wish you had commended the Negro sit-inners and demonstrators of Birmingham for their sublime courage, their willingness to suffer and their amazing discipline in the midst of the most inhuman provocation. One day the South will recognize its real heroes. They will be the James Merediths, courageously and with a majestic sense of purpose facing jeering and hostile mobs and the agonizing loneliness that characterizes the life of the pioneer. They will be old, oppressed, battered Negro women, symbolized in a seventy-two-year-old woman of Montgomery, Alabama, who rose up with a sense of dignity and with her people decided not to ride the segregated buses, and responded to one who inquired about her tiredness with ungrammatical profundity: "My feet is tired, but my soul is rested." They will be the young high school and college students, young ministers of the gospel and a host of their elders courageously and nonviolently sitting-in at lunch counters and willingly going to jail for conscience's sake. One day the South will know that when these disinherited children of God sat down at lunch counters they were in reality standing up for the best in the American dream and the most sacred values in our Judeo-Christian heritage, and thusly, carrying our whole nation back to those great wells of democracy which were dug deep by the Founding Fathers in the formulation of the Constitution and the Declaration of Independence.

Never before have I written a letter this long (or should I say a book?). I'm afraid that it is much too long to take your precious time. I can assure you that it would have been much shorter if I had been writing from a comfortable desk, but what else is there to do when you are alone for days in the dull monotony of a narrow jail cell other than write long letters, think strange thoughts, and pray long prayers?

If I have said anything in this letter that is an overstatement of the truth and is indicative of an unreasonable impatience, I beg you to forgive me. If I have said anything in this letter that is an understatement of the truth and is indicative of my having a patience that makes me patient with anything less than brotherhood, I beg God to forgive me.

I hope this letter finds you strong in the faith. I also hope that circumstances will soon make it possible for me to meet each of you, not as an integrationist or a civil rights leader, but as a fellow clergyman and a Christian brother. Let us all hope that the dark clouds of racial prejudice will soon pass away and the deep fog of misunderstanding will be lifted from our fear-drenched communities and in some not too distant tomorrow the radiant stars of love and brotherhood will shine over our great nation with all of their scintillating beauty.

Yours for the cause of Peace and Brotherhood,
Martin Luther King, Jr.   ["Letter from Birmingham City Jail"]

66. Women in the church

Pope John Paul II, in his letter *On the Dignity of Women,* uses the language of complementarity and mutuality to discuss Christianity's understanding of women's role in redemption and ministry. What does the pope mean by the "anthropomorphism" of biblical language? What was new in Jesus' relationships with women that gives Christianity a special obligation to oppose sexual discrimination? According to the pope, what is the special mission of women in the church?

II. WOMAN-MOTHER OF GOD (THEOTOKOS)

Union With God

3. "When the time had fully come, God sent forth his Son, born of woman." With these words of his Letter to the Galatians (4:4), the apostle Paul links together the principal moments which essentially determine the fulfillment of the mystery "predetermined in God" (cf. Eph. 1:9). The Son, the Word one in substance with the Father, becomes man, born of a woman at "the fullness of time." This event leads to the turning point of man's history on earth, understood as salvation history. It is significant that St. Paul does not call the mother of Christ by her own name, *Mary*, but calls her *woman:* This coincides with the words of the "Proto-evangelium" in the Book of Genesis (cf. 3:15). She is that "woman who is present in the central salvific event which marks the "fullness of time": This event is realized in her and through her.

Thus there begins the central event, the key event in the history of salvation: the Lord's paschal mystery. Perhaps it would be worthwhile to reconsider it from the point of view of man's spiritual history, understood in the widest possible sense, and as this history is expressed through the different world religions. Let us recall at this point the words of the Second Vatican Council: "People look to the various religions for answers to those profound mysteries of the human condition which today even as in olden times deeply stir the human heart: What is a human being? What is the meaning and purpose of our life? What is goodness and what is sin? What gives rise to our sorrows, and to what intent? Where lies the path to true happiness? What is the truth about death, judgment and retribution beyond the grave? What, finally, is that ultimate and unutterable mystery which engulfs our being and from which we take our origins and toward which we move?" "From ancient times down to the present, there has existed among different peoples a certain perception of that hidden power which is present in the course of things and in the events of human life; at times, indeed, recognition can be found of a supreme divinity or even a supreme Father."

Against the background of this broad panorama, which testifies to the aspirations of the human spirit in search of God—at times as it were "groping its way" (cf. Acts 17:27)—the "fullness of time" spoken of in Paul's letter emphasizes the response of God himself, "in whom we live and move and have our being" (cf. Acts 17:28). This is the God who "in many and various ways spoke of old to our fathers by the prophets, but in these last days has spoken to us by a Son" (Heb. 1:1–2). The sending of this Son, one in substance with the Father, as a man "born of woman" constitutes the culminating and definitive point of God's self-revelation to humanity. This self-revelation is salvific in character, as the Second Vatican Council teaches in another passage: "In his goodness and wisdom, God chose to reveal himself and to make known to us the hidden purpose of his will (cf. Eph. 1:9) by which through Christ, the Word made flesh, man has access to the Father in the Holy Spirit and comes to share in the divine nature (cf. Eph. 2:18; 2 Pt. 1:4)."

A woman is to be found at the center this salvific event. The self-revelation of God who is the inscrutable unity of the Trinity, is outlined in the annunciation at Nazareth; "Behold, you will conceive in your womb and bear a son, and you shall call his name Jesus. He will be great, and will be called the Son of the Most High"—"How shall this be, since I have no husband?"—"The Holy Spirit will come upon you, and the power of the Most High will overshadow you; therefore the child to be born will be called holy, the Son of God. . . . For with God nothing will be impossible" (cf. Lk. 1:31–37).

It may be easy to think of this event in the setting of the history of Israel, the chosen people of which Mary is a daughter, but it is also easy to think of it in the context of all the different ways in which humanity has always sought to answer the fundamental and definitive questions which most beset it. Do we not find in the annunciation at Nazareth the beginning of that definitive answer by which God himself "attempts to calm people's hearts"? It is not just a matter here of God's words revealed through the prophets; rather with this response "the Word is truly made flesh" (cf. Jn. 1:14). Hence Mary attains a union with God that exceeds all the expectations of the human spirit. It even exceeds the expectations of all Israel, in particular the daughters of this chosen people, who on the basis of the promise could hope that one of their number would one day become the mother of the Messiah. Who among them, however, could have imagined that the promised Messiah would be "the Son of the Most High"? On the basis of the Old Testament's monotheistic faith such a thing was difficult to imagine. Only by the power of the Holy Spirit, who "overshadowed" her, was Mary able to accept what is "impossible with men, but not with God" (cf. Mk. 10:27).

Theotokos

4. Thus the "fullness of time" manifests the extraordinary dignity of the "woman." On the one hand, this dignity consists in the supernatural elevation to union with God in Jesus Christ, which determines the ulti-

mate finality of the existence of every person both on earth and in eternity. From this point of view, the "woman" is the representative and the archetype of the whole human race: She represents the humanity which belongs to all human beings, both men and women. On the other hand, however, the event at Nazareth highlights a form of union with the living God which can only belong to the "woman," Mary: the union between mother and son. The Virgin of Nazareth truly becomes the mother of God.

This truth, which Christian faith has accepted from the beginning, was solemnly defined at the Council of Ephesus (431 A.D.). In opposition to the opinion of Nestorius, who held that Mary was only the mother of the man Jesus, this council emphasized the essential meaning of the motherhood of the Virgin Mary. At the moment of the annunciation, by responding with her *fiat*, Mary conceived a man who was the Son of God, of one substance with the Father. Therefore she is truly the mother of God, because motherhood concerns the whole person, not just the body nor even just human "nature." In this way the name *Theotokos*—mother of God—became the name proper to the union with God granted to the Virgin Mary.

The particular union of the *Theotokos* with God—which fulfills in the most eminent manner the supernatural predestination to union with the Father which is granted to every human being (*filii in Filio*)—is a pure grace and, as such, a gift of the Spirit. At the same time, however, through her response of faith Mary exercises her free will and thus fully shares with her personal and feminine "I" in the event of the incarnation. With her *fiat*, Mary becomes the authentic subject of that union with God which was realized in the mystery of the incarnation of the Word, who is of one substance with the Father. All of God's action in human history at all times respects the free will of the human "I." And such was the case with the annunciation at Nazareth.

The Anthropomorphism of Biblical Language

8. The presentation of man as "the image and likeness of God" at the very beginning of Sacred Scripture has another significance too. It is the key for understanding biblical revelation as God's word about himself. Speaking about himself, whether through the prophets or through the Son (cf. Heb. 1:1, 2) who became man, God speaks in human language, using human concepts and images. If this manner of expressing himself is characterized by a certain anthropomorphism, the reason is that man is "like" God: created in his image and likeness. But then, God too is in

some measure "like man," and precisely because of this likeness, he can be humanly known. At the same time the language of the Bible is sufficiently precise to indicate the limits of the "likeness," the limits of the "analogy." For biblical revelation says that while man's "likeness" to God is true, the "non-likeness" which separates the whole of creation from the Creator is still more essentially true. Although man is created in God's likeness, God does not cease to be for him the one "who dwells in unapproachable light" (1 Tm. 6:16): He is the "Different One," by essence the "totally Other."

This observation on the limits of the analogy—the limits of man's likeness to God in biblical language—must also be kept in mind when, in different passages of Sacred Scripture (especially in the Old Testament), we find comparisons that attribute to God "masculine" or "feminine" qualities. We find in these passages an indirect confirmation of the truth that both man and woman were created in the image and likeness of God. If there is a likeness between Creator and creatures, it is understandable that the Bible would refer to God using expressions that attribute to him both "masculine" and "feminine" qualities.

We may quote here some characteristic passages from the prophet Isaiah: "But Zion said, 'The Lord has forsaken me, my Lord has forgotten me.' 'Can a woman forget her sucking child, that she should have no compassion on the son of her womb? Even these may forget, yet I will not forget you' " (49:14–15). And elsewhere: "As one whom his mother comforts, so will I comfort you; you shall be comforted in Jerusalem" (66:13). In the Psalms too, God is compared to a caring mother: "Like a child quieted at its mother's breast; like a child that is quieted is my soul. O Israel, hope in the Lord" (Ps. 131:2–3). In various passages the love of God who cares for his people is shown to be like that of a mother: Thus like a mother God "has carried" humanity, and in particular, his chosen people, within his own womb; he has given birth to it in travail, has nourished and comforted it (cf. Is. 42:14; 46:3–4). In many passages God's love is presented as the "masculine" love of the bridegroom and father (cf. Hos. 11:1–4; Jer. 3:4–19), but also sometimes as the "feminine" love of a mother.

This characteristic of biblical language—its anthropomorphic way of speaking about God—points indirectly to the mystery of the eternal "generating" which belongs to the inner life of God. Nevertheless, in itself this "generating" has neither "masculine" nor "feminine" qualities. It is by nature totally divine. It is spiritual in the most perfect way, since "God is spirit" (Jn. 4:24) and possesses no property typical of the body, neither "feminine" nor "masculine." Thus even "fatherhood" in

God is completely divine and free of the "masculine" bodily characteristics proper to human fatherhood. In this sense the Old Testament spoke of God as a Father and turned to him as a Father. Jesus Christ—who called God "Abba-Father" (Mk. 14:36), and who as the only begotten and consubstantial Son placed this truth at the very center of his Gospel, thus establishing the norm of Christian prayer—referred to fatherhood in this ultracorporeal, superhuman and completely divine sense. He spoke as the Son, joined to the Father by the eternal mystery of divine generation, and he did so while being at the same time the truly human son of his Virgin Mother.

Although it is not possible to attribute human qualities to the eternal generation of the Word of God and although the divine fatherhood does not possess "masculine" characteristics in a physical sense, we must nevertheless seek in God the absolute model of all "generation" among human beings. This would seem to be the sense of the Letter to the Ephesians: "I bow my knees before the Father, from whom every family in heaven and on earth is named" (3:14–15). All "generating" among creatures finds its primary model in that generating which in God is completely divine, that is, spiritual. All "generating" in the created world is to be likened to this absolute and uncreated model. Thus every element of human generation which is proper to man and every element which is proper to woman, namely human "fatherhood" and "motherhood," bears within itself a likeness to or analogy with the divine "generating" and with that "fatherhood" which in God is "totally different," that is, completely spiritual and divine in essence; whereas in the human order, generation is proper to the "unity of the two": Both are "parents," the man and the woman alike.

V. JESUS CHRIST

"They Marveled That He Was Talking With a Woman"

12. The words of the Protoevangelium in the Book of Genesis enable us to move into the context of the Gospel. Man's redemption, foretold in Genesis, now becomes a reality in the person and mission of Jesus Christ, in which we also recognize what the reality of the redemption means for the dignity and the vocation of women. This meaning becomes clearer for us from Christ's words and from his whole attitude toward women, an attitude which is extremely simple and for this very

reason extraordinary, if seen against the background of his time. It is an attitude marked by great clarity and depth. Various women appear along the path of the mission of Jesus of Nazareth, and his meeting with each of them is a confirmation of the evangelical "newness of life" already spoken of.

It is universally admitted—even by people with a critical attitude toward the Christian message—that in the eyes of his contemporaries Christ became a promoter of women's true dignity and of the vocation corresponding to this dignity. At times this caused wonder, surprise, often to the point of scandal: "They marveled that he was talking with a woman" (Jn. 4:27), because this behavior differed from that of his contemporaries. Even Christ's own disciples "marveled." The Pharisee to whose house the sinful woman went to anoint Jesus' feet with perfumed oil "said to himself, 'If this man were a prophet, he would have known who and what sort of woman this is who is touching him, for she is a sinner' " (Lk. 7:39). Even greater dismay or even "holy indignation" must have filled the self-satisfied hearers of Christ's words: "The tax collectors and the harlots go into the kingdom of God before you" (Mt. 21:31).

By speaking and acting in this way, Jesus made it clear that "the mysteries of the kingdom" were known to him in every detail. He also "knew what was in man" (Jn. 2:25), in his innermost being, in his "heart." He was a witness of God's eternal plan for the human being, created in his own image and likeness as man and woman. He was also perfectly aware of the consequences of sin, of that "mystery of iniquity" working in human hearts as the bitter fruit of the obscuring of the divine image. It is truly significant that in his important discussion about marriage and its indissolubility, in the presence of "the scribes," who by profession were experts in the law, Jesus makes reference to the "beginning." The question asked concerns a man's right "to divorce one's wife for any cause" (Mt. 19:3) and therefore also concerns the woman's right, her rightful position in marriage, her dignity. The questioners think they have on their side the Mosaic legislation then followed in Israel: "Why then did Moses command one to give a certificate of divorce and to put her away?" (Mt. 19:7). Jesus answers: "For your hardness of heart Moses allowed you to divorce your wives, but from the beginning it was not so" (Mt. 19:8). Jesus appeals to the "beginning," to the creation of man as male and female and their ordering by God himself, which is based upon the fact that both were created "in his image and likeness." Therefore, when "a man shall leave his father and mother and is joined to his wife so that the two become one flesh," there remains in force the law which comes from God himself: "What therefore God has joined together, let no man put asunder" (Mt. 19:6).

The principle of this "ethos," which from the beginning marks the reality of creation, is now confirmed by Christ in opposition to that tradition which discriminated against women. In this tradition the male "dominated," without having proper regard for woman and for her dignity, which the "ethos" of creation made the basis of the mutual relationships of two people united in marriage. This "ethos" is recalled and confirmed by Christ's words; it is the "ethos" of the Gospel and of redemption.

Women in the Gospel

13. As we scan the pages of the Gospel, many women of different ages and conditions pass before our eyes. We meet women with illnesses or physical sufferings such as the one who had "a spirit of infirmity for eighteen years; she was bent over and could not fully straighten herself" (Lk. 13:11); or Simon's mother-in-law, who "lay sick with a fever" (Mk. 1:30); or the woman "who had a flow of blood" (cf. Mk. 5:25–34) who could not touch anyone because it was believed that her touch would make a person "impure." Each of them was healed, and the last-mentioned—the one with a flow of blood who touched Jesus' garment "in the crowd" (Mk. 5:27)—was praised by him for her great faith: "Your faith has made you well" (Mk. 5:34). Then there is the daughter of Jairus, whom Jesus brings back to life, saying to her tenderly: "Little girl, I say to you, arise" (Mk. 5:41). There also is the widow of Nain, whose only son Jesus brings back to life, accompanying his action by an expression of affectionate mercy: "He had compassion on her and said to her, 'Do not weep!' " (Lk. 7:13). And finally there is the Canaanite woman, whom Christ extols for her faith, her humility and for that greatness of spirit of which only a mother's heart is capable. "O woman, great is your faith! Be it done for you as you desire" (Mt. 15:28). The Canaanite woman was asking for the healing of her daughter.

Sometimes the women whom Jesus met and who received so many graces from him also accompanied him as he journeyed with the apostles through the towns and villages, proclaiming the good news of the kingdom of God; and they "provided for them out of their means." The Gospel names Joanna, who was the wife of Herod's steward, Susanna and "many others" (cf. Lk. 8:1–3).

Sometimes women appear in the parables which Jesus of Nazareth used to illustrate for his listeners the truth about the kingdom of God. This is the case in the parables of the lost coin (cf. Lk. 15:8–10), the leaven (cf. Mt. 13:33), and the wise and foolish virgins (cf. Mt. 25:1–13). Particularly eloquent is the story of the widow's mite. While "the rich were putting their gifts into the treasury . . . a poor widow put in two copper coins." Then Jesus said: "This poor widow has put in more than all of them. . . . She out of her poverty put in all the living that she had" (Lk. 21:1–4). In this way Jesus presents her as a model for everyone and defends her, for in the socio-juridical system of the time widows were totally defenseless people (cf. also Lk. 18:1–7).

In all of Jesus' teaching, as well as in his behavior, one can find nothing which reflects the discrimination against women prevalent in his day. On the contrary, his words and works always express the respect and honor due to women. The woman with a stoop is called a "daughter of Abraham" (Lk. 13:16), while in the whole Bible the title "son of Abraham" is used only of men. Walking the *via dolorosa* to Golgotha, Jesus will say to the women: "Daughters of Jerusalem, do not weep for me" (Lk. 23:28). This way of speaking to and about women, as well as his manner of treating them, clearly constitutes an "innovation" with respect to the prevailing custom at that time.

This becomes even more explicit in regard to women whom popular opinion contemptuously labeled sinners, public sinners and adulteresses. There is the Samaritan woman, to whom Jesus himself says: "For you have had five husbands, and he whom you now have is not your husband." And she, realizing that he knows the secrets of her life, recognizes him as the Messiah and runs to tell her neighbors. The conversation leading up to this realization is one of the most beautiful in the Gospel (cf. Jn. 4:7–27).

Then there is the public sinner who, in spite of her condemnation by common opinion, enters into the house of the Pharisee to anoint the feet of Jesus with perfumed oil. To his host, who is scandalized by this, he will say: "Her sins, which are many, are forgiven, for she loved much" (cf. Lk. 7:37–47).

Finally, there is a situation which is perhaps the most eloquent: A woman caught in adultery is brought to Jesus. To the leading question, "In the law Moses commanded us to stone such. What do you say about her?" Jesus replies, "Let him who is without sin among you be the first to throw a stone at her." The power of truth contained in this answer is so great that "they went away, one by one, beginning with the eldest."

Only Jesus and the woman remain. "Woman, where are they? Has no one condemned you?" "No one, Lord." "Neither do I condemn you; go, and do not sin again" (cf. Jn. 8:3–11).

These episodes provide a very clear picture. Christ is the one who "knows what is in man" (cf. Jn. 2:25)—in man and woman. He knows the dignity of man, his worth in God's eyes. He himself, the Christ, is the definitive confirmation of this worth. Everything he says and does is definitively fulfilled in the paschal mystery of the redemption. Jesus' attitude to the women whom he meets in the course of his messianic service reflects the eternal plan of God, who in creating each one of them, chooses her and loves her in Christ (cf. Eph. 1:1–5). Each woman, therefore, is "the only creature on earth which God willed for its own sake." Each of them from the "beginning" inherits as a woman the dignity of personhood. Jesus of Nazareth confirms this dignity, recalls it, renews it and makes it a part of the Gospel and of the redemption for which he is sent into the world. Every word and gesture of Christ about women must therefore be brought into the dimension of the paschal mystery. In this way everything is completely explained.

The Symbolic Dimension of the "Great Mystery"

25. In the Letter to the Ephesians we encounter a second dimension of the analogy which, taken as a whole, serves to reveal the "great mystery." This is a symbolic dimension. If God's love for the human person, for the chosen people of Israel, is presented by the prophets as the love of the bridegroom for the bride, such an analogy expresses the "spousal" quality and the divine and non-human character of God's love: "For your Maker is your husband . . . the God of the whole earth he is called" (Is. 54:5). The same can also be said of the spousal love of Christ, the Redeemer: "For God so loved the world that he gave his only Son!" (Jn. 3:18). It is a matter, therefore, of God's love expressed by means of the redemption accomplished by Christ. According to St. Paul's letter, this love is "like" the spousal love of human spouses, but naturally it is not "the same." For the analogy implies a likeness, while at the same time leaving ample room for non-likeness.

This is easily seen in regard to the person of the "bride." According to the Letter to the Ephesians, the bride is the church, just as for the prophets the bride was Israel. She is therefore a collective subject and not an individual person. This collective subject is the people of God, a community made up of many persons, both women and men. "Christ has loved the church" precisely as a community, as the people of God. At the same time, in this church, which in the same passage is also called his "body" (cf. Eph. 5:23), he has loved every individual person. For Christ has redeemed all without exception, every man and woman. It is precisely this love of God which is expressed in the redemption; the spousal character of this love reaches completion in the history of humanity and of the world.

Christ has entered this history and remains in it as the bridegroom who "has given himself." *To give* means "to become a sincere gift" in the most complete and radical way: "Greater love has no man than this" (Jn. 15:13). According to this conception, all human beings—both women and men—are called through the church to be the "bride" of Christ, the redeemer of the world. In this way "being the bride," and thus the "feminine" element, becomes a symbol of all that is "human," according to the words of Paul: "There is neither male nor female; for you are all one in Christ Jesus" (Gal. 3:28).

From a linguistic viewpoint we can say that the analogy of spousal love found in the Letter to the Ephesians links what is "masculine" to what is "feminine," since as members of the church men too are included in the concept of "bride." This should not surprise us, for St. Paul, in order to express his mission in Christ and in the church, speaks of the "little children with whom he is again in travail" (cf. Gal. 4:19). In the sphere of what is "human"—of what is humanly personal—"masculinity" and "femininity" are distinct, yet at the same time they complete and explain each other: This is also present in the great analogy of the "bride" in the Letter to the Ephesians. In the church every human being —male and female—is the "bride," in that he or she accepts the gift of the love of Christ, the Redeemer, and seeks to respond to it with the gift of his or her own person.

Christ is the bridegroom. This expresses the truth about the love of God, who "first loved us" (cf. 1 Jn. 4:19) and who, with the gift generated by this spousal love for man, has exceeded all human expectations: "He loved them to the end" (Jn. 13:1). The bridegroom—the Son consubstantial with the Father as God—became the son of Mary; he became the "son of man," true man, a male. The symbol of the bridegroom is masculine. This masculine symbol represents the human aspect of the divine love which God has for Israel, for the church and for all people. Meditating on what the Gospels say about Christ's attitude toward women, we can conclude that as a man, a son of Israel, he revealed the dignity of the "daughters of Abraham" (cf. Lk. 13:16), the dignity belonging to women from the very "beginning" on an equal footing with men. At the same time Christ emphasized the originality which distinguishes women from men, all the richness lavished upon women in the mystery of creation. Christ's attitude toward women serves as a model of what the Letter to the Ephesians expresses with the concept of "bridegroom." Precisely because Christ's divine love is the love of a bridegroom, it is the model and pattern of all human love, men's love in particular.

The Eucharist

26. Against the broad background of the "great mystery" expressed in the spousal relationship between Christ and the church, it is possible to understand adequately the calling of the "Twelve." In calling only men as his apostles, Christ acted in a completely free and sovereign manner. In doing so, he exercised the same freedom with which, in all his behavior, he emphasized the dignity and the vocation of women without conforming to the prevailing customs and to the traditions sanctioned by the legislation of the time. Consequently, the assumption that he called men to be apostles in order to conform with the widespread mentality of his times does not at all correspond to Christ's way of acting. "Teacher, we know that you are true, and teach the way of God truthfully, and care for no man; for you do not regard the position of men" (Mt. 22:16). These words fully characterize Jesus of Nazareth's behavior. Here one also finds an explanation for the calling of the Twelve." They are with Christ at the Last Supper. They alone receive the sacramental charge, "Do this in remembrance of me" (Lk. 22:19; 1 Cor. 11:24), which is joined to the institution of the eucharist. On Easter Sunday night they receive the Holy Spirit for the forgiveness of sins: "Whose sins you forgive are forgiven them, and whose sins you retain are retained" (Jn. 20:23).

We find ourselves at the very heart of the paschal mystery, which completely reveals the spousal love of God. Christ is the bridegroom because "he has given himself": His body has been "given," his blood has been "poured out" (cf. Lk. 22:19–20). In this way "he loved them to the end" (Jn. 13:1). The "sincere gift" contained in the sacrifice of the cross gives definitive prominence to the spousal meaning of God's love. As the redeemer of the world, Christ is the bridegroom of the church. The eucharist is the sacrament of our redemption. It is the sacrament of the bridegroom and of the bride. The eucharist makes present and realizes anew in a sacramental manner the redemptive act of Christ, who "creates" the church, his body. Christ is united with this "body" as the bridegroom with the bride. All this is contained in the Letter to the Ephesians. The perennial "unity of the two" that exists between man and woman from the very "beginning" is introduced into this "great mystery" of Christ and of the church.

Since Christ in instituting the eucharist linked it in such an explicit way to the priestly service of the apostles, it is legitimate to conclude that he thereby wished to express the relationship between man and woman, between what is "feminine" and what is "masculine." It is a relationship willed by God both in the mystery of creation and in the mystery of redemption. It is the eucharist above all that expresses the redemptive act of Christ, the bridegroom, toward the church, the bride. This is clear and unambiguous when the sacramental ministry of the eucharist, in which the priest acts *in persona Christi*, is performed by a man. This explanation confirms the teaching of the declaration *Inter Insigniores*, published at the behest of Paul VI in response to the question concerning the admission of women to the ministerial priesthood.

The Gift of the Bride

27. The Second Vatican Council renewed the church's awareness of the universality of the priesthood. In the new covenant there is only one sacrifice and only one priest: Christ. All the baptized share in the one priesthood of Christ, both men and women, inasmuch as they must "present their bodies as a living sacrifice, holy and acceptable to God (cf. Rom. 12:1), give witness to Christ in every place and give an explanation to anyone who asks the reason for the hope in eternal life that is in them (cf. 1 Pt. 3:15)." Universal participation in Christ's sacrifice, in which the redeemer has offered to the Father the whole world and humanity in particular, brings it about that all in the church are "a kingdom of priests" (Rv. 5:10; cf. 1 Pt. 2:9), who not only share in the priestly mission, but also in the prophetic and kingly mission of Christ, the Messiah. Furthermore, this participation determines the organic unity of the church, the people of God, with Christ. It expresses at the same time the "great mystery" described in the Letter to the Ephesians: the bride united to her bridegroom; united, because she lives his life; united, because she shares in his threefold mission (*tria munera Christi*); united in such a manner as to respond with a "sincere gift" of self to the inexpressible gift of the love of the bridegroom, the Redeemer of the world. This concerns everyone in the church, women as well as men. It obviously

concerns those who share in the "ministerial priesthood," which is characterized by service. In the context of the "great mystery" of Christ and of the church, all are called to respond—as a bride—with the gift of their lives to the inexpressible gift of the love of Christ, who alone, as the redeemer of the world, is the church's bridegroom. The "royal priesthood," which is universal, at the same time expresses the gift of the bride.

This is of fundamental importance for understanding the church in her own essence, so as to avoid applying to the church—even in her dimension as an "institution" made up of human beings and forming part of history—criteria of understanding and judgment which do not pertain to her nature. Although the church possesses a "hierarchical" structure, nevertheless this structure is totally ordered to the holiness of Christ's members. And holiness is measured according to the "great mystery" in which the bride responds with the gift of love to the gift of the bridegroom. She does this "in the Holy Spirit," since "God's love has been poured into our hearts through the Holy Spirit, who has been given to us" (Rom. 5:5). The Second Vatican Council, confirming the teaching of the whole of tradition, recalled that in the hierarchy of holiness it is precisely the "woman," Mary of Nazareth, who is the "figure" of the church. She "precedes" everyone on the path to holiness; in her person "the church has already reached that perfection whereby she exists without spot or wrinkle (cf. Eph. 5:27)" In this sense, one can say that the church is both "Marian" and "apostolic-Petrine."

In the history of the church, even from earliest times, there were side by side with men a number of women for whom the response of the bride to the bridegroom's redemptive love acquired full expressive force. First we see those women who had personally encountered Christ and followed him. After his departure, together with the apostles, they "devoted themselves to prayer" in the Upper Room in Jerusalem until the day of Pentecost. On that day the Holy Spirit spoke through "the sons and daughters" of the people of God, thus fulfilling the words of the prophet Joel (cf. Acts 2:17). These women, and others afterward, played an active and important role in the life of the early church, in building up from its foundations the first Christian community—and subsequent communities—through their own charisms and their varied service. The apostolic writings note their names, such as Phoebe, "a deaconess of the church at Cenchreae" (cf. Rom. 16:1), Prisca with her husband Aquila (cf. 2 Tm. 4:19), Euodia and Syntyche (cf. Phil. 4:2), Mary, Tryphaena, Persis and Tryphosa (cf. Rom. 16:6, 12). St. Paul speaks of their "hard work" for Christ, and this hard work indicates the various fields of the church's apostolic service, beginning with the "domestic church." For in the latter, "sincere faith" passes from the mother to her children and grandchildren, as was the case in the house of Timothy (cf. 2 Tm. 1:5).

The same thing is repeated down the centuries from one generation to the next, as the history of the church demonstrates. By defending the dignity of women and their vocation, the church has shown honor and gratitude for those women who—faithful to the Gospel—have shared in every age in the apostolic mission of the whole people of God. They are the holy martyrs, virgins and mothers of families who bravely bore witness to their faith and passed on the church's faith and tradition by bringing up their children in the spirit of the Gospel.

In every age and in every country we find many "perfect" women (cf. Prv. 31:10), who despite persecution, difficulties and discriminations, have shared in the church's mission. It suffices to mention: Monica, the mother of Augustine, Macrina, Olga of Kiev, Matilda of Tuscany, Hedwig of Silesia, Jadwiga of Cracow, Elizabeth of Thuringia, Birgitta of Sweden, Joan of Arc, Rose of Lima, Elizabeth Ann Seton and Mary Ward.

The witness and the achievements of Christian women have had a significant impact on the life of the church as well as of society. Even in the face of serious social discrimination, holy women have acted "freely," strengthened by their union with Christ. Such union and freedom rooted in God explain, for example, the great work of St. Catherine of Siena in the life of the church and the work of St. Teresa of Jesus in the monastic life.

In our own days too the church is constantly enriched by the witness of the many women who fulfill their vocation to holiness. Holy women are an incarnation of the feminine ideal; they are also a model for all Christians, a model of the *"sequela Christi,"* an example of how the bride must respond with love to the love of the bridegroom.

VIII. "THE GREATEST OF THESE IS LOVE"

In the Face of Changes

28. "The church believes that Christ, who died and was raised up for all, can through his Spirit offer man the light and the strength to respond to his supreme destiny." We can apply these words of the conciliar

constitution *Gaudium et Spes* to the present reflections. The particular reference to the dignity of women and their vocation, precisely in our time, can and must be received in the "light and power" which the Spirit grants to human beings, including the people of our own age, which is marked by so many different transformations. The church "holds that in her Lord and Master can be found the key, the focal point and the goal" of man and "of all human history," and she "maintains that beneath all changes there are many realities which do not change and which have their ultimate foundation in Christ, who is the same yesterday and to-day, yes and forever."

These words of the Constitution on the Church in the Modern World show the path to be followed in undertaking the tasks connected with the dignity and vocation of women, against the background of the significant changes of our times. We can face these changes correctly and adequately only if we go back to the foundations which are to be found in Christ, to those "immutable" truths and values of which he himself remains the "faithful witness" (cf. Rv. 1:5) and teacher. A different way of acting would lead to doubtful, if not actually erroneous and deceptive results.

The Dignity of Women and the Order of Love

29. The passage from the Letter to the Ephesians already quoted (5:21–33), in which the relationship between Christ and the church is presented as the link between the bridegroom and the bride, also makes reference to the institution of marriage as recorded in the Book of Genesis (cf. 2:24). This passage connects the truth about marriage as a primordial sacrament with the creation of man and woman in the image and likeness of God (cf. Gn. 1:27; 5:1). The significant comparison in the Letter to the Ephesians gives perfect clarity to what is decisive for the dignity of women both in the eyes of God—the Creator and Redeemer —and in the eyes of human beings—men and women. In God's eternal plan, woman is the one in whom the order of love in the created world of persons takes first root. The order of love belongs to the intimate life of God himself, the life of the Trinity. In the intimate life of God, the Holy Spirit is the personal hypostasis of love. Through the Spirit, uncreated gift, love becomes a gift for created persons. Love, which is of God, communicates itself to creatures: "God's love has been poured into our hearts through the Holy Spirit who has been given to us" (Rom. 5:5).

The calling of woman into existence at man's side as "a helper fit for him" (Gn. 2:18) in the "unity of the two" provides the visible world of creatures with particular conditions so that "the love of God may be poured into the hearts" of the beings created in his image. When the author of the Letter to the Ephesians calls Christ "the bridegroom" and the church "the bride," he indirectly confirms through this analogy the truth about woman as bride. The bridegroom is the one who loves. The bride is loved: It is she who receives love, in order to love in return.

Rereading Genesis in light of the spousal symbol in the Letter to the Ephesians enables us to grasp a truth which seems to determine in an essential manner the question of women's dignity and, subsequently, also the question of their vocation: The dignity of women is measured by the order of love, which is essentially the order of justice and charity.

Only a person can love, and only a person can be loved. This statement is primarily ontological in nature, and it gives rise to an ethical affirmation. Love is an ontological and ethical requirement of the person. The person must be loved, since love alone corresponds to what the person is. This explains the commandment of love, known already in the Old Testament (cf. Dt. 6:5; Lv. 19:18) and placed by Christ at the very center of the Gospel "ethos" (cf. Mt. 22:36–40; Mk. 12:28–34). This also explains the primacy of love expressed by St. Paul in the First Letter to the Corinthians: "The greatest of these is love" (cf. 13:13).

Unless we refer to this order and primacy, we cannot give a complete and adequate answer to the question about women's dignity and vocation. When we say that the woman is the one who receives love in order to love in return, this refers not only or above all to the specific spousal relationship of marriage. It means something more universal, based on the very fact of her being a woman within all the interpersonal relationships which, in the most varied ways, shape society and structure the interaction between all persons—men and women. In this broad and diversified context, a woman represents a particular value by the fact that she is a human person and, at the same time, this particular person, by the fact of her femininity. This concerns each and every woman, independently of the cultural context in which she lives and independently of her spiritual, psychological and physical characteristics, as for example, age, education, health, work and whether she is married or single.

The passage from the Letter to the Ephesians which we have been considering enables us to think of a special kind of "prophetism" that belongs to women in their femininity. The analogy of the bridegroom and the bride speaks of the love with which every human being—man and woman—is loved by God in Christ. But in the context of the biblical analogy and the text's interior logic, it is precisely the woman—the bride —who manifests this truth to everyone. This "prophetic" character of women in their femininity finds its highest expression in the Virgin Mother of God. She emphasizes, in the fullest and most direct way, the intimate linking of the order of love—which enters the world of human persons through a woman—with the Holy Spirit. At the annunciation Mary hears the words, "The Holy Spirit will come upon you" (Lk. 1:35).

Awareness of a Mission

30. A woman's dignity is closely connected with the love which she receives by the very reason of her femininity; it is likewise connected with the love which she gives in return. The truth about the person and about love is thus confirmed. With regard to the truth about the person, we must turn again to the Second Vatican Council: "Man, who is the only creature on earth that God willed for its own sake, cannot fully find himself except through a sincere gift of self." This applies to every human being as a person created in God's image, whether man or woman. This ontological affirmation also indicates the ethical dimension of a person's vocation. Woman can only find herself by giving love to others.

From the "beginning," woman—like man—was created and "placed" by God in this order of love. The sin of the first parents did not destroy this order nor irreversibly cancel it out. This is proved by the words of the Proto-evangelium (cf. Gn. 3:15). Our reflections have focused on the particular place occupied by the "woman" in this key text of revelation. It is also to be noted how the same woman, who attains the position of a biblical "exemplar," also appears within the eschatological perspective of the world and of humanity given in the Book of Revelation. She is "a woman clothed with the sun," with the moon under her feet and on her head a crown of stars (cf. Rv. 12:1). One can say she is a woman of cosmic scale, on a scale with the whole work of creation. At the same time she is "suffering the pangs and anguish of childbirth" (Rv. 12:2) like Eve, "the mother of all the living" (Gn. 3:20). She also suffers because "before the woman who is about to give birth" (cf. Rv. 12:4) there stands "the great dragon . . . that ancient serpent" (Rv. 12:9), already known from the Proto-evangelium: the Evil One, the "father of lies" and of sin (cf. Jn. 8:44). The "ancient serpent" wishes to devour "the child." While we see in this text an echo of the infancy narrative (cf. Mt. 2:13, 16), we can also see that the struggle with evil and the Evil One marks the biblical exemplar of the "woman" from the beginning to the end of history. It is also a struggle for man, for his true good, for his salvation. Is not the Bible trying to tell us that it is precisely in the "woman"—Eve-Mary—that history witnesses a dramatic struggle for every human being, the struggle for his or her fundamental yes or no to God and God's eternal plan for humanity?

While the dignity of woman witnesses to the love which she receives in order to love in return, the biblical "exemplar" of the woman also seems to reveal the true order of love which constitutes woman's own vocation. Vocation is meant here in its fundamental and, one may say, universal significance, a significance which is then actualized and expressed in women's many different "vocations" in the church and the world.

The moral and spiritual strength of a woman is joined to her awareness that God entrusts the human being to her in a special way. Of course, God entrusts every human being to each and every other human being. But this entrusting concerns women in a special way—precisely by reason of their femininity—and this in a particular way determines their vocation.

The moral force of women, which draws strength from this awareness and this entrusting, expresses itself in a great number of figures of the Old Testament, of the time of Christ and of later ages right up to our own day.

A woman is strong because of her awareness of this entrusting, strong because of the fact that God "entrusts the human being to her," always and in every way, even in the situations of social discrimination in which she may find herself. This awareness and this fundamental vocation speak to women of the dignity which they receive from God himself, and this makes them "strong" and strengthens their vocation. Thus the "perfect woman" (cf. Prv. 31:10) becomes an irreplaceable support and source of spiritual strength for other people, who perceive the great energies of her spirit. These "perfect women" are owed much by their families and sometimes by whole nations.

In our own time, the successes of science and technology make it possible to attain material well-being to a degree hitherto unknown. While this favors some, it pushes others to the edges of society. In this way, unilateral progress can also lead to a gradual loss of sensitivity for man, that is, for what is essentially human. In this sense, our time in particular awaits the manifestation of that "genius" which belongs to women and which can ensure sensitivity for human beings in every circumstance: Because they are human!—and because "the greatest of these is love" (cf. 1 Cor. 13:13).

Thus a careful reading of the biblical exemplar of the woman—from the Book of Genesis to the Book of Revelation—confirms that which constitutes women's dignity and vocation as well as that which is unchangeable and ever relevant in them, because it has its "ultimate foundation in Christ, who is the same yesterday and today, yes and forever." If the human being is entrusted by God to women in a particular way, does not this mean that Christ looks to them for the accomplishment of the "royal priesthood" (1 Pt. 2:9), which is the treasure he has given to every individual? Christ, as the supreme and only priest of the new and eternal covenant and as the bridegroom of the church, does not cease to submit this same inheritance to the Father through the Spirit, so that God may be "everything to everyone" (1 Cor. 15:28).

Then the truth that "the greatest of these is love" (cf. 1 Cor. 13:13) will have its definitive fulfillment. [from "On the Dignity of Women"]

67. Faith and liberation

Archbishop Oscar Romero of San Salvador spoke out against the oppression of the poor in his country of El Salvador by unjust economic structures and by terrorism practiced by opponents of social change. He was assassinated in March of 1980 as he celebrated mass, and is revered as a martyr by many throughout Latin America. In the speech below, given on the occasion of his being awarded an honorary doctorate by the University of Louvain (Belgium), he echoes some of the themes of the "theology of liberation"—especially the need for the church to be involved actively in the struggle for justice.

I come from the smallest country in faraway Latin America. I come bringing in my heart, which is that of a Salvadoran Christian and pastor, greetings, gratitude, and the joy of sharing the experiences of life.

I first of all greet with admiration this noble alma mater of Louvain. Never did I imagine the enormous honor of being thus linked with a European center of such academic and cultural prestige, a center where were born so many of the ideas that have contributed to the marvelous effort being made by the church and by society to adapt themselves to the new times in which we live.

Therefore I come also to express my thanks to the University of Louvain, and to the church in Belgium. I want to think of this honorary doctorate as something other than an act of homage to me personally. The enormous disproportion of such a great weight being attributed to my few merits would overwhelm me. Let me rather interpret this generous distinction awarded by the university as an affectionate act of homage to the people of El Salvador and to their church, as an eloquent testimony of support for, and solidarity with, the sufferings of my people and for their noble struggle for liberation, and as a gesture of communion, and of sympathy, with the apostolic work of my archdiocese.

I could not refuse to accept the privilege of this act of homage if, by coming to receive it, I could come to thank the church of Belgium for the invaluable pastoral help it has given to the church of El Salvador. It would not, indeed, have been possible to find a more suitable time and place to say "thank you" than this one, so courteously provided for me by the University of Louvain. So, from the depths of my heart, many thanks to you—bishops, priests, religious, and lay persons—for so generously uniting your lives, your labors, the hardships, and the persecution involved in our pastoral activities.

And in the same spirit of friendship as that in which I expressed my greetings and my gratitude, I want to express the joy I have in coming to share with you, in a fraternal way, my experience as a pastor and as a Salvadoran, and my theological reflection as a teacher of the faith.

In line with the friendly suggestion made by the university, I have the honor of placing this experience and reflection within the series of conferences taking place here upon the theme of the political dimension of the Christian faith.

I shall not try to talk, and you cannot expect me to talk, as would an expert in politics. Nor will I even speculate, as someone might who was an expert, on the theoretical relationship between the faith and politics. No, I am going to speak to you simply as a pastor, as one who, together with his people, has been learning the beautiful but harsh truth that the Christian faith does not cut us off from the world but immerses us in it, that the church is not a fortress set apart from the city. The church follows Jesus who lived, worked, battled, and died in the midst of a city, in the *polis*. It is in this sense that I should like to talk about the political dimension of the Christian faith: in the precise sense of the repercussions of the faith on the world, and also of the repercussions that being in the world has on the faith.

A CHURCH AT THE SERVICE OF THE WORLD

We ought to be clear from the start that the Christian faith and the activity of the church have always had socio-political repercussions. By commission or omission, by associating themselves with one or another social group, Christians have always had an influence upon the socio-political makeup of the world in which they lived. The problem is about the "how" of this influence in the socio-political world, whether or not it is in accordance with the faith.

As a first idea, though still a very general one, I want to propose the intuition of Vatican II that lies at the root of every ecclesial movement of today. The essence of the church lies in its mission of service to the world, in its mission to save the world in its totality, and of saving it in history, here and now. The church exists to act in solidarity with the hopes and joys, the anxieties and sorrows, of men and women. Like Jesus, the church was sent "to bring good news to the poor, to heal the contrite of heart . . . to seek and to save what was lost" (Luke 4:18, 19:10).

The World of the Poor

You all know these words of Scripture, given prominence by Vatican II. During the 1960s several of your bishops and theologians helped to throw light on the essence and the mission of the church understood in these terms. My contribution will be to flesh out those beautiful declarations from the standpoint of my own situation, that of a small Latin American country, typical of what today is called the Third World. To put it in one word—in a word that sums it all up and makes it concrete—the world that the church ought to serve is, for us, the world of the poor.

Our Salvadoran world is no abstraction. It is not another example of what is understood by "world" in developed countries such as yours. It is a world made up mostly of men and women who are poor and oppressed. And we say of that world of the poor that it is the key to understanding the Christian faith, to understanding the activity of the church and the political dimension of that faith and that ecclesial activity. It is the poor who tell us what the world is, and what the church's service to the world should be. It is the poor who tell us what the *polis* is, what the city is and what it means for the church really to live in that world.

Allow me, then, briefly to explain from the perspective of the poor among my people, whom I represent, the situation and the activity of

our church in the world in which we live, and then to reflect theologically upon the importance that this real world, this culture, this socio-
political world, has for the church.

In its pastoral work, our archdiocese in recent years has been moving
in a direction that can only be described and only be understood as a
turning toward the world of the poor, to their real, concrete world.

Incarnation in the World of the Poor

Just as elsewhere in Latin America, the words of Exodus have, after
many years, perhaps centuries, finally resounded in our ears: "The cry of
the sons of Israel has come to me, and I have witnessed the way in which
the Egyptians oppress them" (Exod. 3:9). These words have given us
new eyes to see what has always been the case among us, but which has
so often been hidden, even from the view of the church itself. We have
learned to see what is the first, basic fact about our world and, as pastors,
we have made a judgment about it at Medellín and at Puebla. "That
misery, as a collective fact, expresses itself as an injustice which cries to
the heavens." At Puebla we declared, "So we brand the situation of
inhuman poverty in which millions of Latin Americans live as the most
devastating and humiliating kind of scourge. And this situation finds
expression in such things as a high rate of infant mortality, lack of adequate housing, health problems, starvation wages, unemployment and
underemployment, malnutrition, job uncertainty, compulsory mass mi-
grations, etc." Experiencing these realities, and letting ourselves be affected by them, far from separating us from our faith has sent us back to
the world of the poor as to our true home. It has moved us, as a first,
basic step, to take the world of the poor upon ourselves.

It is there that we have found the real faces of the poor, about which
Puebla speaks. There we have met landworkers without land and without steady employment, without running water or electricity in their
homes, without medical assistance when mothers give birth, and without schools for their children. There we have met factory workers who
have no labor rights, and who get fired from their jobs if they demand
such rights; human beings who are at the mercy of cold economic calcu-
lations. There we have met the mothers and the wives of those who have
disappeared, or who are political prisoners. There we have met the
shantytown dwellers, whose wretchedness defies imagination, suffering
the permanent mockery of the mansions nearby.

It is within this world devoid of a human face, this contemporary
sacrament of the suffering servant of Yahweh, that the church of my

archdiocese has undertaken to incarnate itself. I do not say this in a triumphalistic spirit, for I am well aware how much in this regard remains to be done. But I say it with immense joy, for we have made the effort not to pass by afar off, not to circle round the one lying wounded in the roadway, but to approach him or her as did the good Samaritan.

This coming closer to the world of the poor is what we understand both by the incarnation and by conversion. The changes that were needed within the church and in its apostolate, in education, in religious and in priestly life, in lay movements, which we had not brought about simply by looking inward upon the church, we are now carrying out by turning ourselves outward toward the world of the poor.

Proclaiming the Good News to the Poor

Our encounter with the poor has regained for us the central truth of the gospel, through which the word of God urges us to conversion. The church has to proclaim the Good News to the poor. Those who, in this-worldly terms, have heard bad news, and who have lived out even worse realities, are now listening through the church to the word of Jesus: "The kingdom of God is at hand; blessed are you who are poor, for the kingdom of God is yours." And hence they also have Good News to proclaim to the rich: that they, too, become poor in order to share the benefits of the kingdom with the poor. Anyone who knows Latin America will be quite clear that there is no ingenuousness in these words, still less the workings of a soporific drug. What is to be found in these words is a coming together of the aspiration on our continent for liberation, and God's offer of love to the poor. This is the hope that the church offers, and it coincides with the hope, at times dormant and at other times frustrated or manipulated, of the poor of Latin America.

It is something new among our people that today the poor see in the church a source of hope and a support for their noble struggle for liberation. The hope that our church encourages is neither naive nor passive. It is rather a summons from the word of God for the great majority of the people, the poor, that they assume their proper responsibility, that they undertake their own conscientization, that, in a country where it is legally or practically prohibited (at some periods more so than at others) they set about organizing themselves. And it is support, sometimes critical support, for their just causes and demands. The hope that we preach to the poor is intended to give them back their dignity, to encourage them to take charge of their own future. In a word, the church has not only turned toward the poor, it has made of the poor the special beneficiaries of its mission because, as Puebla says, "God takes on their defense and loves them."

Commitment to the Defense of the Poor

The church has not only incarnated itself in the world of the poor, giving them hope; it has also firmly committed itself to their defense. The majority of the poor in our country are oppressed and repressed daily by economic and political structures. The terrible words spoken by the prophets of Israel continue to be verified among us. Among us there are those who sell others for money, who sell a poor person for a pair of sandals; those who, in their mansions, pile up violence and plunder; those who crush the poor; those who make the kingdom of violence come closer as they lie upon their beds of ivory; those who join house to house, and field to field, until they occupy the whole land, and are the only ones there.

Amos and Isaiah are not just voices from distant centuries; their writings are not merely texts that we reverently read in the liturgy. They are everyday realities. Day by day we live out the cruelty and ferocity they excoriate. We live them out when there come to us the mothers and the wives of those who have been arrested or who have disappeared, when mutilated bodies turn up in secret cemeteries, when those who fight for justice and peace are assassinated. Daily we live out in our archdiocese what Puebla so vigorously denounced: "There are the anxieties based on systematic or selective repression; it is accompanied by accusations, violations of privacy, improper pressures, tortures, and exiles. There are the anxieties produced in many families by the disappearance of their loved ones, about whom they cannot get any news. There is the total insecurity bound up with arrest and detention without judicial consent. There are the anxieties, felt in the face of a system of justice that has been suborned or cowed."

In this situation of conflict and antagonism, in which just a few persons control economic and political power, the church has placed itself at the side of the poor and has undertaken their defense. The church cannot do otherwise, for it remembers that Jesus had pity on the multitude. But by defending the poor it has entered into serious conflict with the powerful who belong to the monied oligarchies and with the political and military authorities of the state.

Persecuted for Serving the Poor

This defense of the poor in a world deep in conflict has occasioned something new in the recent history of our church: persecution. You know the more important facts. In less than three years over fifty priests have been attacked, threatened, calumniated. Six are already martyrs—they were murdered. Some have been tortured and others expelled. Nuns have also been persecuted. The archdiocesan radio station and educational institutions that are Catholic or of a Christian inspiration have been attacked, threatened, intimidated, even bombed. Several parish communities have been raided.

If all this has happened to persons who are the most evident representatives of the church, you can guess what has happened to ordinary Christians, to the campesinos, catechists, lay ministers, and to the ecclesial base communities. There have been threats, arrests, tortures, murders, numbering in the hundreds and thousands. As always, even in persecution, it has been the poor among the Christians who have suffered most.

It is, then, an indisputable fact that, over the last three years, our church has been persecuted. But it is important to note why it has been persecuted. Not any and every priest has been persecuted, not any and every institution has been attacked. That part of the church has been attacked and persecuted that put itself on the side of the people and went to the people's defense.

Here again we find the same key to understanding the persecution of the church: the poor. Once again it is the poor who bring us to understand what has really happened. That is why the church has understood the persecution from the perspective of the poor. Persecution has been occasioned by the defense of the poor. It amounts to nothing other than the church's taking upon itself the lot of the poor.

Real persecution has been directed against the poor, the body of Christ in history today. They, like Jesus, are the crucified, the persecuted servant of Yahweh. They are the ones who make up in their own bodies that which is lacking in the passion of Christ. And for that reason when the church has organized and united itself around the hopes and the anxieties of the poor, it has incurred the same fate as that of Jesus and of the poor: persecution.

The Political Dimension of the Faith

This has been a brief sketch of the situation, and of the stance, of the church in El Salvador. The political dimension of the faith is nothing other than the church's response to the demands made upon it by the de facto socio-political world in which it exists. What we have rediscovered is that this demand is a fundamental one for the faith, and that the church cannot ignore it. That is not to say that the church should regard itself as a political institution entering into competition with other political institutions, or that it has its own political processes. Nor, much less, is it to say that our church seeks political leadership. I am talking of something more profound, something more in keeping with the gospel. I am talking about an authentic option for the poor, of becoming incarnate in their world, of proclaiming the good news to them, of giving them hope, of encouraging them to engage in a liberating praxis, of defending their cause and of sharing their fate.

The church's option for the poor explains the political dimension of the faith in its fundamentals and in its basic outline. Because the church has opted for the truly poor, not for the fictitiously poor, because it has opted for those who really are oppressed and repressed, the church lives in a political world, and it fulfills itself as church also through politics. It cannot be otherwise if the church, like Jesus, is to turn itself toward the poor.

MAKING THE FAITH REAL IN THE WORLD OF THE POOR

The course taken by the archdiocese has clearly issued from its faith conviction. The transcendence of the gospel has guided us in our judgment and in our action. We have judged the social and political situation from the standpoint of the faith. But it is also true, to look at it another way, that the faith itself has been deepened, that hidden riches of the gospel have been opened, precisely by taking up this stance toward socio-political reality such as it is.

Now I should just like to put forward some short reflections on several fundamental aspects of the faith that we have seen enriched through this real incarnation in the socio-political world.

A Clearer Awareness of Sin

In the first place, we have a better knowledge of what sin is. We know that offending God is death for humans. We know that such a sin really is mortal, not only in the sense of the interior death of the person who commits the sin, but also because of the real, objective death the sin produces. Let us remind ourselves of a fundamental datum of our Christian faith: sin killed the Son of God, and sin is what goes on killing the children of God.

We see that basic truth of the Christian faith daily in the situation in our country. It is impossible to offend God without offending one's brother or sister. And the worse offense against God, the worst form of secularism, as one of our Salvadoran theologians has said, is:

> to turn children of God, temples of the Holy Spirit, the body of Christ in history, into victims of oppression and injustice, into slaves to economic greed, into fodder for political repression. The worst of these forms of secularism is the denial of grace by the objectivization of this world as an operative presence of the powers of evil, the visible presence of the denial of God.

It is not a matter of sheer routine that I insist once again on the existence in our country of structures of sin. They are sin because they produce the fruits of sin: the deaths of Salvadorans—the swift death brought by repression or the long, drawn out, but no less real, death from structural oppression. That is why we have denounced what in our country has become the idolatry of wealth, of the absolute right, within the capitalist system, of private property, of political power in National Security regimes, in the name of which personal security is itself institutionalized.

No matter how tragic it may appear, the church through its entrance into the real socio-political world has learned how to recognize, and how to deepen its understanding of, the essence of sin. The fundamental essence of sin, in our world, is revealed in the death of Salvadorans.

Greater Clarity on the Incarnation and Redemption

In the second place we now have a better understanding of what the incarnation means, what it means to say that Jesus really took human flesh and made himself one with his brothers and sisters in suffering, in tears and laments, in surrender. I am not speaking of a universal incarnation. This is impossible. I am speaking of an incarnation that is preferential and partial: incarnation in the world of the poor. From that perspective the church will become a church for everybody. It will offer a service to the powerful, too, through the apostolate of conversion—but not the other way around, as has so often been the case in the past.

The world of the poor, with its very concrete social and political characteristics, teaches us where the church can incarnate itself in such a way that it will avoid the false universalism that inclines the church to associate itself with the powerful. The world of the poor teaches us what the nature of Christian love is, a love that certainly seeks peace but also unmasks false pacifism—the pacifism of resignation and inactivity. It is a love that should certainly be freely offered, but that seeks to be effective in history. The world of the poor teaches us that the sublimity of Christian love ought to be mediated through the overriding necessity of justice for the majority. It ought not to turn away from honorable conflict. The world of the poor teaches us that liberation will arrive only when the poor are not simply on the receiving end of handouts from governments or from the church, but when they themselves are the masters of, and protagonists in, their own struggle and liberation, thereby unmasking the root of false paternalism, including ecclesiastical paternalism.

The real world of the poor also teaches us about Christian hope. The church preaches a new heaven and a new earth. It knows, moreover, that no socio-political system can be exchanged for the final fullness that is given by God. But it has also learned that transcendent hope must be preserved by signs of hope in history, no matter how simple they may apparently be—such as those proclaimed by the Trito-Isaiah when he says "they will build houses and inhabit them, plant vineyards and eat their fruit" (Isa. 65:21). What in this is an authentically Christian hope—not reduced, as is so often said disparagingly, to what is merely of this world or purely human—is being learned daily through contact with those who have no houses and no vineyards, those who build for others to inhabit and work so that others may eat the fruits.

A Deeper Faith in God and in Christ

In the third place, incarnation in the socio-political world is the locus for deepening faith in God and in Christ. We believe in Jesus who came to bring the fullness of life, and we believe in a living God who gives life to men and women and wants them truly to live. These radical truths of the faith become really true and truly radical when the church enters into the heart of the life and death of its people. Then there is put before the faith of the church, as it is put before the faith of every individual, the most fundamental choice: to be in favor of life or to be in favor of death. We see, with great clarity, that here neutrality is impossible. Either we serve the life of Salvadorans, or we are accomplices in their death. And here what is most fundamental about the faith is given expression in history: either we believe in a God of life, or we serve the idols of death.

In the name of Jesus we want, and we work for, life in its fullness, a life that is not reduced to the frantic search for basic material needs, nor one reduced to the sphere of the socio-political. We know perfectly well that the superabundant fullness of life is to be achieved only in the kingdom of the Father. In human history this fullness is achieved through a worthy service of that kingdom, and total surrender to the Father. But we see with equal clarity that in the name of Jesus it would be sheer illusion, it would be an irony, and, at bottom, it would be the most profound blasphemy, to forget and to ignore the basic levels of life, the life that begins with bread, a roof, a job.

With the Apostle John we believe that Jesus is "the Word who is life" (1 John 1:1), and that God is revealed wherever this life is to be found. Where the poor begin to really live, where the poor begin to free themselves, where persons are able to sit around a common table to share with one another—the God of life is there. When the church inserts itself into the socio-political world it does so in order to work with it so that from such cooperation life may be given to the poor. In doing so, therefore, it is not distancing itself from its mission, nor is it doing something of secondary importance or something incidental to its mission. It is giving testimony to its faith in God; it is being the instrument of the Spirit, the Lord and giver of life.

This faith in the God of life is the explanation for what lies deepest in the Christian mystery. To give life to the poor, one has to give of one's own life, even to give one's life itself. The greatest sign of faith in a God of life is the witness of those who are ready to give up their own life. "A man can have no greater love than to lay down his life for his friends" (John 15:13). And we see this daily in our country. Many Salvadorans, many Christians, are ready to give their lives so that the poor may have life. They are following Jesus and showing their faith in him. Living within the real world just as Jesus did, like him accused and threatened, like him laying down their lives, they are giving witness to the word of life.

Our story, then, is a very old one. It is Jesus' story that we, in all modesty, are trying to follow. As church, we are not political experts, nor do we want to manipulate politics through its own internal mechanisms. But entrance into the socio-political world, into the world where the lives and deaths of the great mass of the population are decided upon, is necessary and urgent if we are to preserve, not only in word but in deed, faith in a God of life, and follow the lead of Jesus.

CONCLUSION

In conclusion, I should like to sum up what is central to the things I have been saying. In the ecclesial life of our archdiocese the political dimension of the faith—or, if one prefers, the relationship between faith and politics—has not been discovered by purely theoretical reflection, reflection made before the church has acted. Such reflection is important —but not decisive. Such reflection becomes important *and* decisive when it does indeed reflect the real life of the church. The honor of putting my pastoral experience into words in this university setting has obliged me today to undertake theological reflection. But it is rather in the actual practice of service to the poor that the political dimension of the faith is to be found, and correctly found. In such practice one can discover the relationship between the two, and what distinguishes them. It is the faith that provides the first impulse to incarnate oneself in the socio-political world of the poor, and gives encouragement to actions that lead to liberation and are also socio-political. And in their own turn that praxis and that incarnation make concrete the basic aspects of the faith.

In what I have here laid out, I have sketched only a broad outline of this double movement. Naturally, there are many more topics to be discussed. I might have talked about the relationship between the faith and political ideologies—in particular Marxism. I could have dwelt upon the question of violence and its legitimacy—a burning issue for us. Such topics are frequent subjects for reflection, and we face them without preconceptions and without fear. But we face them to the extent that they become real problems, and we are learning to provide solutions within the same process.

In the short period it has fallen to me to guide the archdiocese, there have been four different governments with distinctive political programs. Over these years other political forces, revolutionary and democratic, have been growing and developing. So the church has had to go on making judgments about politics from within a changing scene. At the present time the outlook is ambiguous. On the one hand all the projects emanating from the government are collapsing, and the possibility of popular liberation is growing.

But rather than listing for you all the fluctuations in the politics of El Salvador, I have chosen to explain what lies at the root of the church's stance in our explosive socio-political world. I have tried to make clear to you the ultimate criterion, one which is theological and historical, for the church's involvement in the world of the poor. In accordance with its own specific nature the church will go on supporting one or another political program to the extent that it operates in favor of the poor among the people.

I believe that this is the way to maintain the church's identity and transcendence. We enter into the real socio-political development of our people. We judge it from the point of view of the poor. We encourage all liberation movements that really lead to justice and peace for the majority of the people. We think this is the way to preserve the transcendence and the identity of the church, because in this way we preserve our faith in God.

Early Christians used to say *Gloria Dei, vivens homo* ("the glory of God is the living person"). We could make this more concrete by saying *Gloria Dei, vivens pauper* ("the glory of God is the living poor person"). From the perspective of the transcendence of the gospel, I believe we can determine what the life of the poor truly is. And I also believe that by putting ourselves alongside the poor and trying to bring life to them we shall come to know the eternal truth of the gospel. ["The Political Dimension of the Faith"]